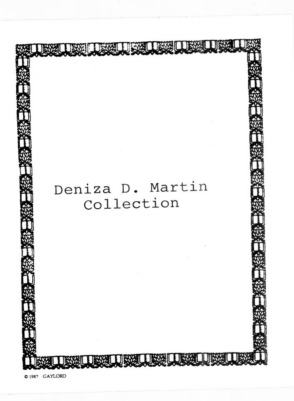

Deniza D. Martin
Collection

THE COURT OF ST JAMES'S

THE COURT OF
ST. JAMES'S

E. S. Turner

ST MARTIN'S PRESS

New York

CONTENTS

ILLUSTRATIONS

Introduction

THIS book sets out to sketch the life of the British Court for a thousand years. It is the story, not merely of kings and queens, but of favourites, jesters, maids of honour, whipping boys, wet nurses, cooks and chamberlains. It is the story of débutantes holding 'train teas,' of ambassadors battling for precedence and of Socialist ministers blushing as they pull on their knee breeches.

Although the book draws its title from St. James's, this is also the story of the Court at Westminster, Whitehall and those other palaces, ancient and modern, through which its history has flowed.

To put ten centuries of Court life into one volume may seem a foolhardy endeavour. Necessarily, the approach has been highly selective. Though the Court has changed mightily in character and influence down the centuries, it still retains echoes of Norman days; therefore there is no option but to start the story at about the time of the Conquest. It is not necessary, however, to describe the Court under every sovereign. Many Plantagenets, bold, proud and foolish, are missing from these pages; but from the Tudors onwards all reigns are represented.

This is by no means a history of kings and queens as such, still less of their policies and achievements. It is not concerned with coronation ceremonial or with the derivation of obscure ritual. Events which are historically hackneyed—like the execution of Charles I, the trial of Queen Caroline and the abdication of Edward VIII—have been passed over in a line or two. The aim has been to give a broad picture of the Court; its changes in atmosphere from reign to reign; the quarrels and controversies which have split it; the attempts to reform it; its revels and progresses; its whimsicalities of etiquette; its

9

strange employments above and below stairs; its influence on manners and taste; and the varying attitudes of the public towards it.

At different times the Court has been the driving force of the realm, an incubus on the realm and an inspiration to the realm. In early days the people looked to it, not only for law and justice, but for rousing displays of wildfire and fountains flowing with wine. Its resplendent days are commonly supposed to have ended with the Stuarts, since when the officers of the Court, gradually shorn of political power, have become a ring of quaintly-titled and gravely courteous functionaries occupied with problems of ceremonial, administration and movement. The story of this slow descent from riotous magnificence, in social terms, is anything but an anti-climactic one.

It is unlikely that modern courtiers describe themselves as such on their passports. The word is old-fashioned and has not the happiest of associations. For the best part of a thousand years courtiers as a class have had an indifferent name. Sycophancy, dissimulation, greed—these were assumed to be their prime attributes (though the abuse frequently came from those who had been disappointed in their desires for preferment and profit). At Court it was each man for himself. The rules were to keep one's countenance at the expense of one's word, to blend a flexible conscience with an inflexible politeness, and so on. William Paulet, first Marquis of Winchester, admitted that he survived the revolutions of four bloody reigns by being a reed, not an oak. In their spare time courtiers were thought to spend their energy practising the art of walking backwards or debating whether to say '*Dieu vous aide*' when a prince sneezed. Today nearly all the sting has gone out of the attack. There is no demand for sycophancy. Courtiers have no expectations of manors or bailiwicks. They have clear-cut duties to perform and they need the skill of a business executive allied to an instinct for ceremonial. They earn no ruder adjectives than 'toffee-nosed' or 'tweedy.'

It is not easy to see the events of the present reign in anything like perspective, but it is probably fair to say (as *Time* has said) that the Court is the scene of a struggle between 'the partisans of a pompous past and the champions of a folksier future.' If it had been left to the traditionalists the Queen would still be touching for the Evil and the Poet Laureate would still be grinding out Birthday and New Year Odes. If it were left to the democratic *avant garde*, the royal family would be escorting the public through their picture galleries. It seems clear, however, that the old exclusivity is crumbling and that there is a growing tendency towards informality. The abandonment of débutantes' parties and the introduction of palace luncheons with actors, sportsmen and record-breakers are only two examples.

At the time of writing, one of the commonest criticisms is that the Queen should spend more time touring the Commonwealth. The Court began as a mobile one and it will be ironic if, after ten centuries, it reverts to that role.

1

An End to Simplicity

IN days of rude simplicity, a king needed little more than a hall, a bedchamber and a box under the bed in which to keep his crown.

For a king with any pretensions to majesty, even in pre-Norman times, the following chief courtiers were essential: a chamberlain, to look after the chamber; a treasurer, to guard the crown and coffers; a marshal, to keep order among nobles and petitioners in the hall; a steward to serve the king his food; a butler to bring him his wine; a churchman to say his prayers; and a constable to repel rogues and wantons.

If he married, his queen would demand her own establishment, consisting in the main of various idle women to keep her amused. His infant sons and daughters would require nurses, rockers and tutors; and in the fullness of time they, too, would demand the apparatus of chamberlains, stewards and butlers.

All too soon, the king would find himself collecting jesters, tasters, cupbearers, pages, poets, grooms, chroniclers, harpers, hornblowers, huntsmen and washerwomen. One half of his court would make meals for the other half and all of them, in winter, would burn his furniture for fuel.

The bigger the court, the less inclined would be the great officers to do any work. They would demand deputies, thus leaving them free to inflate pomp and enforce etiquette, as much for their own magnification as for that of the king.

A courtier who sat in the wrong seat at the board of King Canute was unlikely to repeat his mistake. For his indiscretion, he would be sent to the foot of the table, and his fellow diners were encouraged to pelt him with greasy bones, which he was not at liberty to return. It was a rough but not unfriendly way of teaching precedence.

The need for enforcing a certain formality is further shown by a warning issued to Welshmen who contemplated attending the Anglo-Saxon Court. They were instructed not to strike the Queen or to snatch things from her with violence, under pain of incurring her displeasure.

That affable albino, Edward the Confessor, preserved a reasonable decorum in his Court, but he did not always stand sufficiently on his dignity. The royal funds were kept in a box in his bedroom, and when the King found a thief robbing it (so the tale goes) he urged the rogue to make haste, for if Hugolin, the Norman Treasurer, came along there would not be a penny left for anybody. Hugolin was not amused when he heard of this episode, but the King pointed out that the thief was in greater need than either of them, and there was still enough money left for their purposes. Hugolin was still not amused. The Normans sometimes lacked a sense of humour.

Edward's Queen gave grammar lessons to scholars and embroidered elaborate robes for her husband, who wore them with reluctance; not because they were home-made but because he disliked show. The King had an inadequate sense of tradition and even waived the royal privilege of talking and laughing during divine service. He also waived his marital privileges, thus inspiring much indelicate gossip. Only one enthusiasm distinguished him from an abbot: he liked hunting.

The Bastard out of Normandy put an end to all this foolish simplicity. He showed the Anglo-Saxon nobles how a king should live. Even when stripped for travel, William's Court had a rugged splendour; but at the three great static courts of the year—at Christmas, Easter and Whitsun—he put on a calculated display of magnificence. There were three classes who had to be outshone if he was to retain his crown: the English collaborators, some of whom had been used to a far from threadbare grandeur; the Norman nobles, who lived as petty kings; and visiting ambassadors, ever on the alert for shortcomings in hospitality and manners. So, by royal command, peers and prelates journeyed to Westminster (where the Confessor had left a palace), to Winchester or Gloucester, to see their sovereign wear his crown. These great courts met for business as well as pleasure. Here the policies of the realm were shaped. Here the King got to know his magnates, noting the symptoms of ambition and restlessness, selecting, restraining, counselling and taking counsel. The Court was parliament and government in one. Its deliberations were varied by feasting, by ceremonial, by prayer and the exchange of gifts. A major feast might begin shortly after mid-day and go on until midnight. Once at least, William's board offered delicacies from Constantinople, Babylon, Tripoli, Syria and Phoenicia. The cost of assembling such items today would be immodest; in the Conqueror's day it must have been inordinate. Yet the King's purveyors seem to have been given *carte blanche*. What better way to impress an ambassador, William may have argued, than to offer him dainties from his own distant land ?

The Norman Court set new standards of social behaviour. That jolly swinishness which had distinguished many of the Anglo-Saxon nobles fell away under the influence of what, by contrast, must be called a new elegance. There was grumbling, of course; no one who has been used to four meals a day likes to trim himself to two. Except on special occasions, William's Court dined at nine in the morning and supped at five. The day was free for working or hunting. To be drunk at noon was no longer smart, nor was it the correct thing to clout one's womenfolk.

As the threat of rebellion died out, the Norman standards slackened. Nobles tried to win reputations by serving as many delicacies as their King and banqueting became a ruinous obsession. The rot was completed by William Rufus, who, unless all the monks are liars, imported exotic vices as well as exotic foods. His Court became a byword for strenuous wickedness. Many a historian has preferred to indicate the nature of the Red King's aberrations in Latin footnotes. ' In order that he might indulge his passions with less restraint he refused to marry,' says Dr John Lingard; ' the young nobility courted the favour of their sovereign by imitating his example.'* Rufus's entourage were lustful, avaricious, bold and cruel, first in battle and first in vice.

The Conqueror's men had dressed ready for instant action. Rufus had minions who clad themselves in long flowing garments and, not content with dressing like women, walked like

* *History of England*

them. They wore long hair and long pointed toes to their shoes, a fashion to which moralists have never ceased to take exception. By day these creatures slept. By night they drank, diced and indulged in ' the habits of the ancient Greek and the modern Turk.'*

Another vice which disfigured the Court of the Red King was chivalry, that chivalry which taught that those of knightly status were to be treated nobly and the rest of humanity ignobly. For the high-born, chivalry sweetened human intercourse and dignified the art of knocking other men off horses. For the low-born it was a code which sanctioned mutilation and massacre.

The flaxen, florid monarch who mocked his God and then mocked his own blasphemies lived in spendthrift splendour. Like many a rakehelly monarch he loved to build. The palace of Edward the Confessor at Westminster was not grandiose enough for him, nor was the city of London. Both, he decided, would have to be rebuilt. His principal monument was Westminster Hall, 270 feet long by 74 feet wide. To complaints that it was too big, he retorted that it was a mere bedchamber compared with the palace he proposed to erect beside the Thames. At the same time he extended his father's castle at Windsor. The years were too few for the realisation of his worthier dreams. The king who lived like a beast died like one. With some misgivings they laid the great blasphemer in Winchester Cathedral; and seven years later the tower fell down.

The clerkly Henry I succeeded in imposing some decency and discipline on his followers, if not on himself. After Rufus, a king with mistresses and bastards was a symbol of moral health. Henry was not too busy to marry, though there were some who would have felt happier if he had not married a nun. On the whole, he divided his days admirably. In the mornings he listened to the wise; in the afternoon, after a siesta, he gossiped with the young. 'As far as this world allowed,' says Walter Map, 'his court was without care, his palace free of crowding and confusion.'†

The Court was still an ambulant one. Henry widened his itinerary, wearing his crown at other centres besides West-

* E. A. Freeman : *The Reign of William Rufus*
† *De Nugis Curialium*

minster, Winchester and Gloucester. Aware that his subjects looked on a royal visit as a punishment rather than a privilege, he made some effort to curb the rapacity of his purveyors and the insolence of his followers. For a courtier to wash his horse's feet in his host's wine was no longer worth the risk. Always, the King notified the route of his progresses so that goods might be brought in orderly fashion to market. The result was that wherever the King lay was to be found the biggest fair in the realm, a fair which attracted even visitors from overseas. On vacation days the King allowed access to himself, either in a great house or in the open, 'until the sixth hour.'

In the King's modest list of vices, drunkenness was not included. His Chamberlain, Payne FitzJohn, drew each night a sexterce of wine to assuage the royal thirst, but only rarely was it called for. The Chamberlain and the pages therefore drank it themselves. One night, when they had quaffed it, the King decided he was thirsty and the embarrassed baron had no option but to go down on his knees and make a clean breast of what had been going on. 'In future,' said the King, 'draw two every night from the Butler, one for yourself, the other for me.' No milder king ever castrated a coiner.

The Court of King Henry saddened the clergy by indulging in the effeminate hair styles which should have gone out with Rufus's reign. The shagginess of the courtiers equalled that of their horses. When the Court visited France, Bishop Serlo preached so vehemently against this fashion that Henry had his hair cut as soon as he left the church and his courtiers could hardly do other than follow suit.

One of Henry's clerical courtiers, Rahere, left a finer monument than many a king has done: the still-surviving hospital of St Bartholomew in London. As a young man at Rufus's Court he acquired a reputation as minstrel, mime and jester, and continued in these several capacities until, uncorrupted, he entered the Church. While on a pilgrimage to Rome he fell ill with malaria and vowed to build a hospital for the poor. The site of Smithfield was supposedly suggested in a vision by St Bartholomew, who urged that a priory also be established. Rahere's financial resources seem to have been adequate to the occasion. It was the amiable Norman custom to reward eminent wags with estates (William the Conqueror's 'joculator,' Berdic, was given lands in Gloucestershire) and there were many other perquisites of office. Rahere enjoys a proud and unique position in history. As a class, jesters cannot be said to have been distinguished for works of piety.

Under Henry sprang up two courts within the parent Court: the Exchequer, which handled revenues and expenditure, and the *Curia Regis*, which tackled the accumulated chaos of legal claims, causes and appeals. Each was composed of the great officers of the Household, assisted by carefully chosen nobles learned in the law. In the Exchequer, where the members sat round a chequered cloth, a man was styled a Baron; in the *Curia Regis*, the same man was a Justice; and all the time he was a Household officer. This system, in which one day an officer would attend to the affairs of wardrobe, chapel or cellar, and the next day to the affairs of the kingdom, makes it almost impossible to define comprehensively the functions of any one of them. Each officer was what the King made him.

The policy of centralisation, as practised by the first two Henrys, enabled the King to offset the powers of territorial magnates who lived in sub-regal state in the outer parts of his realm. These did not fail to mock a monarch who gave great offices to clerks and bailiffs. Henry balanced the risks. The Household officers were always under his eye and there was no one else to whom they could look for advancement. Moreover, having once tasted power, they were in no mood to lose it. It was a system which worked well enough if the monarch was a strong man and a shrewd judge of character and capacity. If he was susceptible to female influence, the high appointments would go, if not to relatives, to adventurers. If he had vicious tastes, the way was open to rogues and catamites. If he was saintly, the reins would be seized by orgulous clergy. The story of the Plantagenets is the story of all this and more.

2

The Saddle-Sore Court

OF the Plantagenet courts, the first and most uncomfortably virile was that of Henry II, who in 1154 seized the throne vacated by Stephen but was too busy to sit on it.

No king of England worked at higher pressure. Thanks to his marriage to Eleanor of Aquitaine, Henry's domains in England and France were enormous and could be held down only if he kept continually on the move. All too rarely was he in England but when he was he made his presence felt from end to end of it. The saddle-sore monks who chronicled his reign have left some comical, and probably overdrawn, pictures of Henry on the road, travelling by unbearable stages, like a hard-pressed courier. They would have us believe that the King was capable of halting his Court in the wilds, taking possession of the only presentable dwelling and leaving his knights to contest with drawn swords for the occupancy of hovels. The King's Marshals were supposed to find accommodation for all, but behaved in high and arbitrary fashion towards those who omitted to bribe them. Usually Henry was content with the shortest night's rest and the Court would be on its way at dawn; which meant that horses would start riding down horses and waggons overturning waggons, with hounds baying and hawks snapping, and bishops and barbers, barons and buffoons milling about in fog and confusion. Occasionally the King, having given orders for an early start, would sleep all morning, thus playing havoc with the plans of clerks, carters and packmen. If he announced a late start, he would change his mind and take the road early, to the grief of those who had just been bled, or had taken physic, or who were engaged in shoeing their horses. Just as, in a modern army, the latrine orderly is the first to know of the regiment's intentions, so the prostitutes and liquor sellers who followed the royal progress were credited with having the only accurate fore-knowledge of the King's movements. On the road he would dictate letters, dispatching them from perhaps three places in a day. 'Oh Lord God Almighty,' moaned one of his monks, 'turn and avert the heart of the King from this pestilent habit that he may know himself to be but man, and that he may show a real mercy and compassion to those who are driven after him both by ambition and by necessity.' But the Lord did not listen; and the fretful Court, its clothes threadbare and its mounts broken-winded, deprived of all solace for body and soul, continued to stumble over abominable roads from one soggy end of England to the other, trying to keep up with the Angevin devil.

Though the courtiers would seem to have had the worst of it, Henry got through more work than any of them. He issued charters, listened to pleas, remedied injustices, pounced unexpectedly on his sheriffs and judges. A king was expected to be as zealous in ridding his kingdom of wild beasts as of insolent bailiffs; so, when the Court was reeling with fatigue, Henry would order a day's hunting. His subjects idolised him. Often they would seize him and carry him about 'whither he would not.' In spite of severe jostling, he did his best to listen to every man who sought his ear; though few of his humble English subjects can have received much satisfaction at interviews of this type, since the King spoke not a word of their language. However, the monks of St Swithin, at Winchester, were able to catch their Sovereign's meaning. Prostrating themselves in the mud before him, they complained that their bishop had deprived them of three dishes at meals. When the King asked how many they had left, they wrung their hands and said, 'Only ten.' To which came the answer: 'In my Court I am content with three. Perish your bishop if he does not give you the same.'

Henry's Court at Westminster, when he found time to grace it, was by no means without splendour, but much of it was the splendour of horses, hounds and hawks. Nobody praised the victuals or the cooking. When Henry first took up residence the palace was 'ready to have fallen down,' but Thomas Becket, Henry's Chancellor, rebuilt it in 1163 'with exceeding great celerity and speed.' Even then it tended to be smoky, draughty and sweaty. It was a five-fold dwelling, made up of courtyard, great hall, living quarters, chapel and exchequer house. In the great hall thronged scholars, churchmen and lawyers. They were kept standing for hours as the restless young King circulated among them, absorbing their knowledge. Next day the Court might spend eight hours hunting, after which the King would sit down to dinner, bolt his three courses and then get up again. This meant that his courtiers had to get up too, leaving their food and drink unfinished, and spend the rest of the evening on their feet. In divine service, Henry still dictated, scribbled or sketched.

In stature he was short and bullet-headed, with a protruding abdomen. It has been said that he tried to reduce his girth by exercise and abstinence, but the well-informed Walter Map says that his furious activities were an attempt to dispel his erotic dreams. Another monkish gossip, Gerald of Wales, testifies that the King had swollen legs caused by incessant standing and spurring of unwilling horses. He wore a short plain mantle and was often untidy in his appearance. Now and again, he was a victim of that demoniac possession which made the Angevin princes behave like fiends from the pit. His florid face would grow purple, his eyes would blaze and become flecked with blood. He tried to tear out the eyes of a page, who had to be pulled away scarred and mangled as a trainer is pulled away from a wild beast. Sometimes he visited his rage on himself. When Humet, his minister, spoke in defence of the King of the Scots, Henry threw his cap on the ground, ripped off his clothes, pulled the covers from his bed and finally subsided on the floor, where he gnashed the straw.

Walter Map thought it remiss in the King that, on the rare occasions when he took his ease, he shut himself away and was accessible only 'to those who seemed unworthy of such approach.' This may simply mean that Map himself had difficulty in gaining audience. Or it may mean that Henry was impatient of ceremonialists jostling for the honour of dressing and undressing him. He was too active a man to bother overmuch about etiquette. It was sufficient if people kept their places and did what they were told. Toadies he loathed. When he had occasion to rebuke the Bishop of Worcester, a courtier ventured to add his mite of abuse. The King delivered a fierce rebuke which ended, 'Scarce can I keep my hands from thy eyes.'

Although the weary Walter Map bemoaned that Henry's Court was 'more opposed to the Muses than all the others,' so much so that even humble chroniclers could not keep up with the rush of events, this reign was far from antagonistic to the arts. Many lively and industrious pens were at work. Thanks to the royal influence, nobles began to add poets, as well as buffoons, to their establishments.

For many years, Henry's Court had a rival, a court where a man could get a decent meal, hear witty or scholarly talk and keep up with the trend of fashion. This was the court of Thomas Becket, his Chancellor and first minister of State, whose board was renowned all over Europe for all those things that were absent from the King's table. Becket's house was, over and above, an academy of manners and knightly virtues; among the young men groomed there was Henry's son. Though it drew the *bons viveurs* away from the stale bread and tough meat of Westminster, Henry cherished no ill feelings on this account. He liked to drop in from time to time, perhaps on his way home from hunting, to watch his dazzling Chancellor showing off. Lacking the time and the polish to perform these honours, Henry was grateful to have the aid of an older, worldlier man with the necessary gift of showmanship.

The King's forced marches through his realms presented a disorderly contrast to the famous progress of Becket to Paris, in 1158. His mission was to propose a marriage between Henry's oldest son and the French King's daughter. In the van marched two hundred and fifty boys singing their national airs. Next came the Chancellor's hounds, in couples. Eight waggons followed, each drawn by five horses and attended by five drivers, and each guarded by two men and a fierce mastiff. Two of the waggons contained free ale for the populace; others held the furniture for the Chancellor's chapel, his bedchamber, his kitchen and his wardrobe. After the waggons came twelve sumpter horses, each carrying a long-tailed monkey; a body of esquires leading their knights' chargers; then more esquires, sons of gentlemen, falconers, officers of the household, knights and clergymen, all riding two by two; and finally the magnificent Chancellor, talking serenely to his companions. The peasants who saw this chanting, glittering cavalcade, with its disciplined beasts and birds, asked as they were meant to ask, 'What kind of a man is the King of England, if his Chancellor travels like this ?'

There was a third court in England, that of Queen Eleanor, former wife of the French King and one-time Crusader. Eight years older than Henry, this adventurous divorcée had a reputation for lasciviousness and intrigue. Much of her energy was devoted to softening the harsh edges of chivalry and spreading the adulterous code of courtly love. But her young husband ruled her with a heavy hand and her foolishness fizzled out in the damp airs of Westminster. When he was not present she was able to expand a little, and the relaxed moral climate of her court at Bermondsey helped to offset the attractions of Becket's *ménage*. When Henry fell out with Becket, Eleanor spent much time in Aquitaine, where she and her ladies proceeded with the good work of corrupting masculinity. In the courts of Troyes and Poitiers both young and old were expected to wipe the dung from their boots, to comb their locks, to dress tidily, to pay compliments to each other and to engage in such civilised pursuits as composing poems in praise of other men's wives. With her daughter, the Countess of Champagne, Eleanor encouraged the rewriting of history in accordance with the new conception of chivalry, King Alfred being a notable victim of the process. Queen and daughter held so-called courts of love at which they sought to regulate passion within adulterous channels (only a simpleton would pretend to be in love with his wife whom he had acquired by purchase). Between them they tried to convince men that it was their duty to perform all kinds of imbecile feats in order to win a lady's regard. Englishmen were harder to persuade than Frenchmen.

Whether through Eleanor's influence or not, there was enough slackening of standards in England to disgust John of Salisbury, who served as secretary to Thomas Becket. Men, he maintained, were growing effeminate. They wore gloves in order that their hands might be the softer for fondling women. Not content with singing love songs publicly, they trilled dulcetly and wantonly in church, in a manner more likely to stir lust than devotion. Everywhere fashionable society was obsessed with jesters, mimics, wizards, necromancers and indecent performers of all descriptions.*

The bullet-headed King with his hard-riding Court had the last laugh. Ostentatiously, Becket cut out ostentation when he became Archbishop of Canterbury; his martyrdom was near. Eleanor's inability to leave dangerous ideas alone led her to plot against her husband, who put her behind bars. For long she had known about his Fair Rosamond, but as the propagandist of adulterous passion she was ill qualified to protest. According to Holinshed, the mistress was 'verily a rare and peerless piece in those days.'

Although the structure of Henry's Court was laid down by his predecessors, no clear account of it appears until his reign. The kernel of it was the King's Household, which was divided into five main sections: the great offices of State; the Chapel and Chancery; the Steward's department, or commissariat; the King's Chamber; and the Marshalsea and Constabulary.†

The great officers were listed as Chancellor, Treasurer, Sewers (stewards), Master Butler, Master Chamberlain, Master Marshal and Constable. Of these, the highest-paid was the Chancellor, whose emoluments were five shillings a day, plus one lord's simnel loaf, two salted simnel loaves, one sextary of ordinary wine, one fat wax candle and 40 pieces of candle. Although five shillings was no despicable sum in those days, it is very obvious that a Chancellor like Thomas Becket, a statesman and a policy maker, was not required to live on his Household salary. His income was chiefly derived from fees payable whenever a royal writ was issued. His clerks worked behind a screen in the hall or even in the chapel, which was often used for lay purposes.

The Steward's department had a long chain of offices for storing or processing food and for looking after all the apparatus of the royal table. These included the Dispensary or Pantry, the Bakery, the Larder or *Bouche*, the Butlery or Cellars, the Spicery, the King's Kitchen, the Private Kitchen, the Great Kitchen and Scullery, the Napery and the Ewery or Pitcher House. As the reigns went by so many offices were added—now

* *Policraticus*
† Hubert Hall (ed)—*Red Book of the Exchequer*

a Chandlery or a Squillery,* now a Wafery† or a Scalding House—that the tail of the Court wagged monstrously long. These departments employed a profusion of keepers, counters, spensers, ushers, carters, clerks, cooks, scullions and grooms. The Ewerer functioned not only at the royal board but at the royal bath, being paid a fee of fourpence whenever the King decided to perform major ablutions. Doubtless he earned it, for the second Henry can hardly have been an easy man to bath. The Ewerer was also paid a penny a day for drying the King's clothes on progresses.

The King's Chamber had a by no means excessive establishment. The officers included a Master Chamberlain and various lesser chamberlains serving in rotation. Not the least important appointment was that of the Chamberlain of the Candles, who kept a tight hand on a much-sought and easily filched commodity. In this department were the Bearer of the King's Litter, a Water Carrier and a Laundress.

To the Marshalsea (marshal-seat) and Constabulary, which were chiefly concerned with discipline and protection of the Court, were attached Knights-Huntsmen and lesser huntsmen with all the necessary beasts for pursuing stags, harts, wolves, otters, foxes, hares and cats. Among the office-holders were the Leader of the Limmers (large hounds), the Keeper of the Brachs (hounds hunting by scent) and the Bearward. The Constabulary also controlled a number of miscellaneous servants, ranging from the Keeper of the Hearth and the Keeper of the Tents to the Watchmen of the Treasury and a quartet of Hornblowers.

The gossiping monks who wrote of Henry's forced marches do not seem to have left a description of the Court conducting a cat hunt. It is an omission to be regretted.

To trace, from this point onwards, all variations in titles and responsibilities of every Court officer would be a task of enormous tedium. It is perhaps enough to say that chamberlains, whether plain or Great, Master, Lord or Lord Great, have been concerned with exercising authority above stairs, and with ceremonial. Stewards, however described, have ruled

---

* A depot for wood, coal and rushes
† Confectionery

below stairs and in the commissariat, with the administrative aid of the Board of Green Cloth. The Lord Chamberlain and the Lord Steward, two of the three great officers of the Court today, were originally deputies of the Lord Great Chamberlain and Lord High Steward, who were either too busy or too important to do the work of the Household, exercising their rights only on such occasions as coronations. The symbol of office, for both, is a white wand. The third great officer of today's Court, the Master of the Horse, is descended from the Constable, and has authority over the stables and outside servants. All three of these officers shed much of their political power in the eighteenth century and lost the last vestige of it in the twentieth.

The Chancellor broke away from the Household by the end of the twelfth century, when the Exchequer and Chancery achieved a separate existence.

3

Dung and Diamonds

FROISSART says: 'Between two valiant kings of England there is always one weak in mind and body.'* The Courts of the Plantagenets tended to be alternately hard-centred and soft-centred.

Henry III (1216–72) made the error of encouraging art, music and architecture, thus incurring deep obloquy. Part of the trouble was that he imported Frenchmen to spend English money. It was obvious that his Queen, a greedy French minx, attached an absurd importance to comfort, cleanliness and politeness. Henry tried to trick the philistine barons by financing his operations through his own Wardrobe account, instead of through the Exchequer; which was as if the head of a great business were to ignore the apparatus of his counting-house and build up the petty cash account to the stage where he could buy yachts with it. The barons applied various pressures, with the result that Henry's Court was perpetually in financial straits.

Normally, the birth of an heir to the Throne was an occasion when a certain *largesse* was expected of the monarch. Henry, tired of being crabbed, took the view that it was for his subjects to open their purses. When the various royal messengers returned from spreading the good news, the King enquired of them what gifts they had received. Many of the offerings he considered to be inadequate, and the messengers were told to reject them with scorn. This they did, and held their ground until something more suitable was produced. The episode, says Matthew Paris, cast a dark stain on the King's magnificence. A witty woman remarked, 'God gave us this child but the King sells him to us.'

* *Chronicles*

Some years later, still under pressure to economise, Henry decided to cut down his alms-giving and to reduce the number of tapers burned in churches. At Christmas 1251 he gave no presents. The lavishness of his board had been criticised, so he sought food and lodgings in the houses of clergy of low degree. Hosts of higher status were expected to present him, his Queen and the leading courtiers with costly gifts as well as hospitality. The Queen demanded these, not as a favour but as her due; and the courtiers made it clear that they were interested in nothing less than 'for instance, desirable palfreys, gold and silver cups, necklaces with choice jewels, imperial girdles and the like.' Thus, says the courtier-monk, 'the King's Court became like to that of Rome, prostituting itself like a harlot for gain.'

In 1263, when the Court was under baronial siege, Queen Eleanor tried to sail up the Thames from the Tower to the greater security of Windsor. At London Bridge the mob, crying 'Drown the witch!' flung offal, mud and bad eggs (which, mysteriously, are always available on these occasions) at her barge. She was forced back and sought sanctuary in St Paul's.

One of Henry's Court appointments was that of King's Versifier, a post held by Henri d'Avranches, whose yearly award of two tuns of wine set a happy precedent for later laureates. At the Tower the King kept the nucleus of a royal menagerie. Besides leopards and an elephant, there was a great white bear which helped to earn its keep by catching fish from the Thames. The sheriffs of London were required to produce fourpence a day for the maintenance of beast and keeper and to provide a muzzle and chain.

Only posterity honours a king who spends on architecture. Henry is remembered by his rebuilding of Westminster Abbey. He had a certain amount of trouble with the Abbey monks, who pilfered the Crown jewels, and he decided to keep the more valuable items in the Tower. In his reign Westminster Hall acquired a new importance as a permanent home for the courts of justice. Judges no longer trailed round with the King and his Court.

Those who failed to dip deeply in their pockets in honour of Henry's heir were not to know that the child would turn out to be the most redoubtable of the Plantagenet line. As a youth, the future Edward I was full of the exuberant high spirits which are so rightly looked for in an English prince. With a locust band of 200 horsemen, mostly undesirable aliens, he ranged the countryside, seizing what he fancied. Once he took possession of a priory, expelled its occupants, stole their food and, to

Mummers entertain the Court

round off the jest, flogged the servants. It was important that a prince of the blood should not suffer obstruction on the highway; to drive the lesson home, a youth who failed to give way to Edward was deprived of an ear and an eye. This act is said to have inspired the liveliest speculation as to the nature of the punishments he might introduce as a king (as it turned out, he popularised hanging, drawing and quartering).

For his coronation feast in Westminster Edward ordered his sheriffs to provide 380 oxen, 450 porkers, 430 sheep, 278 bacon hogs and 22,600 hens and capons. The meal lasted a fortnight and, in the view of those who consumed it, did much to atone for Edward's earlier indiscretions. Others may have felt that it was a modest enough gesture from one who had been given Gascony, Ireland, Wales and the cities of Bristol, Stamford and Grantham for a wedding present.

Edward did not maintain an extravagant Court, though he had a sense of occasion. Asked why he did not dress more elaborately, he said, 'I should not be a better man however splendidly I dressed.' That hot temper which cost a hapless youth an ear and eye caused the King to belabour a clumsy esquire who attended him at the wedding of his daughter Margaret. Subsequently the esquire received an *ex gratia* payment of £13 6s. 8d. Some of the royal ferocity was expended on deer which Edward rode down on horseback and dispatched with a sword; and, of course, on Welsh and Scots rebels. The manners of his Court have been described as frank and jovial. On Easter Monday, 1290, the King graciously allowed himself to be 'heaved' in his chair by the Queen's ladies, who invaded his private chamber. They did not desist until he had agreed to pay 40s. to each. At Fingringhoe, Essex, the King lost another 40s. when he wagered that the royal washerwoman, Matilda of Waltham, could not ride with the stag hounds and come in at the kill. Royal washerwomen were made of stern stuff and this one rose admirably to the challenge.

Some further idea of the stresses imposed on an ambulant court may be gained from the Wardrobe account for the period November 1299 to November 1300,* a year when Edward was at war with the Scots. This also affords a pretty illustration of campaigning on a petty cash account. The Wardrobe bore not only the cost of robes and furs, but of victuals and wine, the wages of minstrels, fools and falconers, the expenses of European messengers, the fees of knights, the cost of fortifying and maintaining castles, the wages of engineers, archers and the seamen of the Cinque Ports fleet.

On its way north the Court travelled by horseback, with the exception of the Queen who, being in an advanced state of pregnancy, had the choice of chariot or litter. Her ladies were expected, like washerwomen, to be good equestrians. Between Boston and Lincoln, the King rode in an armoured barge, the

---

* John Topham : *Observations on the Wardrobe Account of King Edward I (1787).*

latticework of which was intended to protect him from missiles hurled by the disaffected.

Various delicacies were procured en route for the Queen, who possibly was beset by those cravings which afflict pregnant women. 'John, the Queen's Fruiterer,' obtained for her apples and pears at various places between Dunstable and North- ampton; and 'Peter, the Queen's Apothecary' kept her supplied with nuts, pomegranates, figs, raisins and sundry spices. The Queen evidently saw no reason why she should be any more uncomfortable than she had to be; there is an entry in the accounts for 'cords, great and small, to hang up the Queen's clothes in her wardrobe.' At Brotherton in Yorkshire the Queen halted her journey and was safely delivered of a son.

Though he travelled with such appurtenances of royalty as minstrels and falconers, the King's own tent was lightly fur- nished, containing little more than a few chairs. The accounts mention four urinals, two of glass and two of copper, for the King.

There are references to venison sent in hogsheads from Sherwood Forest to Hull, for shipment to London; to the dispatch of lampreys from Gloucester; and the upkeep of four she-goats to furnish the King with milk. John de la Lee, Sheriff of Essex and Hertford, was paid an appropriate allow- ance for guarding a 'whale' taken off Mersey Island; for the cost of a cask to put it in; for salt to preserve it and for the expense of carrying it to the Court at Stamford. Whether the 'whale' was intended to be eaten or admired does not emerge.

During the year the King's Butler contrived to spend £6934 6s. 4½d. on wine. It was necessary to buy 32 quarters of coal to burn in the cellars during a period of hard frost in order to save the casks from ruin. The wine destined for the soldiery was rough and sour and doubtless well suited to the onions and garlic which were their main diet.

Not the least commitments were the oblations offered at the various shrines visited by the King on his journeyings, the alms handed out on Saints' days to thousands of paupers and the sums spent on masses for the souls of defunct kings and queens. The King of Cyprus sent a party of friars to England and these too demanded alms. There was also a payment to 'a person from Rome' bringing to the King's son a gift from certain clerks of a buffalo's horn. Those who qualified for the 'royal touch' also received small sums.

Then there were claims for compensation. The prioress of Wilberfosse put in a bill 'for damage sustained by the King's coming there.' Those who had been kicked by the royal palfreys and those whose horses had died in the King's service had to be paid off. Another item was for the repair of St Martin's Church at Charing, Westminster, where walls and altars had been damaged by diggers seeking treasure on the King's orders.

Miscellaneous entries included payments to messengers who brought news of auspicious births or of the fall of beleaguered towns; 'to Martinot of Gascoigne, a fool'; 3d. a day for prisoners in Carlisle Castle; the cost of a step to the chair intended to hold the stone of Scotland; the expenses of the King's door-keeper, a versatile fellow who went 'to Holland to repair the bridges'; and the issue of summer and winter shoes for such varied beneficiaries as the maids of honour, the Welsh archers, the fox hunters and the Queen's Confessor.

The total expenditure of the Wardrobe account for the year was £64,105 0s. 5d., a grievous enough sum in its day. John de Drokensford and John de Benstede, Keeper and Comptroller respectively of the Wardrobe, were also responsible for the receipt of no small share of the Crown's revenues.

The reign of Edward II (1307-27) is notable for the rise and disgrace of the first of the greedy, unscrupulous, overweening Court favourites who cut such an equivocal figure on the stage of history. Piers Gaveston, son of a Gascon knight, was a play-mate of the young Prince, on whom he gained an early, and probably a vicious, hold. Like so many sons of stern rulers, Edward's tastes were for prodigals, fiddlers and low company. Gaveston was handsome, witty, musical, a linguist and a good jouster; that Edward should have preferred his company to that of noble dullards is not surprising. It is unlikely that the favourite had serious political ambitions. He was essentially a pleasure-lover and a plunderer. The tightness of his grip on young Edward may be judged from what happened when the Abbot of Peterborough offered the Prince the gift of a valuable cup. This was declined on the ground that Gaveston had not been offered a similar gift. The favourite, suitably solaced, was then begged to use his influence to make Edward accept his cup. This Gaveston graciously consented to do, sending an officer with the words, 'Go to Lord Edward and tell him I am willing he should receive the Abbot's present.'

Court ladies abroad: Queen Isabella, wife of Edward II, arrives at Paris, 1325, to intrigue against her husband. From Froissart's *Chronicles*

To Edward I, the dependence of his son on Gaveston was nauseating. He decided to break up the association, but had hardly signed the order exiling the favourite when he died. Back came Gaveston, more insolent than ever, and was rewarded, for no visible services, with manors, rents, a castle, vast quantities of jewels, episcopal forfeits, a huge fund collected for the relief of the Holy Land, the earldom of Cornwall and a bride of the blood royal. At the Coronation he wore purple and carried the crown of St Edward. The public behaviour of King and favourite on this occasion threatened a premature end to the festivities. Queen Isabella, having seen her husband's affections lavished on Gaveston, now saw her rival endowed with the presents her father had given her. Gaveston must have known that the game could not last, for much of his wealth he prudently sent out of the country; but while it lasted, he invited fellow Gascons to England to share in the looting. Through their depredations, the Court itself could hardly meet its commitments. The old nobility, for whom Gaveston had insulting nicknames, and whom he propelled from their saddles with contemptuous ease, could stand only so much. Previous kings had seen fit to vest power in Household servants, but these, however unworthy, had not been irresponsible pirates. Gaveston was the *reductio ad absurdum* of the system. So the barons seized him and on a hill near Warwick his handsome head was struck off by a ferocious Welshman. A moral monument built on the spot recorded how 'the Minion of a Hateful King' was beheaded 'by Barons Lawless as Himself.'*

At least Gaveston's end was quick and clean. His royal master, humiliated by his nobles, defeated by the Scots, rationed by the Despensers, deserted by his wife and driven from the Throne, was murdered by the insertion of red-hot rods in his fundament.

The third Edward (1327–77) was intoxicated with the spirit of chivalry, which did not prevent him from hanging his mother's lover. There was a period when he saw himself as a second Arthur. Before the vision faded he pulled down much of Windsor Castle and rebuilt it with a Round Tower on the lines of the Arthurian one. In 1345 he held an international tournament at Windsor. His heralds ranged through Scotland, Burgundy, Hainault, Flanders, Brabant and Germany, offering a fifteen-days safe conduct to all knights and esquires who wished to compete. According to Adam de Murimuth, an indulgent cleric who was present, the revels were uninhibited and the ladies delightfully free with their kisses. 'The joy was unspeakable, the comfort inestimable, the pleasure without murmuring, the hilarity without care.' Even the captive David, King of Scotland, enjoyed the occasion. He was given a fine horse and invited to join in the jousting, which he did with

* W. P. Dodge: *Piers Gaveston*

distinction. Edward revelled in the whole affair. He had found the secret of happy sovereignty: it was to be a royal showman. About this time he conceived the idea of a new order of chivalry, the Order of the Garter, an honour which was intended to promote piety and virtue by force of example. Thanks to Edward's chivalrous obsession, the heralds assumed a new importance at Court. Their function, apart from carrying the King's challenge through Europe, was to give dignity to tournaments and discipline to all forms of ceremonial. From this reign date Norroy and Surroy Kings-at-Arms.

Another of Edward's more popular revels was the one which followed his return from France with prodigious loot from Caen and Calais. For months on end Court and capital frolicked around in expensive clothes, like pirates dressing up in the cargo of a treasure galleon. Never had so many subjects worn French furs and velvets. Hardly a housewife lacked French household linen or utensils.

Orgies like these did the public morals no good. The Court was much blamed for the frivolities and abominations which now became fashionable. Even the clergy succumbed to the lure of dressing up. They wore curled and powdered hair, hung themselves with knives and wore frivolous footwear. In the processions to tournaments rode beribboned women dressed as men, mounted on splendid horses, and indulging in much 'scurrilous wantonness.' One such was Alice Perrers, who rode from the Tower to a great joust at Smithfield dressed as the Lady of the Sun. She became the King's mistress and a menace in the land. Even John o'Gaunt could not ignore the fact that she had the royal ear. In the course of feathering her nest, Perrers sat on the judicial bench to ensure that the judges should decide causes in her favour. When the friendless apostle of chivalry was dying at Sheen, near Richmond, she is supposed to have pulled the rings from his fingers and abandoned him to a solitary priest. Edward, alas, was not the last king to be pillaged in his dotage by a rapacious mistress.

In his prime, he had been a king with *panache* and his Court had attained a splendour which only the next king would surpass. It was not his fault that his espousal of chivalry coincided with the arrival of gunpowder.

*   *   *

When 15-year-old Richard II brought his bride, Anne of
Bohemia, to London, in 1377, four enchanting maidens of his
own age, perched on a tower in Cheapside, blew gold leaf
towards him and threw imitation gold coins under his horse's
feet. The tower on which they stood gushed out red and white
wine for the lieges' refreshment.

The Black Prince's son tried to conduct his Court in the
same fanciful spirit. Surrounding him were a swarm of prodigals who urged him to 'be a king.' The barons, who believed
that if money was to be squandered, it should be squandered
on war, deeply resented the delirious spending in the Old
Palace of Westminster. Richard, as they admitted, had spirit—
had he not galloped out to harangue the insurgent peasants
when Wat Tyler was struck down?—but the life he was living
could lead only to lechery, decay and revolution.

In its heyday, Richard's Court was not so much a court as
a royal city, feeding up to ten thousand mouths daily. This
city laboured mightily for its own glorification. It was not
concerned with commerce, save in so far as it was necessary
to import freaks, luxuries and vices. It was a heaven and a
haven of servants, of whom the lower ones wore simple livery
and the upper ones wore cloth of gold. It was a city of dung
and diamonds. It was a twanging, strumming, tinkling city,
daubed in bright primary colours, scented indoors with trodden
herbs. It was a neighing, barking, fluttering city, half menagerie and half monastery. It was a city with a baker's dozen
of bishops, little concerned with the care of souls; but to make
up for their deficiencies there was a profusion of lesser churchmen, all warranted to be 'in descant clean voiced, well released
and pronouncing, eloquent in reading and sufficient in organ
playing.' It was an ogling, pining city, with top-heavy maidens
waiting to be traded for manors and castles. At its heart was
a literate cell of clerks who kept the records, not only of the
Old Palace, but of the nation. And in the recesses of this city
were hundreds of liveried craftsmen who could fashion anything from a gilded pavilion to an assault tower.

Now and then the occupants of this city forsook their recreations (and rumour said some of their recreations were unspeakable) to form themselves into bizarre processions: sixty
squires on sixty barded coursers, then sixty ladies of high rank

on palfreys, each leading on a silver chain a knight completely armed for tilting. To common men unaccustomed to deferring to women, the sight was both splendid and shaming. Occasionally pride took a toss, as when a Court waggon capsized on London Bridge and spilled its load of maids of honour upside down on their foolish head-dresses.

Hundreds of Cheshire archers, well-paid, insolent men ready to kill at the drop of a glove, guarded Richard's Court and wore his white hart livery. On a notorious day four thousand of them surrounded Parliament, with bows bent, arrows ready. But their authority extended little farther than an arrow's flight. On the roads between Westminster and the royal manors desperate men preyed on the King's messengers. Richard's Clerk of Works, one Geoffrey Chaucer, set off to Eltham to pay accounts and was robbed of his money and horse. He set out again the same day and was again robbed. It did not help his prestige at Court.

Two arts were well understood by the inhabitants of Richard's Court: that of feeding themselves and that of clothing themselves. One Christmas 28 oxen, 300 sheep and innumerable fowls were slaughtered daily. 'In the kitchen,' says Holinshed, 'there were 300 servitors and every other office was furnished after the like fashion.' It was not only the officers and servants, the archers and craftsmen, who had to be fed, but their wives, children and dependants.

The passion for self-adornment verged on mania. There were laws which regulated the amount of silk and fur to be worn by men and women of different ranks, but they were laughed at. 'Yeomen and grooms,' according to Holinshed, 'were clothed in silks with cloth of grain and scarlet over sumptuous, ye may be sure, for their estates. And this vanity was not only used in the Court . . . but also other people in the towns and country had their garments cut far otherwise than had been customed . . . with embroideries, rich furs and goldsmiths' work, and every day there was devising of new fashions to the great hindrance and decay of the commonwealth.'*

William Langland is more scornful. In his *Richard the Redeless* (in modern slang, Richard the Clueless) he describes the system of dressmaking at Richard's Court. The thing to do, he says,

* *Chronicles*

is to buy a length of expensive cloth, slash it into pieces, and then pay seven good stitchers for six weeks to stitch it all together again, thus multiplying the cost of the cloth by twenty. The poet mocks the King's malapert courtiers as 'the sleeves,' because these appendages had to be long enough to sweep the ground as they walked. He could as easily have called them 'the shoes,' for the points of shoes were so long that a cart wheel could have passed over them without coming nearer than six inches to the wearer's toes. For mobility, the ends of the toes were caught up in gold chains to the knees, or even to the waist. The higher a man's rank, the more he weighted his clothes with precious stones; and the heavier his clothes, the more they dragged in the dung. But hygiene was not wholly lacking. Richard is credited with being the first king to use a handkerchief.

His first Queen, Anne of Bohemia, set the feminine fashions of the Court. In particular she is remembered for the great horned head-dress which made women's faces appear to be a third of the way down their bodies. His second wife, Isabella of Valois, had no chance to set any fashions. She was not eight years old when he married her and was only ten when he abdicated.

Those who feasted and strutted amid the bright arras had no illusions about the stability of this Court. Many were up-starts, and it was in their interest to stiffen the King against the powerful boors who bullied him. Richard, unbalanced and passionate, needed little stiffening. Criticism of his Household he regarded as treason. He swore that not a varlet of his kitchen would he discharge at the request of Parliament. When Anne of Bohemia died he pettishly destroyed the palace of Sheen which had failed to exclude the angel of death, and dared Parliament to say anything about it. Yet even Richard occasionally drew the line at extravagance in his entourage. When he found that the Lady of Coucy, Isabella's governess at Windsor, was keeping 18 horses, maintaining several gold-smiths and furriers and building a chapel, he dismissed her. Not long afterwards, the barons dismissed Richard.

The reign was not all waste. In spite of the perversities of dress, it was an age of taste in art and building. To Richard goes the credit for the existing version of Westminster Hall.

Radio Times Hulton Library

Court officers of Richard II. Note long shoes

For its completion he wore a gold gown stiff with pearls and gems. Not even Richard could prevent the Thames from rising on occasions and flooding the Hall. At various times men have rowed about it in wherries.

The medieval pattern was breaking up. There were spendthrift, luxuriant courts still to come, notably that of Edward IV (1471-83) which eventually foundered under a weight of female relatives and concubines. But Richard's Court marked the Plantagenets' zenith.

If Richard had a sense of humour, there is little or no evidence of it. For a glimpse of a jester at work, it is better

to turn to the Court of the fourth Edward. Here flourished
the fool Scoggin, whose jests* would make a daunting chapter
in a history of humour. Many of them were no doubt attributed
to him by men of inferior wit. Supposedly, Scoggin had been
a student at Oxford University, but, believing that 'a Master
of Art is not worth a f——t,' he allowed himself to be introduced to Court by Sir William Nevill. On his first visit there
he drew attention to himself by standing for a long period
under a running waterspout, in an effort to win a £20 wager.
He was quick to learn the ways of the Court and was impressed
by the way in which 'men did leap over the table in the King's
hall to sit down to dinner and supper.' Evidently this had not
been the custom at Oxford.

Like most fools, Scoggin was in the game for the money, and
extracted considerable sums from courtiers and such dignitaries as he met on royal progresses. Once, feeling inadequately
rewarded, he obtained a fat sow and began to roast it under
the palace wall, greasing it liberally and unnecessarily. Asked
for an explanation, he said: 'I do as kings and lords and every
man else do; for he that hath enough shall have more and
he that hath nothing shall go without, and this sow needeth
no basting nor greasing for she is fat enough yet shall she have
more than enough.' This performance was described to the
King, who offered the fool a house in Cheapside. Evidently
it did not wholly satisfy him, for he threatened to fill it with
straw and set fire to it, which caused the neighbours to protest
vigorously. After collecting £40 from them, Scoggin let it be
known that he had abandoned his incendiary intentions. The
King also gave him a mansion at Bury.

Scoggin's jests, though simple-minded and unseemly, cannot
be passed over if we are to understand the sense of humour
of our forebears. Asked why he drew his son up and down the
Court by the heels, he replied, 'Every man doth say that that
man or child which is drawn up in the Court shall be the
better as long as he lives.'

When the Queen sent for Scoggin's wife he told each that
the other was deaf, thus precipitating a strenuous shouting
match. But his crudest jest at the Queen's expense occurred
when he asked her if she would like to have 'horseplay played

* A purported collection appears in Andrew Boorde's *Scoggin's Jests* (*1626*)

in her chamber.' Innocently the Queen replied, 'Yea.' Whereupon 'Scoggin unbuttoned his points and put down his breeches as if he would have bewrayed the chamber and then kicked up his heels and said wehee.' As he was trying to persuade a servant to come and comb him, the Queen exclaimed, 'Out, knave, out of my chamber!' but the fool protested that he had acted thus by her express permission. 'After that the Queen would have no more horseplay in her chamber,' says Andrew Boorde.

For impertinences of this kind the Queen and her ladies proposed to beat Scoggin with stones enclosed in napkins, but he extracted himself from this peril by inviting the greatest whore to strike the first blow.

Much of Scoggin's wit, such as it was, consisted of taking instructions literally. If the King said he had no wish to see the fool's face again, the fool would arrange for the King to see a baser portion of his anatomy. When banished from the realm and told not to set foot on English soil again, he reputedly returned from France with his shoes full of Picard earth.

It would seem that life at Court must have been inexpressibly dull if it needed wit like Scoggin's to brighten it. Even less seemly, perhaps, were the capers of those buffoons who owed their presence at Court to the fact that they were simpletons or monsters, or the possessors of hideous squints. Accustomed from youth to be laughed at, they made a virtue of parading their shortcomings before the royal board. The proudest uniform to which they could aspire was the coat of motley, with trousers in two colours, ass's head and cock's comb; the proudest staff was the stick with a bladder tied to it. Such as these were not given houses in Cheapside or anywhere else. They slept with the dogs, were fed and belaboured like dogs, but were not unhappy.

It has been widely forgotten that one of the functions of a fool was to keep his royal master in a eupeptic state. Laughter stimulates the digestive organs. Thus, a fool was required to give of his best at dinner. Jesters attending the banquets of the lord mayors of London were required to jump into a large bowl of custard, splashing it in all directions.

4

Standing Orders

ANYONE who has served in the armed forces of the Crown will be aware that the daily life of a camp is not always conducted in minutest accordance with standing orders. It is probable, therefore, that the rules drawn up for the courts of kings are only an approximate guide to life as it was lived.

In the latter years of the fifteenth century there were detailed regulations for everything from the laying of a royal table-cloth to the *accouchement* of a queen.* These were drawn up by the lords spiritual, temporal and legal, and if they had been adhered to the life of the Court would have been one of exemplary diligence and gravity. But, as Edward IV well knew, it was impossible to frame rules governing the irrational activities of favourites, female relatives, concubines and Scoggins.

On paper, the mother of Edward IV, the Princess Cecily, lived a life of arduous piety. Her standing orders said that she was to rise at seven, say matins with her chaplain and observe low mass in her chamber, before being allowed to take 'something to recreate nature.' She then went to chapel for divine service and two low masses. Next came dinner, 'during the time whereof she hath a lecture of holy matter.' For an hour afterwards she held audience, then slept for a quarter of an hour, and prayed until the first peal of evensong. Hereabouts came a respite; she was allowed to take wine or ale at pleasure, but not enough to prevent her saying both evensongs with a chaplain. After the last peal, she went on to chapel to hear evensong by note. At supper she was expected to repeat, to

---

* John Nichols: *A Collection of Ordinances . . . from Edward III to William and Mary (1790)*

those about her, the holy matter to which she had listened at
dinner. Once over this hurdle, she was at liberty to indulge
in honest mirth, if she could summon up any, with her gentlewomen. One hour before bed-time she was permitted to drink

Radio Times Hulton Library

The Court of Edward IV

a cup of wine. Then, after taking leave of God in her privy
closet, she retired to bed by eight, having indulged in no exercise other than spiritual. The hardest part of the programme
may have been to sleep for exactly a quarter of an hour when
directed. The King, her son, seems to have entertained doubts
as to whether this exacting schedule was strictly kept. 'I trust
of our Lord's mercy that this noble princess thus divideth the
hours to his high pleasure,' he noted.

Edward's son was brought up at Ludlow Castle. The ordinances for the 'politic, sad and good rule' of his household
directed that there should be no idleness or unvirtuous behaviour. His courtiers were to read to him only 'such noble
stories as behoveth a prince to understand.' Any courtier who
struck another was to be put in the stocks; for a second offence

he was to be dismissed. One of the duties of the Prince's gentle-men was to make him 'joyous and merry towards his bed,' to which he went at eight o'clock. Any member of his entourage arriving late at matins, that is, after the third lesson, was to have nothing to eat but bread and water until dinner. At Easter all had to produce written evidence that they had received the Holy Sacrament. There was a tariff of fines for swearing.

In his own household, the King had a number of youths who came under a regimen nearly as strict as that of his son. These were the henxmen, pages from noble families under-going their apprenticeship to knighthood. They read the newest works on courtesy and urbanity, learned to 'ride cleanly and surely,' engaged each other with all gentlemanly weapons, and studied languages, piping, singing, dancing and 'honest and temperate behaviour.' There was a Master of the Henxmen who sat beside them at the royal board to see 'how mannerly they eat and drink.' Nor were these the only young-sters in the King's care. He stood *in loco parentis* to the golden-voiced boys of the King's Chapel, in the recruiting of whom enormous pains were taken. When their voices broke they were sent at the royal expense to Oxford or Cambridge.

The officers closest to the King were the Esquires of the Body. Their function, and exclusive privilege, was to 'array and unarray' the King in the morning and evening, and to watch over him continuously. Every night an Esquire of the Body attended at the King's Cupboard to 'serve him for All Night.' Thereafter this Esquire, who slept on a pallet in the Presence Chamber, had sole command of the palace, above and below stairs. If urgent dispatches were brought at night, it was his duty, and nobody else's, to wake the King and hand them to him. The royal Chamber held so many sleeping figures—here a gentleman, there a groom, there a page—that the King had little cause to fear the entry of an assassin. His chief con-cern, perhaps, was to surround himself with gentlemen who did not snore.

The Esquires of the Body are not to be confused with the Esquires of the Household, who in later reigns were called Gentlemen of the Privy Chamber, and who were privileged to complete the dressing of the King. Originally their function was to provide cultured, witty and knowledgeable conversation for the Sovereign, to sing or play musical instruments, and to put visitors at their ease. By earning the favour and trust of the King a Gentleman could be readily advanced to high office.

It is noteworthy that while the well-born competed for the privilege of performing menial tasks about the royal person, the shaving of the King's chin was left, and very wisely so, to a professional. Unfortunately, barbers tended to be uncouth fellows. The rules directed that the barber should not begin operations on the King's 'most high and dread person' until an Esquire of the Body or higher dignitary was present. On Saturday nights, unless the King directed otherwise, the barber was to cleanse the royal head, legs and feet, earning two loaves and a pitcher of wine for his pains. As we do not know how often the King directed otherwise, we can form no idea how high and dread he became.

When a king asked for meat, he set in train a complex routine in which nothing was left to individual initiative. The instructions say: '. . . the Sewer shall take the Esquires and go down to the kitchen and fetch the King's meat; and when he cometh up again the Usher shall go to the ewery board and say to the Ewer, Give me a towel that the King shall wash with, and lay it on his shoulder and go therewith into the King's Chamber, and when he cometh there, take the towel to the greatest estate, and stand still till the basin follow . . .' And so on, interminably.

Making the King's bed was not an operation which could be rushed. It required the presence of two Esquires of the Body at the head of the bed and two grooms at the foot, besides a yeoman or groom to carry in 'the stuff' and a Gentleman Usher to hold the bed curtains together. Here is an excerpt from the directions: '. . . the Esquires to gather the sheet round together in their hand on either side of the bed, and go to the bed's head and strike down the same twice or thrice as they come down and shake the sheet at the feet; then lay it abroad on the bed; then lay on the over fustian above; then take a pane of ermines and lay it above; then roll down the bed the space of an ell; then let the yeomen take the pillows and beat them well with their hands and cast them up to the Esquires and let them lay on, as it pleaseth the King best, high or low. . .'

Finally an Esquire of the Body was required to cast holy water on the bed, an act which, one feels, might well have been performed symbolically. When this was done, and the bed was warranted free from daggers and assassins, all who had been concerned with the ritual went off to refresh themselves with bread, ale and wine. No doubt an efficient 'necessary woman' could have made a better, though perhaps not a safer, bed in half the time.

A Queen's bed was made with especial ceremony when she was to be delivered of a child. The walls were hung with rich arras, except for a single window, the floors well carpeted, and the bed covered with ermine and cloth of gold. When her time came, however, there was no question of rushing her to bed. She was escorted in procession by lords and ladies of estate, first to the Chapel to be houseled, then to the Great Chamber for spice and wine, then into her chamber for delivery. When the lords and ladies had departed no man was to enter her apartments. The man-midwife was still three centuries off.

For the christening, the child was carried in a rich mantle of cloth of gold furred with ermine, and preceded by 200 torches. In the church the torches were extinguished, but re-lit after the ceremony at the font. Afterwards the prince was placed in a state cradle of gold, crimson and ermine. He drew his nourishment from a nurse, the Queen having already given adequate demonstration that she was human. Officials were deputed to assay the nurse's meat and drink while she gave suck; and when the infant reached the stage of meat and drink a physician was to stand over the nurse at every meal to ensure that a correct dietary balance was observed.

On marriage, a princess allowed herself to be put to bed by her ladies. Her husband was brought in and sat beside her in his shirt, with a gown wrapped round him. Then a bishop and a chaplain came in and blessed the bed, after which all spectators left the room 'without any drink.' The bride remained out of sight until she visited chapel on the third day, to offer a taper.

When a prince of the blood died, his body was placed in a new chest covered with white damask and bearing a cross of red velvet. An image of the dead man, executed as faithfully as possible, was dressed in his robes and laid over the coffin on a black-draped chariot drawn by six black-draped horses, with the hangings of the chariot rolled up in such a way that anyone could see the Prince's image. Sombre torchmen preceded the hearse night after night until it reached its destination. For their benefit there was a cart bearing spare torches which were lit as required. At night the body was suitably guarded in churches. The regulations do not say who was to undertake the task of making a life-like dummy of a dead prince.

What should have been an informal occasion, the handing of gifts to the King on New Year's Day, was nothing of the sort. First an Usher of the Chamber would go up to the King and say, 'There is a New Year's gift come from the Queen.' The King would reply, 'Sir, let it come in,' and the Usher would then admit the messenger bearing the gift. If the messenger was a knight he would receive ten marks; if an esquire, eight marks. Gifts from other members of the royal family, and from the nobility, were announced in similar fashion, and the messengers rewarded according to a sliding scale. It was directed that the Queen's gifts should not be as valuable as those of the King.

5

Bright and Lusty

THE first of the Tudors, whose crown was picked up from a bramble bush on Bosworth Field, in 1485, probably came as near as any monarch to running his Court in accordance with standing orders. Henry VII contrived to live with prudence and dignity, and without benefit of a Scoggin. During his reign the old 'King's Council,' which had suffered many vicissitudes since Norman days, took on an orderly pattern as a Privy Council, with a careful blending of advisers, administrative experts and Household dignitaries.

Although Henry saved a good deal of money, much of which he invested in jewels, he was no cheeseparer. Ambassadors were well satisfied by the lustre of his receptions. No miser would have built as Henry did. He created the splendid palace of Richmond, the earlier royal dwelling of Sheen having been burned down, and he provided the funds for the chapel at Westminster where he is buried. He inherited an extended and remodelled palace at Greenwich, birthplace of four Tudor rulers.

It was a Court lit by the rising fires of the Renaissance. Scholars, philosophers and poets were welcome in its halls, as they were welcome at the home of the monarch's mother, Margaret Beaufort, the 'Lady Margaret' of Oxford and Cambridge. Nine-year-old Prince Henry, the future Henry VIII, was visited in his nursery by Sir Thomas More and Erasmus. Not only scholars were welcome; so were merchants, discoverers and travellers of all kinds.

A major embellishment added by Henry to his Court was a royal bodyguard: the Yeomen of the Guard of Our Lord the King. His pretext for forming this still-existing corps was that he wished to give new dignity to his coronation ceremony.

There were, at the outset, fifty archers, 'hardy, strong and of agility,' charged with keeping daily attendance on the King's person. This influx of armed men with their dependants caused a certain amount of grumbling in and out of Court, especially as their numbers more than doubled before the King died. Only monarchs like Richard II had found it necessary to employ 'such a furniture of daily soldiers.'

Ruthlessly, craftily, Henry filleted the barons and stiffened the central power. The middle classes were with him. And all classes idolised his son—a son who, as it turned out, could be relied upon to cut down ruthlessly all who threatened the Tudor line.

Outwardly, the Court of the young Henry VIII had a lusty, brainless beauty all its own. In place of a gloomy extortioner (for that was how Henry VII was widely regarded), here was a dashing 18-year-old prince with every claim to the title, if anyone had thought of it, of First Gentleman of Europe. He had a beautiful, if second-hand, wife, at whose first wedding (to his brother) he had danced a jubilant jig in his underclothes. Ominously, Catherine was six years his senior.

This nonpareil among princes was a lover of learning and music, but he recognised that the times called for a certain heartiness. Among the younger nobility there had been too much dancing and gambling, not enough hunting and tilting. By his own example Henry sought to restore the balance.

Surrounding his person, in the roles of Esquire of the Body, Cupbearer, Gentleman of the King's Chamber and so on, was forged as tough a ring of extroverts as the Court of England had ever assembled. With a few notable exceptions, they looked warily on the new ideas, the softening influences from the South. Too much learning, they suspected, was liable to breed not only unmanliness but moral scruple. In Henry they had just the King they wanted—a man ready to ride and wrestle, revel and sing, generous, flamboyant, skilled at arms, courageous, chivalrous. Essentially, the courtiers were men of action. The only art for which they cared was that of self-adornment, and like their master they were slaves to cloth of gold. Their idea of a day's fun was to propel each other from horses, or to pit one part of the brute creation against another—hounds against stags and otters, bandogs against bears, hawks against

herons. Henry himself would wear out eight or ten horses in
a day and yet ride home unsated. Afterwards there was feasting,
with little wit but much laughter. Why cudgel the creaking
brain for persiflage when there were buffoons ready to knock
each other about?

There were poets at Court, but mostly they were roystering
warrior-poets, like Sir Francis Bryan, the one-eyed 'vicar of
hell.' No cupbearer emptied so many cups with his royal
master. His valour in this respect, like that of the King, may
have done a useful service to literature by demonstrating that
it need not be the exclusive obsession of milksops. A later
courtier-poet was Henry Howard, Earl of Surrey, a quarrelsome, full-blooded fellow who wrote his poems on the not
infrequent occasions when he found himself in custody. There
was also Sir Thomas Wyatt, who shares with Surrey the
honour of importing the sonnet from Italy. He was a man of
action and affairs, as ready to cozen an emperor as browbeat
an abbess.

It was a great life for those who did not weaken. If a man
could hold his lance, his liquor and his tongue, if he was ready
to wring the necks of rebels, lead a mission or empty a monastery, and not least, if he could keep his hands off the King's
women, then the good things of life would tumble into his
lap: titles, grants, manors, pastures, bailiwicks, sheriffdoms,
stewardships, keeperships of forests and all the rest. The old
nobility, even the arrogant Howards, were welcome to join in,
provided they did not seek to play the game by their own rules.

The men who made their mark under Henry did not remain
for long periods at Court. They would depart at intervals to
fight the King's battles or conduct his intrigues at foreign
courts, to govern the Irish or maintain prestige at Calais, then
perhaps return to take another appointment under the King's
immediate eye. All of which had a certain liberalising effect on
Court manners. A character in Shakespeare's *Henry VIII* speaks of

> . . . our travelled gallants
> That fill the Court with quarrels, talk and tailors.

When a man lost favour, foreign affectations might be held
against him.

At first, the public did not grudge Henry and his roysterers their fun. Had he not celebrated his accession by executing the two most eminent tax-collectors in the realm? Soon enough his impartial axe would descend on eminent taxpayers too, but meanwhile life was good. Thanks to his father, there was cash and to spare for masques, mummeries, tournaments, pageants by land and water. At Henry's coronation a crown-capped castle was run up at Westminster and from its gargoyles, for days on end, ran three continual streams of wine. But what was a mere wine-filled castle? For the Queen's special delight they lugged up a mobile park, enclosed with pales of white and green, and containing a number of fallow deer frisking nervously among exquisite trees. When the park came to rest before the Queen, the deer ran out and the greyhounds were let slip. Gallant knights then presented the corpses of the deer to the Queen and her ladies.

The building of conceits like these gave gainful employment to scores of needy artificers. The King or his representative might order a ship in full sail, or a gem-studded mountain covered with roses and pomegranates, with internal accommodation for a lady of the mountain and her children of honour; or a forest containing a castle of gold, to be drawn by a lion and an antelope; or another mountain, this time carrying a freight of beasts and savage men, capable of opening up to disgorge a company of knights and ladies; or a Garden of Esperance with turrets at the corners, its banks brightly flowered, with room for six knights to dance with six ladies. Sometimes the artificers scamped their work. There was an unhappy day at Westminster when two lighters, disguised as warships, were set to engage each other in mock battle. One of them broke amidships and a gentleman was drowned. In the other a gun burst and maimed two mariners.*

The Court's passion for dressing up was as uninhibited as that of children in a box-room. Often the more expensive apparel was the gift of the King. Shortly after his marriage Henry and his favourite courtiers clad themselves as Robin Hood and his men and raided the Queen's chamber. The ladies squealed with the delight expected of them. After certain 'dances and pastimes' the visitors frisked off. Once, when the Court went out maying (another excuse for dressing up) they met 'Robin

* Holinshed describes many of these spectacles

Hood' and 200 men in green on Shooter's Hill. The outlaws, who were archers of the King's guard, fired a salvo of arrows with whistles attached, 'so that the noise was strange and loud, which greatly delighted the King, Queen and their company.' The Court were then invited into flowery arbours in the green-wood and regaled themselves on wine and venison.

Most of all, perhaps, the King liked to show off on horse-back. The ladies at their windows encouraged him to prance and caracole. As a jouster he was formidable. In a tournament at Greenwich, in the sixth year of his reign, he and the Marquis of Dorset took on all comers. The King broke 23 spears and bore down a rider complete with horse.

It was to encourage the well-born in deeds of arms that the King formed, in 1509, a new *élite* guard of fifty gentlemen, the King's Spears. Each member of this sumptuous corps had to find his own armour and maintain a servant with javelin or demi-lance and two mounted archers. On foot the Spears were armed with the spiked battle-axe which gave them their name. They were expected to accompany the sovereign on ceremonial occasions and to take part in all tournaments. This *garde du corps* proved too expensive and was allowed to lapse, but was re-created in 1539 as the Band of Gentlemen Pensioners. In the words of one of its later captains, it was to serve as 'a nursery to breed up hopeful gentlemen and fit them for employments, civil and military, as well abroad as at home,' notably as deputies of Ireland, ambassadors, captains of the guard, counsellors of state and commanders in the wars.

Between Henry and Cardinal Wolsey the relationship was not unlike that which existed between Henry II and Becket. The butcher's son lived in outrageous grandeur in two palaces —York Place, in London, and Hampton Court. In his suite of nearly a thousand persons he had all the apparatus of royalty. He kept ten main tables a day. His mules, like his palaces, were hung with crimson velvet. When he walked in procession two great crosses were carried before him and his gentlemen ushers cried, 'On before, my lords and masters, on before! Make way for my Lord Cardinal.'

One day at York Place Wolsey's guests were half-way through a banquet when a salute of guns from the water gate shook the roof. It was obvious that distinguished visitors had arrived. Solemnly, Wolsey sent his highest officer to make enquiries. The officer reported that the visitors appeared to be ambassadors of a foreign prince, and was told to invite them to the banquet. Ushered in by torches, drums and flutes, the strangers entered, vizarded, in splendid robes of cloth of gold laced with silver wire. The Cardinal declared his belief that one of them was of higher status than himself, and eventually, after a good deal of business, the King revealed himself. He was led up to the Cardinal's bedchamber, where a big fire was blazing, to robe himself for the banquet. The guests whose dinner was interrupted had no complaint, for the cloths were whipped away, clean ones laid and the whole meal began all over again.*

The gaudiest display of the reign—and perhaps of any reign —was staged, not at Hampton Court, York Place or Westminster, but on foreign soil. This, the Field of the Cloth of Gold, was a heroic attempt by the King and Wolsey to outdazzle a nation which heavily outnumbered their own. Near the Castle of Guisnes a thousand English workmen built a crystal palace of 437 yards square, with glass windows, and bearing no other adornment than gold and silver. Inside it were state apartments, including a chapel. Near the town of Ardres a similar pavilion was set up for the French king. Henry had 4000 in his train, his Queen 1200. Wolsey fielded his usual immodest suite. It was an occasion of enormous ostentation and enormous distrust. On the first day the French and English hosts, jingling and flashing, rode warily towards each other, then halted, each on rising ground. The two kings rode out towards each other, dismounted and embraced, whereupon their followers mingled with hearty, if spurious, *bonhomie*. A fortnight's feasting, tilting and dressing up followed:

> Today the French
> All clinquant, all in gold, like heathen gods,
> Shone down the English; and tomorrow they
> Made Britain India; every man that stood
> Show'd like a mine. Their dwarfish pages were
> As cherubims, all gilt. . .†

* George Cavendish: *Life of Cardinal Wolsey*
† Shakespeare: *King Henry VIII*

It was the last great jamboree of old-fashioned chivalry, and since it was an event of chivalry the ordinary public were excluded from it. They watched, fascinated, from a distance, herded and threatened by security officials. Other officials carefully counted the number of attendants on each side and tried to ensure that when the monarchs left their pavilions they should do so simultaneously. The whole event, as it turned out, was a success only for security. Politically, the results were as indifferent as the intentions were dubious. Socially, the effects were crippling, for many in Henry's Court 'broke their backs with laying manors on 'em.'

During the decade which reached its climax at Guisnes, the Court's reputation abroad was by no means one of empty exhibitionism. The Pope's envoy in 1517 was not too dazzled by cloth of gold to notice that English manners were exceptionally good. Those who called the English barbarians, he said, qualified for that description themselves. Erasmus thought that Henry's Court, in its concern for learning and piety, was the home of the Muses, a beacon to Christendom. Observers reported, as they reported in Elizabeth's time, that there were more learned men at Court than in any university. It may be that visitors saw that aspect of the Court they wanted to see.

The King, while ready enough to punish his followers for public misbehaviour, in private rode many of them with an easy rein, leaving it to others to tighten up discipline. In 1519 several young gentlemen who had been over-familiar with him were removed by the Council and replaced by a group of 'sad and ancient knights,' and many other appointments were changed.

6

No Private Eating

WOLSEY'S back was not broken by the Field of the Cloth of Gold. He still produced any number of 'excellent fair dames' at his entertainments. His master cook still wore damask satin with a chain of gold. Not all, by any means, grudged the butcher's son his success, but John Skelton, the King's unofficial laureate, did:

> The King's Court
>> Should have the excellence,
> But Hampton Court
>> Hath the pre-eminence. . .*

In 1526 Wolsey, in disfavour on more serious matters, tactfully handed over Hampton Court as a gift to the King. In that same year the Cardinal drew up the Eltham Statutes,† by which he hoped to bring about much-needed reforms in the conduct of Henry's Household. The Statutes seem to have met with the usual fate of standing orders, but they shed a good deal of light on the running of a Tudor palace.

In his preamble, the Cardinal complained that while the King had been away at the wars, striving for the weal of Christendom, a great many abuses had multiplied at Court. It had become the resort of ' boys and vile persons,' 'vagabonds and mighty beggars' and of unkennelled hounds. Locks had been stolen from doors, thus making it easier to abstract tables, forms, trestles and cupboards. The servants, in fact, had taken to pillaging their royal master's home as freely as if it had been the home of a nobleman where the King was staying. On top of it all, there was cheating in the Chandlery and

---

* *Why Come Ye Not To Court?*
† John Nichols: *A Collection of Ordinances*

squabbling in the Squillery. Henceforth, said Wolsey, Gentlemen Ushers and Yeomen Ushers were to watch that no property was filched. Harbingers were to warn those whom they lodged 'that no person presume to take by high words, ravine, violent countenance or other undue means any victuals, fruit, hay, corn, grass, deer, fish or coneys.'

The Cardinal deplored that the Court was the scene of much confusion and annoyance because of the influx of 'sickly, impotent, inable and unmeet persons' whose only function was to eat the food of better men. These were to be replaced by 'persons of good towardness, likelihood, behaviour, demeanour and conversation'; and, if possible, they should also be of good gesture, countenance, fashion and stature. Visitors to Court were to bring to the royal board only their more cultivated and personable retainers. The Knight Harbinger would answer at his peril if unthrifty and common women were not openly punished or banished from Court; and the guards who, with their ill-disciplined boys and servants, occupied the greater part of the King's palace and the adjacent lodgings, were to be cut down in number. Only thus could the King's house become a mirror and example to others.

In the kitchens, the standard of hygiene was low. A grant would be made to the master cooks to clothe their scullions, who either went naked or wore garments of unusual vileness. Henceforth they were not to lie all night around the kitchen fire. Used dishes were to be taken back to the scullery and not left about or given to dogs. No unkennelled greyhounds, mastiffs or other dogs were to be suffered about the Court, but there was a dispensation in respect of 'some few small spaniels for ladies and others.' The keeping of ferrets was prohibited.

Throughout the Court, strict meal times would be observed. On 'eating days' dinner would be at ten o'clock or slightly earlier, and first supper at four o'clock. There was an antisocial tendency on the part of sundry gentlemen to dine in corners and secret places, instead of repairing to the King's chamber or hall, or to the head officers of the Household when hall was not kept. As a result the high officers had been destitute of company at their boards, and their viands had not been used 'to the King's honour.' In future all would dine at their

appointed messes, and to ensure that they did so the clerks of
the Green Cloth were charged with patrolling all secret eating-
holes.

Slothfulness, also, was to be rooted out. Pages were to be
up at seven o'clock to make the fires and rouse the Esquires
of the Body, who were to present themselves, dressed, in the
King's Chamber at eight. If the Esquires slept late, they were
to leave in their nightgowns and go to another room, so as
not to delay the preparation of the Chamber. At eight, a
Yeoman Usher was to stand at the Chamber door to repel
intruders. No ale, water or broken meat was to be dropped
outside the King's door. Grooms were to remove the overnight
pallets and lay straw on the floor, 'purging all filthiness,' so
that the King should find his rooms pure, clean and wholesome. This work was not to be left to inferior servants.

By seven o'clock or sooner six Gentlemen of the Privy
Chamber were to attend 'ready and proper of apparel' to dress
the King, handing him his clothes in 'reverent, discreet and
sober manner' (it appears that the Esquires of the Body put
on the King's foundation garments). No ushers or grooms were
to lay hands on the royal person, or to attempt to assist in the
ritual of dressing, 'except it be to warm clothes.' Doublet,
hose and shoes were to be brought 'honestly and cleanly' to
the door of the Chamber by the Yeoman of the Wardrobe,
who was on no account to cross the threshold. None of the
six gentlemen was to follow the King into his Bedchamber or
any other secret place unless called upon to do so.

It was important that all Gentlemen of the Privy Chamber
should be 'loving together and of good unity and accord.'
If the King was absent there was to be no speculation as to
his whereabouts, no matter what the time of day or night, and
no grudging, mumbling or talking about the way he spent his
time. Pending his return there would be no immoderate, continual gaming nor was the Chamber to be made the scene of
'frequent and intemperate plays'; moderate card-playing and
chess were not, however, excluded. As soon as they became
aware that the King was returning the Gentlemen were to
break off play so that they might stand in respectful attitudes
when he entered. All were to have 'a vigilant and reverent
respect to the eye of his Grace so that by his look or counte-

nance they may know what lacketh or is his pleasure to be had or done.' They were also to see that ushers and grooms stood at a suitable distance from the King, behaving neither too boldly nor familiarly. In general, the Gentlemen were expected to be 'well languaged, expert in outward parts and meet and able to be sent on familiar messages, or otherwise, to outward princes when the cause shall require.' On no account were they to present suits or interfere with causes.

Wolsey had a word of warning for nearly all. Mostly he required them to keep their eyes open and their doors shut, to give daily attendance and not to employ substitutes. Evidently earlier monarchs had been unlucky in their barbers, for he laid down that all barbers should be clean-smelling and of decent conversation, 'without resorting to the company of vile persons or of misguided women,' thus running the risk of infecting the King's person. Ironically, it was Wolsey himself who was to be accused of giving Henry the pox by breathing on him too closely.

The Sergeant of the Acatery* was to spurn inferior meats. He was to attend fairs and markets and make good bargains. Also, yearly, he was to 'attend at the sea coast to make provision of lings and cods for the King's most profit'; and he was to see that the King's pastures were well ordered and suitably stocked with cattle. In the Bakehouse the Sergeant and his clerk were to ensure that bread was baked properly, and not 'drowned with too much water.' The brewers, too, had been abusing their privileges; they were to produce 'good and seasonable stuff without weevil or fustiness and put neither hops nor brimstone in their ale in the pipes so that it may be found good, wholesome and perfect stuff and worthy the King's money.'

So it went on. Three or four times a day, one of the porters at the gate was to search the palace for any boys or vagabonds who, in spite of all precautions, might have entered the palace. His colleagues were to keep a special eye that no waxlights, leather pots, vessels of silver or pewter, wood or coals were smuggled out of the gates. The almoners were to be diligent in distributing broken meats to the poor, and to refrain from embezzling any portions thereof. Finally, Anne Harris, the

* A purchasing department

King's laundress, was to examine the soiled napery to see whether it had been abused, and if so to call the attention of the appropriate officers of the counting-house.

Disappointingly, Wolsey does not seem to have prescribed any code of behaviour for jesters. He heartily disliked Henry's favourite clown, Will Sommers, a lean, stooping Salopian who played elementary practical jokes on him. Sommers specialised in riddles, of which fortunately few have survived. One which is said to have caused the monarch to wax exceeding merry was: 'What is it that, being born without life, head, lip or eye, yet doth run roaring through the world till it die?' The answer was: 'A fart.' One authority says that Sommers slept among the spaniels. Perhaps Wolsey was content that he should remain there.

The Statutes are not entirely minatory. They contain authorised scales of accommodation, diet and expenditure which help to fill in the picture of Tudor Court life. Among them is a scale of stabling and beds for different ranks and degrees of visitors. For cardinals no specific figure was laid down. Dukes and archbishops were entitled to stabling for 24 horses and nine beds. The scale for noblewomen depended on whether they were widowed or whether their husbands were absent from Court; a widowed duchess could demand stabling for 20 horses and seven beds. Farther down the list were Esquire of the Body—five horses, two beds; Master of the Grammar—three horses, two beds; each chaplain—three horses, two beds; the Queen's maids, 'amongst them all'—six horses, three beds.

Obviously nine beds, however overcrowded, could hold only the merest fraction of a duke's retinue. The remainder of his followers, who might be numbered in hundreds, were quartered by the King's Harbingers within a radius of seven miles. It is easy to see that the arrival at Court of a prince of the Church, followed by several nobles and widows of nobles must have imposed a heavy strain on the surrounding countryside; which is sufficient explanation why the Court confined itself to large centres of population. Whether such visitations were a good thing for the local population may well be doubted, but probably much easy money was picked up by the residents.

The King's own horses, under the Master of the Horse and

his Querries (Equerries), took up no small space in the royal stables. They included 30 coursers, eight running horses, four Barbary horses, eight stallions, twelve hobbies and geldings, four running geldings, one mail horse, three battle horses, one stalking horse, one pack horse, seven sumpter horses and five horses for the carriage of the robes—more than a hundred in all. In addition to which there were ten horses for the officers of the Master of the Horse. Under the heading of 'Hackneys of Diverse Officers' was one for the King's fool.

Much has been heard of trenchermen's feats at the Court of the Tudors. At the table of 'the King's Majesty and the Queen's Grace' dinner and supper were divided into two so-called courses, each containing a large number of dishes which were courses and indeed meals in themselves. The menu is not an easy one to read, as it is not always clear which of the listed foods are alternative ones, nor is it even clear what some of the foods are. The first 'course' of dinner was made up of approximately fifteen dishes, beginning with bread and soup and proceeding through beef, venison, red deer, mutton (or young veal) to swan (or grey goose or stork), capons, coneys and baked carp, rounded off with custard or fritters. The second course of some nine dishes began with jelly, ipocras* and cream of almonds, then took toll of pheasants, herons, bitterns, shovelards, partridges, quails or mews, cocks, plovers, gulls, kid, lamb, pigeons, larks, rabbits, pullets, chickens, venison paste and tarts. There were suitable supplies of beer, ale and wine.

The two courses of supper offered a similar range, with variations in the shape of sparrows, plovers, quinces or pippins, 'blank mange,' godwits or teals, and butter and eggs.

On a fish day the King went on a lighter diet. Thus, the first course at dinner would consist merely of bread, soup, ling, eels (or lampreys), pike, salmon, whiting, haddock, mullet (or bass), plaice (or gurnard), sea bream (or sole), conger, porpoise (or seal), carp, trout, crabs, lobsters, custard, tart, fritters and fruit. The second course would comprise a second soup, sturgeon, bream, tench, perch, eels, lampreys, chines of salmon, crayfish, shrimps, tart, fritters, fruit, baked pippins, oranges, butter and eggs.

* Spiced wine

It may well be that a present-day executive, dining on an expense account, can command a greater range of foods than are shown above. But whereas he chooses, perhaps, half a dozen dishes from the range available, Henry was entitled to order everything on the menu at every meal, allowing others to eat what he did not consume.

Under the heading '*Bouche* of Court' the Ordinances set out the meals to be issued to officers and servants of all degrees. The Lord Chamberlain's dinner consisted of a first course of ten dishes, excluding bread, and a second course of six dishes. His supper was of seven and four dishes. Gentlemen of the Privy Chamber had courses of seven and four dishes for dinner and the same for supper. So did 'ladies in presence,' except that they were one dish lighter at supper. Farther down the scale, physicians and surgeons had mere nine-dish dinners and six-dish suppers. Maids, servants, porters and children were entitled to two meat dishes (beef and veal) for dinner and two meat dishes (beef and mutton) for supper. No matter how the higher officials gorged themselves, there must have been times when the poor at the gates gorged themselves no less handsomely on left-overs.

For the guidance of those buying provisions authorised prices were set out. Swans were six shillings the piece; cranes, storks, bustards, 4s 8d; herons, 20 pence; peacocks, 16 pence; fat quails, 4d; cocks, 4d; house rabbits, 3d; rabbits out of the warren, 2½d.; larks, 6d per dozen; sparrows, 4d per dozen; sweet powder, 3d per lb; eggs, from Michaelmas to Easter, 4d per 100. A porpoise, if not exceeding one horse's load, cost 13s 4d; if it exceeded one horse's load, it was to be diligently viewed by a Clerk Comptroller and assessed.

Between eight and nine in the morning the Treasurer and Comptroller of the Household were expected to sit in the counting house, doing their best to eliminate waste, going through the books and punishing offenders. Their clerks, when not looking for hole-and-corner diners, were to watch for un-invited guests at the various tables and sniff the meats in the storehouses.

Certain perquisites were allowed to the toilers in the pro-vision stores. The master cooks, for instance, took salmon tails and pigs' heads as their fees, and shared ox skins with the

Sergeant of the Acatery. The grooms of the Scalding House were entitled to the feathers of the poultry and the yeomen were welcome to the down from the Queen's swans and the 'garbage of poultry.'

In order to discourage violent conduct in his palace, Henry authorised his Lord Steward to conduct a bizarre ceremony* for the maiming of offenders. It required the co-operation of a wide assortment of palace servants.

Anyone, high or low, who struck another to the effusion of blood qualified to play the sacrificial part in this ceremony. At the 'place of execution' the Sergeant of the Woodyard would instal a square block, a beetle, staple and cords, and with these would pin down the victim's right hand. Beside the block was a large fire of coals provided by the Yeoman of the Scullery, and here would stand the Chief Farrier with his searing irons, and the Chief Surgeon, who was to employ them. The Groom of the Saucery was present with vinegar and cold water, and the chief officers of Cellar and Pantry also stood by, the one with a cup of red wine and the other with a loaf of bread to offer the criminal for solace after the deed was done, and to show there was no ill feeling. Linen to wind round the severed stump was produced by the Sergeant of the Ewery. The Yeoman of the Poultry provided a live cock which, when the time came, would be beheaded and applied to the wound. The Yeoman of the Chandlery brought the seared cloths, and the Master Cook a sharp knife, which was to be held upright by the Sergeant of the Larder until the moment of mutilation arrived. Of the various functionaries assembled, the Surgeon and the Master Cook would seem to have been best qualified to perform the act of dismemberment; but the Surgeon at least would probably have grumbled that such an act was contrary to professional ethics. The actual wielding of the knife was delegated, therefore, to an 'officer appointed thereto.' No doubt the jealous representatives of those departments unaccountably omitted—the Laundry, Wafery and Squillery—would be lined up to see justice done.

One who narrowly escaped this punishment was Sir Edmund

* Described in John Chamberlayne's *Magnae Britanniae Notitia* (*1723*)

Knyvet, who struck a servant of the Earl of Surrey in the tennis court at Greenwich. All the grisly preparations were set in motion. Then Sir Edmund begged mercy, suggesting that the King should merely cut off his left hand, so that the right hand might still perform stout and loyal service. This winning speech earned him a free pardon.

7

Luckless Maids

I T is not necessary to trace out all the threads of Henry VIII's matrimonial affairs, except in so far as these directly affected the life of the Court. Five times in all, Henry laid siege to maids of honour in attendance on his queens, seducing two, marrying three and beheading two.

It was no new thing for a king to regard the Court virgins with a concupiscent eye. In theory, these well-born damsels were brought up in great strictness, modesty being by no means the least of the qualities they were required to display. The Court was their finishing school, and if they obeyed the rules, they were assured of the highest matrimonial prizes. As their ward, the Queen could hardly fail to be aware of the fascination they held, not only for her partner but for her princelings, to say nothing of libertine courtiers. Much of their time they were kept sequestered. They trailed after the Queen, prayed when she prayed, sewed when she sewed. But they were not kept in strict purdah. When Wolsey visited the King, his gentlemen would kill time by going to the maids' apartments and chaffing them, rather as Englishmen in Spain in later days went to the convent grilles to chaff the nuns. At feasts, masques and other revels the maids mingled with the hot-blooded throng, giggling not only at the licensed indelicacies of the jesters but at whispered suggestions in their ears. In these circumstances it was impossible to keep the nest of little white birds wholly inviolate.

The first maid to fall to Henry's advances was Elizabeth Blount, who had caught his eye as she danced in the Court revels. At once Cardinal Wolsey, as willing to set up his king with a mistress as to organise his war economy or reform his Household, made the necessary dispositions. Elizabeth's father, who carried a spear for the king, was appointed an Esquire of the Body—the body which was about to deflower that of his daughter. He did not resent the arrangement and there is no reason to believe that his daughter did. It was no mean honour to share a royal bed.

In 1519 Mistress Blount bore the King a son, Henry Fitzroy, whose existence, in the interests of respectability, was not publicised; but before he died at the age of 18 he had become a Garter knight, Duke of Richmond, a lieutenant-general and a lord high admiral. His mother was married by the King to Sir Gilbert Tailbois, who believed that what was good enough for the King was good enough for him.

Next to tempt Henry were the daughters of Sir Thomas Boleyn. Mary and Anne had been maids at the French Court, where the libertinism that came in with the Renaissance had taken a heavier toll of virtue. When they returned to England, they had ways and graces which distinguished them from the English maids. The pliant Mary was the first of the two to unsettle Henry's peace of mind, but he waited until she had been married to Sir William Carey before starting his affair with her. Anne was a very different proposition. As Sir Thomas Wyatt, her childhood sweetheart, knew only too well, she was 'wild for to hold.' Lord Henry Percy, heir to the earldom of Northumberland, also had some association with Anne. Wolsey, in whose household he served, tried to break up the relationship, saying, 'I marvel not a little of thy folly that thou wouldst thus entangle thyself with a foolish girl yonder in the Court.' Percy's father was called to remonstrate with his son and called him 'a proud, licentious, disdainful and a very unthrifty waster.'* Under this pressure, young Percy capitulated. Wolsey was acting on the orders of the King, who seems to have had a husband in view for Anne. As yet the Cardinal had no reason to suspect the depth of the King's interest in her.

Anne's father, like Elizabeth Blount's father, had been in close attendance on the King, as a Knight of the Body. Seemingly, he was happy enough to lay down his daughters, married or unmarried, for his master; but so that there should be no difficulties Henry, as his interest in Anne quickened, made Sir Thomas Treasurer of the Household, showered him with lands

* George Cavendish: *Life of Cardinal Wolsey*

C

and titles, and raised him to the peerage as Earl of Wiltshire. His wife, a Howard, was made a lady in waiting and young Carey also had a place at Court. Anne's brother George was appointed Master of the Buck Hounds, was raised from an Esquire to a Knight of the Body, and then created Viscount Rochford.

In her sojourn at the French Court, Anne had smelled more than a whiff of decaying morals, but when Henry wooed her she declined to accept the status of a mistress. Ambition steeled her virtue, if virtue it was. Her obstinacy is sometimes supposed to have cost Wolsey his career and precipitated the Reformation, but Henry, for his part, did not want another mistress and another bastard. He wanted a legitimate heir, which Catherine was unable to give him.

During Henry's long negotiations with Rome, Anne was installed with suitable magnificence at Greenwich, with her brother George to guard her and welcome the King. Courtiers who saw the way the wind was blowing attended her unofficial court, and that of Catherine was neglected. When the King, at long last, married Anne in defiance of Rome, Queen Catherine was styled Princess of Wales. The heartless Duke of Suffolk, always a good choice for a dirty assignment, was one of those charged with dismissing all members of her household who would not take an oath of loyalty to Catherine in her new status. Most of her retinue were thus swept away. She did not live to see her rival executed. In her pathetic farewell note to Henry she begged him to respect her maids, now only three in number, and to give them in marriage.

When Anne sailed to the Tower, a few days before her Coronation, she was preceded by a vessel containing a great animated dragon which threw wildfire in all directions. Round it were monsters and savages making a hideous din. Yet even such spectacles could not endear the new Queen to the public. When crowned in Westminster Hall, in 1533, she was seen to be in an advanced state of pregnancy. Statesmen called her 'the concubine' and those courtiers who dared not say 'Anne is a whore' conceived the happy idea of teaching the Court idiot to say it.*

Now the maid of honour who had resisted the most ruthless

* Francis Hackett : *Henry the Eighth*

of the Tudors for seven long years had all the privileges of
queenship, including the attendance of noblewomen to hold
up a clean sheet at dinner when she wished to vomit (she first
availed herself of their services at her coronation banquet).
She also had a full complement of maids of honour, with all
the risks attaching to that privilege. The story goes that she
found one of them, Jane Seymour, sitting on the King's knee,
where she seemed very much at home. There were domestic
quarrels, but as Anne could not produce a live son she had
very little hold on Henry. He installed Jane in private apartments at Greenwich, with her brother Edward (the future
Protector Somerset) as Gentleman of the Privy Chamber, in
the role of protector. Even thus had Anne been installed, with
her brother George, at Greenwich. It was a cynical drill, but
if it worked once it would work twice.

In this unhappy situation, Anne was driven to seek sympathy
from Henry's courtiers. It is highly doubtful whether she committed a fraction of the sins that were reported to the King's
ears, but she had many enemies ready to testify to the worst
against her. The crisis came in 1536, at the May Day tournament at Greenwich, when Anne dropped her handkerchief to
one of her supposed lovers in the lists. It was a gesture which
ended an era and cost five courtiers their lives. The King rose
and walked out accompanied by only six attendants. One of
them was Henry Norris, his Groom of the Stole and life-long
friend, whom he now accused of misconduct with Anne.
Norris denied the charge and was sent to the Tower. There he
confessed but later withdrew his confession. Also arrested were
Anne's brother George, Viscount Rochford, who was accused
of incestuous relations with her; Sir Francis Watson and
William Brereton, both Gentlemen of the Privy Chamber,
and Mark Smeaton, a gay young musician who had the *entrée*
to Court but held no place there. All the courtiers were of the
'Boleyn set' and the King's intimate hunting, drinking and
gambling companions. When they were behind bars, Anne was
escorted to the Tower. Among those who sat in judgment on
her was her former suitor, Lord Henry Percy, now Earl of
Northumberland. Before she was sentenced to be burned or
beheaded, at the King's pleasure, he left the Court on the plea
of sudden illness.

From a window of the Tower Anne watched her accomplices and her brother die. Then two days later she herself went to the block. She availed herself of one last queenly privilege, that of being beheaded by a sword instead of an axe. Nobody in England was practised in this art, so the executioner of Calais crossed over to officiate. He may have had guiltier clients but he can have had few braver ones.

Legend has it that, on the morning of Anne's execution, the King was waiting with his huntsmen and hounds on a mound in Richmond Park, listening for the signal gun from the Tower which was to announce the end of a luckless maid of honour. When it boomed faintly up the Thames he exclaimed, like the old-fashioned villain he was rapidly becoming, 'Ha! Ha! The deed is done! Uncouple the hounds and away.' If this story is not true, it would have been necessary to invent it.

The extent of Anne's guilt remains an open question. Every courtier knew that the price of a gallant encounter with the Queen of England was death. It was as reckless a form of treason as could be conceived. But the standards of the Court had grown slack. What envious clerics used to call 'filthy play' and 'lewd behaviour' went on in Anne Boleyn's circle and gossip, malicious or otherwise, undoubtedly magnified indelicacies. The axe which whistled through the King's Chamber inspired, for a while, an affrighted decorum. It is unlikely that Jane, the demure new Queen, ever ran the slightest risk of having her bottom pinched by playful courtiers in the Privy Garden.

Sir Thomas Boleyn, now Earl of Wiltshire, who had been doing so well out of the family shame, was not required to judge his son and daughter; but he helped to convict the others and by so doing found his daughter guilty. His other daughter Mary, Henry's one-time plaything, who had had the misfortune to become pregnant while in a state of widowhood and had been ordered from Court along with an embarrassed gentleman usher, must have been singularly impressed by the fate meted out to a sister who had made such an international nuisance out of her virtue.

Few sorrowed over Anne's death. Even while she lay doomed in the Tower the King was attending banquets, accompanied by minstrels and singers. Eustace Chapuys, the Imperial

Don't look now, but they're executing Anne Boleyn

Ambassador, said that Henry behaved like a man who is happy to get rid of a thin, old and vicious hack and is looking forward to getting a new horse to ride. The Court took its cue from his light-heartedness. Immediately Anne's head was off he married Jane Seymour. But this distressful Queen lived only long enough to give birth to the future Edward VI.

Next, Henry contracted his political marriage with Anne of Cleves, otherwise the 'Flanders mare' or 'Dutch cow.' He accepted her largely on the strength of Holbein's painting; and Holbein, as some think, was lucky not to have been sent to the Tower for misrepresentation of goods. Henry might have done better to adopt the method employed by his father when he contemplated marrying the widowed Queen of Naples, which was to send three emissaries to report, in minutest detail, on the lady's physical characteristics, even to the size of her breasts and paps and the state of her breath. Anne was also recommended to Henry by the Earl of Southampton, who had been Henry's companion from youth and should have known his tastes. Happily expectant, the King decided to waylay Anne in advance of the official meeting. The stolen interview was no less brief and painful than the first encounter of the Prince Regent and Caroline more than two centuries later.

Anne could not be rejected, but her uncouth maids of honour could. One of those who replaced them, Catherine Howard, a girl with a lively past, was unfortunate enough to attract the notice of the King. She was unfortunate, again, in being used as a pawn by the Howard family. Henry, disgusted with Anne, retired her on pension to Richmond and told her that henceforth she was his sister. He then married Catherine, in whom he thought he detected ' a notable appearance of honour, cleanness and maidenly behaviour.' Ere long the Queen's old lovers turned up to embarrass her and one of them was admitted into her personal service. The ineffable Lady Rochford, who had survived the execution of her husband and was now in Catherine's suite, encouraged her to meet her gentlemen friends clandestinely; but dozens knew of these backstairs assignations. Catherine also had a weak place for Thomas Culpeper, a young gentleman of the Privy Chamber, and again Lady Rochford helped the two to meet by stealth. The result was inevitable. Both Catherine and Lady Rochford

Thomas Cromwell shows the portrait of Anne of Cleves to Henry
VIII

went to the block and a number of courtiers were in grave trouble for hiding their knowledge of what had been going on. From now on it was treason for a woman with an unvirginal past to marry a king of England. In the view of Chapuys, most of the maids of honour were thus out of the running. Henry made no more inroads on them, however. His next wife, Catherine Parr, was a virtuous widow who outlived him, though her obstinate ideas on religion put her head in peril.

The King's character, like his body, was deteriorating fast. The nonpareil among princes, the young man who had played Robin Hood, had become a vindictive and suspicious monomaniac. Yet many of the companions of his youth were still with him, full of animal spirits, revelling in any task that called for a show of force and absence of scruple. Loyally, they turned up at Tower Hill to watch their own kin and colleagues beheaded. They were as ready to escort an unwanted queen to the Tower as to ride out maying in the green fields of Richmond with the next one. They would rip a Garter from a disgraced Secretary and then join in the scramble for his lands and sinecures, knowing perhaps that it would be their turn next. The axe had come perilously close to two of them —Sir Francis Bryan and Sir Thomas Wyatt—during the Anne Boleyn investigations, but proceedings were stayed and both remained in favour. Sir Francis was rewarded for his loyal roysterings with grants of Church lands. So was the Duke of Suffolk, who had been an Esquire of the Body when the reign began. He, too, had risked the axe, for he married the King's sister Mary secretly while he still had at least one wife living. Sir William Compton, who began as a page to Henry, did not live to inherit abbeys but nevertheless left property in 18 counties. Assuredly the King was a good man to serve.

It paid not to fly too high. Wolsey could not maintain his grip on the loftiest pinnacle; nor could Sir Thomas More, whose conscience cost him his head; nor could Thomas Cromwell, who had no conscience at all, and was executed just the same. Minor fry whose heads went into the basket included Sir Nicholas Carew, who had held many intimate offices in the early days, including those of Esquire of the Body and Cupbearer. He had also been Master of the Horse and Otter Hunter. His popularity with the King easily survived the day when he was removed from Court, with others, for over-familiarity. But, in 1539, he let it be known that he thought the execution of the Marquis of Exeter had been an arbitrary proceeding, and his master beheaded him. Exeter, too, had been long in favour and a recipient of many honours.

All these courtiers were privileged to die, like gentlemen, on the block. One to whom this honour was not accorded was a former Gentleman of the Privy Chamber, Sebastian Newdigate, who left Court in disgust at the time of the Anne Boleyn negotiations and became a Carthusian friar. He was one of the brotherhood who, denying Henry's title as head of the Church, trooped in their robes to be hanged, drawn and quartered.

The proud, bullying family of the Howards was brutally humbled over and again by Henry. Unable to bear the sight of power going into new hands, they were prepared to cauterise their consciences in the struggle to share it. Old Thomas Howard, the second Duke of Norfolk, who had been on the wrong side at Bosworth, decided that there was no future in captivity and agreed to serve Henry. His new loyalty did not go long untested. In 1521, against all his instincts and sympathies, he helped to find the Duke of Buckingham guilty of treason, and having done so, shed tears which, on a strict reckoning, were treasonable tears. Then he pulled himself together and claimed his reward from Buckingham's lands. His son, the third Duke, had the task of passing the death sentence on his niece, Anne Boleyn. He, too, shed a few tears; but the experience did not prevent him setting another niece, Catherine Howard, on the road to the block. In 1547 he found out for himself how a condemned captive feels as the sands run out. Both he and his poet son, the Earl of Surrey, who had been in and out of favour all his life, were arrested on suspicion of coveting the Crown. First, the Duke watched the building up of a case against his son, who for good measure was accused of advising his sister to offer herself as the King's mistress. Surrey declared that he had said this only in jest. He was also accused of indulging in affected foreign dress and keeping an Italian jester. Miraculously, he was not also charged with introducing the sonnet. For his supposed indiscretions he was beheaded on the spot where he had had the curiosity, or insensitivity, to watch his cousin, Catherine Howard, beheaded. The Duke was saved from the same fate by a matter of hours, for as he waited for the last dawn the King died. Norfolk's verdict on the times was shared by many of the old nobility: 'It was merry in England afore the new learning came up.'

In his last days the King had grown so fat that he had to be moved from room to room by machinery. His hand could not even sign a death warrant. When he lay on his deathbed, a purulent and reeking wreck, his courtiers faced one final problem: who should tell him he was dying? Would this, too, be construed as treason? The Esquires of this very dreadful Body did not choose to take the risk; nor did the physicians; nor did the churchmen; nor did the statesmen. Finally, a Gentleman of the Privy Chamber, Sir Anthony Denny, undertook the assignment. The Defender of the Faith, the Great Erastian, the Father of the Navy, the Occidental Star heard his own death sentence with resignation.

Although the Palace of Westminster was ravaged by fire in the third year of his reign, Henry left a profusion of palaces. To Greenwich, Windsor, Eltham and Richmond had been added Hampton Court and York Place. The latter was confiscated from Wolsey as he passed into disgrace, and was expanded by Henry into a new Palace of Whitehall, with gatehouse, tiltyard, cockpit, tennis court and bowling alleys. In 1532 Henry dispossessed some leprous maidens from a hospital dedicated to St James the Less and on the site built the first Palace of St James, possibly in accordance with plans by Holbein. He drained the surrounding marsh and turned it into a deer park. At this time St James's was little more than a hunting lodge.

Finally, in 1539, Henry obliterated a Surrey village, manor and church to build his extravagant Palace of Nonsuch, laying out its gardens in the Italian style. Later he reserved a tract of land stretching between Nonsuch and Hampton Court as a deer chase. On his death the deer were at once dispersed.

8

Holy Dread

THOSE who sought to bring up the boy King Edward VI, Jane Seymour's son, in a dignity unnatural to his years are reputed to have equipped him with that most farcical of institutions, a whipping boy. Thus, if the monarch scamped his lessons, his offence was expiated, not on his own royal rump, but on that of young Barnaby Fitzpatrick, his companion. Barnaby was the eldest son of the Chief of Upper Ossory, in Ireland, and in his veins was the blood of wild Irish kings. His parents were probably glad enough to get him this humble, but by no means negligible, position at Court. At least, it was more honourable to offer a son as a chopping-block than as a minion.

Barnaby was neither the first nor the last whipping boy in royal annals. In the next century, if Bishop Burnet is correctly informed, the young Charles I had his punishments visited on William Murray, later Earl of Dysart, and the conscience of Louis XIV was stirred by the howls of a boy hussar. Since only a peculiarly depraved youth would be willing to see others regularly punished for his shortcomings, it is probable that the post of whipping boy was something of a sinecure.* Barnaby Fitzpatrick was made a Gentleman of the Privy Chamber by his master and was in no degree warped by a sense of injustice.

The establishment of an infant prince usually contained little more than nurses and rockers, but Edward, from the age of two, had his Chamberlain, Vice-Chamberlain, Comptroller, Treasurer and sundry other dignitaries. When he came to the Throne he was nine years old, and before he was twelve he had written a tract in French against the Pope. The Florentine

---

* In *The Fortunes of Nigel* Sir Walter Scott introduces 'Sir Mungo Malagrowther' as whipping boy to James VI of Scotland (James I)

Ambassador, Ubaldini, noted that certain lords traded on the King's youth by not invariably going down on one knee to address him—'they would not have omitted it with his father.'* But Ubaldini was surprised at the punctilio demanded from the King's sisters, both future queens of England, who were not allowed to sit next to him under the canopy and were lucky if they were offered chairs instead of benches. Princess Elizabeth went down on one knee five times before daring to take her place at table. Princess Mary was required to make similar obeisances. One of her visits caused the King and his counsellors much embarrassment, for her retinue rode through London jingling with rosaries and crosses.

It was a dull, pietistic Court. If it had more exciting days than those on which Bishop Latimer preached in the Privy Garden, they have not found their way into the records. But behind the pietistic façade 'the Court was very corrupt and extremely covetous, especially towards the declining of the King's reign; raking continually from the King (who was fain to borrow) for the enriching of themselves and making preys also of one another.'†

In short, it was a court run by courtiers.

Mary was England's first queen in her own right. As such she enjoyed the goodwill of all lovers of novelty. It was an event which might never happen again for another 500 years and called for fit celebration. Even to Protestants, she was a welcome change after a rather unpleasant little boy and his dubious uncles.

In this blissful dawn, the Court sparkled gaily on borrowed money (Henry having exhausted the coffers). The Queen dressed luxuriously enough to shock. On the eve of her coronation the fountains in Cheapside and Cornhill flowed once more with wine. Only when the country learned that their Queen was proposing to marry Philip of Spain did the mood change.

Suddenly, the rising of young Sir Thomas Wyatt, son of Henry VIII's courtier-poet, gave the Court as ugly a shock as it had suffered since Wat Tyler's men had marched on the capital. It was to have been a nation-wide rebellion in protest against

* F. von Raumer: *History of the 16th and 17th Centuries*
† John Strype: *Memorials*

the Spanish match, but only the Kentishmen under Wyatt rose. As they marched on the capital, the Thames bridges were broken in their path. The Queen was urged to retreat to Windsor, but scorned to do so; instead, she went to the Guildhall to rally the citizens, even offering to abandon her marriage, then withdrew into the Palace of Whitehall. When Wyatt's men reached Southwark, where they came under the fire of the Tower batteries, the Gentlemen Pensioners were ordered to wear their armour in Court. The sight and sound of armed men in the Queen's Chamber set up a doleful wailing among the Court ladies, few of whom expected to survive the night. In command of the Pensioners was John Norris, who at first did not regard the threat as serious enough to warrant the employment of Protestants to guard the Queen's person. When John Underhill, a Pensioner who had recently been jailed for writing an anti-Papist ballad, reported for duty, Norris denounced him as a heretic and ostentatiously struck his name from the register. The 'hot gospeller,' as Underhill was known, left under protest, but as the rebel forces came nearer he returned and was allowed to put on his armour.

The defence of the Palace was hardly up to Thermopylae standards. Outside the gates, when Wyatt's men approached from St James's, was Sir John Gage, the venerable Lord Chamberlain, with a body of guards and gentlemen. He became involved in a brush with the insurgents and appears to have over-magnified the danger. In his rush to get back into the Palace he fell in the dirt and arrived speechless. The rebels loosed a shower of arrows at the gates and windows but made no serious attempt to attack. When Gage fled inside, the gates were locked, an act which angered those Pensioners still outside. They professed to regard it as a slight on their honour and petitioned the Queen, who was watching and praying in the gatehouse, to reopen the gates. She consented, stipulating that the defenders were not to go out of sight, but it is improbable that they had any intention of doing so. When news arrived of Wyatt's capture all the Pensioners went to the Queen, kissed her hand and received large promises. 'But,' says Underhill, 'few or none of us got anything.'* Possibly the Queen, on reflection, decided that nobody had earned a reward.

* Edward Underhill: *Autobiographical Anecdotes*

Soon, gibbeted rebels dangled all over the town. Some 240 more were marched into the tilt-yard at Whitehall, with ropes round their necks, bound in pairs with cords. There they knelt in the mud and begged mercy. Mary directed that they should be pardoned and a great cry went up, 'God save the Queen!'

The next excitement, that same year, was the arrival of a miniature armada bringing Philip of Spain. Philip's advisers had urged him to be affable, even if it went against nature, and at the same time recommended him to wear a shirt of mail under his dress. He drank much English ale in an effort to show himself a good fellow. The marriage feast was held at Winchester and in accordance with Spanish custom only the King and Queen were allowed to sit at the top table. John Underhill, still quarrelling with Norris, helped to serve the dishes. The second course meats were the perquisite of the bearers and Underhill was very pleased with his—a great pasty of a red deer on an enormous charger, which he sent to his family. Many other Pensioners had refused it because it was too heavy.

To please the citizens of London, Philip sent, as a gift, a convoy of twenty bullion carts through the city. For his arrival a notable concession was made: the gibbets were taken down. Soon afterwards, however, the gates of the city were once more decorated with the heads and severed limbs of heretics. At Christmas that year funds were low. Sir Thomas Cawarden, who had been created Master of the Revels* by Henry VIII, grumbled that the Queen would not give him enough to furnish new novelties, but he contrived to mount such spectacles as a masque of cats, ornamented with a profusion of cats' tails (bought at a shilling a dozen) and a masque of apes playing bagpipes.

The Court buzzed with the great Catholic nobility of Europe but the streets buzzed with apprehensive and derisive citizens. At Greenwich, Richmond and Whitehall Philip's grandees with their impossible airs were cold-shouldered when they were not openly ridiculed. A group of his quarrelsome followers drew steel on each other after leaving Court and one was killed on the spot. Mary and Philip took up residence, in a seclusion which was felt to be insulting, at Hampton Court. There the Queen began to detect the first false signs of pregnancy. After

* He is believed to have been the first to hold this office

only 14 months Philip found it necessary to leave the country. The Queen's person was distasteful, but he made a suitable diplomatic excuse. Most of his grandees departed with him, glad to get away from English ale. When they had gone, Mary again prepared for an heir, but what she thought were the symptoms of maternity were the symptoms of mortality. Many of her ladies, notably those with expectations of nursery posts, encouraged her in her delusions long after it was obvious that she could not be pregnant. Under a sick, humiliated Queen, the public life of the Court gradually disintegrated. From a sovereign among courtiers, Mary became an abbess among nuns. Her miseries were not lightened by the need to decide whether, and in what quantities, her heretical subjects should be burned.

Mary's maids of honour were invincibly virtuous, which for once does not mean that their names are lost to history; two of them qualified for full-length biographies by admiring co-religionists. There was Magdalen Dacre, who had been brought up strictly in the old faith and, unlike certain 'profane Dianas' of her day, had eschewed hawking and hunting. At the age of 13 she was appointed a gentlewoman to the Roman Catholic Duchess of Bedford, and showed that she was free from the curse of pride by performing the duties of chambermaid in the middle of the night when that functionary was absent. When Magdalen was 16 the Queen admitted her to Court, which (to quote her confessor-biographer*) was 'a school of virtue, a nursery of purity, a mansion of piety.' Much of Magdalen's time, by day and night, was spent prostrate in prayer. Says her confessor, proudly: 'She never in her life dressed her head or adorned herself by a glass, which in a woman, especially noble and a courtier, may be esteemed a miracle.' He also says that, despising fine raiment, she wore a rude and coarse linen smock, but it is hard to believe that she was allowed to attend State functions like this. Magdalen was a tall girl and in any other context might have been described as Junoesque. She gave incontestable proof of her virtue when King Philip 'youthfully' opened a window of the room in which she was washing her face and 'sportingly' put in his arm, 'which some other would perhaps have taken as a great honour

* Richard Smith: *The Life of Magdalen, Viscountess Montague*

and rejoiced thereat.' Magdalen, without ado, picked up a staff which was lying at hand and belaboured the royal arm until it was withdrawn. The King took no offence. Rather was his respect for English maids of honour greatly intensified. Magdalen's confessor says that if she could act as spiritedly as this when the King merely jested, what would she not have done if the monarch had made a lewd approach? In the Protestant version of this story the King's intentions are, of course, assumed to have been lewd from the start.

'Oh happy Court with such courtiers,' rhapsodises Magdalen's confessor, 'and happy England with such a Court which for virtuous life gave not place to many cloisters and whence as from a fountain-head examples of piety did flow into all provinces of England . . . I desire my countrywomen to consider the notable purity of the maids of honour under Queen Mary and the infamous reproaches which some of them have incurred under Queen Elizabeth.' Though a little regretful that Magdalen should have descended to marriage, he rejoiced that she entrusted her virtue to such an upright young nobleman as Viscount Montague, later Master of the Horse, who also knew how to reject temptation. On a mission to Spain he contracted 'a most perilous and molestful disease' from which, according to the physicians, he could not recover 'unless he had the company of a woman.' This simple cure he resolutely declined, even though it was offered him in a singularly voluptuous wrapping. The same young nobleman, on the death of his mother, upbraided his father for taking a concubine and begged him to dismiss her. 'If I remarry,' said the father, 'it may cost you £30,000.' But the son said he would rather lose that sum than see his father live in sin.

Lord Montague made formal application to the Queen for permission to wed her maid and the Queen gave gracious assent. She herself, with a great train of nobility, attended the wedding at St James's. The mating of two such virtuous natures seems to have aroused unhealthy speculation among the Montagues' domestic staff. One servant, more enterprising than the others, hid under his mistress's bed 'to harken what counsel she at that time suggested to her husband.' Her confessor regards it as typical of the tolerance, lack of vindictiveness and humility of the lady that she did not punish this fellow or even denounce him to her husband. It is an odd story for a priest to publish to the world, but clearly he was carried away with enthusiasm for his subject.

The other maid of honour to enter the history books was Jane Dormer, later Duchess of Feria, who in childhood had been a playmate of the boy King Edward. Only rarely was she allowed out of the Queen's company. Various eminent suitors were dismissed as unworthy of her but she did not complain. She slept frequently in the Queen's room, carved her meat and looked after her jewels. When Jane was ill, the Queen would fuss over her and put her personal litter at the maid's disposal. Eventually Jane married one of Philip's nobles and in the next reign kept open house for Roman Catholic refugees from England.

There is an odd story about one of Mary's maids who had the misfortune to be suspected of wanton behaviour. The Queen, while waiting to go to chapel, was standing in a gallery from which she could see, through a traverse, her maids gathered below. Lord William Howard, 'a merry gentleman,' chucked Frances Neville under the chin and said, loud enough for the Queen to overhear, 'My pretty ——, how dost thou?' Later the Queen's farthingale worked loose and as Mistress Neville bent to adjust it the Queen said, 'God-a-mercy, my pretty ——.' Blushing, the maid looked up to enquire whether she had heard aright. The Queen replied that she had said no more than her Great Chamberlain had said—'May I not be as bold with thee as he?' With simple dignity, the maid defended herself. Lord William Howard, she said, was an idle gentleman and nobody attached any importance to what he said or did, but it was indeed a shock to hear such a word fall from the Queen's lips, whether in jest or earnest. 'A ——,' she said, 'is a wicked, misliving woman.' Bested, the Queen replied, 'Thou must forgive me, for I meant no harm.'*

With her maids, Mary often went out visiting the houses of carpenters, colliers and other persons of humble degree, watching them at table, offering advice and helping to apprentice their surplus offspring. When some of them complained that Court officials owed them money, the Queen would send for her Comptroller and angrily rebuke him for the slackness of

* J. M. Stone: *Queen Mary*

his officials. One of the Household servants was put in the
public pillory for his sins. Mary's solicitude for the humble
was such that she abandoned summer progresses on the grounds
that the requisitioning of carts upset the harvest plans of her
subjects.

The picture of a devout Queen moving informally among the
humble is, of course, only a facet of the picture. As plots multiplied about her, this same Queen slept in nightly fear of
assassination. Her Presence Chamber was heavily guarded by
armed men, as at the time of Wyatt's rising. There is even a
report that she slept in body armour. Of the menfolk in her
Household, only two or three were trusted by her, one of them
being Lord Montague.

Towards the end, Mary only rarely emerged from her
seclusion, perhaps to review her pensioners or watch a tournament. Sickness, fear and impecuniosity combined to keep her
a palace prisoner. Her nostrils may never have caught the
aroma of roast human flesh from Smithfield.

9

Don't Throw the Jelly

IN fifty years, there had been a brutal masculine Court, ruled by a single will; a boy's Court, in which courtiers gave the orders; and a feminine Court of tormented and oppressive piety. With the enthronement of Elizabeth, the conditions were ripe for a Court modelled on, and vigorously animated by, the ideas of the Renaissance.

It is time to look at the Italian conception of courtly behaviour. The sealed pattern of the courtier, on which the Elizabethan gallants, consciously or unconsciously, modelled themselves, was drawn up by Count Baldassare Castiglione in his *Book of the Courtier*, published in Italy in 1528. It was first issued in Britain in 1561, though many of its ideas were already familiar to men of fashion and culture.

Castiglione, who was a courtier in the hill-top castle of Urbino, addresses himself to those with the instincts and outlook of gentlemen. The well-bred courtier, he makes it clear, must steer between the rocks of effeminacy and heartiness. Castiglione has hard words to say about languorous creatures with 'soft womanish faces, curled hair, plucked brows, pampered like wanton women who speak so faintly that they appear to be yielding up the ghost.' He adds:

'Since Nature has not created them women, they ought not to be esteemed as such, but should be banished, like common harlots, not only from the courts of princes but from the company of gentlemen.' Among unmanly habits noted by Castiglione is that of keeping a looking glass in one's cap and a hair comb in one's sleeve. Still less is it necessary to have at one's heels a page carrying sponge and brush.

It is essential for a courtier to keep fit, the better to defend his honour against slander or truth. He should be able to handle all gentlemanly weapons, to hunt, swim, ride, tilt, leap, run, vault and cast stones; but he should not indulge in 'tumbling, climbing upon a cord and such other matters that taste somewhat of the juggler's craft.' Tennis is recommended as a noble exercise in which 'the disposition of the body, the quickness and nimbleness of every member, is much perceived.' Tennis courts were, of course, a feature of Henry VIII's palaces.

A courtier must not attempt athletic feats in front of less privileged mortals unless he is sure of outshining them. He should acquit himself in such a way as to suggest that his prowess comes naturally and has not been practised.

In war a courtier should not indulge in bold feats unless these are likely to be noticed by the right people. The only purpose of going to war is to gain honour, and honour is not gained by risking one's life in order to capture, say, a flock of sheep. In the same way, the only purpose of jousting is to win honour. For this reason one should be careful to be among the first to enter the lists, for women tend to take more heed of the first than the last. All good, sound, sensible advice.

Among softer pursuits, a courtier should be able to sing to the lute, but white-haired men with no teeth should have more sense than to play and sing in the company of women. Lute songs are love songs, and in old men love is only a joke.

Among forms of horseplay condemned by Castiglione are shouldering one's fellows downstairs, hurling bricks at their heads and riding men and horses into ditches. Needless to say, gentlemen who indulge in this sort of thing are unable to contain themselves at table: 'potage, sauce, jellies and whatever cometh to hand, into the face it goeth.' Anything for a laugh, in fact. Whoever can do most of these tricks 'counteth himself the best and gallantest courtier and supposeth that he hath won great glory.' This applies equally to the eating of 'unsavoury and stinking things, impossible to name,' for wagers. Those who will not play this kind of game are deemed 'too wise,' worthy enough to be counsellors, but not ranking as good fellows.

It is not comely in a courtier, says Castiglione, to use outlandish phrases or 'inkhorn terms'. Nor should he make men laugh too much or too often. That is the sphere of the common jester; and jesters, while they must be tolerated, do not qualify to be described as courtiers. Castiglione does not go as far as that eighteenth century mentor of the courtier, Lord Chesterfield, who condemns the act of laughter as ill-mannered and gross in itself.

What of the woman courtier, who is unable to defend herself against slander other than by living a virtuous life and refusing to listen to smut? She must refrain from familiar conversation, unless with old men. Her mind, not her body, should be her major asset. On the dance floor she should avoid 'swift and violent tricks' and refrain from all acts likely to detract from her natural 'sweet mildness,' as for example playing on a drum or blowing a trumpet. These recommendations seem as applicable today to exuberant débutantes as to the young ladies of the Renaissance.

There were other courtesy books besides that of Castiglione, notably the *Galateo* of Giovanni della Casa. In a more special-ised class was a work which, in its English translation, was called *The Court of Civil Courtesy*, 'a pleasant port of stately phrases and pithy precepts' for young gentlemen. Though it did not appear until 1591 it may usefully be considered here.

A major concern of its author is to show his readers how to embroider blunt statements and to give the lie without undue offence. Observations addressed to a superior should be prefaced by 'I pray you, Sir,' 'Will it please you,' 'Marry sir, I tell you' or 'With a good will, if it please you.' When wrongly rebuked by a superior, one should say: 'My lord, these be very ill terms to offer to a gentleman; and I must tell you you offer them to him that would not bear them at many men's hands, but I must bear them at yours. For I confess you be able to over-match me, your train is longer than mine; if I had thought you would have bled me thus, your lordship should have pardoned me for coming to you at this time.'

To a social equal a stronger line may be taken, even this: 'If it were not for troubling this company, I would be your carver with a piece of my dagger; but doubt not that I shall find a time for you.'

There is also a range of speeches which, by alterations in voice and expression, 'may serve in sport or earnest if a man like not to be jested with.' An example: 'I know, sir, your good word is ever at hand for your friends, and I perceive by this I am one of them.'

Praise from a friend should be received with 'I may not take your praise for anything; for the good will you bear me blinds you'; from a stranger, with 'I thank you for your good opinion. I would I could beguile everybody so cunningly as to make them of like mind'; and from a superior, with 'I humbly thank your lordship and I beseech you think that you vouchsafe this courtesy on him that will be as ready to requite it with the uttermost of his service.'

The author admits that it may not always be possible for a gentleman to work off a long and involved compliment: 'the use of long or short sentences must be employed according as he seeth the hearer at leisure.'

There are many hints about meal-time behaviour, including a warning against filling the mouth so full of meat that the lips cannot be held together—'a foul sight and loathsome.' It is unmannerly to call on all and sundry to drink toasts. Any such request should be civilly prefaced with some phrase like, 'Shall I be so bold as salute you with this cup of wine?'

How much the courtesy books did to civilise the rough manners of the Tudors is hard to say. Courtiers did not read these works as monks read Bibles, any more than Elizabeth read a daily chapter of Macchiavelli; but in one way or another the teachings were absorbed. There are many echoes of the Castiglione school in Shakespeare, who in his own way was a notable teacher of manners—with sharp words to describe over-precious behaviour.

10

Dangling Gallants

LIKE Eleanor of Aquitaine, Elizabeth faced the problem of dominating, and at the same time inspiring and invigilating, a Court of men; men who were ambitious, brilliant and ruthless, and whose heads were buzzing with audacious and exotic ideas. Whereas Eleanor trained her rude males to worship women, Elizabeth taught hers to worship one woman. It was a dazzling performance, and though it did not fool all the courtiers all of the time, it fooled most of the courtiers some of the time.

Elizabeth would never have encouraged her ladies to hold courts of love or to read off-colour fables. Although she started her reign with an infatuation for a married man, the Earl of Leicester, although courtiers' wives had little reason to love her, she did her best to enforce standards which approached the puritanical. Her own behaviour frequently set tongues wagging, but she was Queen of England and could be trusted to know what she was doing. The rule was 'Do as I say,' not 'Do as I do.' Always, she took strenuous steps to preserve the chastity of her maids of honour. 'If she knew any of her nobility given to frequenting houses of ill fame,' says Edmund Bohun, 'she treated them with as little respect as she did meaner men.'* Notorious evil-livers found no encouragement at Court.

It may well be that Elizabeth would not have been allowed to ascend the Throne if there had been any suspicion that she would refuse to marry. Until the game of courtship palled, her strutting suitors added immensely to the excitement of her Court and the gaiety of nations. Since it was obvious that the Queen liked to be wooed, her courtiers fell easily into the way of wooing her, couching their addresses in extravagant terms

* *Character of Queen Elizabeth (1693)*

of affection. Basically, the Queen's idea of leadership may have been the same as Nelson's; namely, that warmth of affection should flow along the channels of command. She doubtless felt, also, that men imbued with romantic ardour were more likely to tackle their assignments with eagerness. Unashamedly, she used sex as a stimulant, and we may be grateful that she did, for under a dull phlegmatic queen the country might have gone down in chaos.

Lytton Strachey has said of Elizabeth that 'Nature had implanted in her an amorousness so irrepressible as to be always obvious and sometimes scandalous.'* Other historians have denied her a sensual temperament. Bohun says: 'Though she lived in a royal plenty and was attacked by the blandishments of Nature, and a multitude of external pleasing objects, yet she persisted in the resolution she had taken and with a constant and unmoveable soul preferred her maiden state. . . Though she was almost every night tempted to change her resolution by the luxury, cheerfulness and wantonness of a Court which showed itself in interludes, banquets and pleasures and the things which may provoke the most cool and languid lust, yet she preserved herself from being conquered or broken by them; for the fear of God and a true sense of piety extinguished in her all feminine intemperance and lust.'

It was the Queen's amorousness, according to Strachey, which caused her to be 'filled with delicious agitation by the glorious figures of men.' According to the opposite school, the Queen liked to have handsome men about her only because she believed that majesty was best served by those of arresting and stalwart appearance. Whatever the reason, the Court from Council chamber to Chandlery was staffed by men of splendid physique. It is said that the Queen refused employment to one aspirant because he lacked a tooth. Ushers and porters were expected to be proficient at wrestling and throwing the bar. The idea was that visitors from abroad would go home and report that, while the Court was ruled by a woman, it was none the less a robust one. Those who grew old, toothless and bald in the service were not lightly cast adrift but honourably pensioned.

In selecting a candidate for the peerage, the Queen made

* *Elizabeth and Essex*

'an exact and careful consideration of the nobility of his ancestors, the greatness of his family, the endowments of his mind and the briskness of his parts, of his probity, wisdom and prudence and the strength and vigour of his body, which might enable him to perform some good service to the nation.'* Choosing a favourite was a rather different matter. Elizabeth needed a man who was a projection of herself, who could rise above desk work to entertain emperors and command armies, who could frighten the courts of Europe and yet be brought to his knees by a twitch on the thread. In Leicester she had a counsellor who was also an exhibitionist, a musk-drenched adventurer who could be a honey-tongued companion, a statesman who was proud to be her Master of the Horse.

As life wore on, the Queen found that male beauty and male brains were too rarely found in the same body. Yet she departed from her standards only with reluctance. Much pressure had to be put on her to advance Burghley's son Robert to be Secretary of State. For a long time she refused 'only because he was little of stature and hunchbacked; and she thought it a dishonour to that Board to have a deformed person sit amongst so many eminent and noble persons.'† This, however, is only part of the story; there were other reasons why the Queen withheld advancement from her 'little elf.'

At the start of her reign the Queen caused some surprise by retaining those officers whose duties could only be fully discharged in the service of a male ruler. The pallet in her Bedchamber was occupied by a lady in waiting, but the Esquires of the Body were still in close attendance. Gossip said that Leicester on occasion performed the ritual of handing the royal clothes; if so, it was a service not normally expected of a Master of the Horse. One of the Esquires, Ambrose Willoughby, was commended by the Queen for the strong line he took with the Earl of Southampton, in a dispute which broke out in the Presence Chamber. Southampton, Sir Walter Raleigh and another had been playing primero, and when the Queen retired for the night Willoughby asked them to desist. In some indignation, the Earl struck Willoughby, who closed with him and pulled out some of his hair.‡

* *Bohun*
† *Ibid.*
‡ *Dictionary of National Biography* (Southampton)

There was little future in England for a well-born, ambitious young man other than at Court. Wherever it lay, whether at Greenwich or Richmond, Whitehall or Windsor, it was at once the hub of Government and the hub of the graces. The men who ruled the Court still ruled the country. It drew the leaders of the military and justiciary, the Treasury and the Church. It was the centre of news, in a land without newspapers. It set the fashions of dress, manners and speech. It was the road to adventure, to high military command, to civil and clerical preferment. Whether a man wanted to sack a town or capture a galleon, to find a new ocean, to start a colony, to get a play produced, to win himself some Church lands, to search for the Philosopher's Stone, the road to his ambition lay through Court. Here were the great captains and great patrons, the rising favourites who would help generously if they thought that such help would do them any good, and the established favourites who were capable, on occasion, of disinterested help. There was, of course, no tradesman's entrance to this society. All were gentlemen. Most of them could turn out a sonnet when the mood took them, though they would have scorned to live by their pens. All knew how to live, how to defend their honour and, above all, how to die, whether in battle or on the block. Nothing in the Tudor courtier commands greater awe than the dignity with which he faced the executioner.

To get oneself noticed was the first step. The old nobility were ready, as always, to solicit the best places at Court for their sons, daughters, nephews and nieces. But there were other ways of catching the Queen's eye. Skill with a lance was one. Solicitude with a cloak was another. Sir Christopher Hatton danced his way into the Queen's affections. A broad chest and a good leg, a bold glance, a well-turned compliment—all these could carry a man to the heights. Espying the bright face of Sir Charles Blount, later Earl of Devonshire, the Queen said, 'Fail you not to come to Court and I will bethink myself how to do you good.' In the Presence Chamber she paused on sight of the young Lord Herbert of Cherbury and said, 'God's death, who is this?' The young man's antecedents were explained and the Queen heard with disappointment that he was married. Nevertheless, she looked at him admiringly, gave him her hand

Nonsuch Palace, Surrey in Queen Elizabeth's day. From John Nichols' *Progresses*

to kiss twice, and twice gently clapped him on the cheek. Young Herbert had been noticed; the rest was up to him.

A domesticated courtier, young or old, had small hope of rising. Favourites postponed marrying as long as they could, knowing that the Queen expected all worship to be focused on her. But the greatest handicap in a courtier was a lack of spirit, a dash of melancholy. As a young man, William Herbert, Earl of Pembroke, who suffered from headaches, was accused of cultivating the Queen's favour in 'too cold and weak a manner.' Later he summoned up enough spirit to seduce one of her maids of honour.

Even the heartiest young courtier could not wholly escape languor and frustration. Though the Court was the power-house of England, there were times when its musky air grew enervating, when the ear wearied of the 'lascivious pleasing of a lute,' when the heart was full of an ache inexpressible in a sonnet. There were times, too, when it was obvious that friends were being false and that one was being outsmarted by one's fellow intriguers. The Queen blew hot and cold on the daring projects submitted for her sanction, preferring to keep her gallants dangling. Meanwhile the gallants ran up debts. Sir Robert Carey is an example. 'In all triumphs I was one,' he writes, 'either at tilt, tourney or barriers, in mask or balls; I kept men and horses far above my rank.' Faced with a financial crisis, he made a wager that he would walk to Berwick in 12 days—and won £2000. In his autobiography he mentions this feat in a single sentence. Possibly he was a trifle ashamed that a kinsman of the Queen should have to descend to such mercenary shifts to finance his further attend-ance at Court. The Queen valued Carey not as a pedestrian but as an equestrian. He was a one-man pony express, well equipped to conduct a delicate interview at the end of a furious ride. Eventually he left Court and helped to pacify the Border lands, rooting out thieves and highwaymen. Hearing that he had married, the Queen let it be known that she was deeply offended; but he told her to her face it was her own fault for not giving him a worthier chance to serve her. It was what they all said.

From time to time the Queen's frustrated courtiers slipped quietly away to the wars, hoping to allay the inevitable royal wrath by a display of valour. The first time Essex bolted, Carey was sent after him, located him at Sandwich, and with much ado persuaded him to return. Essex had learned his lesson. Next time, he left London on a Thursday evening and rode into Plymouth on the Saturday morning, having covered 220 miles and shaken off the pursuit of Sir Francis Knollys.

If a man sought the Queen's formal permission to go to the wars, it might well be refused on the grounds that his life was too valuable or that the Queen esteemed his company highly. If permission was graciously granted, the gallant would suspect that his star was waning. It was better to slip off quietly and hope for the best. When the Queen was not at war, her gallants would enter the service of France or Sweden, Hungary or Russia. The battle experience thus gained would be put at her service when required.

A courtier was expected to obtain the Queen's permission even in order to undertake recreational travel. Some did not do so, hoping to placate the Queen later with gifts of scented gloves or other novelties out of Italy. At various times Elizabeth's Government expressed concern at the number of young gentlemen who went abroad ostensibly to learn languages or to finish their education, at great peril to their religion and manners.

When so many mettlesome gentlemen were kept idle at Court, quarrels were bound to be frequent. Sir Philip Sidney was playing tennis at Whitehall when the Earl of Oxford, uninvited, joined in the game. Sidney's objections were brushed aside. When they were repeated, the Earl ordered all players to leave the court. Sidney refused and was called a puppy. A duel was arranged, but was stopped by the Queen, who ordered Sidney to apologise to the Earl on account of his higher rank. Sidney declined. This was only one of many reasons why he left Court. But the prospect of living permanently by his pen was an indignity not to be contemplated. Sidney bided his time, gave a warrant of good behaviour and was taken back into favour.

The Earl of Oxford was himself as quarrelsome a puppy as ever bit the ankles of a court, but the Queen admired his spirit. In youth he killed a cook in the service of his guardian, Lord Burghley (verdict: suicide). In later life he fought a duel with Thomas Knyvet, a Gentleman of the Bedchamber. When both adversaries were temporarily out of action, their followers took up the battle, each side killing an opponent. The Queen then put the Earl under house arrest.

Burghley, the old fox, watched the brash youngsters come and go. He saw a Leicester, who snatched the Queen's hand-kerchief to mop his brow at tennis, who reputedly drank pearls and amber to excite his lust, superseded by the youngster Essex, who sat playing cards 'and other games' with an elderly Queen 'till birds sing in the morning.' But he did not live to see Elizabeth cut off Essex's head. He did his best to save the Queen from too reckless an encouragement of the arts. When Spenser was brought to Court to read instalments of his *Faerie Queen*, Elizabeth was so delighted that she promised the poet £100. Burghley objected that this was an absurd sum to pay for a mere song, to a man who was a mere State messenger. 'Then give him what is reasonable,' said the Queen, so Burghley gave him nothing. Not until Spenser complained to the Queen did he receive his £100. It was as a result of Burghley's snubs that Spenser summed up the courtier's life thus:

'. . . to fret thy soul with crosses and with cares;
To eat thy heart through comfortless despairs;
To fawn, to crouch, to wait, to ride, to run,
To spend, to give, to want, to be undone. . .'

Elizabeth had two weapons for the magnification of her majesty: splendour and etiquette. Though her palaces were economically run, the parade on State occasions was as dazzl-ing as anything mounted by her father. She had at least 2000 dresses, probably hundreds more. Every New Year's Day her nobles gave her magnificent petticoats. Her head-dresses were rigid with pearls and diamonds. When the entire Court dressed up for the entertainment of ambassadors the sight was a breath-taking one. 'I do believe that at some times I have seen very near ten thousand chains of gold stirring,' writes Dr Godfrey Goodman.* The follies of fashion were such that, quite early in her reign, laws were passed (as they had been passed in earlier centuries) reserving the use of velvet, silk or gold embroidery to those of lofty rank. Rapiers, it was ruled,

* *The Court of James I*

were not to exceed three feet in length. At the gates of London were posted officials to trim back offending ruffs and break off rapier points. The French Ambassador was put into a fine fury because officials at Smithfield proposed to cut his rapier down to size. Higher authority intervened and he was allowed to flaunt his diplomatic privilege.

All men addressed Elizabeth on their knees. No man sat when she stood, not even the hoariest ambassador; and the Queen was nearly as fond of standing as the first Plantagenet had been. The only man who turned his back on her, deliberately, had his ears boxed. That was Essex. It was also Essex who, returning hot and travel-stained from Ireland, burst unannounced into her private apartments and surprised her wigless, half-dressed and unpainted. In the following year he went to the block for treason, but his irruption into the Bedchamber had been treason enough. There are times when it pays even the highest to proceed through the normal channels.

Dressed and painted, the Queen was a formidable sight. As she passed through the Presence Chamber on her way to chapel, preceded by her great officers, all fell on their knees as her eyes turned on them. By this time she was accustomed to see men and women lower their eyes on meeting hers, in deference to such glory. Fear of making a *gaffe* bore heavily on some. John Aubrey has a famous story of a young courtier who, when bowing low before the Queen, made an unfortunate noise. This humiliated him so much that he spent the next few years travelling in far places. Other courtiers were less sensitive. That blunt soldier Sir Roger Williams knelt in his new boots to press a petition which the Queen was reluctant to grant. Impatiently she interrupted him and said, 'Fah! Williams, I prithee begone. Thy boots stink.' This the knight denied. 'Tut, tut, Madame, 'tis not my boots that stink but my suit.'

The Queen was not content to preside in static majesty at the Court revels. Until a late age, she danced a galliard with great spirit. In 1596 the Bishop of St David's, Antony Rudd, believing perhaps that it was time for the head of the Church of England to stop strutting on the dance floor, preached a minatory sermon in her presence at Richmond. After sketching the disabilities and infirmities of old age, he invited the congregation to consider how even queens suffered from the dilapidations of time. Elizabeth did not stay the sermon through. With surprising mildness, afterwards, she commented: 'The wisest clerks are not always the wisest men.' But she struck the preacher off her list.

Much ceremony was observed even when the Queen was not present. Paul Hentzner was privileged to see the Queen's dinner table set.* First a gentleman with a rod entered the room accompanied by another with a tablecloth. Both knelt to the table three times with the utmost veneration before spreading the cloth, and knelt again before they retired. Those who brought in plates, bread and salt also bowed with each operation. Then came 'an unmarried lady of extraordinary beauty,' accompanied by a married lady, the latter bearing a tasting knife. After prostrating themselves three times the unmarried lady in the most graceful manner approached the table and rubbed the plates with bread and salt, 'with as much awe as if the Queen had been present.' Next came the Yeomen of the Guard, 'the tallest and stoutest that can be found in England,' bringing in silver dishes. Each was required to taste a mouthful of the dish he had brought in, as a precaution against poison. Meanwhile 12 trumpets and two kettledrums were making the hall ring. At the end a number of unmarried ladies appeared and with great solemnity lifted the meat from the table and took it into the Queen's inner chamber where she chose what she wanted; the rest was then distributed among the ladies of the Court. Hentzner was told that the Queen dined and supped alone with very few attendants. At this time she was 65 years of age.

Raphael Holinshed, who wrote during the Queen's lifetime, gives a curiously confused picture of life at Court. He is at pains to make it sound virtuous but cannot resist the chance to censure unseemly behaviour. With the object of avoiding idleness and preventing transgressions, he says, every office in the Court contained either a Bible or the Acts and Monuments of the Church of England, as well as worthy histories and chronicles. As a result, 'the stranger that cometh into the Court of England upon the sudden shall rather imagine himself to come into some public school of the universities, where many give ear to one that readeth, than into a prince's palace.'

* *Travels in England*

Chaired by her gallants, Queen Elizabeth goes to visit Lord Hunsdon.
From Sir Robert Carey's *Memoirs*

Holinshed confesses that he is no frequenter of courts, so this may have been a flight of fancy. But he had seen, and been much impressed by, the great throng of liveried servants in the palace courtyards, each man with his master's insignia on his sleeve. It was like a throng of peacocks or a meadow bright with flowers.

The 'ancient ladies' of the Court, according to Holinshed, shunned idleness by taking up needlework, silk spinning, studying the Scriptures, reading or writing histories and translating foreign works. They were also skilled in surgery (which means they could attend to minor wounds) and distillation of waters, and were familiar with the ways of ornamenting the female body.

One of these worthy ancient ladies, who are apt to be overlooked in the glitter, was Blanche Parry, chief Gentlewoman of the Privy Chamber and Keeper of the Queen's Jewels. She was appointed a lady in waiting when the Queen was only three and spent the rest of her life in the royal service. Loyal, discreet and unambitious, she kept clear of intrigues and scandals throughout her 80-odd years, but was willing to help an honest man with his suit. Elizabeth esteemed her highly and gave her grants of lands in Herefordshire and Wales. In old age she became too blind to look after the jewels. When she died in 1589 she was buried with the honours of a baroness. The verse on her monument in Bacton Church, Herefordshire describes her as 'a maid in Court, and never no man's wife.' It may, or may not, have been composed by herself:

I lived always as handmaid to a Queen,
    In chamber chief my time did overpass,
Uncareful of my wealth, there was I seen,
    Whilst I abode the running of my glass.
Not doubting want whilst that my mistress lived,
    In woman's state whose cradle saw I rocked,
Her servant, then, as when her crown achieved,
    And so remained till death he my door had knocked. . .

Holinshed says it was a rare thing to find a courtier who could speak no language but his own. Not only were Greek and Latin widely understood, but Spanish, Italian and French could be heard on courtiers' lips. The Queen herself set an example of lingual virtuosity which few of her Court could have emulated. There was the famous occasion when a presumptuous ambassador from Poland, addressing her in Latin as she sat on her throne, began to reproach her for her policies, and to voice what appeared to be threats. The Queen endured it for a while then abused the ambassador heartily in his chosen tongue, to the dazed admiration of the Court. When congratulated—and this was one occasion when congratulations could be sincerely voiced—she said, 'God's death, my lords, I have been enforced this day to scour up my old Latin that hath been long in rusting.'* She was then in her middle sixties.

Not less important than the power to command foreign tongues was the ability to speak a polite version of one's own. After John Lyly published his *Euphues*, the Court revelled in antithesis and clotted, hieroglyphic imagery. 'That beauty in Court which could not parley Euphueism was as little regarded as she which now there speaks not French,' said Edward Blount, writing in 1632. The craze was made to be mocked, and mocked it was. Sir Philip Sidney wrote of 'the dainty wits enamelling with pied flowers their thoughts of gold.' In turn his *Arcadia* gave the Court a new source of affectation, which lasted it well into the next reign. Such cults as these served well to distinguish the courtier from the merchant.

The Court's entertainments were closely controlled by the Master of the Revels. Besides helping to devise masques, he had the responsibility of choosing, cutting and adapting plays. To Edmund Tilney, who was appointed to this post in 1579, fell the privilege of examining the proffered manuscripts of William Shakespeare.

By an act of 1571 all players had to be licensed by a peer or other person of high degree, otherwise their social status was that of rogues and vagabonds. Usually, it was not difficult to find a patron, for there were as many literate nobles willing to form theatrical companies as to have sonnets addressed to them. For their part, the players were content, indeed proud, to wear their master's livery. If a company achieved a good reputation, it would be invited to Court and the patron's prestige would be enhanced. Leicester, in 1572, formed the first licensed company. Some eleven years later the Queen

* Dr. Godfrey Goodman: *The Court of King James I*

had her own players, who wore the royal livery. One of them was the witty Richard Tarleton, an improviser of comic doggerel, reputedly once a Shropshire swineherd.

Not only were Shakespeare's plays produced at Court, but he himself acted in them. The Queen, as is well known, had a liking for the character of Falstaff and requested that he be made to fall in love. Shakespeare was given 14 days to carry out this suggestion and the result was *The Merry Wives of Windsor*.

The theatrical companies suffered what they regarded as unfair competition in the form of two companies of boy players created by the Queen, who drew precocious talent from the choirs of Whitehall, Windsor, St Paul's and Westminster. These youngsters, who were quite at home in the plays of Shakespeare and Jonson, were embarrassingly popular with Court and public. In *Hamlet*, Rosencrantz sneers at the rage for 'an aery of children, little eyases,'* who are 'tyrannically clapped' for their efforts. The early Puritans also disliked the sight of 'Her Majesty's unfledged minions' flaunting about in sinful silk and satin. While these enjoyed royal favour, how could plays ever be suppressed? One boy actor, Salathiel Pavy, who specialised in old men's parts, died at the age of 12. In a rhymed epitaph, Jonson suggested that, so successfully had the lad impersonated ancients, the Fates had failed to distinguish him from one.

Under Elizabeth, the maids of honour were buffeted by many a gust of imperial displeasure, but at least they were spared the block. If they watched their manners and their morals, if they forsook such silly ideas as wanting to choose their own husbands, if they refrained from setting their caps at the Queen's favourites, they could look forward to a reasonably good marriage. Their daily function was to amuse the Queen with light conversation, to sing and play to her, to accompany her on walks and to perform minor acts of ceremonial. Their quarters were in the Coffer Chamber.

Elizabeth regarded herself as the custodian of the maids' virginity and any attempt on it was not far removed from an attempt on her own. Nor was she tolerant of efforts to broaden

* fledglings

their innocent minds. Her waggish godson, Sir John Harington, allowed certain of the Court ladies to see his translation of *Orlando Furioso*, notably that part of it which described the excessive efforts of the two heroes to prove that all women were vulnerable. When this fell into the Queen's hands she sent for the offender, read him a severe lecture and as a punishment ordered him to translate the entire work before entering her presence again. It was a substantial imposition.*

Bohun says that the maids took a wonderful pleasure in the Queen's manners and discourses, and in modelling themselves on her modesty and gestures 'so that they would never suffer any young nobleman to have any familiar acquaintance with any of them if he had not recommended himself to them by some generous manly action in the wars.' Such young gentlemen were by no means scarce, however, and acquaintanceship often became too familiar. On these occasions the Queen took severest action. It is easy to mock Elizabeth for tyrannous interference with the lives of grown men and women, but she saw no reason why her Coffer Chamber should be turned into a brothel, which was what some of her lustier nobles seemed to desire. For their part, the maids rebelled at living in convent conditions until the Queen should condescend, if she ever did condescend, to release them. They can hardly have failed to see, or hear of, occasions when the Queen, as with her French suitors, Simier and Alençon, behaved with alarming lack of discretion. But the Queen presumably knew when to stop.

The roll of maids who did not know when to stop is a long one. Elizabeth Throckmorton, the blue-eyed, blonde daughter of Sir Nicholas Throckmorton, allowed herself to be compromised by Sir Walter Raleigh, and the two guilty lovers were sent to the Tower to cool their ardour. Forty-year-old Raleigh's behaviour was the more disgraceful, in the Queen's eyes, because she regarded him as one of her own devoted celibates. He was her knight in, literally, silver armour, yet he had the insolence to fall in love with one of her waiting women. Only the prodigious success of Raleigh's raiding vessels secured his release. The Queen's hurt feelings were partially assuaged by a cataract of loot. There is no evidence that Raleigh

* G. B. Harrison: *The Elizabethan Journals*

was a philanderer, which is more than can be said for Essex, who in his periods of disfavour looked on the Queen's maids as legitimate prey.

Then there was the scandalous affair of the Earl of Southampton, to whom Shakespeare dedicated his *Venus and Adonis*. He sneaked home from the wars to make an honest woman of Elizabeth Vernon, then sneaked back again. When the Queen found that Mistress Vernon had won herself a title by fornication she ordered her into 'the sweetest and best-appointed lodging' in the Fleet Prison. Southampton was called home, and on arrival was also sent to the Fleet. Though speedily released, his Court career was finished. The Queen would not even allow Essex to give him a military command.

Mary Fitton, a vivacious minx admired by Shakespeare, also found herself with child by a nobleman. She had been in the habit of slipping out of Court, dressed as a man and wearing a white cloak, in order to meet the melancholy Earl of Pembroke (supposedly Shakespeare's 'Mr W. H.'). The gallant Earl admitted paternity but said he had no intention of marrying the lady. Elizabeth gave him a taste of the Fleet and banished him from Court, refusing him permission to travel to forget. He had to wait for the next reign before he became Lord Chamberlain and a Knight of the Garter. Mistress Fitton's punishment was confined to that of bearing Pembroke's child.

There were many other irregular episodes involving maids of honour, ranging from elopements to near-rapes. The courts of justice could not jail those who indulged in sexual licence, but Elizabeth could. In her own Court, she was her own judge. Even betrothals contracted without her knowledge could bring jail to the offenders. Thomas Shirley, son of Sir Thomas Shirley, Treasurer for the Wars in the Low Countries, secretly married Frances Vavasour, one of the Queen's maids, and was sent to the Marshalsea for contempt of Court. Stiffly, Burghley called on Sir Thomas to announce his displeasure at such an act of discourtesy to the Queen, and informed him that if he came to Court the Queen would 'tell him her mind.'

The Queen succeeded in telling her mind to the Countess of Rutland, who connived at the secret wedding of her daughter, Lady Bridget Manners, one of the Queen's favourite ladies in waiting, to a Mr Tyrwhitt. Bride and groom were ordered to London, the former to be put in the custody of a suitable lady, the latter to be jailed. This order had to be repeated before the Countess took action.

Elizabeth's sense of fitness was doubly outraged when she found that Lady Mary Grey, the smallest woman in the Court, had secretly married her Gentleman Porter, Henry Keys, who was the tallest man in the Court. Burghley described this affair as ' an unhappy chance and monstrous.' He was in no hurry to accept the apologies of the guilty parties.*

Worse, much worse, was the offence of marrying without sanction a person of the blood royal. One day when the Queen left Whitehall for a day's hunting at Eltham, her maid of honour, Lady Catherine Grey, who was a great-grand-daughter of Henry VII, slipped down river in a barge and was secretly married to the Earl of Hertford, returning to Court in time for dinner. When her pregnancy became apparent, Catherine was sent to the Tower, where she bore her child. The Earl also was sent to the Tower, occupying a separate suite. The guards seem to have been open to bribery, for a second child was born while they were in custody. This was a gratuitous insult which filled the Queen with fury. The Earl, for his incontinence, was fined £15,000 by the Star Chamber. Of this, £5000 was for deflowering a virgin of the blood royal in the Queen's home, £5000 for breaking out of quarters and £5000 for repeating his wickedness.* Elizabeth remitted £10,000 of this penalty, and in the end the Earl, who was supposed to have had more ready money than anyone in England, disgorged little more than £1000. He did not, however, win his liberty. Burghley was bombarded with letters appealing for clemency to be shown to the couple, but rejected them. It is clear that Lady Catherine bitterly regretted her behaviour. Her quarters in the Tower were by no means spartan, for her bed had damask, the walls were tapestried and she was allowed dogs and monkeys. When the Plague was killing a thousand a week in London she and her husband were moved into the country. After seven years she died, apparently of grief. Hertford spent some nine years in close custody or house arrest.

* Sir Henry Ellis: *Original Letters*

In the Queen's later days the maids found her a very difficult mistress, so much so that they would ' often cry and bewail in piteous sort.' They were too young to offer her true companionship. No real friends remained to whisper to Elizabeth the secrets of the Court; thus, she was the last to learn of events when she should have been the first. Her attendants began to hide mirrors from the rooms and galleries through which she was due to pass, but the maids of honour were there as a mirror of her lost youth. She who had sent John Dee 1500 miles to find a physician or a philosopher who could save a cherished tooth now had a mouthful of black stumps. And the teeth of the maids of honour were white.

Tantrums grew more frequent. The fair Mistress Bridges was abused and even belaboured by the Queen, and along with Mistress Russell was ordered out of the Coffer Chamber. Apparently they had been dosing themselves with physic at a time inconvenient to the Queen and had been taking unlawful short cuts to watch a game of ballon. After spending three days under the roof of Lady Stafford they were readmitted to Court. Lady Mary Howard also behaved in such a way as to provoke the Queen to complain of 'ungracious, flouting wenches.' She had refused to carry the Queen's mantle in the garden, had given a cheeky answer when rebuked, had been absent when required to carry the cup of grace and again absent when it was time to accompany the Queen to prayers. But these were minor offences. As the Queen well knew, Lady Mary had been fluttering her eyes at the Earl of Essex. Biding her time, Elizabeth took a feline, if unqueenly, revenge. On her orders, a rich velvet dress worn by Lady Mary to please the Earl was taken from her wardrobe and brought to the Queen. It was too short for majesty, but majesty nevertheless appeared in it, and asked defiantly, 'Well, ladies, how like you my new-fancied suit?' Pressed for her opinion, Lady Mary had to admit that the gown was too short. The Queen said that it was too short for her and too fine for Lady Mary, 'so it fitteth neither well.' With these few unwitty words, she stormed out.

Any attempt to outshine the Queen was asking for trouble. The game of worshipping Gloriana had to be kept up at all costs. Such an atmosphere should theoretically have turned the maids into a company of colourless, cowed prigs. In fact, it did nothing of the sort. Even in the difficult years there was a good deal of larking about, much of it innocent enough. The maids' high spirits grew too much for Sir William Knollys, Treasurer of the Household, who had a lodging where 'some of the ladies and maids of honour used to frisk and hey about in the next room, to his extreme disquiet o' nights, though he had often warned them of it.' Eventually, made desperate, he took off all his clothes (though one authority seems to think he retained his shirt) and, with spectacles on nose and a copy of Aretino in his hand, entered his chamber in full sight of those who were heying about. 'Now let the reader judge what a sad spectacle and pitiful sight these poor creatures endured, for he faced them and often traversed the room in this posture above an hour.'

The maids suffered other invasions of their modesty. Nearly three centuries later, a maiden queen was told by Lord Melbourne how the ladies of Elizabeth's Court slept in a room with a partition, over which mischievous gentlemen used to peer.

Even in death, the maids did not escape the Queen's interference. Poor Mistress Radcliffe pined and starved her life away after her brother was killed. Somewhat mystified, Elizabeth had the modest maiden's body opened. The anatomists reported that all was well, 'save for certain strings striped all over her heart.' Possibly they were the strings that had held her to the Queen.

11

Mermaids and Wildfire

ELIZABETH'S progresses served the double purpose of shaking the Court out of its too settled ways and of allowing a glimpse of majesty to mortals in the not too distant parts of her realm. In the main, the Queen visited only those great houses where the pattern of Presence Chamber, Privy Chamber and Withdrawing Chamber could be reproduced, and where her domestic offices could be married to those of her host.

In theory, the Queen took charge of the house and made her own dispositions. In practice, her host did all that was necessary, and much that was not, for her entertainment. Elizabeth accepted it all as her due. Her host, she probably reasoned, would not have solicited the honour of a royal visit if he was not anxious to increase his favour or his prestige in his county; it seemed reasonable to let him pay for the privilege. Alternatively, he was perhaps anxious to show gratitude for easy money which had been put in his way by the Queen, so why discourage him? There were occasions, no doubt, when the Queen felt the time had come to help an over-ambitious subject to squander some of his resources. By outshining the splendour of his household she could show his peasantry who was prince and who was not.

Undoubtedly, royal visits bore heavily on some of the Queen's hosts. Twelve times Burghley, self-styled 'the poorest lord in England,' had the honour of entertaining Elizabeth, usually at Theobalds, and each visit cost him between £2000 and £3000. A three-day visit to Lord Keeper Egerton cost that gentleman £2000.

News of an impending visit from the Court had the same stimulating effect on a town that a general's inspection has on a camp. The citizens of Norwich, for instance, 'brushed up their streets, new-polished their houses, removed their dung-hills, new-gravelled their roads.'* Human refuse, in the form of beggars, monsters, idiots and the diseased, was always swept from the royal path. Unlike her subjects, the Queen found no fascination in freaks.

While the Queen's host conferred anxiously with landscape gardeners and pyrotechnic experts, the local poetasters and pedagogues began to hammer out rhymed histories of their towns or long addresses of welcome in Latin. These, unless a merciful heaven sent rain, would be recited to the last syllable on the appointed day. Numerous citizens of suitable condition, age and shape were deputed to play the parts of virgins, sybils, satyrs, nymphs, savages and pilgrims, for it was an unwritten rule that the greenwood must be peopled by such for the great Queen's coming. The gentry scrambled to buy up silks and velvets, regardless of cost. They refurbished their harnesses and put their servants into new clothes.

It may be that the addresses of welcome were no prosier than they are today, but the torrents of verse spilled over the Queen are daunting to contemplate. She showed no impatience, and indeed did much to put nervous performers at their ease. After the Recorder of Warwick had subjected her to a history of his town from the days of the Saxons, discoursed on the various spellings of the town's name, and generally protested his unworthiness to deliver such a 'rude and large speech,' the Queen, who had sat patiently in her coach, said, 'Come hither, little Recorder; it was told me that you would be afraid to look me or to speak boldly; but you were not so afraid of me as I was of you.'

For the Queen's entertainment at Warwick, bands of lusty gentlemen assaulted canvas forts with battering pieces and mortars. Memorable indeed were the fireworks which followed. 'The wildfire falling into the River Avon would for a time lie still and then again rise and fly abroad, casting forth many flashes and flames, whereat the Queen's majesty took great pleasure.' Soon fireballs were raining all over the town, some falling in courts and 'backsides,' others punching holes the

---

* John Nichols: *The Progresses and Public Travels of Queen Elizabeth* (*1788*) on which this chapter is largely based

size of a man's head in roofs. One ball of fire fell on a house where Henry Cowper and his wife were asleep in bed and burned their dwelling about their ears. Such eminent courtiers as the Earl of Oxford and Sir Fulke Greville joined in the task of saving Warwick from the flames. Later, Henry Cowper and his wife were called before the Queen and received £25 12s 8d as compensation. Not a word was said about their want of spirit in electing to sleep through such a royal spectacle.

On all her visits the Queen was dogged by allegorical figures. At the High Cross at Bristol she was welcomed by 'an excellent boy very orderly set forth,' representing Fame. He recited a long poem, then threw her a great garland. At the next gate stood three more boys, Salutation, Gratulation and Obedient Good Will. Salutation piped up as follows:

> All hail, O plant of grace and special sprout of fame,
> Most welcome to this western coast, O pearl and
>   princely dame!

and ended with

> And we poor silly boys that came from school of late
> Rejoice to clap our hands withal as members of thy state.

Obedient Good Will had no opportunity to address the Queen, as time was running out.

Three hundred soldiers accompanied the Queen to her lodging, shooting off their pieces 'in passing good order'; then 130 heavy guns took over where these left off. Afterwards a battle was staged. With little difficulty soldiers overran a minor fort called Feeble Policy and razed it. Throughout the long-drawn noisy action the contestants hurled prodigious quantities of dreadful verse at each other. Two lines will suffice:

> Ah, fie for shame, set hand on sword, in your behalf I
>   blush,
> Bid trumpet sound, advance the pike and give proud
>   Peace a push.

Then came the Earl of Leicester's turn. The 'Princely Pleasures' mounted by him at Kenilworth, in 1575, are said to have cost him £1000 a day. They lasted nearly three weeks. To the wide-eyed countryfolk (among whom is thought to have been William Shakespeare) the occasion must have resembled the meeting of two sovereigns. The gem-girt favourite had numerous regiments and guns encamped in the vicinity, as much for the Queen's flattery as for her protection. Kenilworth had been presented to him by the Queen, and it was for him to show that he had improved the gift. When the Queen reached the first gate six monstrous trumpeters sounded a welcome. The trumpeters were hollow figures and the real trumpets were concealed. The idea behind this conceit was that the castle should seem to be tenanted by King Arthur's men. The porter was a Hercules, who exclaimed: 'What dainty darling's here? Oh God, a peerless pearl!'

The functions prepared for the Queen ran the gamut of Elizabethan entertainment. There was a grand aquatic display in which Triton rode on the back of an 18-foot mermaid and Arion bestrode a 24-foot dolphin. The pool was inhabited by a Lady of the Lake who glided with her nymphs on the surface of the water. Another day there was a pitched battle between thirteen bears and a number of bandogs. 'Such expense of blood and leather was there between them,' says Nichols, 'as a month's licking, I ween, will not recover.'

Several times the Queen hunted. After successfully chasing a hart to its death, she and her followers were greeted by a Savage Man covered with moss and ivy, and bearing an oaken plant in his hand. He stayed the proceedings to conduct a long conversation with Echo. One verse ran:

And who gave all these gifts?
I pray thee, Echo, say.
Was it not he who (but of late)
This building here did lay?

And punning Echo answered, 'Dudley.'

At the end the Savage Man broke his wand in half, like a dismissed chamberlain, and threw away the pieces, one of which hit the Queen's horse on the head, to the dismay of her gentlemen. 'No hurt, no hurt,' exclaimed the patient Queen. She was in an indulgent mood, for when another hart was captured she directed the hunters not to kill it but merely to deprive it of its ears, 'for a ransom.' This was done, and the grateful animal scampered back into the forest.

The Queen did not see all the spectacles designed for her glorification. Like a wise showman, Leicester kept entertainments in reserve. For two or three days together a company of actors wore costume and grease paint ready to perform a long verse play by George Gascoigne, but were the victims of lack of opportunity and unseasonable weather. Gascoigne finally got his chance when the Earl ordered him to devise some farewell words to the Queen. Dressing himself as Silvanus, he intercepted the Queen as she was hunting and apostrophised her, *ex tempore*, as she rode. Occasionally she halted her horse lest he should run out of breath, but he assured her that if his rude speech did not offend he could keep up the tale for 20 miles or more. His harangue, as reported, is an extremely tedious disquisition on the functions of the woodland gods. Eventually there came a welcome diversion when Deep Desire addressed the Queen out of a holly bush.*

At Cowdrey, where the Queen was received by Lord Montecute (Montague), a bower was prepared in the park. Here a nymph presented the Queen with a cross-bow, with which she shot at 30 deer attending her pleasure in a paddock. She killed three or four and the Countess of Kildare accounted for one; the wounded were not listed. Musicians played during this sylvan idyll. In the evening the Court watched sixteen bucks pulled down by greyhounds.

It was not to be expected that the woods of Cowdrey would be free of hoary humbugs. One day the Queen was met by a Pilgrim in russet velvet who led her proudly to an oak which had sprouted not only the royal arms but those of all the loyal gentlemen of the shire. An ivy-clad Wild Man then materialised and said a few suitable words ('all hearts of oak, all in one root'). On another walk the Queen came to a goodly fish pond where an Angler addressed her at length. A netter then drew in his net and spilled all the fish in the pond at her feet. There were other happy surprises, as when the Queen, on a woodland excursion, suddenly came upon two great tables set out for a feast. No wonder she created six knights when she left.

At Norwich the mayor addressed the Queen in Latin. This time she did not feel it incumbent on her to reply in the same tongue. Bad weather preserved her from a speech by 'King

* George Gascoigne: *Princely Pleasures*

Gurgunt, sometime King of England,' but Commonwealth treated her to a rhymed disquisition on weaving. Norwich also devised a charade in which Chastity set about Cupid and turned him out of his coach, then came up to congratulate the Queen on retaining her virginity. In the background Wantonness and Riot flitted enviously. Chastity's maids in waiting, Modesty, Temperance, Good Exercise and Shame-fastness, then sang a ditty to prove that 'chaste life for loss of pleasures short doth win immortal praise,' that 'chaste life hath merry moods and soundly taketh rest,' and 'lewd life cuts off his days.' A bevy of nymphs were scheduled to pop out of caves to greet the Queen, but rain stopped play.

A reception rivalling, and in some ways surpassing, the Kenilworth display was staged at Elvetham by the Earl of Hertford, the same earl who spent many years under arrest for marrying a lady of the blood royal. This was his opportunity to buy himself back into favour. His house was of modest dimensions, so he set 300 artificers busy enlarging it. They also set up halls, bowers and galleries and a royal withdrawing chamber covered with boughs and clusters of ripe hazel nuts; also a whole set of tiled offices for the commissariat.

A major engineering operation was the cutting of a whimsical half-moon pond, with a 'ship isle' 100 feet long and 40 feet broad, pierced by three trees to serve as masts; a fort covering some 20 square yards; and a 'snail mount' in which green hedges spiralled upwards to the summit.

Just before the Queen's arrival the Earl briefed his underlings in a thicket, assuring them that their honour was as much at stake as his. Then he deployed his virgins and posted his poets. The Queen was met two miles away by a train of 300, mostly wearing chains of gold, with yellow and black feathers in their hats. The first poet, dressed in green and garlanded, made a point of wearing boots to show that he was not a 'loose or low creeping prophet.' While he held up the Queen, six maidens were busy removing road blocks set in the royal path by Envy. They then preceded the Queen, strewing flowers and singing

> Oh beauteous queen of second Troy,
> Accept of our unfeigned joy . . .

Arriving at the house, the Queen was saluted by thundering salvoes from the snail mount and the ship isle.

Many strange things happened in the Elvetham pond. From a bower at the far end came a 'pompous array of sea persons,' who swam or waded breast high until they reached the Queen's feet. Virgins in pinnacles played Scottish jigs on cornets. The fort was invested by armed men. The snail mount turned out to have horns of wildfire. Silvanus, in hairy kids' skins, came out of the brake with his ivy-leaved followers and was ducked by the sea gods in a battle of darts and squirts. At the height of the excitement the Queen was presented with a sea jewel. The pyrotechnics included, not merely hurtling wildfire, but a castle of fire and rockets whizzing to their destination on lines. While this was being staged, the Queen and her courtiers banqueted. Two hundred gentlemen, preceded by a hundred torchbearers, carried a thousand dishes. The Earl's confectioners had gone to great pains to make sugar reproductions of all her majesty's castles and arms. Then, having a good deal of sugar left over, they produced a tremendous bestiary of creatures natural and unnatural, and finally a harvest festival of fruits and flowers.

When the Queen left, the performers stood in grief-stricken attitudes along her path. To the Earl she gave an assurance that he would find favour in her eyes, but he did not pitch his hopes too high. A few years later, the Queen, exasperated by the Earl's attempts to regularise the results of his earlier follies, gave him a further taste of the Tower. Ship isles and snail mounts had been conjured up in vain.

Did the enigmatic Queen really enjoy these spectacles? Did she never wince when a squealing Daphne, pursued by Apollo, ran up to beg the protection of the Queen of Chastity? Did she not shudder at the sight of yet another whiskered sage clearing his throat as he unrolled the inevitable scroll? If she disliked these things, she never showed it. She may have reflected that, at the very least, she was bringing fun, feasting and fireworks to subjects whose lives were humdrum, and knighthoods to gentlemen who would otherwise not have qualified for them.

The older courtiers groaned at the thought of setting off on progress. To them, the Queen's answer was that if they

The Earl of Hertford mounts a spectacle for Queen Elizabeth at Elvetham.
From John Nichols' *Progresses*

did not like the idea they could stay behind; but none dared take her at her word. The younger gallants, if Holinshed is to be believed, welcomed progresses as an excuse for larks which would not have been tolerated at Greenwich or Richmond, behaving 'worse than any man shall either hear or read of.' They were, no doubt, cynical enough about these unsophisticated sylvan frolics, but may have preferred the piping of rural poets to the learned disputations of dons at Oxford or Cambridge. Probably they just shrugged, yawned— and accepted their gifts. Some among them may have groaned to see the steadily rising standards of extravagance with which they themselves might have to compete some day. If men were ready to create lakes and islands, where was the thing to stop? The giving of presents was also getting out of hand. When the Queen visited Sir John Puckering at Kew she was presented, on alighting, with a diamond-handled fan. On her way to the house she accepted the sort of nosegay one does not toss lightly to the crowd; it had £400 worth of diamonds embedded in it. After dinner Sir John gave the Queen a pair of virginals, and by night-time he was in her bedchamber begging her to accept a fine gown and 'juppin.'

Progress between towns was at the rate of perhaps a dozen miles a day. As there were scores upon scores of baggage carts, the Harbingers' task was no easier than it had been under the early Plantagenets. The Queen herself rode sometimes on horseback, sometimes in an open litter. Often crowds pressed round her and addressed her without ceremony; on these occasions she gave as good as she got. One Sergeant Bendlowes, of Huntingdonshire, wishing to address the Queen, called to her coachman, 'Stay thy cart, good fellow.' The Queen laughed and gave him her hand to kiss.

Such incidents would be remembered and passed down the generations. With all her state, she had the common touch, this Flower of Grace, this Prince of God's Elect, this Finger of the Lord, this Jewel of the World, this Puissant Prince, this Nurse of Religion, this Starbright Eye, Heaven's Chief Delight, Sweet Beauty's Sun, this Mother Dear.

12

Beautiful Earls

WHEN the great Queen's life was flickering away at Richmond, her courtiers were busy taking steps to safeguard their future. The hard-riding Sir Robert Carey determined to be the first to carry the news of her death to her successor, the Scots King.

As soon as he knew her hours were numbered, he sent a messenger to James at Holyrood. Then he arranged for horses to be waiting all along the road to Edinburgh. The month was March, 1603.

Carey's sister, Lady Scrope, was one of the Queen's ladies. When Elizabeth's heart stopped, she drew a blue ring from a chill finger and dropped it from a window to her brother. The ring was James's own gift and would be evidence enough of the Queen's death. There was an absolute ban on persons leaving the Court, but Carey was allowed out by his brother, Lord Hunsdon, an officer of the Household, who trusted him to do nothing rash. At this point Carey seems to have hesitated; but hearing a rumour that some other messenger might be sent north, he decided to set off. It was between nine and ten on a Thursday morning when he left the city gates and by night he had reached Doncaster, 160 miles away. On the Friday night he slept under his own roof at Widdrington, having covered nearly 300 miles. Early on the Saturday morning he started on the last lap to Edinburgh, reaching Norham about noon. Thereabouts he was thrown heavily and kicked on the head by his horse, losing a great deal of blood. As a result he had to ride at a slower pace and did not reach the Palace of Holyrood until the King had retired to bed. James graciously rose to receive him, digested the stirring news, and as a mark of his appreciation made Carey a Gentleman of the Bedchamber on the spot. The object of the exercise had been accomplished.

The 400-miles ride, like the earlier walk, is baldly described in Carey's reminiscences. There is much one would like to know about it. How many horses did Carey use? How many did he ride to death? What was the cost of such an operation? How good was the signposting? How many miles were covered in darkness?

In the Court at Richmond there was no admiration for Carey's feat but a great deal of indignation because, by disobeying orders, he had tried to win personal advantage from the death of his sovereign. The Lord Mayor of London, in his loyal address to the new King, described Carey's action as 'contrary to all decency, good manners and respect which he owed to so many persons of our degree.' Much of this was merely the anger of officialdom at being 'scooped.' Carey's enemies had long memories, however, and they found ways of cramping his subsequent Court career. But he was first Earl of Monmouth when he died.

He was a successful courtier.

It was customary for a fanciful masque to be followed by a farcical one. The Court of James I fulfilled the latter role in succession to the Court of Elizabeth.

The great Queen, in surrounding herself with handsome male favourites, had given the gossips something to talk about. James, by continuing this policy, opened up a new field of lubricious speculation. Quite early in his reign people were talking about Queen James. The two sovereigns shared few other characteristics, though it was soon apparent that James, like his 'dear sister,' responded to the most oriental flatteries. It is very evident that he was endowed with an unfair share of the seven deadly sins. It is also very evident that his Court was a sink.

On his leisurely way from Holyrood to London James hunted everything that ran and knighted everything that crawled. It has been said that he did not take the ceremony of dubbing seriously, because on one occasion, failing to catch the aspirant's name, he said, 'Arise, Sir What-You-Will.' The name of Sir What-You-Will has come down to us, in one version,

as Everard Rudry Hudinbras Triplin Hipplas, so it is difficult
to fault the King on this point.

Tiresomely, the King's subjects kept crowding round him
when he paused to hunt, but he bore their loyalty with fortitude. Suitors jostled him everywhere. At York he freed all
prisoners save Papists and wilful murderers. At Newark, to
show that he was a king, he hanged a robber without trial.
Near Stamford suitors twelve feet high came stalking out of
the Fens on stilts, preferring a petition against Lady Hatton.
They were told to wait until he had reached London. At
Theobalds the dwarf Secretary of State, Sir Robert Cecil, with
whom he had been in secret correspondence, greeted him in
great state and took his measure. On the outskirts of the capital
James was met by Silvanus, Ceres, Pomona and the rest of
the classical rabble, along with the Nine Muses and the Seven
Liberal Arts (Grammar, Logic, Rhetoric, Music, Arithmetic,
Geometry and Astrology).

The arm which had dubbed three hundred knights was
now growing tired. Title-hunters were told to wait until
after the coronation. Most of those who had been besieging
his Privy Chamber withdrew when they found they would
have to pay their own expenses at Court. The King found
time to inspect the palaces, manors, forests and chases in the
London area, and was delighted to find them well stocked
with slaughter-worthy creatures. For James, oddly enough
in a pedantic sloven, was a keen and indeed pathological
huntsman.

After the nervous rigours of Scotland, life was agreeably
carefree and lavish, but the press of suitors continued to be
an exasperation. 'Those he brought with him wanted means
more than honour; those he found here wanted honour more
than means,' says that sardonic observer, Arthur Wilson, adding that the King supplied both to excess. All those who had
been frustrated in their aspirations, legitimate or otherwise,
by Elizabeth now clamoured for lands, offices, titles, reversions,
grants and pardons. Soon there was a state of tension at Court
between the rapacious Scots and the envious English. Wilson
reports 'the Scots creeping into English lordships and English
ladies' beds, in both of which already they begin to be active.'*

* Arthur Wilson: *The History of Great Britain*

The English scoffed at more than the Scots' rapacity; they despised their uncouth manners and accents.

This friction was keenly watched by the French Ambassador, Count Beaumont, who in 1604 reported to his master: 'He [James] has issued an ordinance according to which he confers on seven Englishmen and a like number of Scots the right of entering his Chamber, hoping thereby to amalgamate them and accustom them to order. They are, however, only become more violent, at which the whole Court is scandalised.'*

In 1605 Ben Jonson was in trouble for exacerbating Anglo-Scots relationships. When the authors of the play *Eastward Hoe* were jailed for mocking the King's countrymen, Jonson gallantly admitted a share in the offence and joined them behind bars, at some slight risk to his ears and nose. He emerged a hero and was soon restored to Court favour.

James had inherited a kingdom in which Protestants, Papists and Puritans spent much of their time accusing each other of lewdness. Tremendous political and social problems awaited his attention, but by hunting hard and often, and by moving from one palace to another, he contrived to shake off the less determined of his ministers, bishops and suitors.

It was delightful to be able to ring the changes on so many palaces—Greenwich, Eltham, Windsor, Hampton Court, Richmond, Nonsuch, to say nothing of excursions to New-market. Elizabeth had run these establishments frugally, but under James they rapidly became the scene of prodigality and riot. Lucy Hutchinson, bitterly Puritan, claims to have seen clearly what was going on. Despite the collapse of the Gun-powder Plot in 1605, 'the Papists lost not their credit at Court, where they now wrought no longer by open and direct ways, but humouring the King and Queen in their lusts and excesses, they found the most ready way to destroy the doctrine of the Gospel was to debauch the professors. The Court of the King was a nursery of lust and intemperance. . . . The generality of the land soon learned the Court fashion and every great house in the country became a sty of uncleanness.'† Mrs Hutchinson may have ascribed undue enterprise to the Papists, but she can hardly have overdrawn the picture of profligacy

* F. von Raumer: *History of the 16th and 17th Centuries*
† *Memoirs of Colonel Hutchinson*

James I about to take assay of the deer. Not all his hunting activities lent themselves to polite illustration. From Osborne's *Traditional Memoirs*

in high places. The day soon came when no one could afford
to be looked upon as other than a rake. 'I would rather be
thought to enjoy such a lady, though I never did it, than
really to enjoy her and nobody know it' was the attitude of
the Court gallant.

James demanded the divinity that surrounds a throne but
he neither looked like a god nor acted like one. There were
times when, in the most alarming contexts, he compared himself with Christ, and possibly, in his dinner-table debates with
sycophantic bishops, he saw himself as Christ and the disciples.
On a more temporal plane, it was agreeable to have great
nobles kneeling before him with food. This helped to foster
the notion of majesty if not of godhead. Unfortunately, having
little or no personal dignity, and being impatient of ceremonial
delays, he gradually let the fences of etiquette crumble, which
only a king like Henry II can afford to do. His Queen, Anne
of Denmark, was equally careless of appearances, scoffing at
her husband's follies without making any attempt to wean
him from them. It has been said that James was never drunk,
but he took heavy wines at such frequent intervals through
the day that it is hard to see how he could ever have been
in anything but a state of stimulation. He was a prodigious
swearer and seemed unable to break himself of the habit of
wishing a pox on his subjects. In his person he was dirty. So
also, at an early stage, were some of his entourage, to judge
from the experiences of Lady Anne Clifford. On a visit to
Theobalds in 1603 she reported: 'We all saw the great change
between the fashion of the Court as it is now and of that in
the Queen's time, for we were all lousy by sitting in the chamber
of Sir Thomas Erskine.'

Gambling was not, perhaps, an outstanding Court vice, save
on Twelfth Night when high play was traditional. At the royal
table in 1607 no one was allowed to sit down unless he could
produce £300. The Earl of Montgomery played with the
King's money and won £150, which he was allowed to keep.
Lord Monteagle lost the Queen £400, which he was not called
upon to defray. On behalf of Prince Charles Sir Robert Carey
lost £300.

Towards his Household the King behaved like a spoiled
child. John Gib, his faithful servant, went on his knees to deny

that he had lost certain papers of his master and was kicked for his pains, at which he packed his belongings and rode sorrowfully from Court. Almost at once the papers were found and Gib was recalled. This time the King went on his knees to his servant and said he would not rise again until he was forgiven. Gib did not relish being asked to pardon a grovelling sovereign but eventually found it necessary to do so.*

The initial rate of spending obviously could not last and James, in 1604, initiated his first economy drive. As an example, he and his Queen cut their consumption of food from 30 dishes of meat a day to 24. Many of those who enjoyed *Bouche* of Court had their privilege commuted to cash. It was the King's opinion that sack (Spanish wine) was being used for wantonness and surfeiting rather than for necessity; its consumption, therefore, was to be cut down. Another proclamation, which sharply reflects on the honesty of those attending the King, laid down that no persons were to send silver dishes out of the Privy Chamber or the Presence Chamber; if meat had to be rejected the silver vessels were to be exchanged for pewter ones at 'Our Presence Door.' To rid himself of the expense of dependents, James revived an old rule which said that if any children, pages, scourers or turnspits presumed to marry they would lose their jobs.

These rules went the way of all sumptuary rules. In 1609 the Lord Treasurer was stopped in the street by a crowd of the King's servants, who refused to let him proceed unless he promised to pay their overdue wages. Tradesmen were declining to deliver goods. 'I feel as if the times of Henry III were before my eyes,' said the French Ambassador.

Masques, of which this was the heyday, ran away with a great deal of money. The most notorious one was staged at Theobalds in 1606 in honour of King Christian IV of Denmark. Cecil, now Earl of Salisbury, was host to both kings, in whose honour he had strewn the avenues with gold oak leaves bearing the word 'Welcome.' A malicious account of the proceedings was penned by Sir John Harington, by now a somewhat disillusioned courtier. The festivities, he says, reminded him of Mahomet's paradise. Each day the ladies abandoned their sobriety and rolled about in intoxication. On one occasion

*Arthur Wilson: *The History of Great Britain*

the performers were supposed to be representing the visit of
the Queen of Sheba to Solomon in his temple. The lady playing
Sheba carried precious gifts to both their majesties, but tripped
over the steps and spilled her casket over the Danish King,
covering him with wine, cream, jelly, cakes and spices. There
was much confusion but he was wiped clean with napkins.
He rose to dance with the tipsy Sheba, but 'fell down and
humbled himself before her,' and was dragged to a couch in
an inner room.

'The entertainment went forward and most of the presenters
went backward or fell down, wine did so much occupy their
upper chambers. Now did appear Hope, Faith and Charity.
Hope did essay to speak but wine rendered her endeavours
so feeble that she withdrew and hoped the King would excuse
her brevity. Faith was then all alone for I am certain she was
not joined with good works, but left the Court in a staggering
condition. Charity came to the King's feet and seemed to cover
the multitude of sins her sisters had committed. In some sort
she made obeisance and brought gifts, but said she would
return home again as there was no gift which Heaven had
not already given His Majesty. She then returned to Hope and
Faith who were both sick and spewing in the lower hall. Next
came Victory in bright armour and presented a rich sword
to the King who did not accept it but put it by with his hand;
but Victory did not triumph long, for after much lamentable
utterance she was led away like a silly captive and laid to
sleep on the outer steps of the antechamber. Now did Peace
make entry and strive to get foremost to the King; but I grieve
to tell you how great wrath she did discover unto her attendants
and much contrary to her semblance most rudely made war
with her olive branch and laid on the pates of those who did
oppose her coming. I never did see such lack of good order,
discretion and sobriety and I have now done.'*

It is only fair to say that there were more temperate Court
masques than this, attaining dazzling heights of ingenuity and
fancy, and combining all the delights of colour, music, poetry,
lighting, flowers, perfume, machinery and women. Notable
among them was the *Masque of Hymen* presented by Ben
Jonson and Inigo Jones. There was an extremely elaborate

* *Nugae Antiquae*

set which is difficult to visualise from the descriptions of it. The proceedings began with Hymen bringing on a bride and Juno a bridegroom. At this point the globe of the world rotated and from its interior leapt eight men masquers, representing the four Affections and the four Humours, who sought to prevent the union. Their interference brought down Reason, crowned with burning tapers, from her throne, to disperse them. About the globe hovered a girdle of clouds in which, mysteriously, a grand concert of musicians functioned, and on the horns, wherever they were, were jewelled ladies who were gently lowered down to dance. Tiresome though the theme sounds, the general effect may well have been as entrancing as anything mounted by the Folies Bergère.

Even to a philosopher like Bacon, masques were a source of much pleasure. In his *Essays* he throws out a few ideas on the subject. Frequent change of scene, he says, is much to be desired, if it can be achieved noiselessly. 'The colours that show best by candlelight are white, carnation and a kind of sea-water green; and oes or spangs [circles or spangles], as they are of no great cost, so they are of most glory.' Very refreshing, at the right time, are 'sweet odours suddenly coming forth without any drops falling.'

Masques were essentially Court entertainments. Nowhere else were the necessary resources of talent and money to be found. The common people tried their hardest to gain admission to such spectacles, but all too often it was their fate to be driven off by officials with rods of office. The subsidising of masques cost many courtiers dearly. Twelve of them put up £300 each for a performance at the wedding of Lord Haddington.

In several of Ben Jonson's masques Queen Anne and her ladies, not always modestly clad, took part. It is clear that Anne's sense of fun sometimes ran away with her. There was a hushed-up occasion when she took part in a *risqué* masked frolic in the town, lost her way and returned to the palace in a cart.

Under James the company of which William Shakespeare was a member received greater encouragement at Court than in Elizabeth's day. As Grooms of the Chamber the actors received cloth for their liveries, plus a great many gifts. Occasionally, to remind them that they were servants, they were required to perform the duties of Court usher, as in 1604 when Shakespeare and his colleagues of the Lord Chamberlain's company waited on the Spanish envoys at Somerset House. It was, no doubt, all grist to the Shakespearean mill. In *Love's Labour's Lost* is a happy description of a Court usher—'the stairs, as he treads on them, kiss his feet.'

The country was becoming inured to the institution of royal favourite. Church and Parliament wearily acquiesced in the rule of beautiful earls. But whereas Elizabeth had exercised some sort of final control over her favourites—beheading one, locking up two—James seemed incapable of reining them back. They accepted his kisses and his titles, threw his money about, bullied him into dissolving Parliaments, sold his offices, forced the wealthy and the up-and-coming to marry their clamorous kin, abused the old nobility and, when faced with a major task of statesmanship or generalship, proved incompetent. They shared the comfortless knowledge that the factions which found it convenient to support them were ready to drop or betray them at a moment's notice. Thus it was all the more necessary to grow rich quickly.

The two best-known of the golden calves were Sir Robert Carr, Earl of Somerset and George Villiers, Earl of Buckingham. Earlier in favour was Philip Herbert, Earl of Montgomery, who was honoured on the morning after his wedding night by a visit from the King in his nightgown; all three then romped in the bed. There was also James Hay, Earl of Carlisle, who had served in the Scots bodyguard of the French king. Unlike most favourites, he had a certain civility and common sense which kept him in favour. His extravagances had a pleasing imbecility all their own. On a mission to Paris he rode to the Louvre on a horse lightly shod with silver shoes. These were kicked off at intervals and scrambled for by the admiring crowd. In Hay's train was an *argentier* who produced new silver shoes as required from a bag and tacked them on.

Like the purveyors of William the Conqueror, Hay delighted in importing great fish from faraway places. From Russia he shipped home sturgeon which were so big that special plates had to be made to carry them. According to one commentator, the necessity of waiting for these to be manufactured could

scarcely have improved the flavour of the fish. Hay also introduced at Court the curiously perverse extravagance of ante-
suppers. These consisted of 'dishes as high as a tall man could
well reach filled with the choicest and dearest viands sea or
land could afford: and all this once seen and having feasted
the eyes of the invited was in a manner thrown away and
fresh set on to the same height, having only this advantage
of the other that it was hot.' On one of these occasions an
attendant of the King ate a whole pie containing an estimated
ten pounds of ambergris, magisterial of pearl and musk, yet
was 'so far from being sweet in the morning that he almost
poisoned his own family, flying himself like the satyr from his
own stink.'*

Sir Robert Carr originally accompanied James to London
as a running page, but as it was not customary for English
kings to keep such retainers he was dismissed with £50 and
a new suit. After spending some time in France he returned
to the English Court and had the good fortune to break a
limb in a tournament. James recognised his former servant,
ordered that he should receive the best surgical treatment and
personally paid him many bedside visits, from which a highly
charged friendship sprang up. Although the King found in
this young gentleman 'no great depth of literature or experience,' nevertheless 'such a smooth and calm outside made him
think there might be good anchorage and a fit harbour for
his most retired thoughts.'†So Carr was appointed to the Bedchamber, where retired thoughts might most readily be shared.
Thereafter his rise was as rapid as it was unmerited; in six
years he was Earl of Somerset. Courtiers quickly recognised
him as a person to be cultivated if they were to gain the royal
ear. Soon he was handling the State correspondence. The King
taught him Latin but failed to teach him manners. In signing
off a letter he was capable of writing, 'And so I kiss your
dirty hands.' Like all his kind, Somerset was barren of gratitude
and full of contempt for the doting elder who lifted him from
obscurity. The major error of his career was to woo and wed
a lovely murderess, the divorced Countess of Essex, who walked
up the aisle of the Chapel at Whitehall dressed in innocent

* Francis Osborne: *Traditional Memoirs*
† Arthur Wilson: *The History of Great Britain*

white. But the scandal of her part (and possibly his) in the murder of Sir Thomas Overbury was late in breaking. Before it did so, Somerset, jealous of the rising George Villiers, had been destroying the peace of the royal Bedchamber with (in the King's words) 'fiery *boutades* coupled with a continual dogged, sullen behaviour.' In a letter of reproach, James asked his favourite what more he wanted:

'Do not all courtesies and places come through your office as Chamberlain, and rewards through your father-in-law as Treasurer? Do not you two (as it were) hedge in all the Court with a manner of necessity to depend on you? And have you not . . . your nephew in my Bedchamber—besides another far more active than he in Court practices? And have you not one of your nearest kinsmen that loves not to be idle in my son's Bedchamber?'

Long before Somerset went out in dazzling disgrace the King was carrying under his dagger-proof doublet the picture of Villiers, a young gentleman of unusual 'symmetry,' who, like St Stephen in exaltation, had the face of an angel (hence the King's nickname for him—'Steenie.') One of Somerset's servants, possibly anxious to further his master's interests, possibly acting under instructions, spilled soup over Villiers, who got up and clouted him, thus risking dire penalties. But Villiers was not born to be mutilated, nor was he a man to be stayed by soup. His first appointment was a modest but intimate one, that of Cupbearer. Before promoting him any higher James invoked the special procedure which he found useful when advancing favourites: he persuaded his Queen to endorse and recommend the candidate. Thanks to this 'rather subtle species of moral obliquity,'* he was able to point out, if the Queen subsequently objected to the favourite's activities, that she had recommended him. Anne raised no special difficulties over Villiers; she had a sense of farce. In little over two years the newcomer was Earl of Buckingham. Soon the Court was aswarm with his rapacious and husband-hunting family, even with their children—'little ones would dance up and down the Privy Stairs like fairies.' The King was always ready to defend his friendship with Buckingham. In 1617 he told the Council: 'I, James, am neither a god nor an angel, but a man

---

* *Dictionary of National Biography* (Anne of Denmark)

like any other. Therefore I act like a man and confess to loving those dear to me more than other men. You may be sure that I love the Earl of Buckingham more than anyone else, and more than you who are here assembled. I wish to speak in my own behalf and not to have it thought to be a defect, for Jesus Christ did the same, and therefore I cannot be blamed. Christ had his son John, and I have my George.' In justification for granting admiral's rank to Buckingham, he said he would rather have a young man whose honesty and integrity he knew than an old beaten soldier. This honest young Admiral, who went about upholstered in precious stones, had zeal, bravery and was not without taste. Although he did not do favours for nothing, he refrained from demanding exorbitant rewards, whatever his mother may have done. The King who had sworn to make him his masterpiece was well pleased with his choice. If Buckingham had possessed diplomatic brilliance and military genius, then indeed he would have been a paragon; as it was, he had the abilities of a good confidential secretary. Because he wielded immense patronage he was the magnet of envy and malice. On the social front, two Court fashions he introduced brought him much censure. He was the first to drive about town in a coach-and-six (as a protest, a venerable aristocrat equipped himself with a coach-and-eight); and he was supposedly the first to popularise the sedan chair, thus reducing his fellow men to beasts of burden. It is a tribute to Buckingham's social charms that he shared the goodwill of Prince Charles (later Charles I).

Suitably enough, the King's most powerful subject wed the country's richest heiress, in the person of Lady Catherine Manners, daughter of the Earl of Rutland. The difficult negotiations to bring this about (the lady was a Roman Catholic) were performed by an ambitious Court chaplain, John Williams, who was a crony of the King. In order to get on in the world, James told him, he ought to do something to help the Duke of Buckingham. For his labours in the vineyard the chaplain was rewarded with the deanery of Westminster. In due time, despite convictions for bribery and suborning of perjury, he became Archbishop of York.

Whether or not James was a practising homosexual nobody knows. One historian will insist that his personal life was pure;

another will describe him as a Christian pasha revelling in the delights of a male harem. Sir John Oglander thought the King was 'wondrous passionate, a lover of his favourites beyond the love of men of women . . . he was the chastest prince for women that ever was, for he would often swear that he never kissed any other woman than his own queen.'* That the King kissed and slobbered over his male favourites in public is well attested. The charitable are willing to believe that the King's addiction to minions was merely the tribute of ugliness to perfection, or the desire of the wisest of mankind to offset his gravity with mirthful and handsome young companions. Francis Osborne says that Somerset and Buckingham went out of their way to look effeminate; 'in w——— looks and wanton gestures they exceeded any part of womankind.' He adds: 'The kissing them after so lascivious a mode in public and upon the theatre, as it were, of the world prompted many to imagine some things done in the tyring house that exceed my expression no less than they do my experience.' He says that Sir Henry Rich, later the Earl of Holland, spat disgustedly after the King had 'slabered' him in the mouth. In 1621 the French Ambassador, Count Beaumont, in his reports to Paris attributed to James conduct which he considered unfit to mention in dispatches, but Paris urgently requested full details and the shy ambassador supplied them.† French ambassadors were always ready to pass on tittle-tattle as news.

Women seem to have found little to praise in James, though they often admired his choice of favourites. The French envoy thought that James's attitude to women was contemptuous. When they were presented to him he would make them kneel and openly exhort them to virtue, scoffing at men who paid them honour. But Oglander testifies that 'a virtuous woman he would both highly grace and commend.' James's Queen never wholly disliked him, nor did he dislike her, even though all they had in common was 'a mutual admiration for masculine beauty.'‡ In official documents, whether they treated of duelling or the reclamation of candle-ends, James referred to his Queen as 'our dearest Bedfellow.'

* W. H. Long (ed): *The Oglander Memoirs*
† F. von Raumer: *History of the 16th and 17th Centuries*
‡ J. H. Jesse: *Memoirs of the Court during the Stuarts*

The game of trying to plant a mistress on a king, in order to influence his policies, was as old as history, but the English nobility had little experience of launching male mistresses. Nevertheless the Howards, as unfastidious as they were unprincipled, did not shrink from the attempt. The Countess of Suffolk was always on the look-out for choice young men 'whom she daily curled and perfumed their breath.' Eventually the plotters found what they hoped might be a rival to Buckingham in the son of Sir William Monson, the explorer, and took great pains to trick him out in what they supposed to be a seductive manner, even to the extent of washing his face with 'posset curd.' When young Monson failed to catch the royal eye, others were propelled into the fray. Their failure was not due to any shyness on their part, for they did their best to out-ogle each other. The Court found it capital amusement but eventually the sniggering grew too loud. The Lord Chamberlain 'told young Monson that the King did not like of his forwardness and presenting himself continually about him,' and bade him be gone from Court.* The Howards, for once, had cause to regret their enterprise. One by one, they were dislodged from Court by Buckingham. The affair of the minions, which occurred in 1618, marked as low a point as the Court had reached in some 500 years.

If James's knighthoods were a bad joke, his baronetcies were hardly to be taken seriously. He conceived the unhappy idea of marketing them at a flat fee of £1000. It was not, in conception, a money-making idea, for the fee was intended to cover the maintenance of 30 foot soldiers for three years in Ireland. The titles were not snapped up as rapidly as James had hoped. When a man could win a peerage with a simper, it seemed hard to pay £1000 for a lesser honour. Yet an openly bought baronetcy was clearly more honourable than some of the titles conferred by the personal pleasure of the Sovereign. In 1618 the earldoms of Warwick and Devonshire were sold for £10,000 each, the King being urgently in need of funds to defray the cost of a hunting tour.

An event which cost a sum equivalent to the proceeds of one hundred baronetcies, or ten earldoms, was the wedding of the Princess Elizabeth to the Elector Palatine. The accounts

* Thomas Birch: *Court and Times of James I*

E

contain such items as: For the Palsgrave's diet at the installation of the Garter, £4000; for diet at his marriage, £2000; for apparel of the Princess Elizabeth, £6252; for furnishing her chamber, £3023; jewels and apparel for her servants, £3914; for naval work of fireworks on the Thames at her marriage, £4800; more fireworks on the Thames at her marriage, £2880; the charges of her journey, £8000; for her transport to Flushing, £5555; paid over to the Palsgrave's agent for her portion, £40,000.*

When James's finances had reached an unusually dire state Buckingham produced a disciplinarian in the person of Sir Lionel Cranfield (later the Earl of Middlesex), a former city apprentice and cloth merchant. This unashamed upstart descended on the Court with all the cold zeal of an accountant determined to check extravagance in a riotous film studio. In 1618 the Rev. Thomas Lorkin wrote to Sir Thomas Puckering to say that Cranfield 'hath troubled much the Household officers at Court by laying down a project to the King of saving him £12,000 a year in his ordinary expenses and yet no man abridged of his allowances; which is, with this condition imposed upon the said officers that either they must make it good or resign up their places unto him.'† Although the King's accounts were in chronic and probably deliberate chaos, Cranfield established order, saying, 'The King shall pay no more than other men do, and he shall pay ready money; and if we cannot have it in one place we will have it another.' He also cut down stealing at Court. 'The truth is,' says Dr Godfrey Goodman, 'that the wonderful waste at Court did draw on a number of Hangbies, whole families of poor people, especially Scots. This made the courtiers in fear of infection and dangerous diseases. They were nasty for want of clean linen. There was much stealing, filching and robbing; it was not safe for men to walk in the night. Thus as poor people do always flock to a common so did they flock here only for diet.'

The spendthrift Hay retired, not without handsome compensation, from the Wardrobe and Cranfield took over. In this notorious department he saved £14,000 a year, to which

* *Memoirs of the Court during the Stuarts*
† Thomas Birch: *Court and Times of James I*

was added a saving of £23,000 in the Household generally. When Cranfield was Lord High Treasurer, says Goodman, the King sold not one foot of land, granted no lease, felled no timber tree and ran into no debts. But he continued to spend more on boots, stockings and beaver hats than all the other kings of Christendom put together.

James had never been ignorant of the fact that his courtiers and officials feathered their nests at his expense, or that his ministers accepted *douceurs*, but he lacked the energy to do anything about it. One of his officers, on his deathbed, wished to confess to the King that he had been cheating him. The King urged him to be of good courage and assured him that all was forgiven. 'I wonder much,' he said, 'that all my officers do not go mad with the like thoughts, for certainly they have as great cause as this poor man hath.'

A new Court post created by James was that of Master of the Ceremonies, whose responsibility it was to receive ambassadors with suitable state, cozening and mollifying them as necessary. Sir Lewis Lewknor with the assistance of Sir John Finett did his ruthless best to preserve peace on the ambassadorial front. In private life the envoys were no doubt amiable gentlemen, but in their public capacities they chose to regard every fancied slight as a deliberate insult to the monarch they represented. Finett's recollections* give some haunting glimpses of pettinesses among the great. Thus, the Spanish Ambassador would regard it as an indignity to be invited to see a masque which had already been seen by the French Ambassador, but each would find excuses if invited to attend a masque at which the other would be present, and each would complain bitterly if invited to no masque at all. The French and Venetian Ambassadors at a royal wedding refused to sit on stools when others had chairs, and objected that the carver stood above them.

Many of these petulant visitors were mightily incensed when they were received on English soil by delegates of, as they thought, inadequate status; but the Russian Ambassador was assured, and apparently believed, that in England it was a greater honour to be received by one lord than by two. Lewknor and Finett worked to a peculiar set of rules which

* *Some Choice Recollections of Sir John Finett*

defined how far the King's coach should be sent to fetch ambassadors of varying pretensions. Whereas the ambassador of a king was to be welcomed by an earl at the least, the ambassador of a duke could consider himself fortunate in being received by a baron. The Master of the Ceremonies also had to soothe wounded feelings when the King decided to cut down the scale of his gratuities to ambassadors. This issue, in turn, led to a domestic quarrel with the Master of the Jewel House, who thought he should have the privilege of handing gifts to ambassadors. Naturally no ambassador could receive gifts without pressing gratuities on those who conveyed them.

What the Court lacked in wit was made up by practical joking, which frequently involved the use of pigs, alive or dead. The King disliked these animals, which was doubtless why they called him 'sow.' The Earl of Pembroke, who hated frogs, was annoyed when James put one down his neck, so he retaliated by placing a pig under 'a particular article of furniture in the King's apartment' at Wilton. One day Buckingham and others sought to cheer the King with a prank which involved dressing up a live pig as an infant and conducting a solemn christening service over it. James was not in a risible mood and walked off saying, 'Fie, fie for shame!' Solomon could be a Grundy.

The King's official jester was Archie Armstrong, reputedly a sheep-stealer who had cheeked his way out of the noose. He blended impertinence with rapacity in the traditional manner. He might be called upon to 'tilt' after supper, riding on the back of another fool, for the Court in its later years liked a session of horseplay. For these and other professional services the King's dizzard was granted a pension of 2s a day for life, made a freeman of Aberdeen and given a patent for making tobacco pipes. He went to Spain with Prince Charles and Buckingham, where, despite a tendency to makes jokes about the fate of the Armada, he was popular with the Infanta and her ladies. He was less popular with Buckingham who, tiring of his insolence, threatened to hang him. His recorded jests were in the usual vein: 'Why is the louse the surest friend?—When all others fall off, it sticks fastest.'

Among the kings who have bored their courtiers silly with their passion for hunting, James occupies a unique place. His behaviour in the field is a study for the psychiatrist rather than the historian. At any time the boundary between sport and slaughter is an elusive one, but James did not regard hunting as sport. He had no respect for a gallant quarry and bitterly grudged the loss of every stag that escaped; and he was capable of riding angrily at anyone unfortunate enough to obstruct his progress. At Theobalds the Queen, trying to show a friendly interest in field sports, loosed off an arrow and hit Jewel, the King's favourite hound. His rage was enormous; but next day he sent Anne a diamond worth £2000 as a legacy from his dead dog.

The moment James lived for was that of the kill. In no time he would be off his horse to make the assay—that is, to make the first cut on the breast in order to judge the extent of the beast's fat. But James found it necessary to cut the creature's throat and rip open its belly; then, having well blooded himself, he distributed blood over his courtiers. As the years passed, he took to paddling in the bellies of newly slain bucks and stags, having been informed that this strengthened the sinews of the legs. Among those who rode with him were servants carrying sweet rich wines with which to sharpen the day's delights. Bad weather he took as a personal affront from the Almighty. Oglander says: 'Being crossed in his hunting by rain he swore it was not rain but ye windows of Heaven were opened; and he could not be drawn out of it; but would sit in it to see whether God would keep his promise in not drowning the world a second time.' If the King sat in the rain, it is not hard to guess where his followers sat. When there was lack of rain, James complained that his dogs' noses were dull.

The King's behaviour when hunting was no Court secret. On the public stage he was shown belabouring a gentleman who had called off the hounds, and cursing loudly because he had been robbed of a bird. As a rider he was bold but ungraceful. They thrust him on his horse and he rode as he was thrust.

In his less bloodthirsty moments the King liked to watch horse racing and is credited with making it a royal sport. Among the tracks he caused to be built was that at Newmarket.

Any goodwill that James had enjoyed with the public at the start of his reign rapidly evaporated. In 1618 his *Book of*

Sports which authorised certain pastimes to be played on Sundays annoyed the London clergy. Their indignation found a convenient focus when James ordered his Court to move to Theobalds on a Sunday and the clatter of his carts disrupted church services. The Lord Mayor, greatly daring, ordered the carts to be halted. James flew into the expected rage, saying that he was under the impression that he was the only King of England, and sent a warrant to the Lord Mayor ordering him to allow the Court traffic to proceed. The Lord Mayor obeyed, saying: 'While it was in my power I did my duty, but that being taken away by a higher power it is my duty to obey.' The King, having won, for once was magnanimous. It is a strange commentary on the popularity of the Court that a lord mayor should have presumed to halt a progress on the grounds that it was a public nuisance.

The sprawling Palace of Whitehall was in a state of some dilapidation during much of James's reign. Inigo Jones drew up plans for a new Whitehall palace of great magnificence, with a profuse sprinkling of statues along its roof. It was to jut out partly over the Thames, on which it would have a frontage of more than 380 yards. James's chances of erecting this were inconsiderable. Only the Banqueting Hall was completed. The plans were occasionally reviewed, modified and sighed over in subsequent reigns.

The court of James's first-born, Prince Henry, was a standing embarrassment to his father in that it diverted the dignified and the chivalrous from his gates to those of St James's and Richmond. It is possible that Henry's behaviour was overpraised by those who were disgusted with his father. The youth is said to have mingled a Christian temper with a Roman virtue, to have had all the pleasant characteristics of youth without any of its irregularities. His court was sober and well-behaved, and had swear-boxes the proceeds of which were given to the poor. James, jealous of his son for drawing away the younger set, exclaimed 'Will he bury me alive?' The jester Archie Armstrong, always one to worry an exposed nerve, drew the King's attention to the way in which, after a visit to Newmarket, most of the high personages followed the Prince and only the servants trailed after the King. For his attempts to cause trouble, Armstrong was tossed in a blanket like a dog by the Prince and his companions. In 1616 the King was relieved of this embarrassing rival court; Henry died from typhoid. By the King's direction there was no mourning. Sully, having put his suite into black, had to revert to normal clothes on his visit of condolence, to avoid paining the King.

Three years later, when Anne died, mourning again presented a problem. Cranfield, knowing the state of her finances, demurred at the high cost of grief. He seems to have been over-ruled. An eye-witness described the Queen's funeral as 'a drawling, tedious sight.' Some 280 poor women formed part of a procession which 'came loggering all along even tired with the length of the way and the weight of their clothes, every lady having twelve yards of broad cloth about her and the countesses sixteen.' These ladies had male supporters, 'else I see not how they had been able to hold out.'*

When James died, Cranfield, that incorrigible accountant, was under a heavy cloud, but it did not prevent him from advancing a characteristic proposal. He recommended that all mourning cloth should be bought in an undyed state and sent to the dyers in gross, 'which is like to save the Crown a good deal of money.'

* Thomas Birch: *Court and Times of James I*

13

Sober but Doomed

EVEN the most censorious Puritans found little cause for complaint in the Court of Charles I. Lucy Hutchinson says: 'The face of the Court was much changed in the change of the King; for King Charles was chaste and serious, so that the fools and bawds, mimics and catamites of the former Court grew out of fashion; and the nobility and courtiers, who did not quite abandon their debaucheries, yet so reverenced the King as to retire into corners to practise them. Men of learning and ingenuity in the arts were in esteem, and received encouragement from the King.'* In dress, the Court set an overdue example of sobriety.

Although Charles trimmed away some useless offices, it was not a frugal Court. Every day the Palace at Whitehall had 86 tables copiously provided with food. The King's table had 28 dishes, the Queen's 24. The others were laden as follows: four tables with 16 dishes each; three with 10; twelve with seven; 17 with five; three with four; 32 with three; 13 with two. In all, about 500 dishes were served at each meal.†

Whitehall was only one of the King's palaces. During this reign St James's took on considerably more royal dignity than hitherto. In all, the King had more than a score of homes, and by the end of his reign all were well and elegantly furnished.

Publicly, Charles was no foe of fun, but in his private life he tended to asceticism. His father had loved the crude horseplay that accompanied the bedding of brides and grooms; but Charles, on his wedding night at Canterbury, when not even an Esquire of the Body was to be trusted, was careful to dismiss his lords of the Bedchamber and personally secure his doors.

* *Memoirs of Colonel Hutchinson*
† Thomas Delaune: *Angliae Metropolis*

As there were seven entrances, the possibilities of non-stop farce were obviously tremendous. But Charles outwitted the Court jokers and next day unbent sufficiently to twit them on their disappointment.

Charles's marriage got off to the worst possible start thanks to the intolerable behaviour of the Queen's French followers. In his marriage articles he had promised the Queen her own suite and liberty to pursue her religion in her own places of worship.

Henrietta, the first Frenchwoman to become an English Queen for 200 years, was the daughter of Henry IV. She was 15 years of age, wilful, vivacious and unstable. She and her followers regarded themselves as missionaries charged with re-converting England to Roman Catholicism. In her train, which was gradually reinforced until it numbered more than 400, were 29 priests, under a bishop not yet in his thirties. He was kept on the aggressive by Madame St George, the first Lady of the Bedchamber, who has been described as handsome and flippant. She quickly fell foul of the King. Also in the suite was the Duchesse de Chevreuse, who caused some comment by swimming across the Thames and back one hot evening.

Henrietta's first court, a joyous occasion, was held on Barham Downs near Canterbury, where her English ladies were presented to her. Many of these she subsequently dismissed. At her first meal with the King in Canterbury there was a hint of trouble to come. It was a fast day, and Henrietta's confessor demurred when he saw the King pressing her to take pheasant and venison. At this stage, the Queen was more concerned to please her husband than her confessor and ate heartily of the forbidden dishes.

All too soon, meals became a battleground between the King's chaplain and the Queen's priests. When the King and Queen dined in a noble house at Titchfield, the chaplain had hardly begun to say grace when the Queen's confessor launched into a sonorous Latin benediction. In some pique, the Protestant gave his rival a smart push and resumed his grace. The confessor then concentrated his benediction on the Queen. Without comment, the King pulled the waiting dishes towards him and instructed the carvers to begin. When the meal was over, chaplain and confessor engaged in a new shouting match, each giving thanks after his own fashion. Charles had had enough; he took the Queen's hand and led her away.

This was not the only affray at Titchfield. When a preacher was conducting a service for the Queen's Protestant followers, in the great hall, the Queen and all her ladies came clattering through the congregation, talking and laughing, forcing the preacher to stop and enquire whether he should continue or not. When he resumed, the Queen and her ladies repeated the invasion from the opposite direction. The young bishop was credited with being the tactician in this affair. A few days later the Protestant preacher complained that he had been peppered with small shot.

Under the marriage agreement, the Queen was entitled to her own chapel. Her followers were displeased to find that, in the meantime, she was expected to observe mass in her Closet. The King forbade English Catholics to attend these services and posted pursuivants at the doors to prevent them entering. French swords were drawn in an effort to secure admission of English adherents.

These were merely the open incidents. Behind the scenes was much plotting and counter-plotting. The Queen's private residence, Somerset House, became the headquarters of a religious resistance movement and a sanctuary for secret papers. It pleased the Protestants to regard it also as a sanctuary of vice.

Charles bore the rising friction with much patience, but it became obvious that he would have to break his solemn promise. He had no wish for war with France or an open breach with his Queen, but he was not prepared to have his Court overrun by insolent 'monsers,' or to see the bold young bishop go striding into the Queen's apartments whenever he liked. Incident after incident laid fuel on his anger. When the King was at worship an Irish earl showed his disapproval by talking loudly in the adjacent chamber. Charles sent a message: 'If he will not come to my prayers, let him get out of my house.' When the Queen's priests complained about the slow progress being made on the new chapel at St James's, the King replied that if the Queen's Closet was inadequate for a mass, they could use the Great Chamber; if that was not big enough they could have the garden; and if space was still cramped they could use the park, which was the fittest place of all. On top of everything there was Madame St George, who conceived it her right to travel in the royal carriage, even when the King was present. Once, he thrust her back with his own hand.

The Queen, who was in tantrums daily, was pulled one way by loyalty to her husband and another way by faith and patriotism. She recognised that some of her suite were acting impossibly, but was sufficiently under their influence to refuse to be crowned with Protestant rites alongside Charles in Westminster Abbey. She even declined to witness her husband's crowning from a vantage point which had been prepared for her.

Protestant rumour-mongers told strange tales of humiliations supposedly suffered by the Queen. John Pory, that indefatigable letter writer, assured one of his correspondents that the 'bawdy knaves' who heard her confession used to ask her how many times in the night the King kissed her. Rumour also had it that Henrietta had been forced by her priests to perform publicly numerous cruel acts of penance. 'Had they not also made her to dabble in the dirt in a foul morning from Somerset House to St James's, her Luciferian confessor riding along by her in a coach? Yea, they have made her to go barefoot, to spin, to eat her meat out of tryne (wooden) dishes, to wait at the table and serve her servants, with many other ridiculous and absurd penances.'* It was also said that she had been forced to walk barefoot to Tyburn, there to pray under the gallows where Jesuits had dangled. It is extremely difficult to see how an English queen could have been forced to indulge in such exercises in the heart of the capital without being attended by an enormous and clamorous mob. Henrietta denied that she had been subjected to any indignities, but Charles did not wholly believe her.

At last he took the inevitable decision to repatriate Henrietta's entire Court, peaceably if possible, but forcibly if necessary. When he called on the Queen at Whitehall to announce his intentions he found her, so the story goes, surrounded by servants frolicking and dancing in her presence. He led her to a private room and locked the door. When she learned his

* Thomas Birch: *Court and Times of Charles I*

decision she flew at him and, in the struggle, smashed the window with her bare hands. About the same time Lord Conway was breaking the news to Henrietta's bishop, whom he had invited for a walk in St James's Park. A tremendous wailing arose from the servants when the royal pleasure became known, and increased as the Yeomen of the Guard, with an active part to play for once, ejected them from their apartments. The King later addressed the Queen's suite at Somerset House and told them they were being expelled because of the havoc they had made in his domestic relations. All of them, he said, would receive one year's pay.

The servants made endless delays and complained incessantly, trying hard to save face, until Charles lost all patience. Buckingham, whom the Queen loathed, was given the task of driving them out 'like wild beasts,' but only after an ultimatum delivered with the full panoply of yeomen, heralds, messengers and trumpeters did they capitulate. It took four days to move the sullen, obstructive convoy to the coast. The operation was not conducted without bloodshed. At Dover a bystander expressed the feelings of many loyal subjects by heaving a stone at the fanciful headdress of Madame St George (possibly it was aimed at her head). At this, an escort described as an English gentleman drew his sword and ran the fellow through, killing him on the spot. This action, according to one historian, was 'inconsiderate.'

The Queen had been kept out of the way during the evacuation. When she returned to London she found that her wardrobe had been pillaged by her followers, who left her with only one gown and two smocks. Some attempt was made to claim back the loot, but only an old satin gown was recovered. Fortunately her Master of the Horse, Count de Lepières, was frustrated in his attempt to take away all her horses. The deportees had the effrontery to present a bill for £19,000 in respect of sums supposedly owing to them.

At the French Court the expulsion caused intense indignation. Marshal Bassompierre was sent over to remonstrate with Charles and to sift the rumours about the priests' behaviour. He ended up by saying a few sharp, soldierly words to the Queen, who thereafter was a changed woman; but not until Buckingham was removed from the scene could a complete reconciliation with Charles be effected. The favourite had infuriated her by telling her that Queens of England who did not behave were liable to have their heads cut off, or words to that effect. In 1628 Buckingham was stabbed to death by a half-pay officer, a fate which might have been avoided if he had worn a chain shirt as advised. Thereafter Charles's marriage was a happy one, even if the Queen's extravagances were sometimes hard to bear. A small French establishment was allowed her and the building of chapels was begun, in the face of heavy criticism. Henrietta drew a younger set around her and took part in plays and masques, as the previous Queen had done. William Prynne's blast against actresses ('notorious whores') was regarded as an attack on the Queen and for this, along with his observations on the Church, he lost his ears.

The Queen's offspring became the subject of religious bickering as soon as they were born. When the Duke of York made his appearance in 1633, Lord Cottington reported: 'The nurse is a Roman Catholic to whom Sir John Tunstone offered the oath of allegiance and she refused it, whereupon there grew a great noise both in the town and Court and the Queen afflicted herself with great passion upon knowledge of a resolution to change the woman, yet after much tampering with the woman to convert her she was let alone to quiet the Queen. Nevertheless this trouble put the nurse into so great a distemper as the physicians attribute the child's sickness to it and now again they are resolved to change her.'*

No King brought greater artistic riches to his Court. In Italy, Holland, France and Spain his agents bought up the works of the masters and shipped them home. Peacham in his *Complete Gentleman* tells how the King had such a liking for ancient statues that he caused 'a whole army of old foreign emperors, captains and senators all at once to land on his coasts to come and do him homage and attend him in his palaces of St James and Somerset House.' A number of these belonged to the Duke of Mantua and others came from the ruins of Apollo's temple at Delos. Of more permanent value were the Giorgiones and Correggios, the Tintorettos and Mantegnas, and the Raphael cartoons. Many of Charles's Italian treasures were found for him by agents of the Roman Church, which hoped

* *Letters and Despatches of the Earl of Strafford*

by this means to build up goodwill at Whitehall. To the distress of the Protestants they succeeded in posting a permanent nuncio to Henrietta's court.

Not content with buying paintings in the European market, Charles sought to bring the great Continental artists to Britain. Rubens, during a harassing period as ambassador, was persuaded to design a ceiling for the Banqueting Hall. From under Rubens' wing came Anthony Van Dyck, whom the King provided successively with a house, a knighthood, a pension and— since his bachelor ways were a little too free—a wife. At Blackfriars, where a private wharf was built so that the King and Queen might more readily visit his studio, Van Dyck embarked on his all-too-short life's task of romanticising Cavaliers, as Lely at a later stage romanticised frail Court ladies. The Queen sat to him at least 25 times.

One of Charles's more specialised craftsmen was his herald painter, Edward Norgate, whom James I had appointed Bluemantle Pursuivant. His task was to illuminate letters to such rulers as 'the Emperor and Patriarch of Russia, the Grand Signior, the Great Mogul, the Emperor of Persia and the Kings of Bantam, Macassar, Barbary, Siam, Achine, Fez, Sus and other far-distant kings.'* Presumably this was the task discharged, in the middle of the eighteenth century, by Sir Thomas Brand, who held the captivating title of Embellisher of Letters to the Eastern Princes.

Ben Jonson enjoyed less favour than in the previous reign. James had given him a stipend of 100 marks ($£67$), in return for which he turned out plays, masques and pageants. It was sweated labour and eventually he petitioned Charles for a rise. The request was couched in indifferent doggerel, ending:

> Please your majesty to make
> Of your grace, for goodness sake,
> Those your father's marks, your pounds.

Charles obligingly raised the salary to $£100$, threw in a terce of Canary wine, and then demanded another masque. There seems to have been a hitch in the delivery of the wine, for the poet was driven to write an angry remonstrance, beginning:

* *Dictionary of National Biography*

> What can the cause be when the King hath given
> His poet sack, the Household will not pay?

The King was not amused, and Jonson had to write a more respectful protest before the wine was delivered.

In Sir Henry Herbert the King had a Master of the Revels who brought an unconscionably serious mind to what should have been a light-hearted office. He deemed it his duty to control, not only the nation's literary output, but exhibitions of dromedaries, games of ninepins and performances by quack doctors. So ruthlessly did he censor Sir William Davenant's play *The Wits* that the author's friends protested. The King personally went through the manuscript with Herbert, restoring certain cuts. Words like 'faith,' 'death' and 'slight,' said the King, could be regarded as asseverations rather than as oaths; but Herbert, who had already been in trouble with the Star Chamber for professional neglect, gave way with extreme reluctance.

If the King's mind did not run along scientific lines, at least he took a close interest in William Harvey's discovery of the circulation of the blood. The stags in the royal parks were put at Harvey's disposal for experiments.

Steadily, Parliament tightened its hold on the royal finances. The resulting economy waves at Court caused a good deal of friction. In 1634 the Gentlemen Pensioners petitioned for their wages, which were two-and-a-half years in arrears. The 'singing men of the Chapel' also made it clear that they were tired of singing for nothing. In the following year the Gentlemen Pensioners found themselves on the list of courtiers and dignitaries ordered by the King to maintain horses 'for the honour and strength of the kingdom.' Even the Archbishop of Canterbury was made responsible for the upkeep of eight cavalry chargers. In 1637 a committee was set up, not before time, to investigate abuses at Court. Whitehall was overrun by families of minor courtiers, for whose benefit unauthorised lodgings were being erected in holes and corners of the mews. 'The King's servants wait pell-mell without any order, lodging still in Court, and feeding there, though they be out of their month or quarter.'* On top of which, the capital was full of country

* *Letters and Dispatches of the Earl of Strafford*

gentry who were idling away their substance and clinging, as best they could, to the fringes of the Court. In that same year Charles ordered them back to their estates to look after their tenantry. Imposition of a few sharp fines speeded the exodus. The ranks of noblemen were also thinned out, less summarily.

The courtiers who remained were not, unfortunately, the cream of the country. Some of them, in spite of hard times, made a very reasonable living. When the Throne toppled, the Earl of Holland—the same Earl who had spat when James I kissed him—put in a claim to Parliament for losses sustained. They were made up as follows: salary as Gentleman of the Bedchamber, £1600; two pensions of £2000; a share in the Customs duty on coal worth £1300; legal fees worth £2000; and sundry lesser emoluments as Chief Justice in Eyre and Constable. It could have been no hardship for him to maintain twelve horses for Charles.

Endymion Porter, that resourceful go-between and art scout, was cushioned from hardship by an annuity, a share in a soap monopoly, a salary for collecting Star Chamber fines, and various wardships and leases of land. His hand was also in the Customs till. On top of it all he undertook successful commercial ventures.

One of Charles's less dependable courtiers was William Murray, a clergyman's son who in childhood is said to have been his sovereign's whipping boy. It is unlikely that any injustices visited on him in this role were responsible for turning him into the oblique and treacherous character he became. Bishop Burnet describes him as well suited to a court, 'very insinuating but very false.' He was of so revengeful a disposition that 'rather than any of the counsels given by his enemies should succeed he would have revealed and betrayed both the King and them.'* When created Earl of Dysart he persuaded the King to antedate the warrant in order that he might have precedence over certain of his enemies. If the Bishop is right, Murray was one of the King's servants who copied his letters while he was asleep and passed on the information to his enemies.

Among the liabilities inherited by Charles from his father was Archie Armstrong, but the jester was unfrocked after a

* *History of my own time*

series of clashes with Archbishop Laud. In the Archbishop's presence, he delivered a grace in these terms: 'Great praise be to God and little laud to the Devil.' After the stool-flinging episode in St Giles's, Edinburgh, he taunted the Archbishop with, 'Wha's fool noo?' It was too much for Laud, who solemnly complained in Council of this insolence. So, in the year 1637, the great men of the land directed that the King's dizzard should have his coat pulled over his head and be discharged from the royal service. This ceremony was duly performed in the porter's lodge. Disgraced but not defeated, the fool clad himself in sables and, since he was no longer in the employ of a living monarch, haunted the tombs of dead kings in Westminster Abbey. When this joke palled, he retired to his native Cumberland, where he jested simple maidens out of their virtue. It is odd that the serious, cultivated Charles should have tolerated a fool in the Court; even more odd that Armstrong should have been succeeded by another fool, Muckle John, a singular fellow who despised money.

The Queen's fancy ran to dwarfs, negroes and monkeys. Borrowing an old Russian idea, Buckingham gave a banquet at which a large cold pie was set before the Queen. When the pie was opened, out stepped the eighteen-inch figure of Jeffrey Hudson, son of a bull-baiter, who bowed and was presented, in both senses of the word, to the Queen. Occasionally he was used by her as a special messenger, as when he went to France to fetch a midwife for the Queen. On their way back, both were captured by a Flemish pirate. In his Court career Hudson, who eventually reached a height of three feet, endured much heartless teasing. Finally he was driven too far. In France, when the Queen went into exile, a waggish courtier, Will Croft, became committed to a duel with the dwarf, who was feeling his dignity as the holder of a commission in Charles's Cavalry. The duel was to be on horseback. Waggish to the last, Croft armed himself only with a squirt, which he discharged; Hudson rode at his opponent and killed him with a pistol shot. For this exploit he was dismissed from the Queen's Court.

Hudson was only one of several dwarfs at Henrietta's Court. Both King and Queen attended the wedding of Richard Gibson, a mannikin with a gift for painting, and his equally diminutive bride. Edmund Waller composed an epithalamium in their honour. Gibson served the King as a page, and his wife attended the Queen.

It was never a happy Court. Charles's cold, stubborn manner, allied to his undependability, did nothing to rally the waverers as the rift with Parliament deepened. In 1642 he and his Queen rode out of Whitehall for the last time, threatened by a huge crowd waving placards with the word 'Liberty.' Henrietta, intriguing furiously, supported her husband to the end. On her various crossings of the North Sea she suffered daunting ordeals. Out from Holland, her ship was tossed for 14 days in a series of great storms, but the Queen bore herself with scornful dignity as her courtiers, fearing imminent death, shouted out their sins to seasick and uncaring Capuchins. When, on a later crossing, her ship was chased by a parliamentary cruiser, she ordered the captain to blow up his vessel rather than allow it to be taken. This, too, created a great wailing among ladies of lesser fortitude, with less to lose.

Charles returned to Whitehall under Parliamentary escort in 1649. On a chill January day he went to his incorruptible crown.

14

'Nothing but Bawdry'

The palace where a king's head was struck from his body lapsed into a frightened calm. No glittering barges called at the river stairs. No poor clamoured for meat at the gates. Those who derived any satisfaction from doing so could march into the Presence Chamber wearing their hats and spurs. The Italian paintings were gathered in and sold for what they would fetch. A bargain hunter bid £4 for the Black Prince's ruby and got it. The crown of Alfred the Great was melted down. Inevitably, the King's Chapel with its ungodly organ, its stained glass and its cloth of gold was a focus for the wreckers. There was talk of selling off Windsor Castle, but Oliver Cromwell turned it into a garrison and cleared out the squatters who over-ran the Home Park.

After the Battle of Worcester, Parliament gave Cromwell the palace of Hampton Court as a country home. He did not take full possession of Whitehall until 1654. At various times he was dogged by would-be assassins, one of whom, Miles Sindercombe, a cashiered quartermaster, decided that the best way to kill him would be to set fire to Whitehall and take advantage of the ensuing confusion. In pursuance of this prodigal plan, he began stuffing combustibles into the Chapel, but was speedily detected.

Gradually, Cromwell surrounded himself with a fair degree of pomp, to the disgust of his more ascetic followers. Lucy Hutchinson admits that he had 'much natural greatness and well became the place he had usurped.'* Nevertheless, 'his Court was full of sin and vanity and the more abominable because they had not yet quite cast away the name of God but profaned it by taking it in vain upon them.'

Much venom was reserved for Elizabeth Cromwell, on

* *Memoirs of Colonel Hutchinson*

whom, in Mrs Hutchinson's view, splendour sat no more happily than scarlet on an ape. The writer of a vicious little work entitled *The Court and Kitchen of Elizabeth, Commonly Called Joan*, published 'for general satisfaction' in 1664, tells how Elizabeth built numerous partitions in Whitehall, 'perhaps afraid of the vastness and silentness thereof.' According to this source, she engaged a surveyor to make her 'little labyrinths and trapdoors by which she might at all times unseen pass to and fro and come unawares upon her servants and keep them vigilant in their places and honest in the discharge thereof.' Soon, however, 'like some kitchen maid partnered by the lust of some rich and noble dotard,' she reached the stage of going about the palace exacting reverences. The anonymous writer is deeply scornful because Elizabeth kept two or three cows in St James's Park and started an 'Office of a Dairy' in Whitehall, complete with milk maids and butter churns. She also had a 'covy of sewers' stitching away all day in the Privy Chamber, all 'indigent godly maidens' and daughters of ministers. The book is filled out with a long list of recipes for the plebeian dishes—like Dutch puddings and Scotch collops of veal—which were made in the Usurper's kitchens. To an unbiassed reader, it seems clear that Elizabeth brought a good deal of common sense to the running of what must have been a housewife's nightmare.

Although he gave away much of his Household money, Cromwell kept a good and hospitable table, at which his military officers often joined him. He was attended by some fifty soberly dressed gentlemen and guarded by scarlet soldiers. The palace was the scene of more prayer than revelry, but once at least the critics saw a spectacle to scandalise them. That was on a night in 1657, when Cromwell's daughters married into the nobility, and there was dancing until dawn to the strains of forty-eight violins.

At Hampton Court, which he did much to embellish, Cromwell lived as many a cavalier would have liked to live: that is, he hunted and he hawked. One of his few extravagances was to import splendid horses—barbs from Tripoli, Arabs from Aleppo. The Court never had better stables than under the Protector.*

*   *   *

* John Buchan: *Oliver Cromwell*

When Charles II reached Whitehall, in 1660, the Palace was not vastly different from when he had last seen it. At once, with limited resources, he set about embellishing it. Enthusiasm for the monarchy, while high, was not such that the King could hope to level the site and erect in its place the dream of Inigo Jones.

So the Whitehall which now faced thirty years of scandalous splendour continued to be developed *ad hoc*. It was less a palace than an agglomeration of inter-connected buildings, straggling for perhaps half a mile along the Thames, with the green fields of Chelsea beyond.

Thomas Delaune, writing in 1690, said: 'Although this palace of Whitehall makes not so glorious a show on the outside as some other stately edifices, yet there is not in Christendom a court more convenient and meet for royal accommodation nor more richly furnished.' In this, its heyday, it had upwards of 2000 rooms. Delaune praised the noble navigable river which carried the barges to its water stairs, and the 'most delectable and spacious park full of great and rare varieties.'* The Thames, to be sure, made a stately approach and offered a flattering background for water parties and fireworks. Also, it was still clean enough for King and courtiers to bathe in it on their picnics. But in flood time it embarrassed Whitehall and Westminster as the Seine never embarrassed the Louvre. One evening, when Lady Castlemaine, the King's mistress, was preparing to entertain him in her lodgings, the cook announced that supper could not be served because the river had extinguished the kitchen fire. Scornfully, Lady Castlemaine urged her servant to rise above such petty obstacles, and he did. The Thames had another disadvantage in that it gave robbers an easy approach into the heart of the Palace after dark.

The boatmen who depended on the Court for a living were a well-organised body, strong enough to defeat a proposal, in 1665, that a bridge should be built across the river at Whitehall. Charles gave them a categorical assurance that no such bridge would be erected while he lived.

It was an admirable palace for a king who loved to saunter. There were galleries and courtyards, a Privy Garden and a bowling green. Near by was St James's Park, its grass no longer

* *Angliae Metropolis*

profaned by Elizabeth Cromwell's cows. Here the King could watch wrestling matches or lay wagers on such of his officers as undertook to walk round it five times in two hours. There were also the Mulberry Gardens, where the *beau monde* frolicked, not always decorously; and there was Hyde Park with its fashionable carriage parade.

So much for bricks and establishments. The spirit of Whitehall was summed up by Macaulay when he wrote that 'half the jobbing and half the flirting of the metropolis' went on under the King's roof.

'Whoever could make himself agreeable to the Prince or could secure the good offices of the mistresses might hope to rise in the world without rendering any service to the Government, without even being known by sight to a Minister of State. This courtier got a frigate and that a company; a third, the pardon of a rich offender; a fourth, a lease of Crown lands on easy terms. If the King notified his pleasure that a briefless lawyer should be made a judge or that a libertine baronet should be made a peer, the gravest counsellors, after a little murmuring, submitted.'*

Suitors had to stalk their game carefully and be nimble on their feet. The King was affable to all he met, but he was a rapid walker and soon shook off the importunate. It was better to try to meet him socially, though there was small hope of taking advantage of him in his cups. To one of his drinking companions who made a request at such a time, Charles replied, 'You had better ask your King tomorrow.' He knew better than to expect gratitude from those whom he benefited. Sooner or later they would be at his funds or his mistresses. Probably he would have echoed Louis XIV, who said: 'Every time I fill a vacant post I make a hundred people discontented and one ungrateful.' When he created the post of Historiographer for James Howell, that author promptly wrote a tactless work on the disappointments suffered by faithful Cavaliers.

In exile, Charles's followers had seen how offices were bought and sold in the French Court and Army. They were quick to spread the same system, not only in the Household but in the new regiments of Horse and Foot the King struggled to

* *History of England*

maintain (these survive as the Life Guards, the Royal Horse Guards, the Grenadier Guards and the Coldstream Guards). Charles showed insufficient resolution in trying to curb the

Charles II makes his triumphal entry into London, 1660

practice of purchase. While one courtier would sell genuine appointments, another, like Thomas Killigrew, sometime Master of the Revels, would sell fictitious ones, among them those of King's Physic Taster and Royal Curtain Drawer. These were no more improbable than many of the genuine appointments. It was all good clean fun and the King did not like to curb high spirits.

For place hunters, the Privy Chamber had potent attractions. Officially, there were 48 Gentlemen of the Privy Chamber, working to a rota, under the Groom of the Stole*. All were knights or esquires who had served the King well or who had other claims on him. They received no allowances other than their food. Over and above the official establishment was a prodigious roll of Gentlemen of the Privy Chamber in Extraordinary, as many as 490 according to one account. The attraction of the appointment may be judged from an order in council issued in 1673, to the effect that all persons holding Privy Chamber appointments, whether in ordinary or extraordinary, were 'absolutely disabled from making use of the same for any pretence of privilege or protection from their creditors, or any other protection.'

No monarch was less of a hermit than Charles. Citizens willing to rise early on a summer morning would see their sovereign strolling with his dogs in St James's Park or throwing food to the strange wildfowl there. As the morning progressed, sightseers and gentlemen-about-town began flocking into the grounds of Whitehall as if it was a fashionable pleasure-ground, which is almost what it was. Security precautions of the modern kind seem to have been sketchy in the extreme. One day in 1661, when there were rumours of risings, Samuel Pepys and certain of his friends were challenged after they had walked in the gardens for four or five hours. The interrogator asked who they were, was told, then apologised. His orders were to challenge 'strange persons.' Ordinarily, the guards at the gates seem to have admitted all who were not in rags and who were not adorned with pistols and cudgels. If further indication were needed of the slack security in Whitehall, it may be found in the fact that the Earl of Rochester at one time kept a spy, dressed in the red uniform of a sentry, whom he posted outside ladies' apartments to watch comings and goings. By this means he supplied himself with up-to-date titbits for his lampoons.

It was the responsibility of the Knight Marshal with his six scarlet-clad provost marshals to clear the Palace precincts of tippling tents and gambling booths, and keep it 'a place of civility and honour.' Common prostitutes and masterless men were turned away. The scrofulous were admitted only on appointed occasions, to be touched by the King.

---

* *There is reason to suspect that this high officer was originally the guardian, not of a vestment, but of the King's close-stool*

The walks and galleries of the Palace were the source of all good stories, of gossip and commercial information. Here gentlemen could discuss the quality of the eunuchs' voices in the Queen's Chapel, or ask each other whether that distant rumble meant that the Dutch had again penetrated the Medway. Those in the King's immediate circle might be privileged to join in the laughter as he told how Rochester's clothes had been stolen the night before by a wench. Persons of 'good fashion and appearance,' but not 'infirm, mean or unknown people,' were welcome to enter the gallery of the Banqueting Hall and watch their sovereign help himself to choice morsels offered by nobles on bended knees. Pepys noted that each man who carried in a dish wiped it with a piece of bread which he popped into his mouth. This was a relic of the days of tasting. In Pepys's opinion, each man should have dipped his bread in the sauce. It is a pity we have not Pepys's comments on the handsome gift the people of Plymouth made to the King on his restoration: a gold wine fountain nearly three feet high. It was in the form of a naked nymph down whose figure the spray descended, the intensity of the flow being regulated by the height of the feeder barrel. The wine ran into a series of receptacles and it was up to the courtiers to empty these before they overflowed*.

Visitors were also welcome, on Sundays, to watch the King worship in the Chapel Royal. There were certain rules to be observed, among them this: 'When we are present no man will presume to put on his hat at Sermon, but those in the stalls on the left hand, which are noblemen or counsellors, or the Dean of the Chapel when we are absent.'† It was the King's pleasure that solemn music should be played in the mornings and evenings, as in a collegiate church, and he was anxious that 'all decent honour and order should be kept.' Both noblemen and others were to observe 'great distance and respect to our person and also civility towards one another.' Appeals for decorum were by no means unnecessary, for the Duke of York and Lady Castlemaine were once seen flirting shamelessly in the Chapel. The King was attended by a Clerk of the Closet, who held himself ready at all times 'to resolve doubts about

---

* Maj-Gen Sir G. Younghusband: *The Jewel House*
† John Nichols: *A Collection of Ordinances*

spiritual matters.' Since Charles tended to fall asleep in church, the Clerk's duties were not unduly onerous. Thirty-two Gentlemen of the Chapel, of whom twelve were priests, accompanied the King to worship. They were appointed, in theory, for their proficiency in singing and assiduity in prayer.

Few of the King's 48 chaplains found the congregation an easy one to address, but more than one divine had sufficient courage to inveigh against the King's favourite recreations, not omitting adultery. Dr Robert Creighton invited his glittering congregation to roll themselves in the dust, and the Bishop of Winchester urged them to turn from gambling, a suggestion which caused visible amusement. It was not at this Court, but at the then Court of France, that a preacher, after announcing, 'We shall all die,' corrected himself and, with a shamefaced look at the King, added, 'Nearly all.'

Even the fish in the tropical tank has its little retreat from ever-watching eyes. Charles's followers fell away by degrees as he passed through the halls which led to his Bed-chamber, which in itself was far from being a private place (incidentally, it was much fouled by the royal spaniels). Up a small flight of steps leading from the Bedchamber was the real sanctuary, the King's Closet, lined with fine pictures and stocked with many other valuables. Only the King and the Keeper of the Closet had keys to this room. Here Charles might sit to artists or discuss his dreams of rebuilding Windsor or Greenwich. It also served as a *venue* for such encounters— political and otherwise—as it was not meet for the world at large to see. Two brothers Chiffinch, Thomas and William, successively held the post of Keeper. William, who took over in 1668, was by far the less scrupulous. He is said to have 'carried the abuse of back stairs influence to scientific perfec-tion.'* Not the least part of his duties was to smuggle wenches of the town up from the river stairs and into the King's apart-ments, afterwards paying them off with the Secret Service money.

Under the Closet was the King's other retreat, a 'pretty place' set up as a laboratory where, with the aid of his favourite physician, he conducted chemical and anatomical experiments. Charles had a *dilettante's* interest in the many new sciences—

* *Dictionary of National Biography*

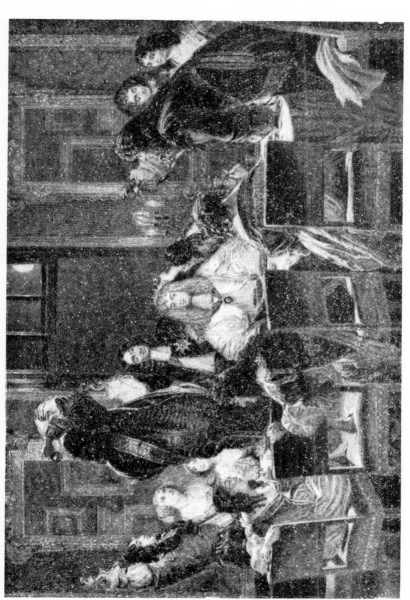

Rake's progress: the Court of Charles II toasts the second Duke of Buckingham

from optics to hydraulics, but not omitting alchemy—which that restless age was exploring. On the establishment of his Court were a Geographer, a Hydrographer and a Cosmographer, rubbing shoulders with such medieval survivors as a Falconer, a Fletcher and a Cross-Bow Maker (though there was now a Hunting Gun Maker). It was at the King's instigation that the Royal Society, to which he gave a charter, explored such subjects as arboriculture, navigation and shipbuilding.

The English Court was accused of aping the French (champagne and wigs being not the least of its innovations), but the French influence was limited. The lethal punctilio of Versailles, which eventually drove the Court ladies to entertain in their beds and baths in order to escape it, found little reflection at Whitehall. Still less did that of the Spanish Court. The King, according to Pepys, was contemptuous of the formality encompassing the Spanish King, 'who will not piss but another must hold the chamber pot.' Doubtless Charles was familiar with the legend of how Philip III met his death in 1621. This unfortunate monarch had been sitting by an over-stoked fire but was prevented by etiquette from doing anything about it. No servants could enter the room, because that also was contrary to etiquette. The Marquis de Potat appeared and was ordered to damp the fire, but explained that this was no part of his duties; it was the function of the Duke of Uceda, who unfortunately had gone out. The monarch had no option but to sit fast, while the fire burned ever brighter. The result was an attack of erysipelas followed by a fever from which he died, with his dignity inviolate.*

Charles's charm carried him through all scrapes. No more affable monarch ever cast his leg over a mistress's garden wall. He could show delightful tact. When William Penn, the Quaker, insisted on wearing his hat in the King's presence, Charles uncovered his own head. 'Friend Charles,' said the Quaker, 'why dost thou not keep on thy hat?' The answer was, ''Tis the custom of this house for only one person to remain covered at a time.'† It was very difficult to be cross with Charles, however monstrous his behaviour or his ingratitude. Even the Prince of Orange must have found it difficult to be angry

---

* I. Disraeli: *Curiosities of Literature*
† J. H. Jesse: *Memoirs of the Court during the Stuarts*

when, on his wedding night, the King closed the curtains of
the bed and exhorted him, 'Now, nephew, to your work. Hey!
St George for England!'

Certainly the King's charm seems to have been strong enough
to induce his servants to work for months, even years, on end
without wages. But by 1666 there was fierce resentment on this
score in the Palace, both among officers and servants. It
followed that perquisites were zealously retained, and, if
possible, enlarged. Pepys saw a Groom of the Bedchamber
administer a 'horrid rating' to an officer of the Wardrobe
because the King had insufficient linen for his person; he had,
it appears, only three neckbands and no handkerchiefs. The
explanation was that there was no money to buy more and that
£5000 was owed to the linen draper. But the real trouble was
that the grooms removed the linen at the end of each quarter
as their perquisite, 'let the King get more as he can.'

Prodigal kings are always under temptation to economise
in wages. In outward show, Charles's Court did not suggest
a hand-to-mouth existence. Delaune says that the Court was
the scene of a prodigious plenty which caused foreigners 'to
put a high value upon the King and was for the honour of the
kingdom.' Each day 240 gallons of beer were dispensed at the
buttery bar for the poor, who also received the benefit of
innumerable baskets of broken meat and bread. Two grooms
and two yeomen were charged with this task. Even though the
best titbits were removed by various officers and servants,
according to their status, the waiting poor fared remarkably well.
The able-bodied among them occasionally jostled for the newly-
minted twopences which the Sub-Almoner scattered in the
roadway when the King travelled. Fearing, perhaps, that
Members of Parliament might look hungrily on the food
given away at his palace gates, Charles used to send his
servants to invite them to share his board. Unfortunately, he
began to offer them more than food.

A monarch of ready wit, surrounded by courtiers who, drunk
or sober, could turn out diverting squibs and libels, poems and
plays, would seem to have had little need of a jester. Unofficially
the duties of this office were discharged by Thomas Killigrew,
who was not above drawing a fee from the Wardrobe in respect
of cap and bells. But the begetter of the Theatre Royal, Drury

Lane, built for the greater honour of His Majesty's Company of Comedians, was far removed from the status of a common jester. He held the appointment of Gentleman of the Bedchamber and his wife was installed as Keeper of the Sweet Coffer on the Queen's establishment. It was within Killigrew's power to persuade the King to attend to business, even though others had failed. When Charles, on a visit to Chatham, flattered himself that he would have made a good shipwright, Killigrew was quick to assure him that he would have done better at any trade but his own. Once, in one of those laborious japes for which jesters were famous, he dressed as a pilgrim and explained that he was on his way to Hell to entreat Cromwell to resume control of the realm, as his successor was always employed on other business. Killigrew's pleasantries annoyed many, notably the Earl of Rochester, whose own wit stung hardest of all. At a banquet given by the Dutch Ambassador Rochester boxed Killigrew's ears, and to the scandal of the Court the King made no attempt to censure this behaviour. Sir William Coventry, incensed at Killigrew's mockery, threatened that he would have his nose slit. This threat was not carried out, but Coventry's nephew, a rash Member of Parliament, later had his nose slit by members of the Life Guards for aspersing his sovereign's morals. Killigrew also clashed violently with Sir Henry Herbert, Charles I's Master of the Revels, who went to great pains to reassert an authority cheerfully infringed by the entertainment industry of the Restoration. In 1673 Killigrew succeeded to the post of Master of the Revels, with the responsibility of licensing such mountebanks as were not already on the Court establishment. His son Harry was a roysterer who could have been sent from Court for many reasons, but was dismissed for calling Lady Castlemaine a wanton.

Sir Henry Herbert was by no means the only office-holder of the old Court who expected to be taken on again in the new one. He was treated with more indulgence than was Sir Henry Mildmay, one-time Keeper of the Jewel House, who had filled in the *interregnum* by teaching ceremonial to the Puritans. In 1660 Charles was inconsiderate enough to ask what had happened to the Crown Jewels and Mildmay tried to flee abroad. He was sentenced to life imprisonment, the monotony to be varied by an annual excursion on a sledge, with a rope round his neck, from the Tower to Tyburn and back. In 1664 this sentence was commuted to one of transportation and Mildmay died on the way to Tangier. His post was given to Sir Gilbert Talbot, who had no intention of sitting all day in a chilly chamber of the Tower watching a collection of baubles. The actual guarding of the jewels was performed by an aged deputy, Talbot Edwards, who was allowed, or rather obliged, to make a living by showing them to visitors. It was this luckless fellow who was battered on the head by Colonel Thomas Blood, disguised as a parson, in his raid on the Tower Mildmay's punishment would have been a lenient one for the man who stole the Crown (and battered it with his mallet to make it fit his receptacle); but Blood, after a personal interview with the King, had his forfeited Irish lands—worth £500 a year—restored and became a gentleman about Court. It is supposed that Charles admired his audacity, but there have been more discreditable .theories.

Ambassadors lost no time in making a battleground of Charles's Court. Having arrived in London, they would gild their coaches, smarten up their servants and then go out to Greenwich for a ceremonial *entrée* by river in the King's barge. At the Tower they would expect to be received with appropriate salutes, every bang being carefully counted, and then ride in the King's coach to Whitehall with an escort of perhaps fifty coaches-and-six. In this cavalcade, precedence was everything. Both the French and Spanish Ambassadors were ready to slay each other's servants in order to secure the place immediately after the King's coach. When the Venetian representatives made their *entrée*, the King persuaded the two Ambassadors, with some difficulty, not to send their carriages, but the pitched battle could not be indefinitely postponed. The next arrival was the Swedish envoy and the whole town turned out to see the fun. It was a popular victory for the Spanish Ambassador, Baron de Batteville, who killed several Frenchmen and wounded a great many more to secure the coveted place, at the cost of only one dead in his own suite. Craftily, the Spaniards had reinforced their harness with chains to prevent it being slashed through. Pepys saw the Spanish coach go by with fifty drawn swords around it. After the affair the French

Ambassador, the Count d'Estrades, was recalled. Charles ruled that no ambassadorial coaches should be sent on such missions in future but his ruling was unpopular, both in diplomatic circles and with the public. Louis XIV briefed his next ambassador, the Comte de Comminges, in great detail. No ambassador was to go in front of him at any time, except that of the Emperor; the Spanish Ambassador was on no account to go on his right, but only on his left; the representatives of Venice were to go behind. As for the splendid envoys of Muscovy, the Comte was to use his discretion whether to allow them to stand on his right when they called on him.*

From a reasonably virtuous start, the Court degenerated swiftly, to the strumming of guitars and the gnashing of cuckolds. Within two years Pepys was reporting that there was 'nothing almost but bawdry at Court from top to bottom.' Evelyn, for his part, was disgusted at the recklessness of the gambling during the Twelfth Night revels. The ladies played 'very deep,' a practice which Charles, for obvious reasons, tried to discourage. At the Groom Porter's, in particular, Evelyn was horrified at 'the wicked folly and monstrous excesses of passion amongst some losers.' It was the Groom Porter who provided the Court with cards and dice and to whom questions arising out of gaming were submitted.

More notorious, in the eyes of the country at large, was the way in which the witty hooligans of the Court—men like Charles Sedley, Charles Sackville and Henry Savile—were protected by their master when they sallied out to slit noses, beat up the watch and riot in, on and around bawdy-houses. Before his reign was long advanced, the King was covering up, not only mayhem, but murder. One whom, in due time, he saved from justice was his natural son, the Duke of Monmouth, who assisted in the slaying of a beadle as he begged for mercy on a Sabbath morning.

Count de Grammont, dismissed from the French Court for making love to a royal mistress, arrived at Whitehall in 1662 and was agreeably surprised at the politeness and splendour of the Court of England. It was 'an entire scene of gallantry and amusement . . . the beauties were desirous to charm and

* J. J. Jusserand: *A French Ambassador at the Court of Charles II*

the men endeavoured to please.' Strictly speaking, says this
rusé Gascon, most of the Court ladies deserved a daily bastinado
for their behaviour. 'I mention no person, God forbid I should,'
he declares, and then mentions several. Conspicuous in the
wicked sisterhood was Lady Shrewsbury. 'I would take a wager
she might have a man killed for her every day and she would
only hold her head the higher for it; one would suppose that
she imported from Rome plenary indulgences for her conduct;
there are three or four gentlemen who wear an ounce of her
hair made into bracelets and no person finds any fault.'*
De Grammont was alluding to the duel in which the Countess's
husband was killed by her lover, the second Duke of Buckingham. It was a three-a-side encounter with cold steel. The
resulting outcry did not disqualify the Duke from becoming
Master of the Horse, a post he bought for £20,000 from the
Duke of Albemarle. He lived openly with the Countess and a
child of the liaison was buried in Westminster Abbey. When
the scandal of their association had lasted six years the Lords
enforced a bond which carried a heavy financial penalty if
they cohabited any more.

The King's private life, which could never be private, set
the standard of Court laxity. According to Bishop Burnet,
whom the King consulted in such matters, there were 'some
things he freely condemned, such as living with another man's
wife; other things he excused and thought God would not
damn a man for a little irregular pleasure.'† Yet Barbara
Palmer (*née* Villiers) was another man's wife when he took up
with her. He created her husband Lord Castlemaine, with the
proviso that the title should pass to the heirs of her body. From
time to time the husband returned from his duties in Ireland
and goggled at the increase in his family. But he could hardly
complain. Charles was King of England and Defender of the
Faith and it was unthinkable that any woman should suffer in
reputation by sharing his bed.

Charles had learned one useful lesson from his father.
When his Queen, Catherine of Braganza, arrived with a retinue
of ill-favoured and presumptuous Portuguese, he lost little
time in shipping her ladies back. He would have been happy to

* *Memoirs*
† *History of My Own Time*

F

return the Infanta too, for he was heard to say that he thought they had brought him a bat instead of a woman. This was an allusion, presumably, to the prominent protruding tooth which held up Catherine's upper lip. The Queen also, according to some observers, suffered from a perpetual 'fluor' or 'nauseous distemper.'

The retinue included, in the harsh words of Count de Grammont, 'six frights, calling themselves maids of honour, and a duenna, another monster, who took the title of governess to these extraordinary beauties.' There were also 'six chaplains, a Jew perfumer and a certain officer probationary without an office who called himself Her Highness's barber.' Lord Clarendon described the suite as 'for the most part old, and ugly, and proud, incapable of any conversation with persons of quality and a liberal education.' Like the followers of Henrietta Maria, they tried to discourage the Queen from adopting English manners and English dress or even learning the English tongue. Any such concessions, they felt, would be inconsistent with the dignity of Portugal. According to one observer, they were so prudish as to refuse to occupy beds in which men had lain.

Notoriously, Charles dallied with Lady Castlemaine on the night that his Queen landed. She was pregnant by him and he did not care to cast her adrift, even if he had dared to try. Equally he did not care for her suggestion that she should lie in at Hampton Court. The Queen refused to meet her husband's mistress, whose reputation had reached the Tagus, but was tricked into doing so at Hampton Court. She then paled, burst into tears, suffered severe bleeding from the nose and fainted. At this point the company retired.

Charles felt insulted. Many of his subjects could have told him that wives and mistresses do not get on well together, but he was determined that they should. How else could a man reign with dignity? It was intolerable that the world should suppose that he was dominated by his wife; this would be a serious reflection on his manliness. On the other hand, nobody would think the worse of him for being anxious to humour a mistress. He decided to appoint Lady Castlemaine a lady of the Queen's Bedchamber, which would be a lesson to both of them. When the Queen rebelled, Lord Clarendon was told to use his influence with her. On this issue, the King showed unwonted vigour and determination. 'Whomsoever I find to be my Lady Castlemaine's enemy in this matter,' he informed Clarendon, 'I do promise upon my word to be his enemy as long as I live.' For Clarendon the task was a distasteful one, the more so as his own wife was not allowed to visit Lady Castlemaine, but he consulted his conscience and found no reason why his career should be wrecked for the sake of a couple of women. He therefore joined in the attempt to break down the Queen's modesty. Lady Castlemaine was installed in apartments adjoining those of the Queen, who refused to speak to her. Catherine sat alone, with a handful of ladies, while the King, his mistress and the rest of the courtiers chatted and joked. After a couple of months she weakened and spoke to Lady Castlemaine. The battle was over, with no honour to anyone. Soon afterwards King, Queen and mistress were seen in a carriage together, and with them was a bastard by another mistress, Lucy Walters (this youth became the Duke of Monmouth). Such was Charles's notion of a happy family outing. Then Lady Castlemaine, who was a Protestant, was seen broad-mindedly accompanying the Queen to chapel. She performed various other duties for the Queen, occasionally laying herself open to snubs, as when she commented on the Queen's patience at the hands of her dresser. 'I have had so much reason to exercise my patience,' said Catherine, 'that I can bear it very well.' Once, the Queen told Lady Castlemaine that she feared the King would catch cold, as he stayed so late at her house. The mistress's answer was that the King always left her apartments and presumably stayed the night somewhere else. Overhearing this, the King sent Lady Castlemaine from Court. Like Samuel Pepys, Catherine doubtless saw Lady Castlemaine's fine underwear fluttering on the line in the Privy Garden, but she is unlikely to have derived the same satisfaction from the sight. Pepys found nothing to gloat over when he visited the Queen's bedroom as a sightseer. It was plainly furnished with a few pious pictures and books of devotion, holy water at her bedside and a lamp which told her the time at any hour.

Having consented to smile on one of her husband's mistresses, the Queen found she was expected to smile on them all. She learned to pause before entering her own dressing-room, having once found the King there making love to one of her maids of honour, Frances Stuart. But Catherine, though she acted merrily enough on occasions, never became wholly inured to insults. She walked out in protest when the actress Mary Davis, whom Pepys called 'the most impertinent slut in the world,' performed at Court; and she cried when Louise Kéroualle was deputed to wait on her at dinner. Her life was one of public insults. Doubtless she saw also the private insults as women of the town were smuggled up the back stairs, from the Thames, to the King's apartments.

By 1668 the popular assessment of the morals of the Court may be judged by the fact that the apprentices who, in that year, stormed and wrecked the more notorious bawdy-houses in Moorfields, reproached themselves for pulling down the little brothels and leaving the big one at Whitehall. The melancholy fact that eight apprentices were hanged for interfering with civic liberties did not prevent the wags from putting out such documents as *The Poor Whores' Petition, to the Most Splendid, Illustrious, Serene and Eminent Lady of Pleasure, the Countess of Castlemaine*. This purported to come from 'the undone company of poor distressed whores, bawds, pimps and panders,' who sought protection for 'a trade wherein Your Ladyship hath great experience and for your diligence therein have arrived to high and eminent advancement.' It was signed on behalf of the sisterhood of Dog and Bitch Yard, Lukeners Lane, Saffron Hill, Moorfields, Chiswell Street, RosemaryLane, Nightingale Street, Ratcliffe Highway, Well Close, Church Lane and East Smithfields. This was followed, in virtuous verse, by *The Prentices' Answer to the Poor Whores' Petition,* then by *The Citizens' Reply to the Whores' Petition and Prentices' Answer* and finally by *The Gracious Answer of the Most Illustrious Lady of Pleasure, the Countess of Castlemaine, to the Poor Whores' Petition.* This contained much useful professional advice on the lines of: 'Give no entertainment without ready money lest you suffer loss. For had we not been careful in that particular we had neither gained honour nor rewards which are now (as you know) both conferred upon us.' The *Gracious Answer* was 'Given at Our Closet in King Street, Westminster, *Die Veneris*, April 24, 1668.'

When so many were prepared to tolerate and cultivate the King's mistresses, it is refreshing to find one who was not. In 1783 the King's Harbinger visited Winchester seeking quarters for courtiers and concubines. What better lodging for Nell Gwyn, he thought, than the prebendary's house? But Thomas Ken refused point-blank, saying that 'a woman of ill repute ought not to be endured in the house of a clergyman and especially the King's chaplain.' It was no doubt a disappointment for Nell, who was at such pains to point out, 'I am the *Protestant* whore,' but the Dean was happy to put her up in his lodging. The King respected Ken's stand, and when the bishopric of Bath and Wells fell vacant ordered that it should be given to 'the little black fellow that refused to lodge poor Nelly.'

If the roll of mistresses, not all of whom have been listed, had a common characteristic, it was that of rapacity; though Frances Stuart must be exempted. The more presentable, or more importunate, were ennobled with names culled from coast and countryside. Lady Castlemaine became Baroness Nonsuch, Countess of Southampton and Duchess of Cleveland. Thus her dishonour was distributed from the Solent to the Tees, from the Atlantic seaboard of Ireland to the banks of Thames. Louise Kéroualle took the titles of Duchess of Portsmouth, Baroness Petersfield and Countess of Fareham. The children these women bore became dukes and also appropriated the names of long-suffering towns. There were patriotic citizens who felt that Nell Gwyn, the people's favourite, might well have had a town allotted to her, if only one of the more disreputable seaports. Bishop Burnet thinks that Nell, 'the indiscreetest and wildest creature that ever was in a court,' was never accorded the 'decencies of a mistress,' but was treated as the prostitute she had been to so many.* It was difficult to give dignities to a woman who was so brutally frank about her function in life. Nevertheless, she was eventually appointed a Lady of the Privy Chamber to Catherine. Comments Samuel Pegge, writing in George III's day: 'This was bare-faced enough to be sure! Had the King made a momentary connection with a lady of that demeanour, the offence might have been connived at by the Queen; but the

* *History of My Own Time*

placing one of the meanest of his creatures so near the Queen's person was an insult that nothing could palliate but the licentiousness of the age and the abandoned character of that lascivious monarch.'*

Undoubtedly Nell developed social aspirations. In the King's presence she is supposed to have said to her son, 'Come here, you little bastard,' pointing out to the King that he had no worthier name. The King took the hint and a few days later the little bastard was Baron of Heddington and Earl of Burford (later he became Duke of St Albans). Financially, Nell was by no means ill treated. She had a fine silver bed and the benefit of a duty imposed on exported logwood. Latterly, like Lady Castlemaine, she received revenues from Ireland, always a useful source of maintenance for the English concubinage. Had Charles lived longer, she might have been Countess of Greenwich.

Although his mistresses encountered snubs from the more fastidious members of society, Charles considered that those he lay with were fit company for the greatest in the land (though this did not apply to Chiffinch's women). He wanted them to be received, not only by the aristocracy, by his Queen and by his ministers, but by each other. Why could not everybody be happy together? Pepys, in 1667, complained that 'the King hath taken ten times more care and pains in making friends between my Lady Castlemaine and Mistress Stuart when they have fallen out than ever he did to save his kingdom.' There was an occasion when the gift to the King of a splendid calash inspired much jealousy between the pair. De Grammont, the donor, noted that Lady Castlemaine, who was then pregnant, threatened to miscarry if she was not the first to ride in it, and that Miss Stuart threatened to be with child if she was refused the honour. The Queen was not without hopes that she might be invited, but this round was won by Miss Stuart. Incidentally, riding in coaches was no recreation for a pregnant woman. No one will ever know how many heirs to the Throne were lost through the jolting of abominably sprung State vehicles.

Although he wanted everyone to be happy, the King objected to his mistresses lavishing their affections, along with

* *Curialia*

his moneys, on other members of his Court. When Rochester tried to steal a kiss from Lady Castlemaine she knocked him flat on his back, but John Churchill, the future Duke of Marlborough, was more amiably received. It was not only the Queen who opened doors and was shocked. Once the King arrived at the Castlemaine apartments as Churchill dropped from the window. 'I forgive you,' said the King later to his gentleman, 'for I know you do it for your bread.' When the King was infatuated with Frances Stuart it was Lady Castlemaine who led him quietly to her rival's bedroom, where the Duke of Richmond was sitting on her pillow. Richmond was banished from Court. At this, Miss Stuart, though hardly one of the most loyal of the Queen's maids, prostrated herself before Catherine, who commiserated with her in her misfortune, and promised to assist her either to enter a nunnery or to marry the Duke. Eventually she became Duchess of Richmond and returned to the Queen's Bedchamber. Even Nell Gwyn was not entirely faithful to the King. Charles found it all very irritating. St Evremond summed it up when he said that 'however docile the English may be in respect of their wives they can by no means bear the inconstancy of their mistresses.'

If the mistresses had confined themselves to their professional services, they would qualify for no more than passing mention. But the tempestuous Lady Castlemaine sought power as eagerly as she sought pleasure and riches. She was credited with regulating, personally, all promotions, spiritual and temporal. As such, she became the focus and the catalyst of infinite Court corruption. She launched Arlington and she helped to unseat Clarendon. The size of her income was a national grievance. When Charles gave her the manor of Nonsuch she sold it to a contractor for its break-up value. Her insolence was such that she was quite capable of inviting herself to stay with the Queen Dowager, Henrietta, at Richmond.

Louise Kéroualle was manipulated for political and religious purposes by the French Ambassador, and the King of France was anxious that she should be brought to bed by Charles at the earliest moment. The country saw in these Court trollops a threat to the nation's independence, its religion, its honour and its finances. Charles had little or no control over them. While he did not woo for political reasons, he could not prevent factions forming around his women. When he was first seen to be infatuated by Frances Stuart (this was not difficult to see, since they were always kissing in corners) his statesmen made strenuous attempts to cultivate the capricious nymph. Her pleasures were simple ones, notably blind man's buff and building houses with packs of cards. The Duke of Buckingham was one of the eager courtiers who passed her the cards and steadied her hand. Between them they built 'the finest towers of cards imaginable.' Miss Stuart was an adept in raising hopes she had no intention of satisfying and when Buckingham sought closer intimacy he was sharply repulsed. Lord Arlington, a dull dog, then tried his hand at card houses, but the lady found it difficult to refrain from laughing when he spoke, so effectively had Buckingham mimicked his manner. He made no attempt to impress her by putting lighted tapers in his mouth, like Anthony Hamilton. In heavy pique, Arlington is reported to have gone away contemplating the introduction of a Bill to prohibit royal mistresses.

Charles may not have been the first King to adopt the cynical practice of drafting his mistresses into the Queen's service, but he effectively confirmed the tradition and later monarchs were pleased to follow it. It was one of the least happy legacies, in the field of manners, left by Charles II. At least his cynicism was slightly less profound than that which prevailed in the French Court, where it was the custom for well-loved royal mistresses, in death, to be laid out on a *lit de parade*, in all the splendour of silver and gold and crimson. Maria Delorme, who had consoled princes, cardinals, marshals, dukes and counts, was displayed in this manner, but the local *curé* objected, successfully, to the virgin's crown which had been set on her head.*

In the rush to lose reputations, the maids of honour were no laggards. If there were artists, like Sir Peter Lely, to flatter their beauty, there were also poets, like the Earl of Rochester, to celebrate their downfall. The major threat to their virtue was, of course, the King, whom they nicknamed Old Rowley after a lecherous goat in the Privy Garden. One day, hearing them singing a song in which Old Rowley figured, he knocked

* C. M. Gray: *The Bed*

on their door, and to the cry, 'Who's there?' answered 'Only Old Rowley.' Pepys thought the 'mad freaks' of the maids were such that 'there be few will venture upon them for wives.' Something more than a mad freak was the mysterious dropping of a babe at a Court ball. The babe was picked up in a handkerchief and removed. Next morning the maids of honour reported early for vindication, but one of them subsequently fell sick and left the Court. Pepys passes on a rumour that the babe was anatomised by the King. The diarist disliked seeing the maids in riding habits, with wigs and hats, distinguished from men only by their long petticoats.

Count de Grammont, who was suspiciously well-informed about the maids' shortcomings, considered that all the Court damsels should have been expelled, if not for irregularities, then for ugliness. The Mother of the Maids was Lady Sanderson who, while no party to the debauching of her charges, allowed young gentlemen to entertain them when she believed their intentions to be honourable. She herself was fond of green oysters and Spanish wine, and many hampers of these and other commodities were brought along by gallants anxious to be in her good graces. Apparently she was neglectful of the first duty of a mother, that of staying up to see gentlemen off the premises. De Grammont was attracted by (among others) Miss Warmestre, of whom he said that 'her consent ran along with her eyes, to the last degree of indiscretion.' Having exceeded the last degree of indiscretion, she left the Court. Then there was the complaisant Miss Bellenden, whose 'chief merit consisted in being plump and fresh-coloured,' and who 'had the prudence to quit the Court before she was obliged to do so.' There was also a Miss Wells who came of a loyal family; 'her father having faithfully served Charles I, she thought it her duty not to revolt against Charles II.'

The Count does not omit to mention the beautiful Elizabeth Hamilton, supposedly the greatest ornament of the Court, whom he married after she had refused many illustrious suppliants. But the *Memoirs* fail to reveal how the marriage came about. It seems that the romance had reached an advanced stage when de Grammont suddenly made for Paris. Elizabeth's two brothers rode hotfoot after him and, intercepting him at Dover, asked him if he had forgotten anything. Cheerfully he admitted that he had forgotten to marry their sister and returned with them in order to do so.

Among the maids of the Duchess of York (Anne Hyde) was the predatory Miss Hobart, whose affections were bestowed on members of her own sex. 'It was not long,' says de Grammont, 'before the report, whether true or false, of this singularity spread through the entire Court, where people being yet so uncivilised as never to have heard of that kind of refinement in love of ancient Greece imagined that the illustrious Hobart, who seemed so particularly attached to the fair sex, was in reality something more than she appeared to be.' This must have been one of de Grammont's little jokes, for it is hard to believe that a whiff of Lesbianism could have revealed such innocence in the Court of Charles II. The aunt of one maid of honour confided to Rochester that she was dubious of Miss Hobart's activities, whereupon Rochester arranged for the threatened damsel to fall into his own hands. The Duchess of York, hearing gossip, ordered Miss Hobart to be removed from the society of the maids and to attend her own person. Nevertheless, Miss Hobart was still in a position to hold *têtes-à-tête* with invited maids in the Duchess's bathing establishment, where she had a closet containing sweets and liquors. De Grammont has a long rambling story about goings-on in this *bagnio*. At one time there was a Court rumour that Miss Hobart's maid was pregnant by her mistress. The opportunity given by this affair to *farceurs* like Rochester, who was heavily involved in it, needs no elaboration.

Rochester had come to Court as a youth of great personality and talent, but he was rapidly spoiled. For five years, on his own admission, he was never sober. Though often sent from Court in disgrace, he was always welcomed back by his master. In one of these periods of disgrace he set up in London as a quack doctor under the name of Alexander Bendo. Among his clients were the maids of the maids of honour. He told one of them that she would have the smallpox and her mistress the great pox within a couple of months if she did not guard against a man in woman's clothes. Messages like this aroused much excited speculation among the maids of honour. Two of them decided to call in person on this too knowledgeable quack and for this purpose they dressed themselves as orange girls. It was an unfortunate disguise, for they were accosted by a notorious gentleman of the Duke of York's household, who wished to hire them on the spot. With great difficulty they shook him off and returned to their quarters without having had the benefit of an interview with Dr Bendo.

The Roman Catholic Duke of York (later James II), who had his establishment at St James's Palace, was a clumsier edition of his brother. His private life had that quality of vulgar farce which was to be more amply demonstrated by Queen Victoria's wicked uncles; but James possessed what the uncles lacked, a conscience. His attempts at cuckoldry were so un-subtle that the wives he ogled had to be packed off into the country by their husbands. One of them was the Countess of Chesterfield (wife of the second Earl) whose rustication pro-vided a catch-phrase to describe such acts of discipline. There-after, susceptible wives were 'sent to the Peak.' The Duke's *penchant* for ill-favoured mistresses, like the skinny Arabella Churchill, one of the Duchess's maids of honour, inspired the King to say that his brother's women must be given him as penances by his priests.

The Duke's real love was the Navy. In times of crisis the rakes and gamesters of Whitehall accompanied him on board the King's men-of-war, where they showed, if not seamanship, commendable spirit. A shameful exception, however, was that Gentleman of the Bedchamber, Henry Brouncker, who lost his nerve and passed off orders, as if from the Duke, to the captain of the *Royal Charles* calling off the pursuit of the Dutch fleet. Most of the Court volunteers, once they found their sea legs, enjoyed the adventure. Some, Court-weary, were encouraged by the Duke to make the Navy their career, to the disgust of the rough tarpaulin captains who had learned their pro-fession the hard way under Blake.

It was the Duke, too, who took a leading role with the Duke of Monmouth in the mock battle of Maestricht as staged at Windsor in 1674. A scale model of that city with all its fortifications had been erected in a meadow. Leading an army of courtiers, the two dukes demonstrated the whole business of siege: the digging of trenches, the exploding of mines, bombardment with guns and grenades. This has been described as the last pageant of chivalry in which a British prince took a leading part. It is a sad thought that this same prince was to find himself under the necessity of beheading his fellow performer some years later.

Towards the end, the royal popularity began to wane. The King's stories of his days of exile were too well known. 'He often began them with a full audience and before he had done there were not above four or five left about him,' says Bishop Burnet. 'This made him fond of strangers, for they hearkened to all his often repeated stories and went away as in a rapture at such an intimate condescension in a King.'*

He had befriended honest courtiers as well as rakes, and had not omitted to encourage artists and craftsmen. Antonio Verrio and Grinling Gibbons embellished the bare castle of Windsor. In Robert Streater, the architectural and decorative artist, he had a most talented Sergeant Painter, and when Streater fell a victim to the stone Charles sent for a special surgeon from Paris to perform the operation. He encouraged Samuel Cooper, the miniaturist. Partly through Buckingham's example, the Court flocked to Simon Verelst, whose speciality was miniature portraits wreathed in coloured flowers. Such patronage turned the painter's head and he had to be put away.

Architecturally, Charles improved both Whitehall and Windsor. The famous Long Walk was laid out by him. He ordered the rebuilding of the neglected Palace of Holyrood but did not live to see the alterations.

Charles's last night before his fatal illness has been sketched by Evelyn:

'I can never forget the inexpressible luxury and profaneness, gaming and all dissoluteness and, as it were, total forgetfulness of God (it being Sunday evening) which . . . I was witness of; the King sitting and toying with his concubines, Portsmouth†, Cleveland, Mazarin etc. A French boy singing love songs in that glorious gallery whilst about twenty of the great courtiers and other dissolute persons were at basset round a large table, a bank of at least £2000 in gold before them; upon which two gentlemen who were with me made reflections with astonishment.'

Next day the King was put in the merciless hands of his

* *History of My Own Time*
† *Louise Kerouelle*

physicians and his soul was left to his chaplains, who prayed the clock round till he died, relieving each other 'every half quarter of an hour.' As there were 48 of them the strain was not, perhaps, excessive.

Debauched though it was, Charles's Court did not corrupt the more stable elements of the realm. The middle and lower classes disliked it for its extravagances, immoralities and French airs; the upper classes either had to loosen their standards in order to keep in the social swim or live as recluses. Though let down by many of his courtiers, Charles was well served by others, not least by the indefatigable Sir Peter Lely, whose flattering likenesses of frail women did 'much to condone in the eyes of posterity the excesses and immoralities of Charles II's court.'*

But Antonio Verrio went one better than Lely. This whimsical Neapolitan, who used to put the faces of his Court enemies on the bodies of satyrs and demons, executed a ceiling at Windsor in which Charles looked down on posterity in the company of Prudence, Temperance and Fortitude.

* *Dictionary of National Biography*

15

Not with a Bang . . .

WITH James II came catastrophe. The Palace of Whitehall which, under his brother, had lived for pleasure and profligacy entered a taut and plot-racked phase in which libertines were forced to look to their religious consciences (for as yet even rakes feared God). Could they, or could they not, bear to watch their King at mass? Many who were unable to do so retired to plot, either at home or across the North Sea; and the Court they left passed into a state of mutinous excitement from which it was delivered only by the beat of alien drums.

On his accession James made some attempt to clean up the Court. The mere fact that he had four illegitimate children by Arabella Churchill and two by Catherine Sedley did not prevent him from denouncing lewdness and profligacy. He paid off his brother's mistress, the Duchess of Portsmouth, who retired to France and, as a gesture to his Queen, removed Catherine Sedley from the company of her gentlewomen. He even tried to eject her from Whitehall, but in this endeavour he was frustrated by the lady's intransigence, his own weakness and the intrigues of those who felt that a Catholic king would be the better for a Protestant mistress. Arabella Churchill was given a pension at the expense of Ireland.

While his reforming mood lasted James dislodged various Court barnacles and did much to discourage open drunkenness and unruly behaviour. The Duke of Devonshire, who used unnecessary violence in expelling one Colonel Culpeper from the Presence Chamber, was chagrined to find himself ordered to pay a fine of £30,000 (the penalty was remitted at the Revolution).

Those who had hoped for a reign of decisive action and

strict attention to business were soon disappointed. It became clear that James's main object was the relief and rehabilitation of Roman Catholics. The reign had hardly begun before Evelyn reported that Romanists were swarming at Court with greater confidence than at any time since the Reformation. Mass was no longer celebrated in holes and closets, but openly and publicly. The gentlemen with the white wands were called from their labours to explain their attitude on transubstantiation. When the priests did not closet them, the King did. If they agreed to support him in his efforts to repeal the anti-Catholic laws, they retained their appointments; if not, they were replaced. Admiral Herbert, a dedicated profligate who combined the appointment of Master of the Robes with that of Rear-Admiral of England, declined to co-operate. 'Nobody doubts your honour,' said James, 'but a man who lives as you do ought not to talk of his conscience.' Herbert nevertheless decided to forego places worth £4000. Rochester gave up his white staff but retained a substantial income. Members of Parliament were subjected to the same ordeal of closeting. Most of them pleaded their conscience; others came out of the Palace with the King's gold in their pockets.

Not all courtiers waited to be closeted. Sir John Reresby tells how the Duke of Somerset, a Lord of the Bedchamber, declined to attend the public entry of the Papal nuncio into Windsor. He was banned from Court and deprived of all his places. The same fate overtook five Gentlemen of the Privy Chamber.*

It was one thing to get rid of Protestant gentlemen from the Bedchamber; it was another to get rid of a pertinacious Protestant mistress. In 1686 the Palace priests were uncommonly mortified when they heard that their sovereign and protector had conferred on Catherine Sedley the titles of Baroness of Darlington and Countess of Dorchester. Even if these titles were intended to soften the lady's dismissal, such favour to a sharp-tongued Protestant baggage was intolerable. The Queen (Mary of Modena) showed her bitterness by abstaining from food and speech for two days. There seemed a risk that she would retire to a convent. In bluntest terms, James was informed by his priests that his wickedness rendered all their

* *Journals and Memoirs*

prayers nugatory. By now, he was heartily shocked by what he had done, and he sent out for a scourge, which was willingly supplied.

Before his accession, James had stimulated the interest of courtiers in the Navy. Now, in his efforts to overawe Parliament and the capital, he made soldiering a Court fashion. His great camp at Hounslow attracted not only the *élite* but their ladies, who found the military life full of quaint and unsuspected excitements. Sparkling reviews were staged on the heath. In the commanders' tents were held feasts—and masses. Yet neither the Army nor the Navy welcomed James's interest, seeing his motives all too clearly.

With perverse industry, James stoked the fires of public and Parliamentary anger against himself. His delight at the birth of a male heir to the Throne, in 1688, was not shared by his Protestant subjects, who would rather have borne the expense of fifty bastards. As the news bitterly displeased them, they decided not to believe it. Obviously, they said, there must have been a plot. The supposed birth had occurred in St James's Palace, which was well known to be infested with priests and foreigners incessantly running disreputable errands along secret passages (Protestants strode boldly through galleries, but Papists preferred to flit about in tunnels and pop up through trapdoors). Of the canards about the royal birth, the most fancied was the one which said that the Queen had merely pretended to be pregnant and that the child was an impostor smuggled into her bed in a warming pan. Bishop Burnet was quite convinced that there had been legerdemain of some sort under the counterpane and was ready to believe all rumours, even if they cancelled each other out. He thought that the witnesses, mostly Papists, had been suspiciously slack in the execution of their duties. For example, 'none of the ladies had felt the child in the Queen's belly.' And when the warming pan was introduced into the chamber 'it was not opened that it might be seen that there was fire and nothing else in it; so here was matter for suspicion with which all were filled.'* Obviously, in the Bishop's view, all those assisting at the birth should have adopted the conjuror's technique and taken pains to display their equipment, with a 'No deception, ladies and

* *History of My Own Time*

gentlemen.' There were 67 witnesses in the Queen's Bed-chamber, of whom some 18, mostly Privy Councillors, stood at the foot of the bed; but even if the midwife had taken the trouble to tour the room with an opened warming pan, rumour would not have been allayed. As it was, there was a rival story to the effect that the Queen had given birth to a sickly child which had died, whereupon another had been substituted (Jesuits being notoriously in the habit of keeping a stock of newly-born babies for such purposes). But the warming pan rumour was best liked.

The Queen was rash enough to recover quickly, thus con-firming the belief that she had never been ill. James, con-temptuous of rumour, ordered grand displays of fireworks. One Thames-side set-piece showed Bacchus with barrels of comesti-bles tumbling from his belly, but the designer played safe with the perilous theme of Fecundity. Poets obliged with the usual odes. Eventually, as rumours continued to grow, James realised that a public enquiry must be held into the circumstances of the birth. This was as humiliating an ordeal as the Throne had yet endured, not only because of the reflections it cast on the King's honour but because of the intimate details which had to be brought under public discussion. It was bad enough for a modest and pious woman to undergo childbirth with a fiend like Judge Jeffreys watching from the end of the bed. It was worse to know that the most intimate processes of her body were being discussed by a conclave of Privy Councillors, judges and nobles. The inquiry disposed of the rumours to the satisfaction of the unprejudiced, of whom there were not many. It was clear in the end that there had been plenty of Protestant witnesses in the Bedchamber. Princess Anne, the King's daughter by Anne Hyde, was jealous of the new heir and said nothing to exculpate the King. She was at Bath when the child was born and her excuse for not being present was that she was breeding and unable to travel. Anne's hostile, even suspicious attitude, deeply pained the King.

The child thus inauspiciously born suffered an initial set-back in health. Because the Queen's other children had suffered from convulsions, it was decided that this one should be fed, not on milk, but on gruel administered with a spoon. The gruel had currants in it and the infant's system rebelled.

Eventually a full conclave of physicians decided that 'His Highness should have the breast,' but not of course the Queen's breast. A hasty reconnaissance of Richmond produced a 'fresh' country woman, the wife of a tile maker, who was in a suitable condition to nourish royalty. She reported for duty wearing her ordinary working clothes, old shoes and no stockings. Only by slow degrees was she rigged out, 'that the surprise may not alter her in her duty and care.'* The Prince's rapid recovery justified the launching of a new rumour: that the wet nurse was the real mother of the child. For her nutritional services she was paid two or three hundred guineas, for which she had no use, and a sum of £100 a year was settled on her. The episode is worth recording if only as an example of Stuart benevolence being bestowed on an honest woman.

The babe doomed to be known as the Old Pretender recovered only a few days before his father woke to the fact that the sceptre was being rapidly prised from his grasp. Off Torbay arrived a fleet of fifty men-of-war and 500 transports, with a recreant son-in-law, William of Orange, in command. James's inner circle swore renewed loyalty to him and then defected, John Churchill among them, to William. His daughter Anne also deserted him. Then, one December morning, the crowds gathering for the King's levee at Whitehall learned that their king had deserted them. Within a week Dutch troops, with drums beating, marched unopposed, save for the scowls of the Coldstream, into the Palace. The secret passages were now innocent of priests, but there were some pretty new chapels to desecrate.

---

* Sir Henry Ellis: *Original Letters*

16

The Chill Falls

T HE Revolution was a bizarre experience for the Princess of Orange who, suitably agog, and from a seemly distance, watched her husband unseat her father. If the throne of England was going abegging, Mary had a better claim to it than William; but William is said to have informed Parliament that he had no intention of becoming a gentleman usher to his wife. It was decided that William and Mary should reign jointly.

William's demeanour when he reached Whitehall was cold and correct. Forgotten, no doubt, was the night when King Charles made him drunk and he had to be restrained from breaking into the quarters of the maids of honour. Mary's behaviour on arrival pained friend and foe alike. She was far too jolly and inquisitive for what should have been a solemn, indeed sombre, occasion. 'Queen Mary wanted bowels,' says Sarah, Duchess of Marlborough. 'She ran about, looking into every closet and conveniency, and turned up the quilts of the beds, just as people do at an inn, with no sort of concern in her appearance.' One conveniency she was expected to take over was the Countess of Dorchester, as a Lady of the Bed-chamber. Haughtily, Mary turned away her head when her father's flame approached; whereupon the Countess protested that she had not sinned more notoriously in breaking the seventh commandment than Mary had done in breaking the fifth.

Side by side in the Banqueting Hall at Whitehall, William and Mary signed the Declaration of Rights. The country had obtained two rulers for the price of one. Nobody dared prophesy how this 'double-bottomed monarchy,' as Bishop Burnet rather unhappily calls it, would work out; but Parliament had the whip hand and did not hesitate, when the occasion demanded, to show it.

William was not greatly interested in the domestic affairs of his new kingdom. He pushed on with his life's work: the frustration of Louis XIV. His Court, when he found time to attend it, was a *farouche* one. Under his scowl, all levity vanished, and more frightening than his scowl was his laugh. The King had no small talk, even in his own tongue. According to Macaulay, 'he praised and reprimanded, rewarded and punished, with the stern tranquillity of a Mohawk chief.' The Princess Anne (later Queen Anne) nicknamed him Caliban. When she called on him he kept her waiting with common suitors, until the Court protested. Then he condescended to send a page to assist her from her carriage.

William was a dangerous man to meet after a night's debauch, or a disastrous session at cards; on these occasions he lashed out with his cane at any servants who displeased him. This could have been overlooked as Dutch boorishness, but there was an outcry when, the day after losing £4000 at basset, he belaboured an English gentleman who rashly preceded him on to the course at Newmarket.

There was little calculated to put William in a good temper. Surrounded by distinguished and undistinguished oath-breakers, by ageing rakes from a court of dishonour, by haughty beldams who expected him to defer to their beauty, he saw no reason for forcing an affability foreign to his nature. Therefore he fell back on his own Dutch advisers. To the Court-frequenting nobility it was like Cromwell and his Roundheads all over again.

Yet the Mohawk chief was human enough to maintain a mistress. Soon after his marriage he had formed a liaison with the squinting Elizabeth Villiers, later Countess of Orkney. This connection caused the Queen much private distress. Elizabeth Villiers was a cousin of the notorious Barbara Villiers, Countess of Castlemaine; thus, a disreputable link was retained with the past. In accordance with custom, William made Ireland support his mistress, but arranged that her revenues should support two old mistresses of James II. Clearly William was not wholly without a sense of humour.

It was not the royal morosity alone that brought paralysis

to the Palace of Whitehall, but the royal asthma. The fog and stink of London caused the King such acute suffering that he withdrew to the kindlier airs of Hampton Court, where he and the Queen lived a private life. This palace proved inconvenient of access to the King's ministers, who had to run the gauntlet of highwaymen in order to collect his signature. The King therefore compromised and acquired the Palace of Kensington from the Earl of Nottingham, but even the road to Kensington was not immune from the attentions of highwaymen. When Lord Halifax told the King that Londoners resented his neglect of the capital, William replied, bluntly, 'Do you wish to see me dead?' Not only the aristocracy were indignant at the virtual dissolution of the Court. The common people missed their fun and fireworks. Some of them even held it against the King that he had discontinued the genial old custom of touching for the King's Evil.

For the Master of the Revels, the early months of the reign were a nightmare. The trouble began when the Queen tactlessly went to Drury Lane to see a performance of Dryden's *Spanish Friar*, which contained such lines as 'A crown usurped, a distaff on the Throne' and 'What title has this Queen but lawless force?' When the audience turned their heads to see whether the Queen had savoured the full aptness of the allusions she took refuge behind her fan. In the interest of good order and courtly discipline, the Master of the Revels found it necessary to take a blue pencil to the works of Shakespeare, deleting passages, scenes and whole acts. *King Lear*, dealing as it does with filial ingratitude, was banned completely. No less perilous was *Richard II*, which treats of the impossibility of washing away the balm from an anointed king. There was a rumour current that James II had died in Ireland, and with this in mind the Master of the Revels struck out an entire act of *Richard III*. When the players objected, they were told that the death of Henry VI would be linked with the supposed fate of James.* Since Shakespeare is notoriously full of apt quotations for all occasions, the task of the Master of the Revels was clearly a most onerous one, and he must have been grateful for those evenings when the Court decided to amuse itself by playing basset.

* Agnes Strickland: *The Queens of England*

Mary possessed many of the social qualities William lacked but found insufficient opportunities to display them. It was said of this Court that the King did nothing but think, the Queen did nothing but talk and the Princess Anne did nothing but eat. Burnet maintains that the Queen did much to improve Court morals and wean ladies from idleness. She kept them hard at their needlework, appointing one to read aloud to all, thus cutting down time which the others might have wasted in individual reading.

Relations between Mary and Anne were deplorable. The Queen, however, did not go so far as to visit her displeasure on Anne's infant, the Duke of Gloucester. Not caring to meet Anne in person, she would send her respects to the infant Duke by a Court official who would recite them in all solemnity to the infant on the nurse's knee and then return, his mission accomplished. Because they knew that Mary loathed her sister, the courtiers neglected Anne's presence. When they suddenly began to flock to her, Anne assumed, cynically but correctly, that her sister must be dying.

Like a loyal wife, Mary helped her husband to improve Hampton Court, on which the talents of Grinling Gibbons and Antonio Verrio were employed. The Queen's own contribution to its splendours was a somewhat intimidating collection of *chinoiserie*. It is to the morose William that posterity is indebted for the whimsicality of the maze.

In 1698 the Palace of Whitehall, scene of so much splendour and wickedness, disappeared in smoke, save for the Banqueting Hall. Suitably enough, the culprit was Dutch. A woman servant in the employ of Colonel Stanley was drying linen too close to the fire, and Stanley's house became alight. It set fire to 150 others, mostly belonging to the nobility. Twenty houses were blown up in a vain effort to arrest the fire, which burned for seventeen hours.

In his loss, the King received no sympathy from the people of London. If the Court had been in residence, they argued, the fire would never have got out of control. William came to look at the ruins and muttered something about having the palace rebuilt, but nobody supposed that he meant it. Gradually private builders began to encroach on the ruins. The principal palace in London was now that of St James's.

*   *   *

An invalid king was succeeded by an invalid queen. Anne was fat and gouty, unable to walk to her coronation. Eighteen times she was pregnant and eighteen times she lost the hoped-for heir. Eventually the Court judged it tactful to stop begging Heaven to fructify her womb. Her consort, Prince George of Denmark, was not taken over-seriously by anyone. He was a plodding, unimaginative type who was a long way from being the inspiration of the Augustan age; though he could always point out that he had hired Sir Richard Steele, at £100 a year, as Gentleman Usher. Had not Shakespeare been content to perform the duties of usher?

At first the Queen tried to give a certain zest and diversification to her Court, but she had little personal interest in the arts, which flourished despite her. All her energy was needed to keep abreast of State business and palace intrigue. Bishop Burnet says she was easy of access and listened politely, but opened herself to few. She was so cold and general in her answers that persons soon got the habit of applying for what they wanted to her ministers. Of her later years, he said:

'She has laid down the splendour of a court too much and eats privately; so that except on Sundays and a few hours twice or thrice a week in the drawing room* she appears so little that her court is, as it were, abandoned.'

Even before her accession, her household had been cob-webbed with feminine intrigue, the spider-in-chief being Sarah Churchill, later Duchess of Marlborough. Sarah's warrior husband had been courtier to three kings: Charles II, whose mistress he had borrowed; James II, whose cause he had deserted; and William III, who had handed him his notice an hour or two after Marlborough had handed him his shirt. Sarah was Anne's Lady of the Bedchamber and a great deal more. The two corresponded cosily under the names of Mrs Morley and Mrs Freeman (Prince George being Mr Morley and the Duke of Marlborough Mr Freeman). This quaint notion emanated from Anne, who thought that friendship such as theirs demanded a form of address appropriate to equals; she begged Sarah not to call her 'Your Highness' at every word. The retreat from etiquette was one which Anne lived

* *Drawing-room receptions were held in Charles II's day. They developed into the feminine version of a levee.*

to regret most bitterly. For Sarah was not content with the role of favourite; she sought to dominate the Queen completely.

On Anne's accession, Sarah was made Groom of the Stole and Mistress of the Robes, and had control of the Privy Purse. The emoluments came to nearly £8000 a year. Hers was the role that Castlemaine, Kéroualle, Sedley and all the mistresses of history had dreamed of. In effect, Sarah was the fountain of honour, with the power to make or break careers. She could dispose of factions and she could dispose of the Queen's cast-off clothes; and in both capacities she aroused hatred and jealousy. For five years her power was almost plenary. As Sir Winston Churchill puts it, 'Sarah managed the Queen, Marlborough managed the war, and Godolphin managed the Parliament.'*

But during these five years the friendship between Mrs Morley and Mrs Freeman was crumbling. Increasingly, Mrs Morley resented being bullied. Mrs Freeman had sown the seeds of her own ruin when she persuaded the Queen to take into her employment a poor and seedy Churchill relation, Abigail Hill, who was appointed one of the Queen's dressers. Once in the palace, Abigail never put a foot wrong; gradually she made herself indispensable to the invalid queen and was taken into her confidence. Her political and religious views coincided with those of her mistress. For some time Sarah was reluctant to believe her suspicions. What had she to fear from a poor, plain, red-nosed relative who was, or ought to be, grateful for her patronage, and who held only a menial position in the palace hierarchy?

For Sarah, the moment of truth came when she discovered, many weeks after the event, that Abigail had been secretly married to a member of Prince George's Bedchamber, Samuel Masham, and that the Queen had been present at the ceremony. This singular event had been staged in the lodgings of the Queen's physician, Dr John Arbuthnot, and had been marked by the withdrawal without explanation of a substantial sum from the Privy Purse, which Sarah held. That the Queen of England should have lent herself to a furtive affair like this says much for the tyranny which Sarah had established. Abigail, though willing to intrigue, was frightened of Sarah's mighty

* *History of the English-Speaking Peoples (The Age of Revolution)*

rages; and the Queen of England was prepared to grace a hole-and-corner marriage for the sake of a quiet life. This was Anne at her least Elizabethan.

After that, there was nothing but bickering and quarrels. Sarah had grown too proud to carry out her duties properly. She handed over fan and gloves with her head averted, contemptuously. Increasingly she stayed from Court, thus ceding more power to her rival; for if there was one thing Anne liked, it was constant attention. The phrase 'Masham and I' in a letter from the Queen brought out all Sarah's venom. Her correspondence contained expressions which few courtiers would have dared to write and few sovereigns to accept. There was a public scene on the day that the Queen rode out, without excessive enthusiasm, to celebrate the victory of Oudenarde. In the carriage Sarah noticed that the Queen was not wearing the jewels in the way that she, as Mistress of the Robes, had set them out for her. This she regarded as an insult to herself, to her husband and to British arms. Obviously, Abigail was at the back of it. All the way to St Paul's Sarah nagged her sovereign and continued to do so on the cathedral steps and in the building itself. Finally the Queen sharply rebuked the Duchess, and the Duchess protested at the strength of this public rebuke.

Abigail's subversive activities were not limited to disorganising the Queen's costume. She had a kinsman in the ambitious Tory politician Harley, whom she used to smuggle up the back stairs into the Queen's presence. Her part in the downfall of the Whigs was far from negligible. Sir Winston Churchill remarks how Abigail exerted influence 'as she smoothed the pillows and removed the slops';* but the Duke of Marlborough, when holding a high military appointment, had been happy to assist the previous two kings to put on their underclothes. Nevertheless, it was a dismal situation. The Duke of Buckingham was goaded to exclaim: 'Good God, how has this poor nation been governed in my time! During the reign of King Charles the Second we were governed by a parcel of French whores; in King James the Second's time by a parcel of popish priests; in King William's time by a parcel of Dutch footmen; and now we are governed by a dirty chambermaid, a Welsh

* *Marlborough*

attorney and a profligate wretch that has neither honour nor honesty.'* The last two characters were presumably Harley and St John.

Much of the quarrelling between Anne and Sarah had been over the filling of Church appointments. The Queen's preferences were not necessarily those of the Whigs, but Sarah would flourish the lists for signature and exclaim, 'Lord, Madam, it *must* be so.' The Queen also resolved that posts in the Household (except military ones) should no longer be bought and sold, as they had been since Charles II's day. In 1702 a proclamation was issued to this effect and Sarah could hardly do other than give it her approval. There were other ways of manipulating patronage than by the crude sale of appointments.

What was needed, also, was a proclamation to ban the sale of non-existent Household appointments, for this abuse was now even more popular than it had been in Charles's day. A venerable courtier living at St James's is said to have offered the post of Vice-Chamberlain to a country gentleman for £7000, of which £4000 was to be paid at once to 'the Queen's foster sister,' £2000 to the outgoing incumbent and £1000 to various agents, including the elderly courtier himself. The aspirant was told that he must walk up and down in the garden at St James's in order that the 'Queen's foster sister' might see whether he had the necessary airs and graces for Court employment. This he did, to the gratification of a housemaid at one of the palace windows. He was then allowed to watch the Vice-Chamberlain hand the Queen from her carriage. The prospect of doing this himself filled him with such ecstasy that he exclaimed aloud that the post was worth another thousand pounds. Overhearing this, the Vice-Chamberlain suspected that his appointment was in peril, and his enquiries laid bare the plot. All that the country gentleman lost was a few guineas and the price of a few drinks. The courtier was not disciplined.†
The whole affair sounds more like the plot of a stage comedy than a serious attempt at fraud; but variations of the theme were practised by confidence tricksters of the day.

Sarah's fall may well have been delayed by her threats to

* Agnes Strickland: *The Queens of England*
† Captain Robert Parker: *Memoirs*

Queen Anne with one of her ministers

publish her correspondence with the Queen. She went about the capital abusing the Queen publicly. One by one the remaining Whigs fell. The message notifying Godolphin of his dismissal was sent by a lackey and left with his porter; in disgust, he broke his staff and threw the pieces on the fire. Sarah waved no wand but she had two gold keys of office which, when the Queen finally plucked up courage to dismiss her, she refused to surrender. The Queen sent for Marlborough and asked him to use his influence on his wife. After a furious scene she threw the keys at his head; he picked them up and bore them humbly to the palace. They were then presented to the Duchess of Somerset and the Privy Purse went to Mrs Masham. Eventually, the unkindest cut of all, the Mashams were ennobled. At first the Queen had been against this proposal, since she felt she could hardly ask a peeress to sleep on a pallet and perform inferior offices. But Lady Masham was not corrupted by ermine. She was shrewd enough to see that it was by the exercise of humble services that she was able to maintain her hold on the Queen.

It would be superfluous, at this point, to say that Anne had little in common with Elizabeth. There were two points of resemblance only: both had a conscientious regard for the business of the nation and both had a passion for hunting. In her early days Anne rode on horseback, but in her more corpulent years she followed the stag in a one-horse, high-wheeled chaise, built to her specification. This, according to Swift, she drove 'furiously, like Jehu'—through fields of high corn if necessary. Her ladies were expected to follow in similar equipages and took many a toss in the process. One August day in 1711 Swift, who was in attendance at Court, complained that dinner was delayed until five o'clock because the Queen had driven 40 miles following stags. It was in that year that a royal race-course was founded on Ascot Heath, where the Queen liked to exercise her horses.

Swift had been sent to Court to try to divert some of Queen Anne's Bounty to the Irish Church. Anne knew nothing of his literary reputation and was suitably horrified on dipping into *The Tale of a Tub*. In his *Journal to Stella* Swift alternately praises and disparages the courtier's life. 'Windsor is a delicious situation, but the town is scoundrel,' he says. He mentions a drawing room so thinly attended that the Queen invited the visitors into her Bedchamber, 'where we made our bows and stood about 20 of us round the room while she looked at us round with her fan in her mouth, and once a minute said about three words to some that were nearest her and then she was told dinner was ready and went out.' Swift was consoled by an invitation to dine at the Green Cloth table. 'It is much the best table in England and costs the Queen a thousand pounds a month while she is at Windsor or Hampton Court; and is the only mark of magnificence or hospitality I can see in the Queen's family; it is designed to entertain foreign ministers and people of quality, who come to see the Queen, and have no place to dine at.' The worst table, in Swift's view, was that of the chaplains, who ate from pewter. He professed to be not primarily interested in the bill of fare, but in the bill of company; the Gentlemen Ushers, for example, were a scurvy gathering. He would have liked to dine with Prince Eugene, but not in the company of seven or eight generals—'they will all be drunk, I am sure.' His proposal to certain of his friends that they should have a sober meal with the Prince was not followed up.

The chief attraction of Court, Swift assured Stella, was that it served as a coffee-house where a man could meet his acquaintances. 'I affect to turn from a lord to the meanest of my acquaintances and I love to go there on Sundays to see the world. But, say the truth, I am growing weary of it.'

Besides getting free dinners, Swift was occasionally offered by the Vice-Chamberlain the use of horses on which to view the countryside. Dr Arbuthnot, the Queen's physician, rode with him. Twelve miles on a mettlesome horse was enough for the Dean. They met a tiresome lady in Miss Forester, 'a silly true maid of honour and I did not like her although she be a toast and was dressed like a man.' All of them had to dismount and stand to attention when they met the Queen. Swift summed up Windsor in two words which generations of courtiers would have been happy to echo: 'bloody cold.'

Not the least notable fact to emerge from Swift's correspondence is that male courtiers shaved only on alternate days. The pain of scraping the face daily was too much to contemplate. Although the Queen accepted stubbly chins, she disliked any slackness over wigs. When an *aide-de-camp* arrived from France in an undress wig she said that, very soon, her officers would come to Court in boots and spurs. Though torpid and withdrawn, she did not allow Court occasions to become slovenly, however ill-attended they might be. She did her best to be gracious to the 'Indian kings' who came to Court to ask her help against the French in Canada. The Duke of Shrewsbury, as Lord Chamberlain, had the privilege of introducing them. It can have been no easy task, as their names were Tee Yee Neen Ho Ga Prow, Ga Sa Yean Qua Prah Ion, Elow Oh Kaom and Oh Nee Yeath Ion No Prow. They presented the white queen with belts of wampum and told her, through an interpreter, that they looked forward to plenty of happy hunting and trading when the French were defeated. The Master of Ceremonies, Sir Charles Cotterel, saw to it that the Indian kings were well entertained.

In the Queen's private life a good deal of informality crept in. She liked to combine the ritual of dressing with her chaplains' prayers. One chaplain, turned out of the room in order that the Queen might put on some of her under-garments, stopped praying. Asked why, he stoutly explained: 'Because I will not whistle the Word of God through a keyhole.'

In praying for the well-being of the royal family the chaplains did not include the Queen's step-brother, the Old Pretender, for whose apprehension dead or alive she was ready to pay £5000. To please her, the palace guard burnt his effigy at the gates one Guy Fawkes night.

A year before she died the Queen had grown so fat that, to spare her the labour of ascending stairs, she was hoisted aloft in a chair-and-pulley apparatus, modelled perhaps on the machinery used by Henry VIII. Her coffin was said, no doubt libellously, to have been almost square.

17

Stately Bosoms

S INCE the Revolution the Court had gone steadily down-hill. Its pomp was becoming only a memory. Art and literature, music and fashion had flourished, but with little or no royal encouragement. The witty, the wise and the beautiful had found no common roof. In popular eyes, the sovereign was a sick hermit and the days of feasting and pageantry were as dead as the days of tournaments, masques and fountains flowing with wine.

Now the throne which had been filled to overflowing by the last of the Stuarts was handed over to a middle-aged, bad-tempered and unappreciative German prince. When they woke him to break the news that an empire had been dropped in his lap he turned over and was soon snoring again. The throne was one he had never sought; why should he lose any sleep over it?

If George I had any virtues other than those of being a Protestant, and an easy-going one at that, he kept them well concealed. He spoke little English and did not propose to learn any more. The obvious course, as he saw it, was to reign over this fractious new dominion with as little effort as was consistent with showing that he was King. If he could use the resources of Britain to buttress his Continental aspirations, so much the better. The Whigs in whose hands he put himself found it no easy task to cajole him into supporting their projects. Happily, however, he had no high monarchical designs, otherwise the reign might well have been a bloody one. Under him, the country had a spell of peace during which it was ruled by an ingenious blend of cunning and corruption, by the suborning of placemen and the tactful allocation of pensions and sinecures. The Court itself was well planted with Sir Robert Walpole's men, who voted as he told them. Without their aid his policies would have collapsed. From this dubious system was eventually evolved the modern two-party system of constitutional government.

The ambitious were quick to appreciate that nothing was to be gained by attempting to fawn on this alien prince. They saw that, in Macaulay's words, 'coronets and garters, bishoprics and embassies, lordships of the Treasury and tellerships of Exchequer, nay even charges in the Royal Stud and Bedchamber, were really bestowed, not by [the King] but by his advisers. Every ambitious and covetous man perceived that he would consult his own interest far better by acquiring the dominion of a Cornish borough and by rendering good service to the Ministry during a critical session than by becoming the companion or even the minion of his prince.'* Macaulay then makes the point that the Hanoverians, lacking though they were in graciousness and affability, in elegance and manners, yet performed their duties better than any ruler who had preceded them; 'for they governed according to law.'

At the coronation, according to Lady Cowper, 'the Jacobites were all there, looking as cheerful as they could but very peevish with everybody that spoke to them.'† When the Archbishop formally demanded the people's consent to this choice of monarch, the Countess of Dorchester (James II's one-time mistress) said to Lady Cowper: 'Does the old fool think that anybody will say no to his question when there are so many drawn swords?' The aim of the Whigs henceforth was to convince the King that all Jacobites were Tories and all Tories Jacobites.

Just as Dutch William had surrounded himself with an inner circle of his own countrymen, so did German George. The establishment he brought over from Germany numbered a hundred, including, notoriously, one washerwoman. His right-hand men were the Baron von Bernstorff and the Baron von Bothmar, and his Private Secretary was a Huguenot, Jean Robethon. The most exotic members of his Household were the valets, Mustapha and Mohamet, who had been captured by the King when he fought the Turks in Hungary. In the ordinary way, Turkish prisoners had little to expect, but the

* *History of England*
† *Diary of Mary, Countess Cowper*

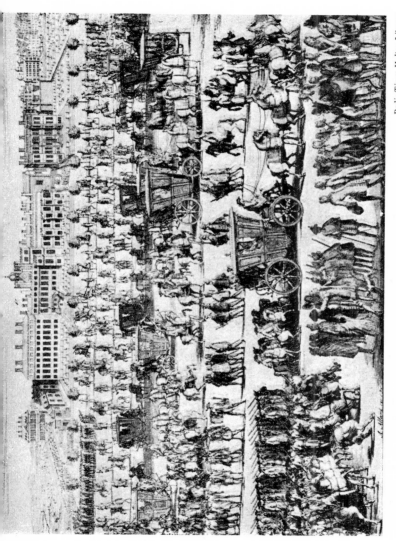

George I arrives at St James's Palace, 1714

G

lot of Mustapha and Mohamet was gratifying beyond all but the most riotous eastern dreams. They adapted themselves readily to the exigencies of life at Herrenhausen and were then equipped to serve as Pages of the Back Stairs at St James's, where they made the most of their many opportunities for self-enrichment. To a suitable audience, Mahomet would tell his story of the death of the King's sister, the Queen of Prussia. She had been a victim, he said, of diamond poisoning, her stomach being worn so thin that he, Mahomet, had been able to thrust his fingers through it at any part.

The lack of a common language cramped the Court both in its social and political roles. Walpole, possessing no German, talked to the King as best he could in fragments of French, English and even schoolboy Latin. At lower levels the language difficulty was equally embarrassing. When the Princess of Wales (later Queen Caroline) was in labour, the German midwife suffered from the delusion that the English ladies had threatened to hang her if the Princess miscarried. No one could explain that this was a misapprehension; but Lord Townshend ('Turnip' Townshend) ran up, shook her by the hand and 'made kind faces at her.' She then performed her office. A dead prince was born but the midwife was not hanged.

For English ladies, the Court offered bleak prospects. There was no female establishment, save in the service of the Princess of Wales. George's Queen was a prisoner in a German fortress, whither he had sent her after the resounding scandal of the Königsmark affair. For feminine consolation he retained German mistresses of frowsty and repulsive mien. Moreover, the German ladies at Court were contemptuous of English-women. The fat Countess of Buckeburg, on a visit from Hanover, voiced her scorn of English ladies of quality, who went about 'as pitifully and sneakingly as they could.' They held their heads down and looked always in a fright, 'whereas those that are foreigners hold up their heads and hold out their breasts and make themselves look as great and stately as they can.' To which Lady Deloraine retorted: 'We show our quality by our birth and titles, Madam, and not by sticking out our bosoms.'*

On this theme, the fourth Lord Chesterfield was not silent.

---

* *Diary of Mary, Countess Cowper*

'The standard of His Majesty's taste,' he said, 'made all those ladies who aspired to his favour and who were near the statutable size strain and swell themselves like the frogs in the fable to rival the bulk and dignity of the ox. Some succeeded and others burst.'

Three broad-minded ladies, veterans of a more liberal day, who did not shrink from matching bosoms with the German women, were the Duchess of Portsmouth, the Countess of Orkney and the Countess of Dorchester. One day all three turned up at Court together. It was left to the Countess of Dorchester to voice the comment which doubtless was on the lips of each of them: 'God, who would have thought that we three whores should have met here!'

In the London mob were men and women who, in their youth, had hissed the foreign mistresses of the Merry Monarch. They now had a splendid chance to show their patriotism by abusing the German mistresses of George I. There was no quarrel with these ladies on religious grounds and little deep-felt objection on moral grounds; it was enough that they were ugly, greedy and German. The two principal targets resembled the ugly sisters of pantomime. The Countess von der Schulenburg, who was 60 years old when the King came to England, was sallow, tall and skinny, and was nicknamed 'the Maypole.' She had been a maid of honour to the King's mother, the Electress Sophia, who once said of her, 'Look at that mawkin, and think of her being my son's passion.' One of the more innocent ways in which she amused the monarch was by cutting out paper silhouettes. The Baroness Kielmansegge reached Britain a little later than her rival, having experienced some difficulty in shaking off her creditors. Forty years old, she was mountainously fat, a cosmetician's benefit and a stay-maker's despair, and was nicknamed 'The Elephant and Castle.' With her generous proportions went a not ungenerous nature. According to Lady Cowper, she complained to the King that the Prince of Wales had been accusing her of flirtations in Hanover. To refute this charge, she produced from her pocket a document in which her husband certified that she had always been a faithful wife. The Princess was not alone in thinking that only a very dubious reputation would require such support.

Both ladies became naturalised and were then peppered with the usual place-names. Schulenburg became Baroness of Dundalk, Countess of Dungarvan and Duchess of Munster in the Irish peerage. Knowing what Irish titles were worth she rebelled, and was created Baroness of Glastonbury, Countess of Feversham and Duchess of Kendal. Kielmansegge became Countess of Darlington. As they came to understand the English governmental system, both waxed rich. Like their master, they had never wanted to leave Hanover, but in this uncivil new land there was yet a good deal of fun to be had out of taking bribes and appointing bishops, especially as both political parties were anxious to contribute to their welfare. Neither of the ladies, however, liked Walpole. At an early stage Schulenburg tried to induce the King's servants to ration their master's punch, for fear he should talk too freely to Walpole. They soon wished they had never listened to her.

In Hanover, where George's heart lay, were other mistresses who came as a welcome change after the Maypole and the Elephant and Castle. Towards the end of his reign he paid Britain a belated compliment by taking an English mistress, with the down-to-earth name of Annie Brett. Her apartment abutted on the garden of St James's, and for greater convenience and prestige she had a door made to enable her to enter it at will. Princess Anne, the Princess Royal, who liked to choose her company, had it bricked up again. Miss Brett reopened the breach and the game might have gone on for long enough but for the death of the King. With his demise vanished Miss Brett's hopes of a coronet. Nell Gwyn, it will be recalled, suffered a similar reverse.

Traditionally, the Tories had been the bulwark of monarchy, but the party was in the wilderness. The task of infiltrating into this forbidding Court, of currying favour with Teutonic trulls, was a daunting one, but it had to be tackled. The Whigs, while much regretting the character of the monarch for whom they had contracted, could not afford to neglect the Court or the opportunities for patronage offered by Court appointments. With luck, there would be seemlier kings later.

Some very odd members of the Whig nobility held office in the new Court. George's first Master of the Horse was that Duke of Somerset who had declined to wait on the Papal nuncio in James II's day. He had grown grand to a point beyond eccentricity. When his second wife tapped him with a fan, he rebuked her, saying, 'Madam, my first wife was a Percy and she never took such a liberty.' For sitting in his presence, his daughter Charlotte was deprived of £20,000 of her inheritance. After two years at the Court of George I he withdrew to his estates, where he communicated with his servants by signs only. When he travelled, the roads were cleared of vulgar sightseers.*

Piquantly enough, the nobleman who became Lord Chamberlain in 1724 was the Duke of Grafton, grandson of one of Charles II's bastards. He discharged his duties with a lazy grandeur suited to his Stuart blood. Neither George I nor George II seems to have doubted his loyalty. He was corpulent and torpid, successfully concealing any intelligence he may have possessed.

Other Whig dukes held Court appointments which called for no great expenditure of effort. On paper they were members of the Government and occasionally they sat in a species of cabinet with the active politicians. It was the Secretaries of State who really transacted the nation's daily business. The ducal function was to exert influence and apply pressure as the party required.

A middle-aged German prince can hardly be blamed for inability to preside with *panache* over a court moulded by Plantagenets, strengthened by Tudors and embellished by Stuarts. To the new monarch, the system contained much that was preposterous. On the first morning after his arrival at St. James's Palace he looked out over the Park with its canal and was told that it was all his. Next morning, Lord Chetwynd, the Keeper of that park, sent him a fine brace of carp from the canal. The King was suitably appreciative, until a courtier explained that he was expected to give Lord Chetwynd's man five guineas for bringing him his own carp out of his own waters in his own park. The King's German suite soon devised their own ways of lining their pockets. Only the cook remained honest, and when he told the King he wished to resign because of the shocking waste in the kitchens he was advised to rob like the rest as the revenues would stand it.

* *Dictionary of National Biography*

Some of the ways in which officers and servants enriched themselves, legitimately, are shown in John Chamberlayne's *Magnae Britanniae Notitia* (1723). Every bishop, on promotion or translation, was required to pay fees to certain of the Household. Typical exactions were £10 to the Lord Chamberlain, £5 to the Groom of the Stole, £1 6s 8d to the Clerk of the Closet, £1 5s to the Master Cook, £1 to the King's Barber and £1 to the Gentleman of the Ewery. An archbishop was shaken down for double fees. Similarly the various ranks of noblemen, on the creation of their degrees of honour, paid financial fealty to chamberlains and bottle-washers. A less frequent windfall was to be expected when the King's eldest son was created Prince of Wales and Earl of Chester. On this occasion the Earl Marshal of England held out his hand for £30, the Sergeant Porter for £20, the Cook of the Privy Kitchen for £10. The latter two also received £6 and £2 respectively from the Prince in his capacity as Earl of Chester, but the Earl Marshal received nothing. It was perhaps thought unfitting that an earl should give a gratuity to another earl.

Chamberlayne also lists 'a bill of homage fees due to the King's servants from all Towns Corporate through which His Majesty shall pass.' These included £5 for Gentlemen Ushers, £1 10s for the Surveyor of the Ways and 10s for the King's Coachman. The total came to the fairly modest one of £37 6s but may well have caused grumbling among oppressed ratepayers.

George had never flattered himself that he was God's elect. The ritual of touching for the Evil had been revived by Anne, but George would have nothing to do with mumbo jumbo. Ceremony also he disliked; and his efforts to compromise between pomp and privacy had ludicrous results. The mob found vast amusement in the sight of the King's progresses by sedan chair. Six footmen would precede the royal chair, which was flanked on each side by six Yeomen of the Guard, and bringing up the rear would be the two jealous concubines each in her chair with attendants. It was a spectacle which inspired not only catcalls but more dangerous forms of derision.

The Stuarts in their heyday had dined in public with great lords kneeling to offer them meat and wine, or to wash and dry their sticky fingers; and there had been more great lords to dress and undress them. The new King preferred to dine in private, served by his own retainers, and to let his tame Turks pass his clothes. There were times when domestic routine was irritatingly interrupted. On the first Ash Wednesday after George's accession, as the Prince of Wales (later George II) was sitting down to supper, a courtier entered and with great solemnity imitated the crowing of a cock, after which he announced that it was ten o'clock. The Prince, convinced that he was the victim of a tasteless practical joke, was ready to exact retribution, but it was explained to him that this was a Court custom dating from the Plantagenets. The King's Cock and Cryer was charged with crowing the hours during Lent, the intention being 'to remind wicked sinners of the august effect the third crowing of the cock had on the guilty apostle St Peter.'* This happy custom, which is ill-documented, may or may not have been introduced by a royal confessor.

The only art which George can be said to have fostered is music. Handel had served in his entourage in Hanover but had strayed to the fold of Queen Anne, who paid him £200 a year. When George came to the English throne the truant Handel was nervous about showing up, but an old Hanover ally is said to have devised a scheme by which the King, in the course of a water party on the Thames, was serenaded by Handel's music from a following barge. Whether or not this is true, the composer came back into favour. The King often went to the opera, but preferred to sit quietly at the back of an ordinary box, with one of his mistresses and perhaps an illegitimate daughter. Sometimes he attended command performances of plays at Hampton Court.

It was the least endearing characteristic of the Hanoverians that fathers and their first-born sons heartily detested each other. George loathed, not only his son but his son's wife Caroline of Anspach ('cette diablesse'). The family split wide open in 1718, after a row at a christening. The Prince and Princess were turned out of St James's and were virtually homeless, their children being retained in the Palace by the King. They then took Leicester House and conceived a diabolical revenge: they would make themselves popular. Thanks to

* *Gentleman's Magazine,* 1785. See also Dr. J. Doran's *History of Court Fools*

Caroline they succeeded, holding a profusion of drawing-rooms and receptions and attracting the gayer elements of society. The King was incensed and let it be known, not only in his capital but in the capitals of other nations, that those who attended his son's court need not expect to be received at St James's. Inevitably, the *verboten* court at Leicester House became the resort of the Opposition, who were by no means ashamed to exacerbate a private quarrel. Pitting sons against fathers was just as much fun as launching mistresses and minions. At length the estrangement became such an open scandal that the Whigs forced a reconciliation, but when King and Prince appeared under the same roof the atmosphere was still tense, and the rival groups of courtiers faced each other as if in battle array.

Caroline's ladies were a sprightly group whose apartments attracted such wits as Pope, Gay and Swift. Among the Prince's gentlemen were Lord Chesterfield and Lord Hervey. The maids of honour flirted much and, like modern débutantes, had their own slang, which included words like frizelation and dangleation. Among them were Mary Bellenden, who was regarded as the best-looking; Mary Lepell, witty and graceful, who married Lord Hervey and so disillusioned him that he described marriage as a 'shining stink'; and Mrs Henrietta Howard, who became the Prince's mistress. The Prince at one time set his cap at the giddy Miss Bellenden, but seems to have been at a loss to know how to conduct the attack. One evening, sitting beside her, he began to count his money, which the lady regarded either as an insult or an inexcusable *gaucherie*. Leaping up, she capsized the Prince and his funds, and made her escape while he was picking up the coins. Secretly, Miss Bellenden married a Colonel Campbell, and the Prince never forgot or forgave. Her correspondence, which was not meant to be preserved, gives a glimpse of the gamy language used by a Court beauty of the period.* Writing to Mrs Howard, she said: 'I now take my leave; only adding one piece of advice, which is, take the utmost care of your ——, for I left all the —— in London in danger.' Comments her editor, John Wilson Croker; 'What the danger was to which any part of the female person was at this time more particularly exposed

† Included in *Letters of Henrietta, Countess of Suffolk*

history does not inform us.' Another time she wrote from Bath to say that she had just paid a bill 'as long as my arm and as broad as my ——.' This time Mr. Croker expresses the hope that Miss Bellenden's allusion will escape the generality of readers; 'she, and the age she lived in, mistook these indelicacies for wit.' Wedlock failed to sober Mary Bellenden, who still palpitated for a bit of scandal. After four years absence from Court she wrote to Mrs Howard to enquire whether any of the maids were 'like to lose what they are weary of', and adding, 'Pray God they do not stay with you till my son is old enough to —— them all.' This time the editor forbears from comment. Horace Walpole says that the author of these letters was regarded by her friends as the most perfect creature they had ever known.

Mary Lepell enjoyed a distinction unique among maids of honour: she had held from birth a cornetcy in her father's regiment. It took the military authorities more than 20 years to decide that this arrangement was not in the best interests of the service. Happily Mary had friends who saw no reason why she should be struck from the public payroll because of a mere quibble; Lord Sunderland arranged with the King that she should draw a pension instead. It is fair to say that if cavalry commissions had to be given to women, the maids of honour were probably best qualified to hold them. They were better riders than many who called themselves cornets, and risked their necks almost daily in the hunting field.

In the gardens of Hampton Court, by moonlight, Mary Lepell and Mary Bellenden unburdened themselves to Pope. In a letter he says: 'We all agreed that the life of a maid of honour was of all things the most miserable and wished that every woman who envied it had a specimen of it. To eat Westphalia ham in a morning; ride over hedges and ditches on borrowed hacks; come home in the heat of the day in a fever and (what is worse a hundred times) with a red mark on the forehead from an uneasy hat—all this may qualify them to make excellent wives for fox hunters. As soon as they wipe off the sweat of the day they must simper an hour and catch cold in the Princess's apartments; from thence (as Shakespeare has it) to dinner, with what appetite they may, and after that, until midnight, work, walk or think as they please. I can easily believe no lone house in Wales with a mountain and a rookery is more contemplative than this Court: as a proof of it I need only tell you that Miss Lepell walked with me three or four hours by moonlight and we met no creature of any quality but the King, who gave audience to the Vice-Chamberlain, all alone, under the garden wall.'

Mrs Howard had been in the Princess of Wales's employment some ten years before the Prince became noticeably involved with her. According to Horace Walpole, her propriety and decency were such that her friends 'affected to suppose' that her relations with the Prince were platonic. Her husband, as Groom of the Bedchamber to the King, was in an invidious position once the two courts became estranged. An obstreperous cuckold, he tried to recover his wife by legal and ecclesiastical process and then threatened to kidnap her from her carriage. For a while she was virtually a palace prisoner. It would have made an agreeable scandal if an angry subject had raided a royal home to rescue his spouse from a state of adultery. Walpole says that, eventually, the husband was bought off for £1200, but this has been disputed.

George I died in 1727, having made not the least effort to achieve popularity. 'In private life,' as Lady Mary Wortley Montagu has testified, 'he would have been an honest blockhead.' His Court had been one in which dullness was enlivened only by domestic scandal. And it was already cocooned in corruption.

18

'*J'aurai Des Maîtresses*'

IF cash could have produced taste and magnificence, the Court of George II should have been a dazzling one. Both political parties were anxious to please him, and Parliament authorised him an annual income of £800,000, with £100,000 for the Queen. The investment turned out to be an unrewarding one. Although, in youth, George had shown signs of being an Anglophile, he could not be bribed out of a belief that all wit and wisdom, beauty and loyalty resided in Hanover. His habit, even in his own family, was to snap and snub.

The Court was run on severely economical lines. Sir Robert Walpole grumbled that never had there been less to be got and more to be done. His only gift from the King was a flawed diamond. No mistresses were paid more than the minimum wages of sin. Occasionally the King allowed a glimpse of himself at Sunday dinner at St James's. A young lady who attended a Court reception in 1728 reported as follows:

'We had ogling and tweezing and whispering and glancing; no eating or drinking, or laughing and dancing; there was standing and walking and fine ladies' airs; no smart repartee and not one word of prayers.'*

The young lady was Mrs Pendarves, later Mrs Delany, whom Burke was to describe as the finest bred woman in the world.

After a shaky start, the method of government was worked out thus: Walpole bought his men and nominated them to the Queen and the Queen recommended them to the King, who pretended that he had chosen them. Between them, the shrewd Queen and her shrewder Prime Minister, whose industry was as gigantic as his belly, held almost complete power. They shared a perfect mutual understanding, even if at times they

---

* Lady Llanover (ed.) *Life and Correspondence of Mrs. Delany*

detested each other. The King had one thing in common with Charles II: he did not wish the world to think that he was dependent in any way on his wife. Caroline therefore took great pains to save his face. But the public was not deceived:

> You may strut, dapper George, but 'twill all be in vain.
> We know 'tis Queen Caroline, not you, that reign.

Walpole's opponents made the mistake of trying to reach the King through his mistress, Mrs Howard, now Countess of Suffolk. They wasted their time, for she had no influence. Her published letters show some candid glimpses of the effrontery with which posts were solicited.* Mrs Pitt, mother of the great Chatham, wrote to enquire whether there was any chance of her brother being offered a Bedchamber vacancy, adding 'if you think it proper (as he has been informed it is usual to make presents on such occasions) I will bring you a thousand guineas to dispose of to whoever is proper, but desire his name not to be used in vain.' Such was the belief in the Countess's influence that when Admiral Sir John Jennings, Governor of Greenwich Hospital, found himself unable to attend Court through infirmity, he did not send his apologies through the usual Service channels but through the boudoir of the Countess of Suffolk.

As a go-between, the Countess was eclipsed by the Baroness Sundon, who held an inferior appointment in the Queen's Bedchamber. This decorous lady held aloof from the more skittish and disreputable elements of the Court and had more influence with the Queen than the Countess of Suffolk had with the King. Walpole often chafed at her 'interference.' She was addressed in flattering terms by nobles with axes to grind and by clerics in search of the preferment which Walpole grudged them. Also she was on good terms with such men of letters as Steele, who on the Hanoverian succession had found himself Surveyor of the Stables at Hampton Court. Lord Tyrconnel asked her to try to obtain the post of Poet Laureate for Richard Savage, who not long before had been preserved, by the intercession of the Countess of Hertford, from the death penalty for murder. The Duke of Grafton, as Lord Chamberlain, preferred to give the post to Colley Cibber. To show he

* *Letters of Henrietta, Countess of Suffolk*

had no hard feelings, Savage wrote a birthday ode for the Queen and was paid £50 a year for his pains. A kinsman of Lady Sundon, the Bishop of Killala, wrote from Dublin to say, among other things, that a student of that city faced execution for a fatal assault. 'As nobody can confer a favour with a better grace than His Majesty, you are the best judge whether you will think it proper to apprise him of it.'* It is difficult to know which is the more remarkable: that a Bedchamber woman should have a life thus dropped in her hands, or that a Bishop should regard his duties to humanity as sufficiently discharged by mentioning such a matter in the course of a rambling letter to a female courtier. It was not unusual for Lady Sundon to receive requests for advice on etiquette. The Countess of Berkshire had learned that the Queen proposed to drop in on her for a dish of coffee and was uncertain what formalities should be observed. Even Kielmansegge begged a favour, describing herself, not inaccurately, as 'a dull and silly woman.' Another correspondent asked for assistance in obtaining apartments at Somerset House; another in finding a husband for a young lady; another sought the modest appointment of rocker in the royal nursery. Those who were crude enough to send money with their applications were rebuffed, but Lady Sundon did not decline all gifts. She was said by Horace Walpole to have been presented with diamond ear-rings for procuring the Earl of Pomfret the post of Master of the Horse (among his first acts was to dismiss one of the Queen's chairmen for being on 'too good an understanding with highwaymen'). The ear-rings were worn by Lady Sundon at the house of the Duchess of Marlborough, who exclaimed: 'How can the woman have the impudence to go about in that bribe?' Lady Mary Wortley Montagu replied: 'Madam, how can people know where wine is to be sold unless there is a sign hung out?' The Bishop of Killala, on becoming Bishop of Cork, sent Lady Sundon a gift of rather indifferent linen and some bottles of usquebaugh sealed with the figure of St Patrick in black wax. It is only fair to say that Lady Sundon often did favours with no expectation of reward.

Nowhere is the background to the reign described with more feline wit than in the pages of the exquisite Lord Hervey, who

* K. Thomson (ed.) *Memoirs of Viscountess Sundon*

served as Vice-Chamberlain. In this capacity he had nothing to do, once he had made up his face, but 'carry candles and set chairs.' His chosen function was that of gossip-bearer to the Queen, of whom he saw far more than did Walpole. He was, of course, Walpole's man, and dutifully carried the gossip of the Court back to the Minister. When Walpole's crudity antagonised the Queen, Hervey's wicked urbanity won her over to his master's views. He might spend many hours of the day in her company, if not in the Bedchamber then at the breakfast table or in the hunting chaise. Of the men in Caroline's life, two were bears and one was a butterfly.

The King does not seem to have resented Hervey's attendance on his Queen. He thought it unseemly, however, for Hervey to write verses; such exercises should be left to 'little Mr Pope.' George had a notorious aversion to 'bainting, blays and boetry' and could not understand the Queen's interest in the intellectuals of the day. He showed enthusiasm for the fashion of masquerades, as fostered by John James Heidegger, a Swiss of breath-taking ugliness whom he made Master of the Revels. These functions offered the Court an ever-welcome opportunity of dressing up. It was not unusual for the King to find himself in the company of splendidly attired monarchs of an older day and to receive curtseys from a number of Mary Stuarts. By their nature, masquerades became a cover for wanton behaviour. Sultans were seen making love to nuns and not all the nuns were female. Heidegger was denounced by a Middlesex jury as the source of all vice and immorality. In an effort to placate prudish opinion, masquerades were renamed ridottos, as a suspect night haunt acquires respectability by changing its name. One of the more memorable masquerades of the reign was that given by the Venetian Ambassador in 1749, when Elizabeth Chudleigh, then maid of honour to the Princess of Wales, appeared in flesh-coloured, flesh-tight silk as Iphigenia. The Princess threw a veil over her and the other maids were so affronted that they cut her. Many guests were under the impression that she appeared naked, as were the news writers.

Apart from masquerades, the King's enthusiasms embraced gambling, soldiering and hunting (but he mocked the Duke of Grafton for hurling his twenty stone about the countryside in pursuit of such a puny creature as a fox). Often, he would set aside a night's winnings for the benefit of an indigent servant and once he won £1000 for the new foundling hospital. In one of his gouty periods he heard that his subjects were wagering ten guineas to a hundred that he would not live longer than twelve months. He at once paid 50 guineas for five risks. Never, he said a year later, had he pocketed 500 guineas with greater pleasure. When it was known that the King proposed to lead his soldiers on the Continent, underwriters offered to pay four times the stake money if he failed to return.

The King's journey to the wars—he was the last British sovereign to lead his men in battle—provided employment for a group of palace servants whose posts had long been regarded as a sinecure: the six Yeomen Hangers and two Yeomen Bedgoers. These took care of all the royal baggage and put up the King's bed each night on the road. They were also prepared to pitch the royal tent if necessary. At Dettingen the King's exploits, though militarily of no great account, temporarily brightened his reputation at home. Among the virtues of the first two Georges, bravery is the first that springs to mind.

The manners of the Court took on little *finesse* from the coarse and peppery King. At drawing-rooms he could be affable, especially towards those ladies who were good-looking. But he was incapable of hiding his feelings. When really angry he would kick his hat or wig about the room. He also kicked the quack Joshua Ward who straightened his dislocated thumb with a sharp jerk, but rewarded him royally afterwards. If he disapproved of the politicians he was called upon to decorate he did not hesitate to show it. He threw the ribbon of the Garter across one nobleman, muttering angrily, then turned his back on him.

If the King's manners lacked *finesse*, so did those of some of his male subjects. Lord Chesterfield, writing to his son, says: 'How many men have I seen here, who, after having had the full benefit of an English education, first at school and then at the university, when they have been presented to the King, did not know whether they stood upon their heads or their heels! If the King spoke to them they were annihilated; they trembled, endeavoured to put their hands in their pockets, and missed them, let their hats fall, and were ashamed to take them up; and, in short, put themselves in every attitude but the right, that is, the easy and natural one. The characteristic of the well-bred man is, to converse with his inferiors without insolence, and with his superiors with respect and with ease. He talks to kings without concern; he trifles with women of the first condition, with familiarity, gaiety, but respect . . .'

Twice, the Court of George II was convulsed by disputes in which faction found it convenient to march under the banners of art. The first of these storms broke over the head of the poet John Gay, who had hovered about George and Caroline when they were Prince and Princess of Wales. In the hope of obtaining favour he had cultivated the Countess of Suffolk, with no success, and had written flattering verses about Caroline, dropping the crudest of hints as to his expectations. He had also dedicated his *Fables* to a royal duke. It was a difficult period for writers, for Walpole's idea of literary patronage was to distribute bribes up and down Grub Street. On George II's accession, Caroline offered Gay the post of Gentleman Usher to the infant Princess Louisa, a sinecure worth £200 a year. A man of less conceit would have jumped at it, but Gay chose to regard the offer as an insult. Swift sided with him:

> Say, had the Court no better place to choose
> For thee, than make a dry-nurse of thy Muse?
> How cheaply had thy liberty been sold
> To squire a royal girl of two years old. . .

In the following year *The Beggar's Opera* was produced, and Gay was both rich and famous. The Court, fancying itself mocked, was displeased. When Gay sent the script of his next opera, *Polly*, to the Lord Chamberlain he received a sharp shock: the work, he was informed, was on no account to be produced. The Lord Chamberlain's orders came direct from the King. Behind this decision, probably, was Walpole, who was a main target of abuse in the new work. At this point, the Tories stepped in. Gay was assured by friends both old and new that the Lord Chamberlain's ban was a disgrace and that he ought to retaliate by publishing the opera in book form. The Opposition made fine sport out of canvassing for subscribers. Gay was a *protégé* of the beautiful, eccentric Duchess of Queensberry, a lady who once turned up at a Court drawing-room wearing an apron and, on being asked to remove it, threw it in the face of a lord in waiting. The Duchess invited subscriptions within the Court itself, and told the King she had hopes of securing a contribution from him, even offering to read the play to him in his Closet. The King laughed it off, but next day the Duchess received a visit from the Vice-Chamberlain who informed her that she was forbidden the Court until further notice. She acknowledged the command in a saucy letter to her sovereign, saying she thought it would have been 'the highest compliment that I could pay the King to endeavour to support truth and innocence in his house.' This letter she showed to the Vice-Chamberlain, who winced and asked her to write another one. When he read the second letter he decided to accept the first.

In sympathy with his Duchess, the Duke of Queensberry handed in his resignation as Vice-Admiral of Scotland. The episode created wild excitement. Swift chuckled mischievously, saying that in one bound Gay had become 'one of the obstructions to the peace of Europe.' As a martyr, the poet did very well, for the publication of *Polly* brought him far more than he could have made out of its stage presentation; but he was expelled from the Whitehall apartments which he had long occupied.

The other storm broke over Handel. Secure, as he felt, in the royal favour, the composer had been taking an arbitrary attitude towards his public, giving them the kind of music he thought was good for them. Many of the nobility preferred the new Italian style of opera, and the Prince of Wales, determined not to like what his father liked, sided with them. An open break came in 1733 when an Italian *maestro* quarrelled with Handel and was set up by his coroneted supporters in a rival opera house in Lincoln's Inn Fields. Here the best singers in Europe were engaged and the prospects for Handel soon looked bleak. Loyally, the King and Queen sat almost alone in the freezing Haymarket Theatre listening to the works of their favourite. On one such occasion Lord Chesterfield is said to have slipped out quietly, not wishing it to be thought that he was intruding on the royal privacy. The Princess Royal supported the King, remarking sarcastically that the nobility would soon be playing in their ermine and coronets in the orchestra at Lincoln's Inn Fields. When the strife was at its height, Opposition hostesses took good care to arrange card parties and other functions to clash with Handel's oratorio days. Even *The Messiah* was boycotted. The King's view was that nothing like this could have happened in Hanover. 'He did not think setting oneself at the head of a faction of fiddlers a very honourable employment for people of quality or the ruin of one poor fellow so generous or good-natured a scheme as to do much honour to the undertakers, whether they succeeded or not.' In fact, the King contributed actively to Handel's ruin. The taste of the Prince of Wales swung back to Handel and the King refused to be seen in the same theatre as his son. Handel went bankrupt, but came back strongly a few years later.

Frederick, Prince of Wales was a vexation to his parents for most of his life. To show what he thought of his son, the King proposed to give him only £50,000 a year, instead of the £100,000 which he himself had enjoyed before his accession. Caroline called the Prince an ass, a liar and a monster, and wished him in hell. As to his morals, she had no illusions. As to his sexual potency, she had the gravest doubts. He was quite capable, in her opinion, of persuading someone else to beget his heir (later in the century, young men advertised in the newspapers offering to perform such services).

The Queen's suspicions were powerfully reinforced when Frederick's princess, Augusta of Saxe-Gotha, was brought to bed in furtive circumstances well calculated to start another warming pan legend. The *accouchement* was as undignified as any in royal annals. For his own mysterious reasons, the Prince smuggled his wife at the last minute from Hampton Court to St James's, where the necessary equipment had to be borrowed or improvised. In her distress, the Princess had the ministrations of the Prince's ex-mistress, Lady Archibald Hamilton, who was one of her attendants. The King sent his son a thundering rebuke and ordered him and the Princess to leave St James's as soon as Nature permitted. With a fine sense of irony, they eventually made their home at Leicester House, where the King, as Prince of Wales, had held his forbidden court in the shadow of his father's wrath. In the next reign the pattern would be repeated, the only difference being that the scene of the son's exile would be Carlton House.

Frederick and Augusta were the parents of George III, whose birth in 1738 also created a domestic crisis. He was premature and not expected to live, but the gardener's wife hired to suckle him was more optimistic. She took the babe to bed with her, an act which was considered disrespectful to a prince, however young. When protests were made, the nurse told the family they could suckle the child among themselves. The objections were withdrawn.

Memoirs of the reign show that the ceremony of putting princes and princesses publicly to bed on their nuptial night was still gloatingly observed. The bridegroom, having been ritually disrobed, would be marched into the bedchamber in his nightshirt or dressing-gown, and with a long white lace cap on his head. Then he would climb into the bed and sit beside his bride, in her rich *négligée*, while the quality came in to admire them. If photography had been invented, doubtless they would have been photographed. Macabre indeed was the scene when the Princess Royal married the Prince of Orange. He was a hunchback and his nightgown did nothing to flatter him. Caroline told Hervey that when she saw this monster enter her daughter's bed she nearly fainted. The Princess doted on her bridegroom and made 'prodigious court' to him. She assured the King that she would have married him if he had been a baboon. 'Well, then, there is baboon enough for you,' said her father. Frederick and Augusta also went through the bedding ordeal, the King condescending so far as to help his son into his nightshirt.

Even when all allowances are made for the morals of the day, the example of family life set by the Court was less than felicitous. The King indulged in gallantries because he thought they were expected of a sovereign and a gentleman. To his credit it must be said that his mistresses were not suffered to frolic in his coffers or appoint his bishops; they filled a purely utilitarian role. Possibly the best-remembered picture of the King is of a portly, pop-eyed figure pacing the drawing-room of an evening, watch in hand, waiting for nine o'clock. That was the hour when, as everyone knew, he called on the Countess of Suffolk.

Caroline accepted her husband's extra-marital exercises as inevitable. As mistresses went, the Countess of Suffolk was discreet, not excessively ambitious and not unduly greedy. Caroline was anxious to retain her as long as possible. She could always be disciplined or humiliated, if necessary, by being given disagreeable duties in the Bedchamber. Sometimes the Countess suspected that the Queen was picking on her. There was bickering about the right way to hold a basin. When she first became Lady of the Bedchamber the Countess had asked Dr Arbuthnot to enquire of Lady Masham the details of Bedchamber etiquette as practised in the days of Queen Anne. Lady Masham duly explained whose duty it was to hand the Queen her shift, to put on her shoes and gloves, to give her her fan, and who should be permitted to look on when she washed her hands.

That other problem of Queen Anne's day—where and when the chaplain should pray during the royal toilet—was never satisfactorily settled. Caroline directed that prayers should be said in an outer room, on receipt of a signal from one of the Bedchamber women. The chaplain then did his best in a room which contained a large painting of a naked Venus.

The Countess of Suffolk's charms began to fade and she grew increasingly deaf. By 1734 the King was visibly bored with her and she withdrew to a villa at Twickenham, leaving him no one with whom to converse except the members of his own family. They found him tiresome. The Princess Royal expressed the wish that he would find another mistress and stop annoying her mother. On a visit to Germany, in 1735, he sighted a delectable new quarry in the person of Madame Walmoden and he went to much trouble, in his letters to the Queen, to describe the stages in his conquest of her. It seemed the most natural thing in the world for him to give his wife the details. When this liaison became known, Sir Robert Walpole urged the Queen to invite Madame Walmoden to Britain. The King's absences were not only disrupting the conduct of the nation's business but were inspiring virulent ballads and demonstrations at his expense.

Finally he returned, and as if to make amends held an un-usually large drawing-room, kissing his way through it as fast as he could without saying a word. He appeared to forget Madame Walmoden for a while. Instead, Lady Deloraine, governess of his younger children, caught his eye and he spent much time 'talking bawdy' to her. Soon Lady Deloraine was claiming credit for keeping the King in Britain.

Then, in 1737, Caroline died, not before urging the King to marry again. His sense of propriety rose through his grief and he protested, '*Non, j'aurai des maîtresses.*' To this the Queen wearily said, '*Ah, mon Dieu, cela n'empêche pas.*'* She had been the chief ornament of the Court, which now lost such modest elegance and distinction as it had possessed.

Caroline was not long dead before Walpole, anxious as always to ease the task of government, was urging the princesses to put suitable women in their father's way. Not for the first time they were thoroughly shocked by the Prime Minister's crudity. By now Lady Deloraine, whom Walpole distrusted, was boasting to the princesses about their father's interest in her. She came to grief, not through a slip of the tongue, but by an act of horseplay. At a game of cards one of the royal children pulled the chair from under her. It was the sort of joke warranted to amuse the King, who laughed heartily. She took her revenge by pulling the chair from under him. After this breach of etiquette, as one writer has described it, Lady Deloraine's interest, never great, steeply declined.

Madame Walmoden duly came to Britain, was presented at Court and became Countess of Yarmouth. It is, perhaps, superfluous to say that she drew revenues from Ireland. She, too, played cards with the King's daughters, but nobody pulled the chair from under her. The Opposition sounded her out and found her an empty vessel.

None of the mistresses took Caroline's place in the King's affections. George had loved his Queen deeply, in his fashion.

It was a period which one would prefer to leave on a more fragrant note. The Georges perfumed their palaces with a very refined and exclusive brand of rose water, distilled in Germany, whence (as they insisted to the end) came all the felicities of life. A former maid of honour, writing of the early years of

* Lord Hervey: *Memoirs*

George V's reign, said that this perfume was still used in all the royal homes.*

Another Georgian innovation, the abolition of finger bowls at Court, lasted until our own times. It had become a habit among secret Jacobite supporters to pass their wine glasses surreptitiously over their finger bowls before drinking the royal toast. By this sleight they persuaded themselves that they were drinking to the King over the water. Edward VII, confident that the Jacobite threat had passed, caused finger bowls to be restored.

* Katharine Villiers: *Memoirs of a Maid of Honour*

19

Sinecures for M.P.s

G EORGE III had a taste for political corruption equalled only by his distaste for moral slackness. The result was a Court which reeked of jobbery even as it blushed with respectability.

The King, who came to the Throne at the age of 22, having already sown his one wild oat, was entitled to call himself an Englishman, and did. He had been brought up by his devious parents, Frederick and Augusta, in an atmosphere of plotting and family rancour. He was under the influence of his Groom of the Stole, Lord Bute, who initiated him in the technique of political bribery. Nobody could have foreseen that this young monarch would develop strong autocratic ambitions, that he would choose to fight the Whigs by their own dirty methods and put his personal nominees—the 'King's friends'—into every appointment within his enormous patronage. Equally nobody could have foreseen that he would shock society by siring fifteen legitimate children and remaining obstinately faithful to his Queen. Here was a king who, instead of planting mistresses in his Queen's household, contented himself with planting politicians.

Queen Charlotte had nothing frivolous about her. She had been recommended to the King largely on the strength of a confidential report by Colonel (later General) David Graeme, a courtier of elegant and fascinating manners and with 'all the knick-knackery of fashion about him.' On the instructions of the King's mother, he had taken the waters and played lotto at various Continental courts, listening to such gossip as he could stimulate about the personal qualities of the various eligible Protestant princesses. He reported moderately on Charlotte's personal charms and, in the event, George was a little disappointed on first meeting her. But he made no complaint. Nor did Charlotte.

William Hickey has left a merry account of the Coronation. He was a boy in his father's party which occupied one of the 'nunneries' at the top of the great columns supporting the Abbey roof. This eyrie had cost fifty guineas to hire, so Hickey *père* felt the family had a right to make themselves at home. The day before the ceremony he sent in a quantity of cold veal, ham, tongue, meat pies, wines and liqueurs, and during the long hours of waiting the party tucked into this feast, which was prepared by two servants. When the Archbishop was preaching his sermon, not all the spectators in the various 'nunneries' could hear, so they continued eating. 'The general clattering of knives, forks, plates and glasses that ensued produced a most ridiculous effect and a universal burst of laughter followed.'* Even at Coronations in our own day, the nobility have not been too shy to eat and drink in Westminster Abbey.

The unseemly scene at his anointing may have rankled in the mind of the young King, who made it clear that State ceremonial must be fitly conducted and all traditional observances kept up. 'I will have no innovations in my time,' he said. It was not long before he had an opportunity to show his displeasure at ill-conduct in his presence. There was a Court ball at which the Russian, French, Spanish and Imperial Ambassadors, jealous as ever of their precedence, became involved in a seating squabble in the presence of ladies, pushing and protesting with all the subtlety of country bumpkins trying to sit beside a pretty dairymaid. The affair resulted in the French Ambassador challenging the Russian to a duel on the way home, but honour could not be satisfied because the gates of St James's Park were locked. Next morning the King heard of the challenge, forbade the encounter, and directed through the Lord Chamberlain that in future ambassadors should not claim precedence at balls.†

Firm action like this was welcome, for the Court was heartily sick of the pretensions of ambassadors. But George's idea of royal ceremonial proved to be a shade too domesticated for some of his nobility. Came the day when the great men of the

---

* *Memoirs of William Hickey*
† J. H. Jesse: *Memoirs of the Life of George III*

land were called upon to abase themselves in front of a dais ornately laden with the royal children. At the head of the group was the seven-year-old Prince of Wales, in scarlet and gold, complete with Garter; beside him his six-year-old brother Frederick, Bishop of Osnaburg, in blue and gold, wearing the insignia of the Bath; four-year-old William and two-year-old Edward wearing Roman togas; and the three-year-old Princess Royal sitting on a sofa. Only one-year-old Augusta was missing. The nobility never forgot this charade, nor did the caricaturists.

The palaces of Windsor, St James's and Hampton Court, however well suited to ceremonial, were ill-adapted to the needs of a philoprogenitive king. In 1761 George bought Buckingham House, later to become Buckingham Palace, to serve as the royal married quarters. As the family grew up they spent a good deal of time in rural domesticity at Kew, where the King's mother earned the gratitude of posterity by building up the botanical gardens. At Windsor the problem of billeting a quiverful of young princes and princesses, with their attendants, in the straggling, dilapidated castle was a harassing one. To ma¹e the rounds of his family, the doting father had to climb cold turrets and cross wet courtyards. Major rebuilding was called for, but the political game ran away with all the available funds.

What the first two Georges did with their money was always something of a mystery. Some of it went on bribery, and much no doubt towards improving the delights of Herrenhausen. The third George, though his table was frugality itself, though he maintained no mistresses, though he abjured pomp and pageantry, lived from hand to mouth and his servants and tradesmen perpetually clamoured for their pay. An income of £800,000 was inadequate to run the royal palaces and the King's own political party at the same time.

The establishment which sustained this pinchpenny domesticity was a vast, patched-up, ramshackle affair designed for a lustier day. Every year it grew less suited to a life of elegance, but in the multiplicity of its useless and redundant appointments it was as splendidly adapted for political corruption as for private peculation. The offices are to be found set out in

such works as John Chamberlayne's *Magnae Britanniae Notitia*,
the *Court and City Register* and *Court and City Kalendar*. It does
not follow that the three great officers of the Household—the
Lord Steward, the Lord Chamberlain and the Master of the
Horse—necessarily supplied the compilers with the full or
correct lists of office holders, or with the correct salaries. The
pages of these works of reference are full of maddening in-
consistencies, making accurate analysis almost impossible, yet
they offer a useful broad picture of a *ménage*, sprawling and
anachronistic, in which Groom of the Stole, Rat Catcher,
Portrait Painter and Page of the Back Stairs found themselves
on a common pay-roll.

The relative status of those who regulated work, revelry,
river transport, recreation, arts, ceremonial, dress and blood
sports may be roughly deduced from a survey of those who
were styled Master. At the foot of the scale, with salaries of
£100, were the Master of the Barges and the Master of the
Revels (the latter had a yeoman to assist him). The Master
of the Tennis Court received £132 13s 4d. A representative
rate for the arts was £200, as paid to the Master of the Musick.
Frequently the post of Master of the Mechanicks appeared as
unsalaried, but once it was occupied at £200 by a gentleman
with the letters D.D., F.R.S. after his name. Comfortably above
the arts came the dignities, in the persons of the Master of
the Ceremonies, at £300, and the Master of the Jewel Office,
at £450. At the top of the scale were such noblemen's appointments as Master of the Great Wardrobe, at anything from
£800 to £2000, and Master of the Horse, at £1266 13s 4d.
The plum posts (though they were expensive to maintain)
were those of Master of the Harriers, at £2000, and Master
of the Buck Hounds, at £2341.

A random dipping into the lists suggests that many minor
appointments were created, abolished, reintroduced and
abolished again, but these vicissitudes may be due to careless-
ness or inconsistency on the part of the compiler or to a lack
of assistance received at Court. One year would be listed a
Keeper of the Lions, Lionesses and Leopards in the Tower;
the next, a Surveyor of His Majesty's Revenues Arising by
Fines, Forgetfulness and Sums of Money called Greenwax
Money. Another year the Keeper of the Orchard Gate would

achieve a mention, along with the Porter of the Outward Port of His Majesty's Castle at Windsor. Next year it would be the turn of the Carrier of All His Majesty's Letters and Despatches Between His Court or Palace of Residence and the Post Office; or of six Table Deckers, charged with decking the tables of the Lords and Ladies of the Bedchamber, the Women of the Bedchamber, the Gentlemen Waiters, the Officers of the Guard and the Chaplains; or of the Keeper of the Ice House, the Distiller of Milk Water, the Keeper of the Fire Buckets, the Heater of Water for the Horses, the Pumper at the Mews, the Cistern Cleaner, the Water Engine Turner and the Deliverer of Greens.

The list of tradesmen in the royal service—Sedan Chair Maker, Pin-Maker, Card-Maker, Spatterdash-Maker, Fish-Hook Maker and so on—is at first sight exhaustive but contains notable omissions. One of the busiest functionaries in a royal palace was the bug-exterminator, but while Rat-Catcher and Mole-Taker were listed, Bug-Taker was not. In the *Public Advertiser* of 1775 Andrew Cooke, of Holborn Hill, described how, over a period of 20 years, he had 'cured 16,000 beds with great applause,' and expressed indignation at the pretensions of a rival who styled himself 'Bug Destroyer to His Majesty.' Cooke himself claimed to have operated successfully in many apartments of the King's Palace.

Among the best-paid servants were the laundry staffs, but it may be that they had heavy expenses to meet. A Body Laundress in 1761 was paid £400, equal to the combined salaries of a Historiographer, a Master Huntsman, a Groom of the Confectionery and the Embellisher of Letters to the Eastern Princes. In 1777 a Sempstress and Starcher was also paid £400. In the royal chapels it was more profitable to wash surplices than to save souls. The Confessor of the Royal Household was paid £36 10s, less than a Lutenist at £41 10s. An Organ Blower at £20 was better off than a Bellringer at £15, but the Tuner of the Regalls received £56. One Dr Nares was paid £24 per head for boarding ten children and £80 for teaching them. Organists and composers received twice the emoluments of priests in ordinary; the latter were paid the same rate (£73) as the Gentlemen of the Chapel who had to listen to them. In addition to the King's own chapel there were

Lutheran, Dutch and French chapels with their own preachers, readers, deputies, sextons and porters.

At all times the medical establishment seemed more than adequate for the shedding of the royal blood or the irrigation of the royal gut. There were suitable financial distinctions between physicians, surgeons and apothecaries, and also between those who attended the Household and those who attended the Person. George III's establishment for 1761 shows an anatomist in the person of Nathanael St André, who in 1726 had made a fool of himself by certifying that, in his presence, Mary Tofts of Godalming had given birth to two rabbits or portions thereof.

Other members of the royal family had their separate establishments, each of which resembled the King's Household in miniature. An adult Prince of Wales might have a hundred officers and servants on strength. He would need four gentlemen, half a dozen grooms and four pages to see him to bed the year round. Besides a Chancellor, a Master of the Horse, Equerries and so forth he would require an Attorney-General, a Solicitor-General, two 'counsel learned in the law' and a whole string of watermen. An infant Prince of Wales, as in 1763, would require a governess, a sub-governess, a dry nurse, a wet nurse, a necessary woman and two rockers. In accordance, no doubt, with the law of supply and demand, the wet nurse, at £200, was paid £50 more than the dry nurse. Since there was a lingering suspicion that the morals of a nurse might be imbibed along with her milk it was important that she should be carefully selected, and virtue in this respect may well have claimed its reward.

The reward seems, indeed, to have lasted long beyond the period of lactation, for in 1777 nine wet nurses were listed in the *Court and City Register* as drawing £200 a year in respect of past professional services to specified princes and princesses. Ranking above this bountiful band in the nursery was the sprightly Miss Peggy Planta, the English teacher, who was paid only £100 and may well have felt that the maiden state was financially unprofitable.

Dowager princesses and royal dukes had their full complements of dignitaries, even to bargemasters and watermen. The Duke of Cumberland in the 1760s had an establishment noticeably strong in gamekeepers, huntsmen, footmen, grooms and rough riders, but including also a painter, a draughtsman, a limner, a confectioner, a sempstress and a necessary woman. In the establishments of junior princesses, the bigger salaries were earned by dancing and music masters.

The royal patronage extended far beyond the King's palaces. The King owned parks, so there had to be rangers and keepers of those parks. He owned waters, so there were keepers of waters. He owned works, so there were surveyors, paymasters and comptrollers of works. He owned tin, so there were an assay master and a supervisor of the tin. At Whitehall and St James's he owned engines, so there were keepers of engines. Not least, he owned gardens, so there was a Master Gardener of All His Majesty's Royal Gardens in England.

One of the more sonorous and ancient appointments, held by a nobleman, was that of Warden and Chief Justice in Eyre of All His Majesty's Forests, Chases, Parks and Warrens on the North Side of Trent. South of Trent another nobleman held a similar appointment. It may be assumed that Surveyor General of All His Majesty's Woods was a full-time appointment, if conscientiously carried out. How much more exacting, therefore, was the task of a Surveyor-General of All His Majesty's Honours, Castles, Lordships, Forests, Chases, Parks, Woods, etc, in England and Wales. Many posts of this type seemed to overlap, but no doubt the Warden and Keeper of the New Forest came to a working agreement with the Woodward and Keeper of the Underwood and Trees in the New Forest.

The number of Members of Parliament in the royal establishments can be discovered from the *Court and City Register*, the editor of which, perhaps mischievously, went out of his way to set an asterisk against their names. In 1777 the Members in the Lord Chamberlain's office included the Vice-Chamberlain, the Secretary to the Lord Chamberlain, one Lord of the Bedchamber, five out of the 12 Grooms of the Bedchamber (at £500 each), and three Gentlemen of the Privy Chamber. Other Members above stairs were the Master of the Robes, the Comptroller of the Great Wardrobe, a yeoman of the Jewel Office and a printer. The Lord Steward's office led off strongly with the following Parliamentarians: the Treasurer (£1200),

the Comptroller (£1200), the Cofferer (£500), Deputy
Cofferer, the Master of the Household, a Clerk to the Green
Cloth and two Clerks Comptrollers. In the Master of the
Horse's department, remarkably enough, no Members of
Parliament had infiltrated. The Duchy of Cornwall employed
four Members as Lord Warden of the Stannaries, Surveyor-
General, Auditor and Receiver-General. The Queen had five
Members on strength and the Duke of Gloucester two. Several
more were to be found among the Rangers and Wardens. All
the other branches of the Government, from the Board of
Works to the Pipe Office, were well sprinkled with legislators
who could be relied upon to exercise the King's vote.

20

A Blast by Burke

BY 1769 the cost of corruption had left the King with a deficit of £500,000, which Parliament made up with little demur. By 1777 he was £600,000 out of pocket. His servants' wages were a year and a half in arrears, his tradesmen on the brink of ruin. This sad state had been caused, as the Opposition justly pointed out, by nothing but the purchase of 'baneful and unbounded influence.' Money which should have gone to make the King 'splendid, magnificent and generous' had been applied 'to the most fatal purposes, whilst a great monarch was reduced to straits which would have been disgraceful to a private gentleman and the lustre of the Crown was obscured and tarnished in a manner before unknown in this country.' The critics also complained that the royal accounts were shrouded in 'Egyptian darkness.' They were 'fabricated to perplex, not to inform,' the reason being that the truth could not bear the light. No vouchers were produced for expenditure; no collateral was shown; no explanations were given; and huge sums were spent on 'secret service.' Parliament grumbled, but voted the King enough money to enable him to continue bribing it.

It was left to Edmund Burke to mount the big attack. Towards the end of 1779 he began sounding the fanfaronade for his Plan of Economic Reform. This proposed, among other things, the overhaul of the Royal Household and the abolition of scores of offices, notably those of treasurers, comptrollers and cofferers; the partial extermination of sinecures; a reduction of secret pensions; and a curtailment of redundant offices in the independent jurisdictions of Wales, Cornwall, Chester and Lancaster. He said: 'There is scarce a family so hidden and lost in the obscurest recesses of the community which does not feel that it has something to keep or to get, to hope or to fear, from the favour or displeasure of the Crown.'

Early in 1780 Sir George Savile presented to Parliament a petition by 8000 angry Yorkshiremen demanding the sweeping away of sinecures and corrupt pensions. Then, on February 11, Burke made one of the great speeches of Parliamentary history.

First, he gibed at the tomfoolery, both financial and litigious, which went on in the Crown lands—petty regions which possessed 'the apparatus of a kingdom for the jurisdiction over a few private estates; and the formality and charge of the Exchequer of Great Britain for collecting the rents of a country squire.' The system existed, he said, solely in order to multiply offices and extend influence.

Then on the subject of the royal palaces, Burke let himself go. These, he said, had lost 'all that was stately and venerable in the antique manners without retrenching anything of the cumbrous charge of a Gothic establishment.'

'Our palaces are vast inhospitable halls. There the bleak winds, there "Boreas and Eurus and Caurus and Argestes loud," howling through the vacant lobbies and clattering the doors of deserted guard-rooms, appal the imagination and conjure up the grim spectre of departed tyrants—the Saxon, the Norman and the Dane; the stern Edwards and fierce Henrys—who stalk from desolation to desolation through the dreary vacuity and melancholy succession of chill and comfortless corridors.'

Basically, the royal establishments were built on the principle of purveyance. 'In former days when the Household was vast and the supply scanty and precarious the royal purveyors, sallying forth from under the Gothic portcullis, to purchase provision with power and prerogative instead of money, brought home the plunder of an hundred markets and all that could be seized from a flying and hiding country, and deposited their spoil in an hundred caverns, with each its keeper. There every commodity received in its rawest condition went through all the processes which fitted it for use.' Yet, centuries later, the King retained 'Buttery, Pantry and all that rabble of places which, though profitable to the holders and expensive to the State, are almost too mean to mention.' Why not put the catering out to contract, as the King of Prussia did?

The Household, Burke thought, resembled Old Sarum in

having more representatives in Parliament than constituents. He instanced many of the superfluous offices. Why could not the Lord Chamberlain take over the Great Wardrobe—a department which in a few years had cost the Crown £150,000 for 'naked walls or walls hung with cobwebs.' Its purpose was not 'to furnish the palace with its hangings but the Parliament with its dependent members.' What was the point of a Removing Wardrobe? Why should a Jewel Office exist 'for the sole purpose of taxing the King's gifts of plate,' when that was surely a Chamberlain's duty? Why maintain an Office of the Robes when the Groom of the Stole held a sinecure? These establishments, useless in themselves, had three useless Treasurers—'two to hold a purse and one to play with a stick.' Why pay a man £100 a year, with an assistant also at £100 a year, to regulate some matter not worth twenty shillings? Everybody knew the answer; that these dignitaries were paid for their vote in Parliament, not for their diligence in administration, cookery or catering.

Burke recalled how Lord Talbot, a former Lord Steward of the Household, had made a bold attempt to impose economies in the royal kitchens, but had been frustrated on all sides because of the principle which laid down that one person should do the work while another drew the emoluments. On that rock his efforts split.

'The King's domestic servants were all undone; his tradesmen remained unpaid, and became bankrupt—because the turnspit of the King's Kitchen was a Member of Parliament. His Majesty's slumbers were interrupted, his pillow was stuffed with thorns and his peace of mind entirely broken—because the turnspit of the King's Kitchen was a Member of Parliament. The judges were unpaid; the justice of the kingdom bent and gave way; the foreign ministers remained inactive and unprofited; the system of Europe was dissolved; the chain of our alliances was broken; all the wheels of government at home and abroad were stopped; because the turnspit of the King's Kitchen was a Member of Parliament.'

For a reason not very flattering to royalty, Burke had decided not to advocate cutting down the number of high officers in personal attendance on the King. Men of condition, he said, loved to attend a court, and even more so did their wives; but

H

if the inevitable constraint that went with attendance were not compensated, the Court would soon be deserted by the nobility and the most serious mischief would follow. For kings, left to themselves, were naturally lovers of low company. They were so elevated above all the rest of mankind that they were apt to hate the nobility, who resisted them. The nobility were as willing 'to act the part of flatterers, tale-bearers, parasites, pimps and buffoons as any of the lowest and vilest of mankind could possible be'; yet they would not descend to be a match for Italian eunuchs, mountebanks, fiddlers and players. It was therefore necessary to contrive such an establishment as would bring into daily and hourly contact with the sovereign a great number of his first nobility; 'though they are not much the better for a court, a court will be the better for them.'

Burke proposed, however, to discourage the nobility from keeping the King's buckhounds, staghounds, foxhounds and harriers. 'These serve no purpose of utility or of splendour . . . It is not proper that great noblemen should be keepers of dogs though they were the King's dogs.'

There was a risk, which Burke did not overlook, that by decreasing the public and ostensible means of influence the fund of private corruption would be increased, and bribes would be paid out under the headings of 'secret service,' 'special service' and 'various payments.' This was doubtless why he was reluctant to urge the sweeping away of all sinecures. Often these were hereditary and the subject of family settlements; to have wiped them all out would have caused social and political chaos. But that did not stop him mocking the system. A rebellion of thirteen Lords of the Bedchamber, he said, would be far more terrible to a Minister than a revolt of thirteen colonies. On his first appearance at Court after an insolvent Christmas quarter, he would be assailed by a clattering of white sticks, a storm of gold keys, a shower of Georges and Thistles, 'a tumult which could not be appeased by all the harmony of a New Year's Ode.'

Lord North said that Burke's speech was one of the best he had ever heard. He then set about destroying the Bill, which he did successfully in committee. John Dunning, later Baron Ashburton, won the Commons' assent to the view that the influence of the Crown was increasing and ought to be diminished. In 1781 Burke returned to the attack and was beaten again. The King, meanwhile, was in a state of deep umbrage. Did they really expect him to say in his Speech that he proposed to root out the corruption which had so long disgraced his Household? But pressure was relentless and in 1782 a number of concessions were granted. Says Sir Nathaniel Wraxall, who lived through those exciting years:

'Many persons of high rank reluctantly disappeared from about the King's person and Court in consequence of Burke's Bill. The Earl of Darlington quitted the Jewel House and Lord Pelham the Great Wardrobe; the first of which offices owed its institution to Elizabeth, while the latter remounted to the times of the Plantagenets. The Earl of Essex laid down the Stag Hounds, as did Lord Denbigh the Harriers; while the disasters of Saratoga and Yorktown were thus felt by rebound through every avenue of St James's.'*

Other posts which went into the discard were those of Treasurer of the Chamber, Cofferer of the Household and six clerkships in the Board of Green Cloth. The valuables of the Jewel House and Great Wardrobe were put in the care of the Lord Chamberlain. From this year, too, the appointments of Lord Chamberlain and Lord Steward ceased to carry Cabinet rank. Mysteriously, the Master of the Buck Hounds survived the purge.

Wraxall was a traditionalist who believed that the maintenance of high-sounding, even if useless, offices 'diffused over the Throne itself a Gothic grandeur calculated to protect and to perpetuate the sanctity of the monarchical office.' No adventitious aid, he felt, should be despised.

One result of Burke's reforms, according to Wraxall, was that the Prime Minister was unable to procure the parliamentary attendance of his adherents. After 1784 Pitt had little to bestow except peerages. Burke is supposed to have said that he blamed himself for the increase of peerages under Pitt. And even Burke, alas, tried to secure a rich sinecure for his son.

Suppression of the Jewel Office involved the King in one episode of high embarrassment. In order to prorogue Parlia-

* *Historical Memoirs of My Own Time*

ment it was necessary that his crown and sceptre should be borne to Westminster, but neither the Lord Chamberlain nor the Lord Steward would order the Keeper of the Jewels at the Tower to liberate these treasures for the occasion. The Home Secretary's office eventually gave the necessary instruction. It was now the turn of the Master of the Horse to refuse to authorise the use of any of the King's carriages for transport purposes. Finally 'four or five stout police agents' were authorised by the Bow Street magistrates to transport crown and sceptre in two hackney carriages (presumably a vehicle for each). They were to travel by an indirect route and to have the blinds pulled down.

In the event, crown and sceptre made the furtive journey there and back in safety. Wraxall thinks that if the baubles had been captured the great economy campaign would have been thrown into ridicule. At this remove, it does not appear that the economy campaign was at fault but rather the three great officers of the Household, all of whom richly merited dismissal on the spot.

At the humbler levels of the Court the economy cuts also caused a good deal of feeling. Mrs Papendiek, Assistant Keeper of the Wardrobe and Reader to the Queen, whose husband was a page, expressed indignation at the admission of persons of inferior rank to certain appointments. The newcomers 'felt no interest, neither duty nor respect; and as to fidelity, such was not understood.' The Queen informed Mrs Papendiek that privations would be felt all round, not least by those servants who had hitherto lived like gentlemen; but the new policy was to admit more strangers to employment.* By strangers she seems to have meant English.

One of the new servants to whom Mrs Papendiek took particular exception was a stable hand whose sluttish wife had attracted the eye of the young Prince of Wales. An appointment had to be made which would ensure the wife's accessibility at Court, so the husband was appointed valet and hairdresser to the Prince. 'Mr Mills,' as he now called himself, was, in Mrs Papendiek's words, 'a dressed-up horror, impertinent and disgusting.' The pages, obliged to consort with him, begged to be relieved of their posts, but in vain. They do not seem to

† *Court and Private Life in the Time of Queen Charlotte*

have been distressed by the fact that Mills had ceded his wife to the Prince; it was his manners they disliked.

The considered view of Mrs Papendiek on royal economies deserves to be cited in full:

'It is a dangerous expedient to call the attention of the public to economies practised in the Royal Household. It degrades every regulation and as the inferior classes always look with a jealous eye upon the great, any changes that may be deemed absolutely necessary should be accomplished as quietly and privately as possible. It is not improbable that the wonderful change in our Royal Household was brought on by Edmund Burke's reform in the Civil List; and that this led through many trifling channels to the destruction of the French king, for in his country also the cry for economy was raised and soon spread far and wide.'

21

Crass Respectability

W HEN he exchanged the role of party leader for that of father figure, George III won back much of the popularity he had forfeited.

The long struggle with the Whigs, followed by the loss of the American colonies, had left deep scars. On a May morning in 1785 the King braced himself for the unkindest cut of all: the reception of the first American Ambassador to the Court of St James's. Into his Closet, making correct obeisances, was ushered the portly wigged figure of John Adams, who then delivered an unexceptionable short speech expressing the hope that two nations linked by ties of blood and language would be able to work closely and amiably together. The King replied with suitable magnanimity and John Adams bowed out. At subsequent Court functions when the American Ambassador was present the King felt unable to maintain this standard of magnanimity and Queen Charlotte was glacial to Mrs Adams.

The Court became the first in British history to commend itself, by its way of life, to the middle and lower middle classes. The great families, the leaders of wit and fashion, who had been used to a dull, immoral Court, were now visibly bored with a dull, moral Court. For sheer crass respectability there had never been anything like it. A king who romped with his children, who ate boiled mutton and turnips, who never got drunk, who lived as a farmer, who chatted to yokels and asked housewives how the apple got into the dumpling, a king who liked nothing better than to make buttons (having learned the knack from a German in Long Acre) and who laughed immoderately at a clown trying to eat a seven-foot carrot was, in their opinion, no fit ornament of the Throne.

Peter Pindar was one of those who mocked the King for an inability to leave the housekeeping to others:

The mail arrives! hark! hark! the cheerful horn,
To majesty announcing oil and corn,
Turnips and cabbages and soap and candles,
And lo, each article great Caesar handles!

Yet the King, on formal occasions, declined to forgo the least mark of respect. In minor ways he and his Queen even intensified etiquette. When the occasion demanded, both could put on a brave show. The royal arrival at Bulstrode Park from Windsor in 1778, as observed by that *grande dame*, Mrs Delany, was a very engaging spectacle. Outside the great house the Duchess of Portland had drawn up all her servants, as had been the custom in Elizabeth's day. The royal cavalcade, colourful and glittering, was led by two grooms on horseback, followed by the handsome 16-year-old Prince of Wales and his brother Frederick, also on horseback. Next came the Master of the Horse, with four mounted servants, then a two-horse phaeton containing the King and Queen. After this rolled up a long string of coaches containing princes and princesses, ladies and gentlemen, governors and governesses, preceptors and pages, each coach attended by grooms and footmen and each separated from the next by two horsemen. The reckoning was: 56 personages, 33 servants.*

Such a cavalcade demanded, and exacted, the right of the road—with whips, if necessary. On one occasion Mrs Delany was riding in a carriage with her nephew when angry shouts were heard and a scarlet-liveried horseman shouted to her postillion, 'Stop, for His Majesty is on the road.' The postillion, ignorant of etiquette, was for contesting the order; Mrs Delany screamed 'Stop!' at him from one window, her nephew from the other. Afterwards she had a hot debate with her nephew who complained of arbitrary power, while she insisted that these marks of respect should be kept up.

To his credit, the King was quick to discourage his postillions and even his Equerries when they made to slash at unsophisticated road users who were slow to give ground. But it was still the King's highway.

* Lady Llanover (ed.) *Life and Correspondence of Mrs. Delany*

The monarch made no attempt to shirk his duty at levees, which were held twice or even three times weekly. Parson Woodforde once saw the King and Queen being carried to St James's in sedan chairs and remarked, 'The King did not look pleasant, but the Queen did.'* The very frequency of levees led to a thin attendance. Sometimes the King would arrive before the guests and then send a Groom of the Bedchamber to reconnoitre and report back. At mixed receptions the King was not without presence of mind. When a kilted colonel bowed very low and displayed an unsuitable part of his anatomy, the monarch exclaimed, 'Keep the ladies in front, keep the ladies in front.'

The King's affability and desire to please were in marked contrast to the manner of Louis XVI, who hardly deigned to glance at people presented to him. At the Court of St James's the conversational rules were simple. No one spoke until addressed by the King, after which it was merely necessary to follow his lead and refrain from contradicting him. Only the King could introduce a new topic. The strain of initiating conversations with scores of people, many of whose faces were unfamiliar, and nearly all of whom were content to respond in polite or dazed monosyllables, was one of royalty's heaviest burdens (as it still is). Queen Charlotte found it even more of a strain than did her husband. The King, though eager to be gracious, had an exasperating habit of interjecting 'What? What?' or 'Hey?' which disconcerted his listeners. This mannerism grew to be a national joke.

Among themselves, the Royal Family kept up a curious formality in their modes of address. The princesses called the Queen 'Mamma,' but their father was always 'the King'; and the Queen, if she chanced to enter a room in which the King was present, would say, 'Ah, Your Majesty is here.' Both the Prince of Wales and the Princess Royal were referred to as such by their brothers and sisters, never by their Christian names; but the brothers and sisters used Christian names among themselves.

The society journals did not hesitate to voice their dissatisfaction over the lack of fashionable display at Court, one of the more waspish critics being the writer calling himself

* *Diary of a Country Parson*

'Man Milliner' in the *European Magazine*. This arbiter of good taste was capable of writing, as he did in 1782, that 'just as the spirit of novelty had sprung up and our buttons as well as the cut of our coats had undergone a very pretty change, Her Majesty's sister made a most unseasonable exit and we have been condemned to boil in black for the whole of the month.'

In the following year, 'Man Milliner,' describing the scene on the Queen's birthday, complained that 'Her Majesty, as is common on her birthday, had nothing remarkable on.' The following year he commented that the display was the least splendid and least festive on record. 'Indeed, it is not much to be wondered at when it is considered this illustrious person-age looks with inattention on every pleasure out of the bosom of her family. The propriety of this in a crowned head I shall leave to the reflection of my readers.' Nevertheless 'Man Milliner' had to admit that the Queen's dress was trimmed with 'a most inestimable rich sable and point lace.'

These were days when male attire was described even more lovingly than that of the female, and when keeping up with the fashions was a worry for both sexes. Not all courtiers met the challenge as shamelessly as one functionary who attended a levee in green velvet made up of bags which had been issued to him to hold office papers. For the Birthday Ode of 1784, according to the *Town and Country Magazine*, 'the gentlemen appeared in a diversity of the spring colours; a number of silver tissues with light grounds were worn. The prevalent colours were buff, blue, pale pink and lilac.' The Prince of Wales, as usual, 'was by far the most elegant in the drawing-room; His Highness was in a pearl-coloured silk embroidered with silver pearl and foil.' Another time, the Prince appeared 'in cardinal blue velvet richly embroidered with silver down the seams,' wearing his hair 'in two curls on a side, not so Germanised as it has been of late.' Once, when he wore an air balloon satin embroidered down the seams with silver, the effect was such that 'the seat of majesty was forgot' and all eyes were directed towards the Prince. On this occasion he had a new carriage of great beauty, the outside in 'high gold,' festooned with parti-coloured gold, and with fluted columns at each corner; and, of course, servants in magnificent livery.

The eyes of the society gossip writers were attracted by other facets of the scene than the purely sartorial. Thus, it was noticed on this occasion that the Prince showed his usual vivacity, 'particularly in company with the Hebes and daughters of Venus who conversed with him.' What the King said, if anything, about the presence of daughters of Venus in his Court was not reported.

The King's attire was not wholly overlooked by the gossip writers, but it could usually be dismissed with a remark like 'His Majesty wore purple uncut velvet, quite plain.' When he appeared in a suit of maroon velvet embroidered with gold, 'Man Milliner' said, 'This colour was too high for a complexion so florid as His Majesty's and it was observed by the circle he never wore a dress so unbecoming.' The Prince of Wales suffered also from the too-florid Guelph complexion; on romantic occasions he went to the trouble of having himself bled to a suitable pastel shade.

'Man Milliner' faithfully described not only dresses but scents. In 1794 the perfumes which predominated at Court were lavender water and Olympian dew; 'the latter indeed was refreshing in the circle near Their Majesties.' He noted also the colours which were patriotically fashionable. Thus, in 1783, the favourite hues for ribands were 'Eliott's red hot bullets' (as fired by the defenders of Gibraltar) and smoke (as of the camp of St Roche).

Masquerades also provided an excuse for fashionable note-taking. At one of them, by way of a novelty, a live goose was hung upside down and the revellers, as at a country fair, competed to pull off its head. Not everyone was convinced that this form of entertainment was suited to polite society. In 1783 'Man Milliner' described a masquerade at the King's Theatre at which the Prince of Wales attended. Supper was served in two sittings. The first was for the Prince's Court friends; 'the second repast was shared among a select few of the frail sisterhood whose names we decline to mention on this occasion.' Only one name was given, that of 'the Perdita' (Mrs Mary Robinson), who was said to be at the head of the Cyprian detachments. 'Man Milliner' did not miss much. Once, in a dramatic criticism, he reproached an actor because 'the use of two buttons, which men in general are most attentive to, was neglected.' One feels that he would not have overlooked similar laxity even in the Prince.

The King's loathing for intimate Court journalism was profound. His disapproval of a son who had taken to roystering with whores and Whigs is unlikely to have been abated by a character study of the Prince of Wales published in the *New Town and Country Magazine* in 1789. This said that 'a generous people like the people of England readily pardon errors that proceed from the mere intemperate levity of youth.' If the Prince had a warm attachment to the opposite sex, then the blame must be laid to Nature 'as having impregnated the most accomplished of her offspring with the largest share of the generous impulse.' But the public were confident that he could be reclaimed from 'the seductive charms of women and the bewitching smiles of Burgundy,' and would some day make England great.

As a father, George III flattered himself he had done his best to bring up his offspring properly. The Prince had been made to dig allotments; he had been well flogged, along with his right reverend brother, the Bishop of Osnaburg, with a long whip; and his mother had been careful to surround herself with only the plainest maids of honour. Yet, at Carlton House and at Brighton, the boy had embarked on a career of resolute libertinism. The sons of whom the King had hoped so much would live to be described by the Duke of Wellington as the damnedest millstones that ever hung about a Government. In an age of moral squalor in high places, they were not helped by the example of the King's own kin, the least of whose faults was that of marrying beneath them. His brother, the Duke of Cumberland, incurred a £13,000 penalty for breaking up a marriage and passed on the bill to the King; his sister, the Queen of Denmark, involved herself in spectacular disgrace. In 1772 the King revenged himself on his family, born and unborn, by securing the passage of the Royal Marriages Act, which forbade members of the royal family to marry commoners without the King's consent. In Parliament, an apprehensive Member described this measure as one 'giving leave to the Princes of the Blood to lie with our wives and forbidding them to marry our daughters.' The King saw it as an essential safeguard against the introduction of disgraceful elements into the Royal Family. He refused to receive at Court the two brothers—the Duke of Cumberland and the Duke of Gloucester—whose marriages to commoners had rendered the Act necessary.

Even at the best of times, the King had been on uneasy terms with his Household. His zeal for economy was as much resented by the humblest servants as by the highest. An Equerry bemoaned that after a hard day's hunting the King refreshed him with nothing better than barley water. Hence, it is not surprising that the King found more difficulty in filling the post of Equerry than any other. Even the maids of honour complained that the King had cheated them of their supper; eventually they wrung from him an allowance instead.

At an early stage he had clashed with his Household over the exaction of vails, or gratuities, from visitors to Court (Samuel Pepys was a victim of the practice in his day). It was an abuse which reigned in all noble households, not least in that of the Duke of Newcastle, whose cook would calmly hand back silver and demand gold. The victim whose protests in due course reached the ears of the King was Jonas Hanway, the philanthropist and friend of climbing boys. Asked why he did not dine more often with those of high station he replied, 'I cannot afford it.' In a series of letters to the Duke, Hanway pointed out: 'Perhaps your guest has not consumed the value of a shilling and he gives six servants half-a-crown each in return for it.' He also commented on the way in which 'the master of the house, with all the adroitness he can exert, shuns the sight of his guests when they leave his doors that he may not be a spectator of a practice at which he is equally ashamed and scandalised, notwithstanding the universality of it.' The more highly organised servants would cut the harness of guests who failed to contribute to their welfare.

The Duke showed Hanway's letters to the King who, suitably impressed, paraded his servants and threatened them with dismissal if they demanded vails. They left his presence 'not very well satisfied' and at once held a protest meeting below stairs. It was difficult to threaten a monarch, but there were ways of insulting him without incurring undue risk. When next the King went to the theatre the servants also attended in a body and openly abused him for his interference with their 'rights.' Says Robert Huish: 'His Majesty bore all their taunts and uproar with the greatest composure, nor did he retire from the theatre until the whole of the performance was finished.'*

In 1787 there was a major domestic upheaval which began with the discovery of a louse on the King's plate at dinner.

A crisis at the royal board: George III asks, 'Is this your louse?'

Its source was not clearly established, but George decided to take no chances and ordered all his kitchen staff to have their heads shaved. This decree was at once attacked as one more befitting an oriental despot. The cooks were proud of their hair and had no desire to walk out in the Mall looking like convicts. They addressed to the King a written protest which 'for boldness of language and the assumptions of importance it abounded in was scarcely ever equalled by any servant of any master in common life.'† It appears to have made the reasonable point that the cooks were no more likely to breed vermin in their heads than any other Court servants. Nevertheless, all

* *Memoirs of George III*
† *Ibid*

the cooks were shaved with the exception of one spirited youth who refused and was dismissed. The incident was not one on which fashionable ladies could afford to say too much, for their own elaborate head-dresses, when opened up after four or five weeks, were often found to be vermin-ridden.

Peter Pindar was not likely to overlook an affair like this. He published *The Lousiad*, notable more for impudence than literary merit. His satire was felt to merit prosecution, but the Lord Chancellor pointed out that the Crown could not be sure of a verdict; if the prosecution failed, they would all look a parcel of fools.

In another field, the King tried to scotch an abuse which, nearly two hundred years later, is still a running scandal: the claiming of diplomatic immunity by lawless servants of foreign ambassadors. It was a common custom for persons fearing arrest to get themselves enrolled, on payment of a trifling sum, as members of a diplomatic suite, after which they were able to thumb their noses at their creditors. Even the King was defied in this way. In 1786 his steward sold a number of sheep to a butcher who refused to pay for them, and when pressed revealed that he was in the suite of the French Ambassador. The King ordered the Ambassador to take suitable action and laid down that the domestics of foreign ministers should be made amenable to the laws of the country. Today, as is well-known, they are not.

The services of George III to the arts were not excessive, but they were far from negligible. He subsidised, and housed, the Royal Academy in its early years and did not outwardly protest when Sir Joshua Reynolds, whose painting and politics he disliked, was chosen as its first president. The King's interest in what he called 'my Academy' was always close, sometimes cantankerous. He told Hoppner that he did not approve of red and yellow trees and that artists should go out and look at Nature. Gainsborough received little royal encouragement. The King's favourite painter was the Quaker Benjamin West, whom he tacitly supported through one of the most comical controversies in the annals of art. West, inspired by the death of Wolfe, announced that he proposed to paint the scene and to show the contestants in the uniforms worn on the battlefield.

George III receives a deputation of ministers. By Gillray

Hitherto it had been a tradition that the participants in battle scenes should be represented in Greek or Roman attire, no matter what the period of the battle. Reynolds, with archiepiscopal support, tried to dissuade West from this heretical endeavour, but West said that togas had not been worn on the Plains of Abraham and he did not see why he should be expected to falsify history. After the painting was completed, Reynolds withdrew his objections; but the choleric James Barry still maintained that an outrage had been committed and, as a protest, painted the death of Wolfe with all the characters in the nude. When this was hilariously received, he resigned from the Academy in dudgeon. The King in due course asked West for a copy of his painting. If he sometimes treated the members of his Academy sharply, no one can be very surprised. West, his *protégé*, was bitterly attacked for his apparent monopoly of the royal favour. Eventually he was stung into revealing that in 33 years he executed 64 paintings for which he received £34,187, a sum which he thought not excessive. When the King went permanently mad, West was dislodged.

For a royal portraitist, an important qualification was that he should be a rapid worker. When Zoffany began painting his picture of the royal family there were ten children to be incorporated in it. Because, at various times, members of the family were unable to sit, work proceeded slowly. One day a messenger arrived with the news that another prince had been born and must be included. With reluctance the painter obliterated much of what he had done to make room for the newcomer. Long before the work could be completed another messenger came to inform him of the birth of a princess. Zoffany again redisposed his canvas but once more failed to keep abreast of events. To his mortification, a maid of honour announced the birth of still another princess. At this news, he is said to have turned the painting to the wall. When the King enquired how the work was progressing, he was told that, as there appeared to be no bounds to the increase of the royal family, the artist did not know what bounds to set to the canvas, for it was already full. 'And so is my quiver, and therefore I must be happy,' replied the tolerant King.*

Although convinced that there was much sad stuff in Shake-

* Huish

speare, the King liked to send for Mrs Siddons to give dramatic readings. Mrs Delany has left an account of such an occasion. Standing at a candle-lit desk, Mrs Siddons read two acts of *The Provok'd Husband* and Queen Catherine's last speech in *Henry VIII*. In Mrs Delany's view, the actress behaved with great propriety. She was allowed three pauses to go into the next room and refresh herself, in a manner not stated, for half an hour each time. In such high regard did the King and Queen hold Mrs Siddons that they appointed her Preceptress in English Reading to the princesses.

It is widely forgotten that the King once proposed the creation of a special order of knighthood for literary men: the Order of Minerva. There were to be 24 beneficiaries, ranking after Knights of the Bath. Once the news got abroad there was so much squabbling and jockeying among those who aspired to the letters K.M. after their names that the King abandoned the idea and, says Huish, 'the self-elected Knights of Minerva returned to their garrets.'

22

A Novelist Answers the Bell

IT will always seem odd that a Queen of England, casting around for a respectable and respectful young lady to lace her stays, should have picked on a short-sighted female novelist with a tendency to twitter.

No doubt Queen Charlotte regarded her offer of £200 a year, with board and honour, to Fanny Burney as a brave and discriminating act of literary patronage. All Miss Burney had to do, in return, was to give up literature.

Happily Miss Burney's pen was not stilled. When not lacing stays or laying out petticoats, she wrote a captivating, if sometimes disingenuous, diary of her five years of gilded servitude at Windsor and Kew.* Because she was an outsider, she noted numerous little oddities of etiquette and behaviour which those bred to courts would have deemed it unnecessary and below their dignity to mention.

Miss Burney served Queen Charlotte from July 1786 to July 1791, and was privileged to see the King go mad. Her post was the modest one of Keeper of the Robes, by no means to be confused with that of Mistress of the Robes, held by the Dowager Duchess of Ancaster. She performed her duties in conjunction with the disagreeable Mrs (actually, Miss) Schwellenberg.

Before being offered her appointment, Miss Burney had several palpitating contacts with royalty. These occurred, without prior notice, under the roof of Mrs Delany, who lived by grace and favour of the King in a house at Windsor. Quickly Miss Burney learned the first rule to be observed when a king drops in to tea: the company must break apart and 'fly off to distant quarters,' in other words, spread themselves around

* Austin Dobson (ed.): *Diary and Letters of Madame d'Arblay*

the room, in order to give the King space to circulate and
to allow him to confer with the individuals of his choice. From
this moment no one was allowed to sit, unless the King said
so, and no one who had been addressed was permitted to leave
without permission. During these early visits Miss Burney could
not disguise her admiration for 'the sweetness of the Queen
and the consideration of the King in each making me a party
to their general conversation before they made any particular
address to me.'

Mrs Delany, as hostess, was in no state to bustle about.
Rather was it the King who bustled about her. (When she
had been a guest of the Duchess of Portland the King had
shown great solicitude for her comfort and the Queen, noticing
her embarrassment, once said, 'Sit down, sit down. It is not
everybody has a chair brought them by a king'). The duties
of hostess were discharged most felicitously by the 13-year-old
Georgina Port, Mrs Delany's poised if precocious great-niece.
When the party flew to action stations, Miss Port would place
herself near the door. Then she would glide backwards, feeling
behind her for the door handle, let herself out and return with
more candles (only the rich and ostentatious habitually lived
amid bright illumination). After this she would glide out again
for tea, bringing it to the King on a large salver, with bread
and butter and cake. Over her arm would be a napkin on
which the King would wipe his fingers.

If the Queen called, her tea was set on a small table in
front of her. Even when she did not drink tea, the table was
placed in position. It helped her, as Miss Burney explains,
'to look comfortable, for certainly it takes off much formality
in a standing circle.'

Miss Burney was short-sighted. A good pair of spectacles
might have saved her much embarrassment but etiquette forbade the wearing of spectacles at Court, as Burke found to
his discomfiture. This ban, which lasted into Victorian times,
also existed in the French Court, where courtiers sometimes
peered through devices called 'perspectives' when they fancied
themselves unobserved. It was a nasty moment for Miss
Burney when she fancied the Queen had curtseyed to her, but
could not be absolutely sure. 'I was hardly ever in a situation
more embarrassing; I dared not return what I was not certain

I had received, yet considered myself as appearing quite a monster, to stand stiff-necked, if really meant.' The King, who was talking to her at the time, saved her from further embarrassment by drawing the Queen into his conversation; then Miss Burney curtseyed and all was well.

To her relatives, Miss Burney wrote playful directions for behaviour in the presence of royalty. Coughing and sneezing must be avoided, even at the cost of a burst blood vessel. Neither a hand nor a foot must be stirred. 'If by chance a black pin runs into your head you must not take it out.' Any resulting tears must not be wiped away; blood must be let trickle. It was permissible to bite the inside of the lips so long as no outward dent was created.

Miss Burney could still joke; but then came the sobering talk of a royal appointment for her. Ironically, it was her father who had long been anxious to secure a place, that of Master of the King's Band. This had already been promised him, and on the death of John Stanley, the incumbent, Dr Burney was anxious to remind the monarch of his existence. A Court functionary advised him to go to Windsor but to content himself with being seen by the King—'take your daughter in your hand and walk upon the terrace.' The King, Dr Burney was assured, was more likely to respond to a delicate hint of this type than to a direct application. This hint turned out to be too delicate altogether. The Burneys duly patrolled the terrace at Windsor with the loyal populace, who pressed themselves to the walls as royalty approached and then closed in to follow. Miss Burney was extremely embarrassed. 'There is nothing that I know so very dejecting as a solicitation,' she wrote. To his chagrin, Dr Burney was not addressed by the King, but his daughter was; and an offer of a place was made, not to him, but to her. He did his best, however, to be grateful for the honour done his family.

The Queen is said to have made minute inquiries into Miss Burney's fitness for a post which was widely coveted by women of fashion and status, and who possessed a knowledge of dress and jewellery which this tremulous novelist lacked. Miss Burney was told that she would have a two-room apartment in the Queen's Lodge and the services of a footman, and that she would dine at Mrs Schwellenberg's table along with Equerries, readers and the Queen's male guests—bishops, peers and commoners—whom etiquette would not permit to sit at meals with their royal hostess (only carefully selected ladies dined with the Queen).

With many misgivings, Miss Burney accepted.

Quickly, she found that the exigencies of etiquette she had learned in Mrs Delany's house were as nothing to those which fell to be observed in the Queen's house. Among the rules which she had to find out for herself were that no one must pass the open door of an apartment in which royalty was present, and that the way to attract the attention of the Queen, if her door was shut, was not to knock, but to grate the key in the lock. Mrs Schwellenberg did not tell Miss Burney what to do but was ready to admonish her when she made mistakes.

In the first days, Miss Burney was nigh overwhelmed by the Queen's tact in requiring her to do little more than stand and watch Mrs Schwellenberg presiding over the royal *toilette*. 'Sweet Queen! She seems as fearful to employ me as I am myself to be employed.' Panting with privilege, flushed by a sense of incompetence, she stood and watched one ugly elderly woman dress and undress another ugly elderly woman.

Miss Burney was 'inexpressibly discomfited' when she learned that she had to dart into action on the summons of a bell— 'it seemed so mortifying a mark of servitude.' But she persuaded herself that it would be very inconvenient for the Queen always to send a messenger and that a bell was, in fact, a lesser interruption than the arrival of a messenger. In time she ceased to blush at the ringing of the bell, unless someone else was present.

Gradually the daily routine established itself. Miss Burney rose at six, put on her morning gown and cap, and awaited her summons. When she reached the presence Mrs Thielky, the German wardrobe woman, had finished dressing the Queen's hair. The two of them then set about clothing her person, Mrs Thielky handing the garments in the appropriate order to Miss Burney. ''Tis fortunate for me I have not the handing them! I should never know which to take first, embarrassed as I am, and should run a prodigious risk of giving the gown before the hoop and the fan before the neckerchief.' By eight o'clock the Queen was ready to accompany the King to the chill chapel for prayers. Miss Burney breakfasted alone, reading a book.

The Queen was dressed, but not dressed for the day. During the morning Miss Burney chose and arranged clothes for the Queen's more formal *toilette*, which began at a quarter to one. If it was a birthday of any member of the family—and birthdays came thick and fast—new clothes were invariably worn. Mrs Schwellenberg assisted at the formal dressing. Between them they removed the Queen's gown and put on her 'powdering things' before admitting the hairdresser. The Queen was not entirely idle during her *toilette*, for it was then that she liked to read the newspapers. Before the messy business of powdering, she would send Miss Burney away, 'with a consideration not to spoil my clothes that one would not expect belonged to her high station.' It is sad to find Miss Burney in the ranks of those who marvel when royalty observe common civilities. At this stage she would go away to read another chapter or two and was then recalled to finish dressing her mistress. An attendant of Miss Burney's status was not allowed to leave until she was authorised to do so. The Queen would say, 'Now I will let you go,' in a permissive rather than a dismissive manner. Miss Burney learned that this observance was a mark of respect to her; mere wardrobe women and pages walked in and out on their errands unnoticed.

At three o'clock Miss Burney would be free and would have two hours in which to reflect on the larger life she had abandoned. At five she dined with Mrs Schwellenberg and the Equerries, and then had coffee in Mrs Schwellenberg's rooms, which were more luxurious than her own. Towards eleven she would eat a little supper. Then, between eleven and midnight the Queen would summon her again in order to be undressed. This represented another twenty minutes stint.

Often, Miss Burney seems to have cut things fine, for she says that when she arrived half-dressed in the Queen's room she was allowed to go back and finish—or was she sent back? Once, in her half-dressed state, she met an Equerry and fled discomfited back to her room. On another occasion she reported for duty conspicuously late, and the Queen in a dry voice said, 'Where have you been, Miss Burney?' It became evident that the Queen who could so subtly create an atmosphere of confidence could also create an atmosphere of disapproval.

Miss Burney professes to have been in great trepidation at the prospect of being asked to read to the Queen. Especially did she dread the daily newspapers, which were full of comment calculated to inflame the royal blood pressure. (Anyone who thinks that Miss Burney was unduly sensitive should ask himself whether he would be happy reading the more critical issues of, say, the *Daily Mirror* to the present occupant of the Throne). Miss Burney was broken in on a volume of *The Spectator*. Her voice was husky but the Queen made no comment. At least she was allowed to sit when reading; the Queen's male readers were expected to stand at a desk.

Once the Queen suggested that Miss Burney, instead of reading to her, should write something for her. She obliged with some decorous lines comparing the Queen's trappings to Venus's cestus, Diana's crest and Minerva's helmet. Miss Burney was becoming quite the courtier.

Short-sightedness still caused her agonies. 'I never know whether they look at me or at someone beyond me, nor whether they notice me or pass me regardlessly.' In a society where a glance or a gesture meant so much, her handicap must have been a formidable one. Out of doors, it was the custom for all, as soon as they sighted the King in the distance, to halt and press themselves against walls and hedges until he had passed. Miss Burney, returning to the Lodge, advanced right up to a group of persons before she recognised the King among them. Aware of her infirmity, the King behaved graciously.

Temperamentally, as well as physically, Miss Burney was never meant to be a courtier. Her self-esteem led her to brood over snubs. From the outset, diffidence prevented her from asserting herself against Mrs Schwellenberg and demanding the right to entertain. As it was, she could offer no hospitality or refreshment to friends who called. Mrs Schwellenberg thought little of Miss Burney's background and had no wish to have her table vulgarised by the presence of literary folk. Those of Miss Burney's friends who sensed her difficulty urged her to go to the Queen and ask permission to invite guests, but Miss Burney could not screw up her courage even to ask for an evening off. An importunate French novelist tried hard to get Miss Burney to introduce her into the royal circle and was fended off with utmost difficulty. Though her rooms were private, servants, officials and even princesses were liable to call in unexpectedly. Miss Burney was very cautious not to admit men, or if it was necessary to do so, to keep them standing. At Kew, where the royal couple lived very informally, the risk of royalty walking into a *tête-à-tête* was even greater than at Windsor.

Miss Burney did not feel herself free to choose her own correspondents. Madame de Genlis wished to write to her, but she was a very public character with many enemies. If it was known that such a person was corresponding with a member of the royal household, what would the world say? More important, what would the Queen say? After making herself miserable worrying about this problem, Miss Burney went, abjectly, to the Queen and asked her advice. This was to the effect that she should decline to correspond on the ground that she was too busy. The Queen indicated that she had heard many tales to the lady's disadvantage. 'Poor Madame de Genlis!' wrote Miss Burney. 'How I grieve at the cloud which hovers over so much merit!' The reader grieves at the apprehension which hovered over such sensibility.

Mrs Schwellenberg, that grim archetype of a Hanoverian courtier, is described by Macaulay as 'a hateful old toad-eater, as illiterate as a chambermaid, as proud as a whole German Chapter, rude, peevish, unable to bear solitude, unable to conduct herself with common decency in society.'* That she was a toad eater (as Peter Pindar also alleges) seems unlikely. She kept pet toads in a glass house complete with table and ladder, fed them on live flies and encouraged them to croak. She would no more have eaten them than an old maid would eat her parrot. There is no evidence that she was even a toady.

Mrs Schwellenberg tyrannised, not only over her inferiors, but over the Queen. No one could gain access to the royal presence without her permission, and her rooms were tactically sited to this end. Though her domination was domestic, not political, it occasioned much strong feeling. According to Mrs Papendiek, the King was dissuaded with difficulty from sending the dragon home. Joseph Planta has testified that Mrs Schwel-

* *Edinburgh Reveiw*, January 1843

lenberg was better served and attended than the Queen herself. Her servant waited at the step of her door to save her the fatigue of ringing the bell. She was wont to say that what might be good enough for the Queen was not good enough for her.

Meals at Mrs Schwellenberg's table were eaten, as often as not, in gloomy tension. The hostess did not care for witty, worldly conversation, especially if it was conducted without reference or deference to her. Equally she disapproved of those taciturn Equerries who ate their food rapidly and then made excuses to leave. If an Equerry or a guest chatted away to Miss Burney, Mrs Schwellenberg would glower; and Miss Burney, knowing that 'Cerbera' was watching, would be unable to do herself justice. Not all Equerries were anxious to chat to Miss Burney, for modest military men had no wish to figure in a novel. Miss Burney was expected to reserve her conversation for the upstairs *tête-à-tête* with 'the Schwellenberg' and if she lingered chatting at the dinner table it was the worse for her. There was little to discuss with Mrs Schwellenberg, apart from the oddities of toads and royalty. The strain of being 'agribble' was heavy, so they played cards.

The resident or visiting oddities among whom Miss Burney's lot was cast included Mr Webb, a Windsor musician who instructed the young members of the family. He had a misshaped nose which sprawled all over his face, and, in order to spare the King's feelings, he held a nosegay in front of it. Nine-year-old Princess Sophia solemnly warned Lady Cremorne, on a visit to the Lodge, that she must on no account laugh at Mr Webb's nose—'that is only to be pitied.'

A very trying character was 'Mr Turbulent,' otherwise the Rev. Charles de Guiffardière, a French reader to the Queen and her family. He was too cordial to Miss Burney, too gallantly vociferous; he 'rattled' too much; and worst of all, he was always making grimaces in her direction. She was terrified that his peculiar expressions would be intercepted and queried. In this instance her short sight seems not to have protected her.

The Equerries, in the main, were polite, affable and somewhat bored colonels. Miss Burney has been accused of fancying that they were in love with her. Often they would be sent for by the King, who had bolted his dinner, before they had finished their soup. One of them grumbled at the royal passion for fiddling—'all that fine squeaking'—which kept him on his feet for two hours in the concert room of an evening.

There were also the proud Papendieks. George was a Page of the Presence and his wife was an Assistant Keeper of the Wardrobe. They were not the types to welcome outsiders into the service. From Mrs Papendiek's own account* of life at Court, it emerges that she and her husband were not too proud to claim such perquisites as the leavings of meals and wines served to royal personages, plus left-over candles. Papendiek had his own standards, however; 'whatever remained untouched he took, but anything that had been tasted he allowed the page's man to take.' Another page, Magnolley, grasped all the left-overs he could, tasted or otherwise.

Miss Burney's best-mannered visitors appear to have been the princesses, whom the Queen sometimes sent to her on errands. Once there was a rap at the door and the Princess Royal entered with the Queen's snuffbox which needed to be replenished. If a princess could call on such a mission, a mere novelist could hardly object to executing it. Of such episodes, Miss Burney wrote: 'Every little commission with which she [the Queen] has yet entrusted me she has contrived to render highly honourable by giving the princesses some share in them.'

A visit by the Duke of Clarence (later William IV) was a more strenuous ordeal. Once he dropped in at Mrs Schwellenberg's table on the King's birthday. His sailor language was too uncouth for the prudish Miss Burney to print. He was in extremely high spirits and called for many rounds of champagne for the Equerry and the 'Queen's philosopher,' otherwise one of the Queen's readers. Loudly he bawled at the servants, gave one of them a violent slap on the back and declared that, if he were not going to a ball, he would have got drunk himself. The others drank with many protestations; they were afraid of becoming 'droll' or 'up in the world.' From time to time William kept referring to his '—— tailor' (Miss Burney's censorship probably makes this sound worse than it was). To Mrs Schwellenberg he said, 'Hold your potato jaw, my dear,' patted her, recollected himself, took her hand,

* *Court and Private Life in the Time of Queen Charlotte*

'pretty abruptly kissed it' then flung it hastily away. 'Dat Prince Villiam,' as Mrs Schwellenberg called him, was onerous company.

Though professedly anxious not to put a foot wrong, Miss Burney committed curious errors of tact and tactics. As a minor example, she asked the Queen if she had finished with the *Morning Herald* because one of the Equerries wanted to read it. The Equerry, when he heard this story, was scandalised. Miss Burney was forbidden to put forward suits or petitions, yet she did so on several occasions. One was on behalf of a poor man who had been shipwrecked. The Queen gave him some money but, in a kindly way, urged Miss Burney to beware that she was not imposed upon. Next she forwarded a petition for a pension on behalf of a woman imprisoned for debt, and was told, again very gently, that she was usurping the Lord Chamberlain's function. Thereafter Miss Burney was obliged to hurt the feelings of many who sought to take advantage of her place at Court; but when her brothers began to press her for help—one wanted a headmastership, the other a ship of 32 guns—she again plucked up courage to intercede.

Some variation of monotony was offered by royal progresses, which gave Miss Burney new glimpses of how things were done in the fashionable world, but the insolence of the servants in noble houses ruined much of her pleasure. There was, for example, that memorable visit to Lord Harcourt's, at Nuneham. No arrangements had been made for receiving Miss Burney and her companion, Miss Planta, the English teacher. The two wandered through the awesome corridors and eventually plucked up courage to ask a 'prodigious fine servant' for directions. He bowed slightly and passed on without replying. 'We met two more of the yellow-laced saunterers with whom we had precisely the same success,' writes Miss Burney. 'I think I never remember to have felt so much shame from my situation as at that time.' Miss Planta was used to such happenings and thought it all a joke. The two addressed more servants, all of whom promised to send someone else, but did nothing. In the end they were led to their rooms by the princesses.

The insults were not yet over. Miss Burney and Miss Planta were summoned tardily to a meal with a distant shout of 'The supper waits' and 'The Equerries want the ladies.' Later Lady

Harcourt was unusually courteous to the pair, as if in atone-
ment for the behaviour of her intolerable servants.

The royal party went on to Oxford. Here the King, knowing
the *gauche* ways of collegiates, wisely modified the hand-kissing
ceremony so that the scholars would not have to walk backwards down steps. Even so, the elderly scholars committed
all the faults, turning their backs on their sovereign as if they
were in a common room, or, if they marched backwards,
stumbled and collided with those behind them. Some, ashamed
to kneel, raised the royal hand to their mouths; others knelt
on both knees and could with difficulty rise again; others rose
by tugging on the King's hand to lift themselves.

In a visit to a college library Miss Burney witnessed a *tour
de force* by Lady Charlotte Bertie which seemed 'as difficult as
any feat I ever beheld at Astley's or Hughes's.' Lady Charlotte
found herself trapped at one end of the hall in close proximity
to the King, who was talking to a professor. To have walked
away would have been contrary to etiquette. Resolutely, she
faced her sovereign and then began to march backwards down
the centre of the room on an injured ankle, with never a look
round and never a stumble, covering 20 yards with as much
poise and aplomb as if she had been entering the room. Fanny
Burney was similarly trapped, but extracted herself by a succession of slow advances and retreats, and a simulated interest
in the pictures on the walls. Miss Planta, who was with her,
had no qualms; she 'fairly ran off.' After that experience, Miss
Burney claims to have advanced prodigiously in the art of
walking backwards, without looking round, feeling giddy, trip-
ping, or treading out the plaits in her train.

When the King lost his reason in 1788 the Court moved
to the whistling corridors and bare boards of the Palace of
Kew, where the windows had to be sandbagged to keep out
the cold. Here, however, the monarch could be sheltered from
curious eyes. Miss Burney's duty was to rise early and obtain
the latest bulletin from the royal physicians, a squabbling and
jealous band. One February day in 1789 she underwent the
most alarming experience in her life. She was walking in the
garden, and once again her short-sightedness prevented her
from seeing the King until it was too late. Terrified, since she
did not know what state of mind he might be in, she began

to run, the King ran after her and the physicians and attendants ran after the King, begging him not to exert himself. Finally they appealed to Miss Burney to stop running, and she obeyed. The King put his arm round her and kissed her, whereupon Dr John Willis beamed as if this was the most natural action. The King opened his heart to Miss Burney and resisted the efforts of his physicians to move him on. 'I have lived so long out of this world I know nothing,' he protested.

Towards the end of her five years Miss Burney was herself living under great stress. To fortify her shattered health she took wine, opium and hartshorn. Mrs Schwellenberg was not able, or willing, to believe that she was at breaking point; nor, for a long time, was the Queen. But eventually she was allowed to go and was awarded a pension of £100. Soon afterwards she secured what she had been unable to obtain at Court: a husband.

She bore no grudge against the Queen. Though vices might be as well avoided at Court as anywhere, 'and particularly in this Court,' she yet would not urge young people to go there. Jealousy, narrowness and selfishness were the mischiefs of the courtier's life. Miss Burney herself absorbed some unfortunate prejudices during her term of service.

Mrs Papendiek has a scornful account of Miss Burney's last days at Court. She says that Miss Burney informed the Queen that she had written a novel and would like the Queen to title it and to give permission for it to be dedicated to her. The Queen promptly said that she would do neither of these things, 'as it would not be consistent with her feelings to encourage or even sanction novel writing, particularly under her own roof. She added that she perceived a want of cheerfulness and pleasurable attendance in Miss Burney and always felt certain that whenever she rang the bell the pen was laid down with regret.' Since Miss Burney preferred to serve her public rather than her Queen, it might be better for her to depart.

'Poor thing, she bowed out,' says Mrs Papendiek.

23

The Clown of Parnassus

Consider one hundred marks a year,
besides the wine and the disgrace !—
Lord Byron, on the Poet Laureateship

N O Court functionary attracted more derision during the eighteenth century than the Poet Laureate. No Court function was more dreaded, by those with any claim to sensibility, than the performance of the New Year and Birthday Odes.

If the Georges had cherished any regard for poetry they would have rejected the laureate's twice-yearly tributes and allowed the appointment to lapse into a sinecure. As it was, once the tendering of New Year and Birthday Odes had been begun, no monarch had enough taste or courage to cry 'stop' and no laureate had the temerity to mutiny.

Gibbon believed that custom rather than vanity perpetuated an office which was 'first invented by the Caesars of Germany.' He did not think any age or court could produce 'a similar establishment of a stipendiary poet who, in every reign and at all events, is bound to furnish twice a year a measure of praise and verse such as may be sung in the chapel and, I believe, in the presence of the Sovereign.'*

The laureate was an irregular descendant of the versificators who served the Plantagenet kings. In most reigns there were poets who sought to rhyme themselves into Court favour, but only a very few were styled, or styled themselves, laureates. The activities of Spenser and Jonson have already been noticed. No laureate had more flexible principles than Dryden, who took the King's money when it was available and insulted

* *Decline and Fall of the Roman Empire*

him when it was not. Deposed in 1689, he was succeeded by Thomas Shadwell, who must share the blame for instituting the January and June odes. He launched them in the same spirit that a soldier, anxious to curry favour, will devise an ill-conceived new line of 'bull,' like polishing the lid of his boot-blacking tin. Authority, delighted, then decrees that the practice shall continue and the soldier is roundly cursed by all those who must follow his example.

With Shadwell the post of Poet Laureate became a political office within the gift of the Lord Chamberlain, and for a century to come its incumbent was the clown of Parnassus. Poets of distinction spurned the appointment, or, like Gray, dared not accept it because of the way in which the office was lampooned. The victims preferred to think that the abuse spilled over them was prompted, if not by jealousy, then by political animus rather than professional scorn.

Not only were the laureates of the eighteenth century men of indifferent talent, but they were of indifferent presence and manners. A biographer of Shadwell says: 'He seems to have been naturally coarse and was grossly indecent without designing to corrupt.' *The Lord Chamberlain, when asked why he made this appointment, replied: 'I do not pretend to say how good a poet Shadwell is, but I am sure he is an honest man.' Shadwell was fortunate enough to be appointed Historiographer as well, the combined salary amounting to £300. After him came Nahum Tate, son of a scholar called Faithful Teat, whose name would seem to have been intended for a wet nurse in a Restoration comedy. Tate has been described as 'an honest, quiet man with downcast face and somewhat given to "fuddling" '; he died in the Mint while hiding from his creditors. Among his works were translations of Ovid's *Art of Love* and of a French poem on syphilis. Next came Nicholas Rowe, trained as a lawyer, who held a variety of minor State appointments. He was succeeded by Laurence Eusden, who had qualified for the post by writing outrageously flattering verses on the marriage of the Duke of Newcastle to Lady Henrietta Godolphin. Eusden was a man of parts. Four years before his appointment he had recited some indecent verses before mixed company at a public function at Cambridge;

* *Dictionary of National Biography*

four years after his appointment, he took Holy Orders. He died a drunkard.

Colley Cibber, actor-dramatist, is a fancied candidate for the title of the worst laureate of them all. A Walpole nominee, he combined, as an anonymous wit said, the functions of poet and fool. At least he had no illusions about his merits. Industriously he circulated squibs at his own expense and laughed when they were repeated to him. William Whitehead, a *protégé* of the Jersey family, followed with 48 official odes. Belaboured by the wits, including Dr Johnson, he circulated *A Pathetic Apology for All Laureates, Past, Present and to Come*. The feeble torch was handed on to another clergyman, the Rev. Thomas Warton, more notable as a historian than as a poet. He was a fat little man of slovenly habits who 'gobbled like a turkeycock' and frequented taverns. The century was seen out by Henry James Pye, a squire, magistrate and Member of Parliament, who had been loyal to Pitt. During his tenure the terce of Canary wine was commuted to a sum of £27.

It is not easy to picture the performance of an official ode at the Court of St James's, and the contemporary diaries are not very helpful. Sometimes, it appears, the ceremony was staged in the Chapel, at other times in the drawing-room. Certain vocal parts were sung by special performers and others were sung by the gentlemen and children of the Chapel Royal. The ode had to be concocted in uneasy conjunction with the music master. Possibly the two men beat out their strophes and antistrophes with the mutual jealousy of Gilbert and Sullivan, possibly with the cold-blooded cynicism of a modern lyric writer and tunesmith in Tin Pan Alley. Whitehead was urged by William Mason, a fellow poet, to farm out his lines to hirelings who would shorten or lengthen them as the exigencies of the music required, just as Handel's 'poetical subalterns' had adapted their metre to the needs of his oratorios. It is charitable to assume that many of the odes were subjected to this treatment. The task of the choralists must have been difficult in the extreme, as many of the lines were virtually unsingable; but in practice the words were mercifully drowned out by the instrumentalists.

Usually, a laureate would take one of three main themes.

He would concentrate on eulogising the monarch; he would breathe fire and patriotism in times of war; or, in peace, he would sing the mingled glories of Commerce, Culture and Connubial Bliss. Alternatively, he could always fall back on the Seasons ('Again imperial Winter's sway Bids the earth and air obey. . .').

Personal eulogy was carried to celestial heights by Nahum Tate, who made many a bid for the laureateship before he secured it on Shadwell's death. An imagination so powerful that it could picture Charles II sitting up in Heaven's White Hall could effortlessly portray William's queen reporting at the same place:

> With robes invested of celestial dyes,
> She towers, and treads the Empyrean skies;
> Angelic choirs, skill'd in triumphant song,
> Heaven's battlements and crystal currents throng.
> The signal's given, the eternal gates unfold,
> Burning with jasper, wreath'd in burnish'd gold. . .

It was a high-flown version of the latter-day 'In Memoriam' notice:

> The angels with their harps cried 'Come!'
> And through the Pearly Gates stepped Mum.

The mere word 'George' aroused in the laureate breast the same excitement that a lover derives from contemplating the name of his beloved. The adjectives 'great' and 'glorious' went easily with it. Only one thing could be better than a George and that was a dynasty of Georges. This is how the panting (or perhaps tongue-in-cheek) Eusden hailed the coronation of George II:

> Hail! Mighty monarch whose desert alone
> Would without birthright raise thee to a throne.
> Thy virtues shine peculiarly nice,
> Un-gloom'd with a confinity to vice. . .
> How exquisitely great, who can'st inspire
> Such choice that Albion mourns no more thy sire. . .
> Avaunt, degenerate grafts, or spurious breed,
> 'Tis a George only can a George succeed.

I

Colley Cibber did not flinch from depicting George II as co-regnant with Jove. In 1732 he had a vision:

> Yet farther, Britons, cast your eyes,
> Behold a long succession rise
> Of future fair felicities.
> Around the royal table spread,
>   See how the beauteous branches shine!
> Sprung from the fertile genial bed
>   Of glorious George and Caroline.

In 1761 it was William Whitehead's turn to hail a new George:

> And who is he, of regal mien,
>   Reclined on Albion's golden fleece,
> Whose polished brow, and eye serene,
>   Proclaim him elder-born of Peace?
> Another George! Ye winds convey
>   Th'auspicious name from pole to pole. . .

The world of the patriotic odes was one in which the patience of Albion's virtuous sons was for ever being exhausted by the pride and licentiousness of vainglorious Gallia (deluded Gaul, for short), proud Iberia and cozening Rome. In spite of the severe lessons they had been taught by Great Henry and Great Eliza, these powers were for ever letting loose Bellona's crimson car, tearing the golden wreath from Ceres' brow and striving to grasp the Trident of the Main. Thus, the sons of Albion ('A chosen race, to Freedom dear, Untaught to injure, as to fear') were seduced from the paths of Commerce and Culture to conduct laborious, but in the end successful, wars beyond the hyperborean mists, in the Arcadian snows or on the reeking Asian shore.

At the New Year, a poet might hail the Panacean dews of Peace, but by the King's Birthday he would be driven to deplore how, once more,

> . . . passion baffles reason's boasted reign.
> And half the peopled world is civilised in vain.

The trouble with Gaul and Iberia was that they were governed by blood-seeking despots, not by broad-visioned

Georges enthroned on Virtue's adamantine base. As Whitehead put it:

> O happier far the well-mixed State
> Which blends the Monarch's with the Subject's fate,
> And links the Sceptre to the Spade!

It was conceded that Gallia had richer soil than Albion, but
this very richness bred habitual excess. Whitehead, in 1758,
did not deny all virtue to Gaul, but he drew an appropriate
moral:

> Give to France the honours due,
> France has chiefs and statesmen too,
> Breasts which patriot passions feel,
> Lovers of the common weal.
> And when such the foes we brave
> Whether on the land or wave,
> Greater is the pride of war,
> And the conquest nobler far.

But by 1794, when the frantic sons of rapine had stained
every dewy sod with civic blood, when Anarchy's insatiate
brood had choked the empurpled flood with corpses, Pye
seemed doubtful whether there could ever be another *rapproche-
ment*:

> Say, shall Britannia's generous sons embrace
> In folds of amity the harpy race,
> Or aid the sword that coward fury rears
> Red with the widow's blood, wet with the orphan's tears?

All that Albion wanted was to be left alone to roll the tribute
of lands with inferior climates and morals into the mouth of
Thames. In this endeavour she had the whole-hearted support,
as a rule, of Neptune. Occasionally one of these less happy
lands was privileged to contribute a royal virgin, with whom
the custodian of Albion's honour would condescend to indulge
in Hymen's soft delights.

In the main, the poetical style of the laureates ran to a
flatulent standard of its own. Not even a connoisseur of bad

verse can say confidently, 'That is a Pye,' or 'This is a White-head.' Sometimes there was a comical echo of Milton:

> But come, thou foster deity,
> Fairest Unanimity!

Or there might even be an unconscious anticipation of Kipling:

> So Edward fought on Cressy's bleeding plain,
> A blooming hero, great beyond his years. . .

At one thing the laureates excelled: expressing the correct sentiment at the correct time. They gushed over new-born babes as the repositories of parental virtue; how should they know that the babes would grow up into libertines and wicked uncles? When the Prince of Wales (later George IV) imported his erratic princess in 1795 Pye detected heavenly virtue beaming from Beauty's blushing eyes and exulted over 'kindred fondness and connubial love.' It turned out to be the most disastrous royal match on record. But virtue was not the only lost cause the laureates cherished. Whitehead in his last ode looked confidently to the day when the American colonies would 'court again the fostering breast.'

George III gave his laureates a chance to sing unhypo-critically of connubial bliss, but he would almost certainly have resented any poetical intrusion into his fertile, genial bed. He had no desire to hear lickspittle odes. Probably he would have abolished the twice-annual performances but for his anxiety not to diminish any of the outward observances calcu-lated to fortify majesty. As it was, his laureates found him not the easiest taskmaster. In 1769 he told Whitehead that he wished to hear no personal praises of himself on his birthday and no references to politics ('insatiate Faction') or the Govern-ment. Under this somewhat negative direction the poet pro-duced an ode picturing the King as patron of the arts, doing his best to found Athens in Albion. Afterwards the King told him: 'You did right, very right, Mr Poet. You reminded me of my favourite play, *Much Ado About Nothing.*'

In 1778 the long-suffering Whitehead blotted his record. During the performance of the New Year Ode strong signs of displeasure were noticed on the royal face. Afterwards a lord in waiting conveyed to the Laureate the Sovereign's censure for bringing the Almighty into the ode: 'It is in His sacred temples I delight to hear His praise and I consider it impious to convert a joyous ode into an anthem or a psalm; let me not know it repeated.'*

The best course was to stick to Sceptre and Spade, which usually Whitehead did.

His successor, the Rev. T. Warton, sought to show that the King not only patronised the arts, but disciplined and purified them. In 1785 he wrote:

'Tis his to bid neglected genius glow,
And teach the royal bounty how to flow.
 His tutelary sceptre's sway
 The vindicated arts obey,
And hail their patron king:
 'Tis his, to judgment's steady line
 Their flights fantastic to confine,
And yet expand their wing;
The fleeting forms of fashion to restrain,
And bind capricious Taste in Truth's eternal chain.
Sculpture, licentious now no more,
From Greece her great example takes,
With Nature's warmth the marble wakes
And spurns the toys of modern lore. . .

Not the easiest task was that which befell Warton when he came to compose the Birthday Ode of 1789. How would the monarch respond to references, however tactful, to the madness from which he had recently recovered? Warton used his first twenty lines in comparing the King's reappearance with the sun re-emerging after a storm. There was a brief reference to 'the monarch's aweful fate,' and all the rest was thanksgiving. The King seems to have been satisfied.

In 1790 there was no New Year Ode, a mystery which caused much speculation. Peter Pindar was inspired to write an 'Ode on No Ode,' asking whether Caesar's bards no more enjoyed the run of his kitchen.

In the end, it was the recurring madness of the King which brought the Odes to an end.

* Huish: *Memoirs of George III*

24

Fish Swam Down the Table

IN the Waterloo decade, the British taxpayer was privileged to maintain two major courts—one for an incurable madman and one for an incorrigible spendthrift.

Through the galleries of Windsor roamed the old King in his violet dressing-gown, playing a harpsichord here, haranguing an invisible senate there. As madmen go, he was well liked, but there were those who chafed at the expense of maintaining him. Members of Parliament kept rising apologetically to ask whether it was really necessary to spend £160,000 a year upholding the splendour of a court which His Majesty could neither appreciate nor see. Why maintain four Lords of the Bedchamber when all he needed was two keepers? Why retain 30 saddle horses and 28 carriage horses for the use of a sovereign who never went out of the castle gates? And did the Queen really need an extra £10,000 a year to travel from London to Windsor to visit her husband?

But Members felt happier when attacking the extravagance of the Prince Regent. When the Regency began he had been voted £100,000 to buy himself 'an outfit,' but the sum had been mysteriously squandered. It had certainly not been spent on, or by, his wife, Caroline of Brunswick, from whom he was irrevocably estranged. The sum had been poured into the gilt belly of Carlton House. How (asked the critics) could one man use so many beds, so many ottomans, so many clocks? How could one man lap himself in so much silk? Opinions varied on what should and should not be cut down. In 1815 George Tierney, a trenchant critic, said he had no wish to trim the establishment of the Master of the Horse, as he considered there was something 'national and manly' in encouraging a fine breed of horses. This gave Samuel Whitbread the chance to illustrate the low regard in which fine horseflesh was held by the Regent. An illustrious foreigner, Prince Platoff, had presented to the Prince the war horse which had carried him through many successful campaigns. Such a horse, Mr Whitbread thought, should have been pampered, and allowed to pass the rest of its life 'in a sort of riotous felicity.' Instead, it was used to draw a dung cart at Hampton Court.

It was left to Lord Castlereagh to point out that the Prince Regent was the only individual in Europe exercising the functions of sovereignty who had not a variety of palaces. Besides his temporary quarters at Windsor the Prince had only Carlton House and the Pavilion at Brighton; and the Pavilion was his own property. St James's Palace had been half-destroyed by fire in 1809.

There was some justice in Castlereagh's remarks. Visiting foreigners who had seen the splendours of Sans Souci and Schönbrünn would remark that the British seemed to set little value on a sovereign if they could give him nothing better than Carlton House. Many commoners had far more imposing palaces. Even a Paris hotel could outshine a British royal home. The Prince Regent undoubtedly faced considerable handicaps in his attempt to revive such glories as seemed suited to an Age of Victory. Back in 1762, when he was less than an hour old, twenty waggons of captured treasure had rumbled past his windows, and before he was six days old Havana had fallen. But riches, in this later war, came less bountifully. By perseverance, by ignoring savage political carping, the Prince was able to mount a few gaudy set-pieces. But he had come too late to power and he was haunted by his ill reputation. A mob which in its heart relished magnificence was inspired to throw stones at the Prince of the Mighty Isle, or to call after his carriage, 'Where's your wife, Georgie? Where's your wife?' They were not to know what an impossible wife Caroline was.

Carlton House, off Pall Mall, had seen many vicissitudes since the 21-year-old Prince first established it as a depot for whoremongering and boroughmongering. Externally it was, as Canova said, 'an ugly barn.' In an effort to lend it importance, a colonnade of pillars had been erected in front of the forecourt; since they supported nothing, they were a target for architectural purists. At the rear of the house were splendid and spacious gardens, with a grove of ancient trees in which nightingales sang. In these grounds the Prince's grandfather had built such refinements as a cascade, a saloon paved with Italian marble and a *bagnio*.

There was little the Prince could do to dignify the exterior of this dilapidated barn, but he set out to embellish the interior with a Roman disregard for expense. In 1789 the *New Town and Country Magazine* described Carlton House as 'a national ornament and the only habitable palace Great Britain can boast.' It considered that the Prince had turned the tide of fashion in favour of England. Amid this florid magnificence the Prince held a rackety court to which flocked the pride and the sweepings of Debrett and the Army List; bucks, wits, buffoons, scholars and fugitives from debtors' prisons; and ladies of much vivacity and little scruple, among them Letitia Lade, one-time mistress of Sixteen-String Jack, the highwayman, who had been hanged at Tyburn. On the fringe of this society hovered tailors and hatters, shoemakers, jewellers and decorators. Beyond these was a dingier fringe of procuresses, pawnbrokers, pugilists, duns, demireps, bailiffs, gamesters and 'financiers' eager to speculate in the royal IOUs.

When the Regency began, Carlton House entered a phase of less raffish magnificence. In June 1811 the Prince held a much-admired and much-criticised ball which had two declared objects: to celebrate the birthday of his father and to benefit artists 'who by the illness of their sovereign and the discontinuance of the accustomed splendour of the Court had been deprived of many advantages in their respective pursuits.' It is not everyone who would wish to celebrate in lavish manner the birthday of an insane father, but the Prince evidently thought it would have been in worse taste not to pay formal honour to the King. (Not long before, enormous crowds at Windsor had waited several hours 'in great suspense' to see the King ride out on his white horse Adonis, chatting agreeably, and apparently normally, with two of his daughters). Queen Charlotte, like most people, considered that the real reason for holding the ball was to celebrate the birth of the Regency; coldly, she declined to attend. Caroline was not invited, although her ladies and gentlemen were, and Maria Fitzherbert,

A MORNING RIDE.

Master and servant: The Prince of Wales (George IV) and Sir John MacMahon. By Gillray

the Prince's unofficial wife, was informed that she must not expect to grace the top table. 'You know, madam, you have no place,' said the Prince. To which she replied: 'None, sir, but such as you give me.' Mrs. Fitzherbert also stayed away; and she stayed away for good.

The mere absence of the Queen and of the Prince's two wives by no means dulled the brilliance of the occasion. A contingent of Bourbons, headed by the Comte de Lisle (brother of the executed Louis XVI) had no hesitation in accepting. The first carriages began to arrive at Carlton House at eight in the morning and the gates were opened at nine. Sedan chairs unloaded their occupants at a separate entrance. Although, according to the *European Magazine*, the utmost order and regularity were observed, the last arrivals did not enter the house until nearly one. The entire mansion was thrown open. To the bemused guests, it appeared that thickets of roses and geraniums had marched in among the porphyry and the ormolu, the bronze and the ebony, and that the normal contents of the house had spilled out into the gardens. Tables laden with silver ran in all directions: across the main hall, through the library and the great vaulted conservatory, and then out into the grounds, under awnings. The conservatory, with its fan tracery and coloured windows, challenged comparison with a Gothic cathedral. Out on the lawns were a number of marquees, linked by screened board-walks. At suitable points were *chevaux de frise* to keep away intruders.

To receive the Bourbons, the Prince had lined a room with blue silk, ornamented with gold *fleurs de lys*. 'The amiable daughter of Louis XVI naturally attracted the Regent's chief attention, the pleasing effect of which was clearly discernible on her woe-worn but interesting countenance,' said the *European Magazine*. The Prince, who wore the uniform of a field-marshal, was on the summit of his form, 'dividing his attentions with the most polished address.'

At the top table, all the guests were of the rank of marquis or above. According to one computation, the entire company included 14 dukes, 15 duchesses, 15 marquises, 16 marchionesses, 98 earls, 85 countesses, 39 viscounts, 107 lords and as many ladies of the same rank, besides 'barons, counts, admirals, generals, etc.' Some 60 servants attended to the needs of the top table. Among those waiting directly on the Prince were twelve footmen in State liveries and a servant clad in ancient armour.

Chairs had been set for 2000 guests but more than that number arrived. The overflow were seated in alcoves and lacked nothing save a close-up glimpse of the rivulet which ran the length of the main tables, threading under fantastic bridges and creating a pleasing murmur. It was fed from a silver fountain which sprang under a temple in front of the Regent, and its banks were covered with green moss and aquatic flowers. As an added enchantment, 'gold and silver fish were by a mechanical invention made to swim and sport through the bubbling current, which formed a cascade at the outlet.' Not all the fish, regrettably, survived the excitements of the passage.

Like all the Prince Regent's functions, this one was chokingly hot. The main ballroom, where the floor had been chalked in stylish arabesques, could not be used, but in the gardens and elsewhere, to the strains of four bands, dancing went on until six the next morning. Everywhere was a riot of lamps. 'The *coup d'oeil* of the whole,' in the view of the *Annual Register*, was 'inexpressibly delightful and even magically impressive.' The *Gentleman's Magazine* enthused over 'a line of female beauty more richly adorned and a blaze of jewellery more brilliant than England probably ever displayed before.'

The Duke of Buckingham thought the whole occasion in bad taste, especially at a time when weavers were starving in Lancashire and on Clydeside. 'However, the *fête* was eminently characteristic of its princely designer and nothing more need be said of it.'*

Within a week Carlton House looked down on a sorry spectacle. The Prince directed that the public be admitted to gaze for themselves on the scenes of splendour of which they had heard and read. On the third day several thousands were waiting by seven o'clock in the morning. Soon there was a crowd of 30,000 extending back to the Haymarket. It became clear that those who had arrived after eleven o'clock would not gain admission, which was regulated to 200 at a time. The crowd began to surge angrily. In the forecourt four 'delicate

* *Memoirs of the Court during the Regency*

females' were picked up nearly lifeless, their clothes almost completely torn off. One had been trodden until her face was black. Within the building, the pier glasses which had multiplied scenes of magnificence now multiplied scenes of distress, as shoeless and gownless women, with their hair hanging down their shoulders, wandered weepingly in search of retiring rooms, only to be confronted by more mirrors. Some of them were unable to leave until new clothes had been brought. Outside, the crowd continued to press. At one time they 'literally carried away the Horse Guards for several paces,' until the animals reared and knocked down more delicate females. Lord Yarmouth appealed to the crowd to stop pushing, but without much result. Later the Duke of Clarence, who was used to raising his voice, was more successful. Lord Yarmouth, Colonel MacMahon and Colonel Bloomfield paid every attention to the casualties.

There were other great balls and Court occasions during the first lustrum of the Regency, notably one in honour of the Battle of Vittoria. Early visitors danced on the lawns, in sunlight, before they dined. The belle of the ball was Princess Charlotte, the Regent's daughter. Captain Gronow notes that she danced with the Earl of Aboyne, who had danced with Marie Antoinette and lived, as Lord Huntly, to dance with Queen Victoria.*

The Prince tried hard to be the royal showman of Europe, but his efforts were ill appreciated by the European monarchs who came to London in 1814. The Czar chose to stay at Pulteney's Hotel. Both he and the King of Prussia persisted in trying to do things privately and informally; ceremonies were dodged and invitations ignored. It was as galling to the Prince as to the public, who expected czars and emperors to act as such. Eventually the Allied monarchs were persuaded to ride for a whole afternoon in Hyde Park, which did much to mollify the capital. Blücher was the popular hero. When he arrived at Carlton House the crowd surged inside the forecourt and the throng was such that the Prince, on a happy inspiration, ordered the doors of the great hall to be opened. There the crowd saw the King lay a blue ribbon across the Marshal's shoulder and present him with a diamond medallion.

* *Reminiscences and Recollections*

'A Voluptuary Under the Horrors of Digestion.' A Gillray study of the future George IV (1792)

Both then bowed politely to the uninvited sightseers, who were wildly appreciative. At Christ Church, Oxford, Blücher gave an address in his own language, speaking powerfully but unintelligibly. Immediately afterwards the Regent, 'with a condescension which did him the highest honour, undertook to interpret the sentiments of the brave warrior.' On a big occasion, the Regent was usually equal to the task.

The Czar, having shown little politeness to the Prince's current 'consort,' Lady Hertford, was tactless enough to ask to see the mad King and the disgraced Princess of Wales. He saw the latter at the opera, and the Regent was unable to avoid bowing in her direction.

The Prince's other home, the Pavilion at Brighton, also made the transition from raffishness to respectability. In the earliest days life there was like Mr Belloc's Midlands: sodden and unkind. Drinking under the table was the rule, and a newcomer would be plied by the Prince with a quick succession of toasts, ending up with a concussive brandy called Diabolino. With his sailor brother, the Duke of Clarence, the Prince would engage in heavy bouts with the formidable old Duke of Norfolk (the 'Jockey'), whose aversion to soap and water was such that his servants could wash him only when he was drunk. The libations were so heavy that Mrs Fitzherbert persuaded the Prince to take evasive action, and he would slip away to answer 'urgent' correspondence. The Duke of Clarence was left to uphold royal prestige. Once even the dirty Duke said he must decline the oppressive hospitality of the Pavilion and called for his carriage. Instead of heading back to the splendours of Arundel the coach, unknown to its occupant, went round and round the Palace lawn. When the Duke woke next morning he was in bed in the Pavilion.

The Prince's heavy drinking did not always make him the easiest of dancing partners, but this was the opportunity for a lady to show her tact. If he seemed unusually giddy after a tour of the floor, it was for her to affect giddiness too.

The Creeveys were guests at the Pavilion soon after the turn of the century. They soon tired of the life there. 'To be sent for half an hour before dinner or perhaps in the middle of one's own was a little too humiliating to be very agreeable,' says the diarist. His wife, who played up to Mrs Fitzherbert, found life at Brighton 'horribly dull.' The sub-tropical heat and stink made her sick and she had headaches till noon. She mentions one curious occasion when the Prince led his guests to the map-room for air-gun practice. One courtier hit the ceiling, another a door, and Lady Downshire contrived to hit a fiddler in the dining-room.* (Ten years or so later, air-guns were to be discharged at the Prince as he drove through the streets of London). Such were the recreations at the Pavilion when news came of the death of Nelson. This, for once, seems to have sobered the Prince, and he stayed in his rooms. But soon he was organising a victory ball and then another for the dependants of those who fell.

Not until about 1820 did the Pavilion attain its full exotic magnificence. The transition had been a curious one. When the lines of the building had been chaste and refined, behaviour under its roof had been anything but chaste and refined; as it went Chinese, behaviour had improved; and in its last florid Indian phase life within its walls was like that of a very decorous casino. Its begetter surveyed the finished work with the pride of a chef who has just put the finishing touch to a saccharine extravaganza. Only one thing could enhance its delights: the sound of his own voice, accompanied by a great orchestra. Mostly, the world was baffled by what it saw. Hazlitt thought that the genius of architecture had been attacked simultaneously by the megrims and the dropsy, but it is hard to follow him when he says that 'a greater dearth of invention was never seen.' Princess Lieven nicknamed the Pavilion the Kremlin and said that nothing like it had been seen since Heliogabalus. She found the fashion of half-lying on cushions effeminate. All agreed that the Prince was un-English in his passion for indoor warmth. Others made appropriate jests about a palace in which the palm-tree pillars holding up the kitchen ceiling burst out into fronds of copper, the great domed stables were reached by an underground passage from the house, and the horses enjoyed the benefit of a fountain. Greville said that pipes costing £600 had been installed to bring in salt water to the bathroom, adding that the Prince had not

* Sir Herbert Maxwell (ed.): *The Creevey Papers*

bathed in the sea for 16 years. The royal girth alone made such an indulgence unthinkable. But Brighton, too, had been expanding and it became obvious, now that a fortune had been spent on the Pavilion, that it was a very unsuitable home for a fat man. It was too exposed to the eyes of sightseers.

The Princess of Wales was admitted to neither of these establishments. Foolish, half-crazy Caroline, who was too *mixing* and too *missish*, who had arrived in Britain primed with strange new ideas about personal hygiene and the knowledge that the price of adultery in one of her position was death, lived a frustrated, sometimes ribald, life under her own roof. To dignify her retinue, she had a portrait painter and a historical engraver. According to the Duke of Buckingham, the best passport to her society was the possession of 'a certain sprinkling of intelligence with a good flow of animal spirits.' Several of her friends were celebrated for their 'independence of moral obligations.' Though much had been done to humiliate her, she had found wry amusement in watching the Prince's efforts to free himself from Lady Jersey, that disreputable young grandmother whom, in the best Stuart tradition, he had assigned to her as lady in waiting on her arrival in Britain. Regularly Caroline committed acts warranted to embarrass the Prince and please his enemies. When out walking, she would drag her waiting women along unsuitable streets and talk to strangers. In 1806 she had survived the Delicate Investigation by four lords charged with ascertaining whether she had borne an illegitimate child. When her husband became Regent and it was clear that there was no place for her at Court, she set off on a scandalous tour of the Continent, gathering rogues and parasites as she proceeded. At a ball at Geneva she appeared as Venus, bare above the waist, and when she waltzed 'the *terrae motus* was dreadful,' to quote her lady in waiting, Lady Charlotte Bury.*
The Princess returned from these unseemly capers in time to make a scene at her husband's Coronation, from which she was excluded. The Prince's Court then combined in an all-out effort to furnish evidence which would convict her of adultery, but Brougham successfully blocked the charges. Happily, George IV was the last British sovereign to take a wife unseen.

* *Diary Illustrative of the Times of George IV*

25

Unorthodox Courtiers

THE Prince Regent's character was not one to attract courtiers of scruple. Rogues and oddities surrounded him for much of his life. Yet, until his later days, he rarely allowed his royal dignity to be infringed by any of them. It never paid to talk too freely at the Prince's Court. 'Hear what you like but say as little as possible' was the rule. Lord Rigby, Master of the Ceremonies, when asked by the Prince at dinner whom he should marry, replied that, although he was drunk, he was not drunk enough to give advice on the marriage of the Prince of Wales.

George Brummell, though he might be the arbiter of tailoring, was not the arbiter of manners. The Prince informed him that the place for his snuff-box was not on the royal table but in his pocket. A supposed request from Brummell, 'Ring the bell, George,' had severe consequences. The wayward Lord Barrymore put his hat on a chair in the Prince's private room and received this rebuke: 'My lord, a well-bred man places his hat under his arm on entering a room and on his head when out of doors.'* Anyone who turned up at a Court function improperly dressed was liable to receive a message expressing the Prince's displeasure. This was equivalent to being ordered to leave.

Rather than surround himself exclusively with sprigs of nobility, keen though some of them were to pander to his pleasures, the Prince preferred to select his courtiers from other walks of life. One of his first Equerries, appointed by his father, was General Gerard Lake, later the scourge of the Mahrattas, a polished, gentlemanly Guardsman who sought, not wholly successfully, to steer the Prince from his early excesses. The

---

* Captain R. H. Gronow: *Reminiscences and Recollections*

Prince seems to have found more joy in the company of a licentious sailor, Rear-Admiral John Willett Payne, whose valour at sea was matched only by his profligacy on shore. He was appointed by the Prince to the posts of Private Secretary and Comptroller of the Household, and furthered his young master's pleasures with a will.

Another rumbustious fighting man to enter the Prince's service was Colonel George Hanger, an Irishman who had the reputation of being fit for all company from St James's to St Giles's. Schooled, after a fashion, at Eton and Göttingen, he fought three duels before he was twenty. His manners were unpredictable and his appearance, in Hessian plumes, was bizarre; but he was a useful companion when it came to shooting at chimney pots or riding horses upstairs, and the Prince thought him well worth an Equerry's pay. He is pilloried in numerous Gillray cartoons. George Cruikshank shows him, cloven-footed, with a gin-drinking woman under each arm and another at his feet. The *Gentleman's Magazine*, which published an obituary in 1824, tried to make the best of him: 'He was formerly admitted among the convivial companions of his present Majesty, but as the Prince advanced in life the eccentric manners of the Colonel became somewhat too free and coarse for the royal tastes.' The Colonel's person 'was disguised by the singularity of his dress,' but he was 'capable of serious exertions of friendship.' After his spell as Equerry, Colonel Hanger, pressed by creditors, spent some time in the Fleet Prison (a not uncommon address for the Prince's friends), and afterwards set himself up as a coal merchant. Although entitled to call himself Lord Coleraine, he chose not to do so, perhaps to spite the punsters. He wrote various works and is remembered by his stern advice on the protection of game. Any gentleman vexed by poachers, says Hanger, should mount a six-pounder on his roof and, at irregular intervals, send salvoes of clay balls and glass marbles whistling through his coverts. It was a day of eccentric military gentlemen, and Hanger was less outrageous than one of the Duke of Cumberland's *aides-de-camp*, Colonel Disney, 'a hare-brained, half-cracked sort of fellow,' who once beguiled the tedium of waiting at Windsor by wandering into the Queen's Bedchamber, where he put a golden vase 'to a use not to be named to ears polite.' For this offence, his master sought to inflict summary chastisement, which the Colonel evaded. He died heartbroken on the second anniversary of his enormity.*

A good deal of oddity marked Louis Weltje, Clerk of the Kitchen, a grotesque little German with a grotesque little wife. He is thought to have been a gingerbread seller in the streets of London and later a pastrycook. In the 1780s he conducted a hard-drinking, hard-gambling club near St James's, where at least one masquerade was held in the Prince's honour. As Clerk of the Kitchen he was once called to the royal table to answer a complaint that the soup had an odd flavour. He dipped a spoon in the tureen, sipped a sample, and exclaimed indignantly, 'Boh! Boh! Tish ver goote.' Then he laid down the spoon on the tablecloth and went back to his kitchen.†

Weltje had a taste for higher things than soup, for the Prince sent him to Paris to buy furniture and hangings. It was Weltje, again, who selected for the Prince his first house at Brighton, bought it and leased it to him, and superintended the first alterations to it. Thus he has some claim to be called the founder of the Pavilion. The little German enjoyed the Prince's favour until one of his daughters, without permission, married a cook in the Prince's household. Indignantly, Weltje asked the Prince to dismiss the cook, but was counselled to forgive and forget. Weltje nagged, then tried to bully, and the Prince solved the problem by dismissing both of them. Until he died, however, Weltje remained the Prince's landlord. He found it no easier to obtain settlement of his dues than anybody else, but he seems to have succeeded in his ambition to leave enough money for his 'posteriors.'

If the Prince liked a man's company, he would find some way of fitting him into the establishment. George Colman the younger, that indelicate actor-dramatist, was introduced to the Prince by the Duke of York, who extracted him from the King's Bench Prison for one night to attend Carlton House. There the unabashed debtor entertained the greatest debtor in the land and then returned, doubtless with a reeling head, to his jail. In 1820 he was appointed lieutenant of the Yeomen of the Guard, a post which in the ordinary way was obtained by purchase; but, thanks to the royal indulgence, he was

* *Gronow*   † Henry Angelo: *Reminiscences*

allowed to have it free, with the right to sell it when he wished. Four years later Colman was made Examiner of Plays. The responsibility of office seems to have sobered him, for he was possibly the most prudish censor on record.

But these were small fry. It is time to look at one of the most enigmatic figures in the Prince's intimate circle, the Irish-born Colonel (later Sir) John MacMahon, the natural son of a butler and a chambermaid. As Keeper of the Privy Purse, Private Secretary and Secretary Extraordinary (all of which titles he held before the Regency began), he was custodian of many scandalous secrets. Thomas Raikes describes him as a little obsequious man, with a red pimpled face, his head on one side, and always dressed in a blue and buff uniform; a 'prodigious foil' to his Master and always ready to execute any commissions, however complicated.* Huish's version of the Colonel's early career is that after starting life as an actor he joined the regiment of Lord Rawdon (the Earl of Moira) where a talent for pimping was rewarded with an ensigncy. By lending his wife to a royal duke he worked his way up to the rank of lieutenant-colonel, by which time he was ripe for employment as a Chiffinch at Carlton House.

Huish, who describes MacMahon as purveyor-general of female beauty to the royal harem, shakes his head for many pages over the wickedness of this pliant satellite. Once, it seems, MacMahon while riding in the coach to Bath made the acquaintance of a Marlborough clergyman with two beautiful daughters. Afterwards he wrote a 'most private' letter to his master, beginning, 'Sir, Ever alive to the obtaining possession of any object which may contribute to your royal pleasures, I hasten to inform your Royal Highness that chance has thrown me into the company of two most lovely girls . . . who, from their apparent simplicity and ignorance of the world, may be soon brought to comply with the wishes of your Royal Highness.' He described the elder as bearing some resemblance to 'Hillisberg' (an actress whom the Prince had pursued) and the younger as of a more languid beauty. 'From the knowledge which I possess of your royal tastes the elder will be the object of your choice.' MacMahon said that he would at once devise some plan to bring the girls to London.

* *Journal*

It reads remarkably like the kind of letter that G. W. M. Reynolds might have concocted for his marathon penny dreadful, *The Mysteries of the Court.* How, one wonders, did this remarkable epistle come into a historian's possession? Huish goes on to describe in scandalised detail the steps by which the rustic clergyman was flattered into coming to London and how the girls were passed into the hands of fashionable procuresses. To help him in such operations, according to Huish, MacMahon had a secretary, Marable, who joined in the game of flattery and corruption. Their favourite rendezvous was the 'Horse and Groom' at Streatham, where the Prince would call, as if by accident, in his coach.*

MacMahon began to attract public attention when he was appointed by the Prince Regent to the sinecure of Paymaster of the Widows' Pensions, at £2000. Nearly 30 years earlier this post had been recommended for abolition. In January 1812 many Members rose in Parliament to attack the appointment, while making it clear that they were not attacking MacMahon. Indeed, they went out of their way to praise him. Creevey said he had 'the good fortune to be well acquainted with the gentleman and he sincerely believed that a more honest and faithful servant never lived in the court of any prince whatever.' Whitbread declared that MacMahon was a man of whom he had never heard an evil report, so blameless was his conduct, both public and private. Sheridan said the Colonel's service with the Prince had been highly honourable. Brougham also praised him, but thought the appointment was an insult to the Colonel and to Parliament. Were all these Members talking with tongue in cheek?

The gallant Colonel was himself a member of the House, though he rarely appeared in it. In February 1812 he found time to speak in his own defence. He told how he had served in the Army for 21 years, seven of which were spent in the American war. If ill-health had not forced him to retire he would have been a lieutenant-general. 'Life at this moment seems to promise me but too short a span to ever requite by any services the abundant over-payment which the generosity and noble heart of my master has heaped upon me for 16 years past in acts of kindness and affection—acts which have been

* *Memoirs of George IV*

of so delicate and peculiar a nature as to bind my life heart and soul in eternal love and affection to him.' Members seem to have held back their tears. The Colonel said that in the matter of his sinecure, which he insisted was no sinecure, he would implicitly bow to the will and pleasure of Parliament. He had, of course, no other choice; and the House voted by a majority of three in his disfavour. Two months later William Henry (later Lord) Lyttleton, speaking on the Sinecure Offices Bill, said of MacMahon that the public who paid him knew of no services he had performed. It was notorious that the Regent was hemmed in by minions. Lyttelton said he would rather give hundreds of thousands to a Nelson or a Wellington than a single farthing to a Gaveston or a Despenser. A garbled version of this reached MacMahon, who thought Lyttelton had called him a gamester and a spendthrift, and protested indignantly. When told what Lyttelton had really said, he apparently made no further objection.

The Prince, annoyed that his favourite was deprived of his sinecure, at once appointed him Private Secretary at £2000 a year. This sparked off another row in Parliament. Why should the King require a secretary? George III did not have the benefit of one until he went blind. Why should the secrets of the Privy Council pass through a third party? What were the King's ministers for? Whitbread pointed out that Mac-Mahon already drew £1000 as Keeper of the Privy Purse, £1000 as Auditor of the Duchy of Cornwall, and £500 as secretary to the Prince in his ducal capacity. With this new office he would receive £4500 a year, 'which was very well.' Not long afterwards Lord Castlereagh announced that the salary of Colonel MacMahon would be paid through the Privy Purse, and his listeners cried 'Hear! Hear!' But Parliament was still unhappy about the nation's secrets passing needlessly, as they thought, through a courtier's hands. George III's Private Secretary, General Sir Herbert Taylor, had performed his duties with great discretion, and was trusted by both parties; MacMahon, in spite of extravagant lip service to his integrity, enjoyed no such confidence.

Nor was MacMahon's stature enhanced when, in 1813, he was revealed trying to bribe and bully the editor of the *Star* into abandoning his support of the Princess of Wales. He was seen distributing guineas for drinks among a score of the newspaper's printers.

In 1817 MacMahon, having devoted himself to the bottle after the death of his wife, was near the end of his tether. The sight of a confidential secretary disintegrating with drink was not one to increase the Prince's peace of mind. MacMahon was persuaded to leave for the West Country and Sir Benjamin Bloomfield took over his duties. When the Colonel died the *Gentleman's Magazine*, in a most respectful obituary, spoke of his 'very cultivated understanding' and described him as one of the best letter-writers of his time, but forbore to comment on the fact that he left £90,000. Others were not so reticent. Creevey, who had praised MacMahon in the House, said in his diary that Lady Beauchamp had paid the Colonel £10,000 to have her husband raised from a baron to an earl. His opportunities for selling honours were obviously enormous and doubtless he could have amassed much more if he had wished to do so.

Sir Benjamin Bloomfield had been an impecunious Gunner officer attached to the Prince's own regiment, the 10th Hussars, and had been taken under the princely wing by virtue of a gift for music and ingratiation. He had held the appointment of Chief Equerry, among others, before taking over the Privy Purse. Creevey blackens his character thoroughly and suggests that as the price of keeping his master's secrets he demanded an Irish peerage, the Order of the Bath and an embassy to a crowned head, all of which, along with the rank of lieutenant-general, came his way. He gave up the Privy Purse in 1824 to Sir William Knighton.

Bloomfield's fall was attributed to the enmity of Lady Conyngham who, by the time the Prince became George IV, in 1820, had ousted Lady Hertford from the royal favour. The third noble grandmother to bewitch the King, Lady Conyngham took upon herself many of the privileges, and none of the responsibilities, of Queen Consort. Her husband already owed to this liaison three Irish titles—a viscountcy, an earldom and a marquisate. He now became Lord Minster in the English peerage and was given a staff to wave as Lord Steward.

As 'Lady Steward,' the Marchioness went from one audacity to another. Like George I's mistresses, she did not shrink from wearing the Crown jewels. When entertaining at her town house she had her dinners cooked in the kitchens of St James's Palace and transported in specially-made containers. A fire was lit in her kitchen for such dishes as required heating on the spot, but the coals probably came from the Palace. She ordered carriages as required from the King's stable. Her family began to infiltrate into the Household and to use the royal servants. To all appearances, the King and the Conynghams were a *ménage à trois;* but the lady tired rapidly of her sovereign's maudlin affection, while losing none of her desire to rid him of his resources. The stage was soon reached when he came to her for tea and sympathy and received only tea and scorn.

Even before his father died, the King had become reluctant to appear in public. As far back as 1812 Leigh Hunt had been jailed for calling him, among other things, a fat Adonis, and Lamb had mocked him as the Prince of Whales. Cartoonists had needled him intolerably, even making fun of that ingenious engine which, at a time when his health was impaired, had been rigged up to enable him to mount a horse. It took the form of a chair built to be propelled up a ramp to a platform, and then raised to allow a horse to stand underneath; at a signal, the rider was lowered gently into the saddle. If this was the creation of the Master of the Horse's department, then clearly that department was earning its money, but it was all very humiliating for a man who had once ridden from Brighton to London and back in a day.

When Queen Charlotte died in 1819 another embarrassment befell the ruler. She had always received ladies at drawing-rooms; now he would have to stand in her place exposing his paunch to the eyes of young and merry women. Stay-makers and tailors struggled heroically (a coat might cost £300 by the time the alterations were completed) but Nature was incompressible. Levees were a lesser ordeal, but a certain slackness seems to have crept into the conduct of them. In May 1821 the *London Gazette* contained this arresting paragraph:

'The honour of knighthood having in two recent instances been surreptitiously obtained at the Levee, His Majesty, for the purpose of effectively guarding against all such disgraceful practices in future, has been pleased to direct that henceforth

'Inconveniences of a Crowded Drawing Room.' By George Cruikshank

no person shall be presented to His Majesty at the Levee by the Lord in Waiting to receive the honour of knighthood unless His Majesty's pleasure shall have been previously signified in writing to the Lord in Waiting by one of His Majesty's principal Secretaries of State.'

How could knighthoods be obtained surreptitiously? In one instance, it seems, a lord in waiting 'more good-natured than precise' saw a gentleman muttering to himself in a worried manner and asked what was the trouble. The gentleman replied that he was waiting for a certain earl who had promised to present him to the King for the honour of knighthood. As time went on, he showed more and more distress, and then asked the courtier if he would have the great goodness to make the presentation, both as a favour to himself and to his noble friend. This was done and the new knight paid over his fees of £112. Some time later, a similar success was achieved by another trickster. 'These two knights, we understand, cannot be unknighted,' said the *Globe*, 'but it has been intimated to them by authority that their titles will never be acknowledged nor inserted in the *Gazette*.' In the view of *The Times*, it would have been an act of justice towards genuine knights to publish the names of the impostors.

If MacMahon was a controversial figure, so was the ex-apothecary and man-midwife, Sir William Knighton, who dominated the King's last years. This smooth climber was first commended to Carlton House by Lord Wellesley. Later Knighton said: 'I understand the praise bestowed on me on this occasion was that I was the best-mannered medical man he [the King] had ever seen.' His professional colleagues became jealous and somebody tried to ruin him by saying that he had spoken offensively of the King's conduct towards the Princess of Wales. After becoming physician at Court, Knighton made the acquaintance of MacMahon by whom, says his widow, he was speedily admitted to terms of intimacy; a condescension which Lady Knighton seems to have considered as an honour. On MacMahon's death Knighton, as one of his executors, found some highly confidential papers. At once he took these to Carlton House and placed them, 'without comment or condition,' in his master's hands. His master, impressed by this singular display of honesty, if honesty it was, made Knighton

Auditor of the Duchy of Cornwall, and then, when Bloomfield fell into disgrace, Keeper of the Privy Purse. In effect, he also became Private Secretary.

Thereafter Knighton discharged the duties of the Privy Purse 'with the unshrinking firmness which its embarrassments required,' to quote his widow.* Soon his hand was everywhere. He wrote, for instance, to the architect Nash pointing out that the Pavilion roof was leaking because of faulty mastic (pans had to be set out all over the floors) and requesting him to do something about it. All tradesmen were compelled to get their accounts approved by Sir William in writing. The King grew to depend on him, wrote him letters beginning 'Dearest Friend' and appealed to him 'for God's sake' to report to him. According to Lady Knighton the King co-operated bravely in cutting out riotous expenditure; it was 'gratifying to observe the readiness of His Majesty to second the endeavours of his servant on this desirable point.'

Lady Knighton lists many mysterious missions to various parts of Europe undertaken by her husband in the royal service. Sometimes he travelled for days and nights on end, with no other rest than he could obtain sleeping in his carriage. From the great reticence in which these journeys are wrapped, and the urgency with which they cropped up, it is assumed that they were undertaken for the purpose of tidying up the loose ends of the King's loose life: paying off mistresses, buying up letters, reclaiming IOUs and so forth. Certainly Knighton must have cursed the range of his master's philanderings. In 1824 he went on a journey of 1600 miles, to an unstated destination, and shortly afterwards he was sent to Sardinia. Once, the discreet physician admitted to his wife that these journeys were embarrassing both publicly and privately. In his letters home he deplored the immoralities of the people among whom he travelled, but he was full of pride in the service of a royal profligate, whom he described as 'one of the cleverest and most accomplished men in Europe—full of benevolence.'

As time went on, and the King deteriorated bodily and mentally, only Knighton had the power to make him attend to business. By some, it was assumed that the physician

* Lady Knighton: *Memoirs of Sir William Knighton*

prospered by blackmailing his helpless master; by others, that he must be a fool if he did not. He and Lady Conyngham were thought to be in thieving alliance, neither trusting the other, neither daring to expose the other's activities. Greville says that the King, in the moments when his self-respect reasserted itself, expressed loathing for Knighton and cried for someone to assassinate him. In Parliament and press 'the man-midwife' did not escape criticism; these attacks, says his widow, were of 'unmerited illiberality.'

It is very difficult to like Sir William Knighton, or to give him credit for doing any more than putting the royal accounts in order. Among modern writers on the period who have handled him severely is Philip Lindsay,* who says that 'Knighton, while robbing the cash box, strove more to turn his master's thoughts towards heaven than to keep them on the earth earthy.' Doris Leslie dismisses him as a professional toady.† For the defence, a medical writer, Harley Williams, has paid Knighton a high tribute 'as a guardian of his royal patient's soul,' as one who performed 'that fundamental service . . . of providing mental assurance.' The King put absolute trust in him and without him would never have attained such repose as he did; so runs this argument.‡ But it is an argument which could equally have been held to justify the conscientious labours of MacMahon, who made no pretence to be a physician; or even of Lady Conyngham, who provided a mother figure of sorts for the King's consolation.

During the late 1820s the Court virtually ceased to exist. The man who once animated it slopped about in a dressing-gown and so did his Master of the Robes. Laudanum and cherry brandy, both in desperate quantities, dulled the pain of an outraged constitution. Buckingham House, which the King acquired in 1818, would have been a more private home than Windsor, but the future palace was in the throes of what were humorously called repairs, and these were to go on, to the high indignation of Press and Parliament, for two decades, until the palace had been rebuilt. In 1828 the housebreakers

* *The Loves of Florizel*
† *The Great Corinthian*
‡ *The Healing Touch*

descended on Carlton House and soon left not a trace behind—
save for those pillars which now adorn the National Gallery.
Meanwhile the King had made himself a fanciful retreat at
Virginia Water, where he built a Gothic ruin and a fishing
temple, and installed a menagerie. Here, to the music of the
royal band, cruised a splendid yacht, 'freighted with noble and
ignoble beauty.' The Rev. G. H. Croly says that, in order
not to be seen when travelling to Virginia Water, the King
ordered trees to be planted along miles of avenues, from which
the public were wholly excluded. Where these rides opened
towards the public thoroughfares of the park servants were
stationed to keep sightseers away. The King of England was
a sight not fit to be seen. Only by the connivance of servants
could the curious delights of Virginia Water be seen by the
unauthorised.*

The King had another bolt-hole in a little orangery under
the lip of the North Terrace at Windsor. Hard by was a dark
underground chamber lit by an overhead shaft, with mirrors
on the walls to improve the light. Here the King's sisters,
who had once grumbled that the King kept them like nuns in a
convent, now voluntarily spent their days like rats in a hole.
They had always been glad of a chance to scuttle from the
limelight. When the Court was at Weymouth, they used to
hide with their mother in an eight-seater bathing machine
drawn as far as possible out into the sea. There, as in their
consumptive cavern at Windsor, they read, sewed and gossiped.

Even when in the grip of gout, dropsy and all his other
disorders, the King—like the bloated Henry VIII in similar
distress—still indulged his passion for building. Under his
direction, John Nash reshaped London, creating many a noble
terrace and thoroughfare. At the hands of Sir Jeffrey Wyatt-
ville, Windsor Castle took on its present silhouette. The King's
urban monuments, Buckingham Palace excepted, survived to
be exceedingly praised by those who did not have to pay the
bill, and even the exotic tastes for which he was mocked became
a cult. It was at the King's instigation that the nation bought
John Julius Angerstein's collection of old masters, which
became the nucleus of the National Gallery.

The moribund King was a bad patient and drove his personal

* *Personal History of George IV*

staff to the verge of despair. But his Pages of the Back Stairs, at least, had their reward when, little more than a month after his death, the contents of his wardrobe in all their antic profusion were sold off by the King's Upholder,* a Mr Bailey, of Mount Street. The proceedings lasted a fortnight. Prices ranged from £200 for a sable pelisse, the gift of the Emperor Alexander, to five shillings a pair for a vast collection of shoes. Cambric and silk handkerchiefs fetched a guinea each, although the pages said they were worth only seven shillings. A cellar of snuff went for £400. At the end the pages divided £15,000 among them. The post had always been one with perquisites.

The Times, which mentioned the sale briefly,† had earlier said some hard things in its obituary of the King, though it did him the honour of reversing its column rules. Accused by an evening newspaper of having overstepped the bounds of taste, *The Times* replied that if it had any further provocation from blockheads afflicted by 'haberdasher loyalty' it would tell a great deal more, compared with which its earlier remarks would seem not merely forbearance but panegyric.‡

Many old observances fell away during the reign of George IV and were not missed. Among these were the New Year and Birthday Odes. In 1813 Sir Walter Scott was offered the laureateship, but declined, and Robert Southey was approached. An intermediary in the negotiations was John Wilson Croker, to whom Southey wrote saying that twenty years earlier he would have been glad to furnish odes on demand upon any subject, but that now he would approach the task like a schoolboy, with a sense of incapacity. 'But if these periodical exhibitions were dispensed with, and if I were left to write upon great events, or to be silent, according as the spirit moves, I should then thankfully accept the office as a mark of honourable distinction, which it would become.'§

Southey added that, of course, it must not be thought that he was laying down terms to the Prince. In the event, he wrote a number of State odes, on topics ranging from the bombardment of the corsairs' nest at Algiers to the death of Queen

* Upholsterer
† August 18, 1830
‡ July 17 1830
§ Louis J. Jennings (ed.): *The Croker Papers*

Charlotte. Wordsworth, who succeeded Southey, was not afraid to treat the office as a sinecure.

Among Court hangers-on there were some who chafed at the disappearance of former privileges. Nicholas Carlisle, appointed a Gentleman of His Majesty's Honourable Privy Chamber, awoke belatedly to the fact that there were no longer any perquisites attaching to the appointment. Brooding, he published in 1829 a book* deploring, among other things, a recent legal decision to the effect that a Gentleman of the Privy Chamber could no longer expect to be protected from arrest for debt (in earlier times the post had been much coveted for this reason). 'Why the Law should lend its aid to an unnatural intrusion upon the Prerogative, and should treat with asperity those privileges which were confirmed by the wisest council of the State is worthy of serious if not mournful consideration; as an admission of even the most minute advance upon ancient royal rights may lead to bitter repentance.' This aggrieved Gentleman could think. of no other explanation than that Mutability which governs all Human Affairs.

The *Westminster Review*, paying Carlisle the honour of taking his book seriously, took leave to doubt whether the constitution was really imperilled 'because a person holding a nominal appointment in the King's Household may not snap his fingers at some industrious artisan whom he has defrauded.' It then delivered this magisterial homily:

'The duties of a Gentleman of the Privy Chamber were once performed by the "Valets of the King's Chamber"; and in times when it was deemed an honour for people of birth and talents to render the most menial services to the Sovereign's person the appointments were held by gentlemen; but in our more civilised days, though the situation is not absolutely abolished, it has fallen into desuetude for the very obvious reason that our monarchs are assisted to dress and undress by their valets; to have the bell answered by their footmen; and to send their letters either by "messengers" or orderly dragoons.'†

And yet, said the *Westminster*, here was a man sighing in a thick octavo volume for 'the truly important, most dignified

---

* *An Enquiry into the Place and Quality of the Gentleman of His Majesty's Most Honourable Privy Chamber*
† April, 1830

and highly intellectual employment of sitting in the King's anteroom in readiness to bring him his sacred small clothes or to tie his royal garters.'

In this reign, the Herb Strewer performed her decorative duties for the last time. At the Coronation she and her garlanded maidens, dressed in white and scarlet, tossed fragrant herbs and flowers in the path of the procession from the Abbey to Westminster Hall. Efforts to revive the custom in later reigns were unsuccessful.

George IV died at a time when the masses were beginning to demand cheap sensational fiction, with a strong radical flavour. Inevitably, the facts and legends of his life were woven into many a 'penny dreadful,' and it is due to the authors of these works, perhaps even more than to Thackeray in his *Four Georges*, that the Court of George IV acquired in Victorian times its reputation for flat-out debauchery. In such works as *The Mysteries of the Court*, by G. W. M. Reynolds, and *Confessions of a Page*, by E. L. Blanchard, appear all the shady characters of the Prince's youth: Lady Jersey, the Lades, Colonel Hanger and Colonel MacMahon.

Reynolds, whose *Mysteries* ran in weekly instalments from 1850 to 1856, was one of the first to hit on the happy literary recipe of sex-and-Socialism. He gave many a luscious description of life at Carlton House, on which had been lavished so much 'gold wrung from the very vitals of the toiling millions.' The Prince is pictured waking from his usual morning hangover in a room littered with cosmetics, liquor bottles, whips, boxing gloves, duelling pistols and a 'pile of indecent pictures just imported from Paris and the more calculated to inflame the imagination because the designs and the colours were executed with an artistic perfection and a natural truthfulness well worthy of better subjects.'*

---

* Compare Thomas Moore's vision of the Prince at the dawn of a new day:
> Methinks the P . . . . e in whiskered state
> Before me at his breakfast sate;
> On one side lay unread petitions,
> On t'other, hints from five physicians . . . .
> *Here*, tradesmen's bills, official papers,
> Notes from my lady, drams for vapours,
> *There*, plans of saddles, tea and toast,
> Death warrants and the *Morning Post*.

Voluptuous tight-rope dancers entertain The Prince of Wales in his private rooms at Carlton House. From G. W. M. Reynolds' *The Mysteries of the Court*

It is difficult to know why the Prince needs these when, according to Reynolds, his walls are already hung with inflammatory classical paintings: Lucretia struggling in the arms of Tarquin, Cleopatra with Antony's head on her naked bosom, Mars and Venus sporting on a couch, Andromeda lashed naked to a rock, and many more.

The Prince's private bathroom is 'fitted up with every Oriental splendour and adorned with full-length mirrors in every direction.' There are voluptuous ottomans, buffets covered with wines, and vases filled with perfumes; and, of course, the heat is tremendous. As the Prince is about to perform his toilet the custodian of the private staircase, Tim Meagles, a horsy rogue, ushers in 'The Amazon,' otherwise the lascivious Lady Letitia Fluke (presumably Lady Letitia Lade), dressed as a man. She boxes a round or two with Meagles and is knocked out by him. Almost at once she is on her feet again, and says to the Prince: 'I envy your royal highness the possession of a bathroom contiguous to your sleeping chamber. I must positively make Sir John (her husband) have one fitted up for me.' After which the least the Prince can do is to invite her to share his bath.

Another morning the Prince, shortly after waking, is entertained, in a perfumed room with two fires, by 'six beauteous votaries of the Terpsichorean art.' Dancing degenerates into licence. Then the King enters unexpectedly and says, 'Hey-dey! Am I in Carlton House or in a luxurious brothel? 'Pon my word, George, your taste is very vicious—very vicious indeed.' He comes to tell the Prince that Lord Malmesbury is off to the Continent to fetch him a wife.

After marriage the Prince's private entertainments become a shade more fanciful. One evening he sits back watching three girls dancing on a tight rope stretched across his room. Their motions combine 'all the fascinating graces of the art with the most exquisite refinement of sensual provocation.' The dance lasts an hour, with intervals for champagne poured out by the Prince in person. The dancers have strong heads, even if their morals are weak.

Blanchard's work describes, among other things, Colonel MacMahon's traffickings with the underworld. One of his intimates is the procuress, Mrs General Hamilton, of whom the author confidently asserts: 'Hundreds of blooming victims were by this high priestess of debauchery annually sacrificed on unhallowed altars.'

Knowledgeable footnotes helped to give these accounts an air of authenticity. By hundreds of thousands they were doubtless accepted as a reasonably accurate picture of Court life under the fourth George.

26

Prudery and Prejudice

OF William IV's Court little need be said. The once hard-swearing, hard-drinking sailor had become a garrulous old gentleman of 65, very proud to be a king, very anxious to be affable to his subjects. Whereas George IV had shut himself from sight, William went out of his way to mingle informally with the public. He would even walk about London drawing a crowd behind him. Once he was kissed by a woman near White's; another time, his German Queen in her coach suffered her hand to be held by a rapt female admirer. The courtiers, especially those who had to bundle the King away from the mob, thought it all quite dreadful.

It was a galling day for William when the public, disliking his attitude to the Reform Bill, declined to cheer him in the street. Disgustedly, he spat over the side of the carriage. At this a voice cried, 'George the Fourth would not have done that.'

The old salt tried to do what was expected of him, always provided it did not clash too much with his comfort. At drawing-rooms he kissed the ladies on the cheek, sometimes getting their feathers in his mouth and their thick make-up on his lips. He was the last monarch to perform this sticky civility. Before his coronation he showed some repugnance at the idea of being bussed by bishops, but was told he must suffer spiritual salutations as well as temporal ones. He was fond of giving toasts and making speeches at his dinners, an innovation which Greville thought smacked of a tavern rather than a palace.

If the diarists are to be believed, William's Court was crushingly dull. At Windsor there would be a small bored company sitting round a mahogany table—'the Queen knitting or netting a purse, the King sleeping and occasionally waking up for the purpose of saying, "Exactly so, Ma'am," and then sleeping again.'* Queen Adelaide declined to receive ladies of doubtful reputation, a category which included actresses, ennobled or otherwise. Her attitude is not surprising when it is remembered that her husband had lived with the actress, Mrs Dorothea Jordan, for 20 years. The palaces buzzed with FitzClarences born of this union.

The King liked staying at the Pavilion, to which he was no stranger. Greville observed the Court there, 'very active, vulgar and hospitable,' with King, Queen, princes, princesses, 'bastards' and attendants constantly moving about the town.† At St James's William and Adelaide resented having to move their papers and belongings out of their apartments in order to hold levees and drawing-rooms. The King's ambition was to live a domestic life in Marlborough House, with a tunnel linking it to St James's. He had no great desire to take over Buckingham Palace, unless it was warranted comfortable and not too ostentatiously gilded, but the builders were busy on it during most of his reign. At one time, after a fortune had been spent on it, he toyed with the idea of turning it into a Guards barracks.

To his credit, William remedied certain abuses which had crept into the Court under his immediate predecessors. For example, ambitious civilians had been in the habit of buying themselves into the Yeomen of the Guard, and royal favourites had been appointed as its officers. The bodyguard once known as the King's Spears had also suffered dilution and was in no state to guard St James's Palace against Chartists or other dissidents. Under William it was re-titled the Honourable Corps of Gentlemen at Arms and, with the Yeomen of the Guard, once more became the pride and refuge of military men.

Politically, the King expected his Court to support his measures. In 1830, when Lord Grey mentioned to him that two of the Household had voted against the Reform Bill, he dismissed them at once. George III could not have acted more quickly. Lord Howe, the Queen's Chamberlain, was also turned out for the same offence, much to Adelaide's chagrin. Questioned in Parliament, Lord John Russell explained that

* *The Creevey Papers*
† *Greville Memoirs*

Lord Howe had offered his resignation after the vote and it had been accepted. Lord Howe denied this point-blank. He said that, long before the Bill came up, he had told the King he would vote against it, and had been assured that he was at perfect liberty to vote as he liked; thus, only a positive request by Lord Grey could have resulted in his dismissal. The Chancellor of the Exchequer then took shelter behind the prerogative. Nothing could be clearer, he said, than the right of the King to retain or dismiss his own servants, and it would be contrary to his duty to say why the prerogative had been exercised.

Among those dissatisfied with this explanation was Queen Adelaide. She continued to sulk and refused to appoint anyone else to the vacancy.

The Court did not yet stand above the political battle.

With the accession of 18-year-old Victoria hopes of a lively, distinguished and yet decorous Court were widely revived. The dreadful uncles were thinning out. Could she live down their past?

'Her Court was pure,' testifies Tennyson, but he was not writing of the first Court the Whigs gave her. This was a spotted one. It contained an inordinate representation of Pagets, a high-spirited family which, according to Lord Melbourne, made a point of never learning anything. It was he, of course, who was responsible for their preponderance in the Household. Of the three great officers, the Lord Steward was a Paget and the Lord Chamberlain was married to a Paget; these were, respectively, Lord Uxbridge and Lord Conyngham, son of the notorious Marchioness. Roger Fulford has revealed that both these gentlemen installed their mistresses on the Household staff.* Two daughters of Lord Uxbridge accompanied the Queen on walks and other Paget girls turned up as train-bearers or sang to the company after dinner. Not the least noteworthy of the family was Lord Alfred Paget, the Queen's Equerry, a dashing horseman whom the Queen thought 'remarkably handsome in his uniform of the Blues.' Court gossip said that the Queen admired more than Lord Alfred's horsemanship. Certainly she took pains to admire his dog. She noted in her diary an occasion

* *The Prince Consort*

when he went 'to see his father's leg which is buried at Waterloo' (his father was the Marquess of Anglesey, who commanded
the cavalry on that field.)

Other Pagets came and went, among them Lord George
Paget who was to ride in the Charge of the Light Brigade,

The Court of the young Queen Victoria

keeping a cigar between his teeth all the way to the guns. It was
not surprising that the press referred to Buckingham Palace
as 'the Paget clubhouse.'

Without a doubt, the Queen was ignorant of the cynical way
in which the Lord Chamberlain and Lord Steward had made
their amatory dispositions under her roof. They must have
shown considerably more discretion than Lord Palmerston who,
when Secretary for Foreign Affairs, was found in the wrong
bedroom at Windsor, with a very weak story. Much of the
Queen's animosity towards him in later life sprang from her
knowledge of this incident.

The Queen could hardly have been unaware of the worldly

past of her Prime Minister, Lord Melbourne, who on her accession had just been through the divorce courts for the second time in the role of co-respondent. On each occasion his name had been cleared.

If the Household smelled here and there, so did the palaces. Like the notorious military hospital at Scutari, Buckingham Palace was built over a sewer, the effluent from which invaded its kitchens. Its water closets, like those of Belgravia at large, had unmentionable habits. Windsor Castle was made noisome by a variety of ill-sited cesspools. Its rooms were chill and smoky. A number of its chimneys could be swept only by open defiance of the laws against the use of climbing boys (at one time girls were pushed up its flues). But the Queen clapped her hands over these desirable residences. Almost at once she moved into Buckingham Palace and was so pleased that she conducted her friends all over it, even into the kitchens. St James's now ceased to be a royal residence; it was used for ceremonies only.

The shortcomings of the Court, moral and physical, could not be cleaned up overnight. Meanwhile the girl Queen tried, by no means without success, to bring animation to its social life. Brilliance could not be forced, for the public, though professedly anxious to see pomp and pageantry, was unwilling to pay for it. The Queen gave dinner parties and set up a small orchestra to play during them. Once a week there was dancing. Among the more picturesque Court diversions were the riding excursions when the Queen with her Household officers would set out in a cavalcade perhaps thirty or forty strong, ranging out to the fields and lanes of Harrow, to Richmond Park or to Acton, and returning, pleasantly stimulated, through a huddle of carriages and omnibuses. In her diary she would record how they had ridden twenty-two miles (three exclamation marks), or galloped for three miles without stopping. Once, she came a cropper, and it is perhaps unnecessary to say that the horse which threw her—Uxbridge—was also a Paget.

Four persons, three of them foreigners, and all sharing varying degrees of public distrust, contended for the honour of guiding Victoria. They were the meddling Baroness Lehzen, the Queen's former governess, who was her confidante in domestic matters and acted as an unofficial Lady Steward;

the high-minded Baron Stockmar, another physician turned politician; King Leopold of the Belgians, the Queen's uncle; and Lord Melbourne, an elderly cynic who seemed ideally cast for the role of corrupter of innocence. The Queen's mother, the Duchess of Kent, whose aspirations had so vexed William IV, had hoped to sit at her daughter's elbow, but had been very firmly pushed on one side by her.

Lord Melbourne had signally neglected to cultivate Queen Adelaide, preferring to chaff her maids of honour, and she had found it difficult to forgive. Victoria could not complain of lack of attention. It is a familiar story how Melbourne fell in love with the Queen as an uncle might fall in love with a niece, and how she in turn idolised him. He spent a great deal of time in her company, sitting bolt upright instead of sprawling indolently as was his wont (he was more fortunate than his successors in that he was allowed to sit). 'His situation,' said Croker, 'is certainly the most dictatorial, the most despotic the world has ever seen . . . Wolsey and Walpole were in straight waistcoats compared to him.' But Croker conceded that 'his temper and feelings lead him to no great abuse of his enormous influence.'* Other statesmen looked on enviously, recognising that Melbourne's charm showed up their shortcomings. 'I have no small talk and Peel has no manners,' said the Duke of Wellington.

The Prime Minister guided the Queen in matters of Court etiquette as well as of State. When she was asked to receive a lady who had been rejected by Queen Adelaide, Lord Melbourne advised her not to reverse such a decision at this early stage. Then, treading on delicate ground, he urged her as a general principle to turn away only those persons who had been found guilty by courts of law. If nothing was proved against them, they should be received, irrespective of gossip. It was a useful working rule, but it meant in practice that the only social sin was to be found out. On the subject of chaperonage and the waltz, the Prime Minister supported the Queen's views; she was in favour of the former, not of the latter.

Victoria learned fast. Soon she was ready for trial flights on her own. It was observed that when she laughed she showed her teeth, but she could show her teeth without laughing. She

* Louis J. Jennings, (ed.): *The Croker Papers*

made it clear that she was unwilling to be browbeaten by her high officers. The Duchess of Sutherland, her Mistress of the Robes, was 'so handsome and nice,' but this did not save her from a rebuke for being half an hour late. The Queen differed with her Master of the Horse, Lord Albemarle, on his claim to ride with her in the State coach to Westminster. Albemarle consulted the Duke of Wellington, who said, 'My good fellow, the Queen can, as she pleases, make you go inside the coach or outside the coach or run behind the coach like a tinker's dog.'

Self-will and inexperience, along with a certain prudishness, brought tribulation in their train. The first scandal of the reign broke over the hapless head of Lady Flora Hastings, the Duchess of Kent's gentlewoman, whom the Queen already disliked (it seems that Lady Flora had mocked the royal passion for caraway seeds). A change in Lady Flora's physical appearance, coupled with the knowledge that she had shared a coach from Scotland with the unpopular Sir John Conroy, the Duchess of Kent's more-than-confidential secretary, caused Victoria's ladies to suspect the worst. Baroness Lehzen ensured that their gossip reached the ears of the Queen, who did insufficient to discourage it. With great reluctance and indignation, Lady Flora submitted to a physical examination and the medical verdict exonerated her, without making her any more popular at Court. Lord Hastings, her brother, having vainly sought redress or apology, handed the correspondence to the press. *The Times*, apologising for inflicting such matters on its readers, explained that this was the newest stage in 'the late disgraceful (atrocious would not be too strong a word) intrigue at Buckingham Palace—an intrigue the victim of which was as pure and high-minded a being as breathes, and the purpose of which was to mortify the mother of the Queen in order to inflame dissension in the royal family.'* *The Morning Post* also took a strong line, saying that Lady Flora was 'the victim of a depraved Court.'

It emerged from the correspondence that the Dowager Marchioness of Hastings had written to Lord Melbourne demanding the dismissal of Sir James Clark, the Queen's physician. She used the phrase 'atrocious conspiracy.' But Lord Melbourne knew how to reply to angry dowagers:

* April 17, 1839

Victim of **Court** gossip: Lady Flora Hastings

'The demand which your ladyship's letter makes upon me is so unprecedented and objectionable that even the respect due to your ladyship's sex, rank, family and character would not justify me in more, if indeed, it authorises so much, than acknowledging that letter for the sole purpose of acquainting your ladyship that I have received it.'

With the highest respect, he then signed himself her ladyship's obedient and humble servant.

Publication of the correspondence whipped up intense public indignation and the Court, which had enjoyed so much initial goodwill, became wildly unpopular. The Tories detected a deliberate plot by the Whig ladies of the Bedchamber. Greville thought the whole affair was the sort of thing that only happened in the servants' hall, where housekeepers were wont to accuse still-room maids of frailty.

Not very long afterwards, Lady Flora became mortally ill as a result of the condition which had engendered false suspicions. (It may have been the same disease which deluded Mary Tudor). The Queen was persuaded at long last, by Lord Melbourne, to call personally on the victim, and it is possible that Lady Flora received a private apology. Her death served to inflame afresh public anger against Queen and Court. From that august forum of public opinion, the fashionable enclosure at Ascot, Victoria was hissed by the Duchess of Montrose and Lady Sarah Ingestre, an incivility which drew from the young Queen the comment that 'those two abominable women ought to be flogged.'

Before Lady Flora died, another Palace storm arose. Trouble had been foreseen in the Bedchamber ever since the accession, when Lord Melbourne had thickly planted the Household with Whiggish ladies and gentlemen. He was alleged to have said that not so much as a Conservative cat should mew about the palace. In the *Quarterly Review* of July, 1837, John Wilson Croker, the Tory spokesman, warned of the danger of surrounding the Queen with 'hot and therefore offensive partisans . . . we know to what unhappy and scandalous scenes a departure from this wholesome understanding gave rise in former reigns.'

It was neither constitutional nor desirable, thought Croker, that 'the Sovereign should be enclosed within the circumvallation of any particular set, however respectable—that in the hours of business or amusement, in public or in private, she should see only the repetition of the same family faces, and hear no sound but the different modulations of the same family voices . . . The Sovereign should not be reduced to such a state of unconstitutional dilemma as not to be able to change the ministry without also changing the Mistress of the Robes or the maids of honour—or vice versa, the Mistress of the Robes or maids of honour without also changing her ministry.'

The crisis Croker foresaw duly happened. In 1839 the Whigs resigned and Sir Robert Peel was called on to form a Government. He decided he could not do so unless the Sovereign gave him public proof of her confidence by dismissing some of the Whig ladies about her person. Peel had none of the ingratiating address of Melbourne and his stiff, awkward manner caused the Queen to take umbrage. Wilfully, perhaps, she misunderstood his request, which was not for a clean sweep of all her ladies but a pruning out of those in the rank of Lady of the Bedchamber and above. She assured him that she did not talk politics with her ladies, but he was still dissatisfied. Then this haughty announcement was issued from Buckingham Palace:

'The Queen, having considered the proposal made to her yesterday by Sir Robert Peel, to remove the Ladies of the Bedchamber, cannot consent to adopt a course which she conceives to be contrary to usage and which is repugnant to her feelings.'

The Duke of Wellington supported Peel, but the Queen decided she would not be intimidated. To Melbourne, who had been in favour of compromise, she wrote: 'Do not fear I was not calm and composed. They wanted to deprive me of my ladies and I suppose they would deprive me next of my dressers and housemaids. They wished to treat me like a girl but I will show them that I am Queen of England.' If Peel were to resign on this issue, Victoria considered, he would cut a sorry figure. Already, in her eyes, he had forfeited respect; 'I never saw a man so frightened,' she wrote after he had left her presence.

Melbourne pointed out that Peel had a good case but he was reluctant to antagonise the Queen. When Sir Robert resigned, Melbourne consented to form another Government. At a State ball the Queen did not conceal her jubilation. The more sentimental members of the public rejoiced with her; but the more serious-minded recognised the situation for what it was, the defeat of a political party by the sovereign. In high Tory circles the Queen's unpopularity was never greater; Melbourne tried to take much of the blame, as well he might. It was not long before the Queen realised she had overplayed her hand. Later that year Lady Sandwich, wife of a Tory peer, was invited to join the Household.

What the Queen needed, clearly, was the steadying influence of a husband. In 1840 she proposed to, and was accepted by, Prince Albert, of Saxe-Coburg-Gotha, the first royal love match for perhaps a century. At this stage, if Stockmar is to be believed, Albert was a young man with a dislike of intellectual labour and was politically apathetic; but the Baron vowed to cure him of these deficiencies and to preserve him from the 'English faults' which had so disfigured the royal family in recent memory.

When Albert demurred at having his household chosen for him, the Queen treated him firmly, even severely. Gradually, prodded by Stockmar, he made it clear that he was not content to spend the rest of his life passing the blotting paper. By slow degrees he established mastery, not only over Victoria's affections but over her mind; and by the time of his death he had achieved considerable mastery over her politicians.

Between Albert and Victoria, at the outset, there was a clash of interests. He wanted to get away from London; she loved the capital. He wanted to invite men of culture to the royal board; she feared she would be unequal to their conversation. He wanted to remove Lehzen; she wanted to retain her. On all these points Albert got his way.

In the first ten years of marriage, Victoria produced seven children. The birth of the Prince of Wales, in 1841, occurred only a day or two after an outbreak of unwitting lese-majesty in Rotten Row. As the Queen and her Consort were taking a carriage airing, a well-dressed gentleman on a high-mettled horse dashed past them. Said *The Times:* 'The fact of breaking through the etiquette of the road, which is on all occasions to give precedence to royalty, was not unnoticed by Her Majesty's outriders, who galloped after the gentleman and brought him back to Lt-Col. Arbuthnot and Col. Wylde, the Equerries in waiting. The person pleaded ignorance of the prohibition established by etiquette with regard to passing royalty and after apologising for his rude behaviour he was allowed to depart.'* It is difficult to know on what grounds he could have been detained.

The timing of the Prince's birth was of deep concern to many. Various lord mayors and mayors expected to receive baronetcies or other honours in celebration of the event, but there was a risk that the delivery would take place just after their terms of office had run out, and the honour would fall to their successors. *Punch* said that for a fortnight the Lord Mayor of London had not slept a wink, nor had his lady smiled. It pointed out that twins—one to be born on November 8 and one on November 9—would be an effective compromise. Other interested parties were the subalterns on guard duty at St James's Palace. It was traditional, on those rare occasions when the sovereign gave birth to an heir, for the officer then commanding the guard to be raised to the rank of major. The guard was relieved at 10.45 p.m. on November 9 and three minutes later the tardy Prince was born. The problem was: should the promotion go to the officer of the old guard or the new? The Commander-in-Chief, Lord Hill, decided in favour of the officer commanding the old guard. Both new and old Lord Mayors of London received their baronetcies.

It had been known for some time that an heir was on the way and several ladies of good position had solicited the honour of nursing the Prince. According to one historian, the Queen herself selected a wet nurse from among the domestic staff at Claremont, a property owned by King Leopold. But *The Times* published a delightfully embellished version of this story.† It said that shortly before the birth the wife of a royal under-servant, Mrs Brough, who had recently given birth to a child, travelled from the country to London with her husband. She had no special ambition to be the Prince's nurse, but hearing that numerous ladies with no better qualifications than

* Nov. 10, 1841
† Nov. 18, 1841

her own were at Buckingham Palace soliciting the appointment, she decided to join them. Four physicians examined her, seemed satisfied and told her that if the birth occurred within three weeks she would be called to London. This duly happened. Mrs Brough was met by a royal carriage, like a maid of honour, and was driven to the Palace. Both the Queen and the Consort saw Mrs Brough's own child and expressed concern that it should be placed to another wet nurse and liberally provided for. *The Times* recalled that the last royal wet nurse had received £500 and thought there was a good chance of Mrs Brough receiving double that sum for suckling an heir to the Throne. The moral of this story—that one should never lightly pass by a queue—has not been lost on the women of Britain.

In the same year that the Queen was fortunate enough to find a husband suited to her station, her cousin Prince George of Cambridge, whose family had hoped that he and Victoria might marry, fell in love with an actress, Louisa Fairbrother. He did not ask for permission to wed, knowing that it would almost certainly be refused under the Royal Marriages Act. Believing that his private life was his own, he married Miss Fairbrother morganatically; that is, on the understanding that neither she nor her children would have any claim to share his rank or possessions. Thereafter, as Prince and later as Duke of Cambridge, he kept his public and private careers strictly separate. His wife was known as Mrs FitzGeorge and had three distinguished sons. It took some time for Victoria to grow used to the idea of an actress in the family, but when Mrs Fitz-George died in 1890 she sent the Duke an affectionate message of sympathy.

27

Reforms—and Criticisms

B OTH Prince Albert and Baron Stockmar were vexed by the ill-government of the Queen's Household. One day when the Queen sent Stockmar to complain that the dining-room was always cold he received from an official the explanation: 'You see, properly speaking, it is not our fault; for the Lord Steward lays the fire only and the Lord Chamberlain lights it.'

To Stockmar's delight, Albert gave him the task of investigating the running of the Household and he produced a catalogue of follies suggestive of the demarcation idiocies in which trade unions indulge today. The root of the trouble, he contended, was that all the important Court appointments were political ones; a person's qualifications for the post were purely secondary. In some ten years there had been five changes of Lord Chamberlain, six of Lord Steward. The three great officers all lived outside the palace, and were thus unable to inspect their departments. The result was that they delegated their authority, 'a fact which almost daily is productive of consequences injurious to the dignity, order, discipline and security of the Court.'

During the three preceding reigns the Lord Steward and Lord Chamberlain had squabbled over the right to control the ground floor rooms, claiming or renouncing authority according to their personal whims. Both officers were agreed on one point, however: the control of the outside of the palace belonged to the department of Woods and Forests, a branch notorious for its lethargy. One result of this was that 'as the inside cleaning of the windows belongs to the Lord Chamberlain's department the degree of light to be admitted into the palace depends proportionally on the well-timed and good understanding between the Lord Chamberlain's office and that of the Woods and Forests.'

As far as Stockmar could discover, the Lord Steward was supposed to control the housekeepers, pages and housemaids; the Master of the Horse looked after the footmen, livery porters and under-butlers; and the Lord Steward was responsible for the rest. Only the Lord Steward had a resident representative in the palace, the Master of the Household. The scope of this individual's activities was extended or diminished by successive great officers, and the confusion was such that he was in effect a nullity. Two-thirds of the servants, having no resident master, were free to do as they liked. They came and went unobserved and uncorrected, absented themselves from duty and were free to commit any excess. 'If smoking, drinking or other irregularities occur in the dormitories, where footmen etc. sleep ten and twelve in each room, no one can help it.'

The Baron pointed out the sad results of this lack of system on royal hospitality. There was no one to attend to the comfort of the Queen's guests on their arrival. No one showed them to and from their apartments. No gentlemen of the Household knew where visitors were lodged. Guests at Windsor had been known to wander for an hour in search of the dining-room; their only recourse was to send a servant, if they could find one, to the porter's lodge for assistance. From the point of view of security, the system was equally deplorable. Already the notorious urchin Jones (In-I-go Jones) had shown how easy it was to break into Windsor and to hide under furniture in the royal suite. A would-be assassin could have done his deed far more easily and safely in this ill-run palace than in the public street. Yet the blame for the Jones affair, as Stockmar pointed out, could not be fixed on the Lord Chamberlain, who had an alibi in Staffordshire, and who in any event was not responsible for the porters; nor on the Lord Steward, who had nothing to do with pages near the Person; nor on the Master of the Household, who was a mere subordinate.

Stockmar listed other infelicities arising from divided rule. Besides supplying fires for the Lord Steward to light, the Lord Chamberlain provided lamps for him to light, clean and trim. If a pane of glass or a cupboard was broken in the scullery the procedure was this: the Chief Cook signed a requisition and had it counter-signed by the Clerk of the Kitchen. It was then taken to the Master of the Household, thence to the Lord Chamberlain's office for authorisation and thence to the Clerk of Works under the office of Woods and Forests. The result was that panes and cupboards stayed broken for months.

The Baron bravely refrained from recommending that the three great officers should be abolished, or alternatively that they should be compelled to perform their duties. Instead he urged that they should delegate firm authority to one resident official.*

Conducting a few personal investigations of his own, the Prince was puzzled to find that 35s a week was being spent on 'Red Room Wine.' Not without difficulty he discovered that when George III was nearing his end a certain room at Windsor, hung in red, was used as a guard-room, and that five shillings a day had been authorised to buy wine for officers. The idea of terminating this grant when the guard-room closed had obviously aroused repugnance, and no difficulty was found in transferring it to a new recipient. At the time of the Prince's investigations, the money was going into the pocket of a half-pay officer holding the nominal post of under-butler at Windsor. He was considerably pained when he was invited to perform the duties of his office.

When the Prince approached Sir Robert Peel to discuss possible reforms in the Household, the Prime Minister said he would regret any changes which would decrease the value of the appointments held by the three great officers and render them 'less an object of, ambition than they are at present to very distinguished members of the House of Peers.'

Eventually Prince Albert obtained absolute authority for the Master of the Household over all the servants. He cut the salaries of 80 housemaids, who worked only six months of the year, from £45 to a maximum of £18. He abolished the custom whereby new candles were installed daily in the public rooms, regardless of whether or not the existing ones had been lit (these were the footmen's perquisite). In so doing he incurred much odium from those servants who had been brought up in a tradition of splendid waste. Gradually law, economy and

* *Memoirs of Baron Stockmar* (ed. by his son)

decorum found in Windsor Castle and Buckingham Palace an unwonted habitation.

A disciplinary hand was also needed in the 'grace and favour' residences within the gift of the Queen, for the privileged residents were not above such impertinences as sheltering debtors. The Lord Chamberlain seems to have handled this abuse firmly. At various times members of the Royal Household tried to escape prosecution for debt by pleading immunity. In 1855, when a royal chaplain tried this game at Buxton, he was struck from the list and restored to the jail from which he thought to have freed himself.*

The Prince Consort also strove to tighten etiquette in the Court. He ruled that no man should sit in the Queen's presence except at dinner. To keep the score even, the Queen ruled that no maids of honour should sit in the presence of the Consort—or speak to him unless addressed. When Lady John Russell, wife of the Prime Minister, visited Buckingham Palace soon after her confinement, the Queen allowed her to sit, but took good care when the Prince joined the company to have a very fat lady sitting in front of Lady Russell, lest he show his displeasure. Notoriously, the Queen kept her Prime Ministers standing. To Lord Derby, when he was recovering from a long illness, she expressed her regrets that etiquette would not allow her to permit him to sit. Disraeli, during an attack of gout, was invited to take a chair, but judged it tactful to decline. Queen Elizabeth had kept her courtiers standing too, but she had stood with them.

The maids of honour were closely watched. At Windsor they were not allowed to go unchaperoned farther than the parapet of the East Terrace. In 1846, because there had been many queries about the maids' duties, a framed and glazed copy of new standing orders was installed in their room, much to their disgust. The Queen advised them to lock their bedrooms at night, saying that she always did. One of them, Eleanor Stanley, has put on record that, although mistletoe was hung in the Castle at Christmas, the ladies and gentlemen of the Household were not encouraged to take advantage of it.† The Prince's name was never remotely linked with that

* Vera Watson: *A Queen at Home*
† *Twenty Years at Court*

of a maid of honour. He rarely went anywhere without an Equerry, and this was ascribed as much to a desire to protect his reputation as to enhance his dignity.

In the early years of marriage the Queen and the Prince were in the habit of playing such card games as commerce, old maid and *vingt-et-un*—which the vulgar call pontoon—with their immediate entourage. Even in this diversion etiquette established itself. Courtiers who lost to the Sovereign were required to pay in new-minted coin, a stock of which the ladies and gentlemen in waiting always kept in readiness. This custom was still maintained in Edward VII's reign. It is not easy to picture Baron Stockmar calling the equivalent of 'pontoons only' and scooping in the royal cash. In fact, he did not play cards and usually went to bed early. It was a sign of his status that he was allowed to retire before the Queen and Consort. The maids of honour were expected to sing and play musical instruments. By day they indulged in battledore and shuttlecock with the Queen and sometimes joined the children in 'romps.' Eleanor Stanley thought the princes and princesses were 'dear little things, putting out their fat bits of hands to be kissed and making their civil speeches.'

Even at this period of her life the Queen had an unhealthy obsession for mourning. When the Princess Sophia Matilda of Gloucester died the palace blinds were kept half down, music and cards were stopped and the only recreation allowed was looking at albums. In memory of the Duchess of Saxe-Coburg the Queen had all the windows darkened save for a tiny slit of light. Her mother, the Duchess of Kent, who now had her own home at Frogmore, hated dark rooms but did not want to offend her daughter by disobeying the rules. She therefore posted a look-out and on the Queen's approach her servants rushed to close shutters and pull down blinds. For special events mourning was relaxed. The maids of honour found it all 'too plaguy' to wear black one day, white the next for a princess's birthday, and then to plunge back into the depths of sorrow.

The Prince often rode out with the royal buck hounds. He did not dislike fox hunting so much as he disliked English fox hunters (they, for their part, were astonished to find him a skilled and fearless rider). His apparent liking for blood sports and his efforts to initiate his gentle wife into such activities aroused a good deal of condemnation. There was a famous visit by Victoria and Albert to Gotha, where a picturesquely barbarous exhibition was staged in a clearing of the forest. The Queen and the other guests were invited to sit in a pavilion covered with fir branches, opposite large canvas hangings which concealed another entrance to the clearing. At a signal the canvas was pulled away, and to the cry of the *chasseurs*, a number of stags and hinds raced into the enclosure. There they were shot down, some 55 head of them, to the music of a large band. Let *Punch* continue the story, in a 'Sonnick, sejested by Prince Halbert gratiously killing the Staggs at Sacks-Coburg-Gothy:

> Britannia's Queen let fall the purly tear,
>   Seeing them butchered in their silvan prisns;
> Igspecially when the keepers who stood round
>   Came up and cut their pretty hinnocent whizns.'

Victoria tried to be polite about the entertainment and to appreciate its medieval charm, but she wrote in her *Journal*: 'As for the sport itself, none of the gentlemen like this butchery.'

Little though they cared to follow any precedents set by the Prince Regent, Victoria and Albert nevertheless organised several large balls with the stated object of helping depressed trades. In 1842 was held the Plantagenet Ball, designed for the benefit of the Spitalfields weavers. It was the first function of its kind to be held in Buckingham Palace. Victoria, dressed as Queen Philippa, wore some £60,000 worth of jewels on her stomacher. Albert appeared as Edward III. The next most resplendent figure was the Duchess of Cambridge, as Anne of Brittany, with her own court of one hundred. When the plans for this event were announced the King of the Belgians wrote to say that there was lively apprehension in France because of a suggestion that in Anne of Brittany's procession King John of France was to be represented as a prisoner in chains.

The next function of this type was the *bal poudré* of 1845, when the costumes worn were those of the time of George II. According to the *Annual Register* the *outré* head-dresses were a trying ordeal for the ladies and the unaccustomed high heels robbed them of grace in their gait, but they 'sacrificed themselves to historical propriety.' Certain gentlemen in Highland garb also teetered round on the high heels of the period. One critic thought that the gentlemen in their powdered wigs failed to catch the peculiar manners of the time and therefore did not completely realise the picture. It is unlikely that these functions greatly appealed to the Queen's sober statesmen. On this occasion Sir Robert Peel was said to look remarkably stately, but Palmerston seemed to shrink away under his 'unwonted habiliments.' The Duke of Wellington, who appeared as 'Butcher' Cumberland, was recognisable only by his nose. 'The scarlet hung loosely about him and the nether garments were so ample as to give him a more aged and shrunken appearance than he would have had in a more becoming costume.' By contrast Lord John Russell looked twice his ordinary size in full wig and capacious coat. Lord Cardigan, that notorious martinet, had the 'true jack-boot stride and swagger' as an officer of the 11th Dragoons at Culloden, thus confirming the widely held view that he had been born a century too late.

Six years later was held a Restoration ball. Although certain gentlemen appeared as specific historical characters, no attempt seems to have been made by the ladies to identify themselves with the illustrious courtesans of Whitehall. The Consort cut a chromatic figure in a coat of rich orange satin, brocaded with gold, crimson velvet breeches and lavender stockings. As stylish as any was the United States Minister in blue velvet, richly trimmed with gold lace, a gold baldrick and a scarlet velvet mantle: this was said to be the costume of a governor of a New England colony of the period.

Soon after her marriage Victoria, under Albert's influence, began to lose her taste for London. In 1844 she bought Osborne, in the Isle of Wight, a secluded estate 'free from all Woods and Forests and other charming departments.' Four years later she leased Balmoral, recommended by her physician, Sir James Clark. The Pavilion at Brighton failed to please; Victoria's taste ran to extravaganzas of tartan rather than of *chinoiserie*. In 1847 nearly 150 furniture vans carried away the treasures from the Prince Regent's Xanadu. These were distributed among the other palaces. Henceforth the capital was to see less and less of the Queen.

The Court's failure to patronise the higher culture pained certain sections of the press, notably *The Times*. This newspaper was one of several which lost their tempers when the Court succumbed to the blandishments of Phineas T. Barnum and granted an audience to 'General' Tom Thumb. The dwarf was so well received that he was invited to return. In the words of the *Court Circular* 'his personation of the Emperor Napoleon elicited great mirth and this was followed by a representation of the Grecian statues, after which the General danced a nautical hornpipe and sang several of his favourite songs.' The Queen presented him with gifts and a coat of arms, after which 'the General made his *congé* amidst the congratulations of the royal party.' One of those who shared the mirth was the Queen of the Belgians. In view of the General's repertoire, it is perhaps as well that the French Ambassador was not present. Clearly royalty had not yet lost the interest in dwarfs which had characterised the Court in earlier centuries.

There were those who thought the reception of Tom Thumb at Court less exceptionable than the visit of Robert Owen, the godless Socialist from the north. But Victoria was learning, or being persuaded, to receive representatives of all parties, however distasteful their views.

One branch of culture the Court did much to popularise, and that was music. Mendelssohn was a frequent visitor in the early 1840s. The Consort believed music to be the ideal outlet for that natural craving for excitement which drove an untutored populace to drink and dissolute behaviour. 'Music acts directly on the emotions,' he said, 'and it cannot be abused, for no excess in music is injurious.' Sir Richard Holmes has said: 'Never, in the history of any art, has royal patronage so rapidly provoked the sleeping genius of a race into activity.'*

Before Victoria's accession Parliament had tidied up some of the abuses attaching to Civil List pensions, and the Sovereign was freed of the temptation to raid the secret service money for improper purposes. The Crown, however, was given permission to create new Civil List pensions to the modest value

* *Edward VII: His Life and Times*

The theatre comes to Windsor Castle, 1849. *Illustrated London News*

of £1200 a year. Although the awards under this heading were mostly trivial, many of them engendered hard feeling against the Queen and her ministers. The anonymous author of *Court Jobbery or the Black Book of the Palace* (1848) reminded his numerous readers that Civil List pensions were intended, in Parliament's own words, for 'such persons only as have just claims on the royal benevolence, or who, by their personal services to the Crown, by the performance of duties to the public or by their useful discoveries in science and attainments in literature and the arts, have merited the gracious consideration of their Sovereign and the gratitude of their country.'

Yet, said the indignant author, Civil List pensions were being given to Court butterflies and State caterpillars. 'Why, there are absolutely persons on this list of pensioners (drawing hundreds a year from the impoverished taxpayer) who are living in the greatest splendour—keeping horses, carriages and servants—giving dinner and evening parties—entertaining 1200 visitors at a time to a *fête champêtre*—with a box at the Opera— whilst the widow and two children of a meritorious police officer, who was murdered at Deptford while in execution of his duty, are fobbed off with £8 6s 8d a year each.'

The pensioners fell into these broad categories: former Court and State servants; literary men and women; widows of distinguished wrecks and suicides; and dependants of policemen or individuals injured in riots.

Rashly, Victoria awarded a block of pensions to her old teachers of German, Italian, French, music, dancing, singing and writing. Some of them already had good incomes, or were married to persons who had. There was even £400 for Baroness Lehzen, for 'faithful services.' This pension, said the author of the *Black Book*, was a shameful one, but only in so far as it was paid from the Civil List. It should have been found, along with the others, from the Privy Purse. Much harder to defend was the sum of £1000 paid in two instalments in 1845 to Mlle Augusta Emma d'Este, 'in consideration of her just claims on the royal benevolence.' This woman was the illegitimate daughter of the late Duke of Sussex, the Queen's uncle, whose marriage had been dissolved under the Royal Marriages Act, thus bastardising the offspring. Mlle d'Este suffered no financial stringency and was about to marry a wealthy judge,

Sir Thomas Wilde, later Lord Truro, a Lord Chancellor. The author of the *Black Book* found it difficult to see in what way Mlle d'Este had merited the gratitude of the country, and described the whole affair as 'a shameful and atrocious job.' He used even stronger adjectives—among them gross, rascally, villainous and infamous—to describe the award of £1000 to the aged Sir John Newport, for zealous and efficient services as Chancellor of the Exchequer of Ireland and Comptroller General of the Exchequer of the United Kingdom. This 'public cormorant for 50 years' was to be paid five-sixths of the available money for the year, probably in order to persuade him to resign.

It was a favourite theme of this critic that public men whose health had failed them or who had left their widows destitute ought to have taken out insurances while they were in good financial health. Why should the taxpayer pay for their improvidence?

Some of the awards to the Republic of Letters also occasioned indignation. The payment of £300 to William Wordsworth was perhaps little enough for a man 'if liable to be called on to write an eulogistic ode upon such an occasion as the late installation of Field-Marshal the Prince Consort as Prince Chancellor of Cambridge'; but the facts were that Wordsworth was not in want and at the time of the award was Distributor of Stamps for Westmorland and Cumberland at £2000 a year (offices which he passed on to his son). Pensions of £300 to the blind Lady Morgan, 'the celebrated Irish novelist,' £200 to Tennyson, and £100 to the widow of Tom Hood (who wrote *The Song of the Shirt*) were not grudged; and the £200 for Leigh Hunt was styled an act of justice affording 'some compensation for the pecuniary and personal sacrifices Mr Hunt had suffered from the advocacy of principles the truth of which is now, happily, fully acknowledged.'

Miscellaneous awards included £25 to each of two men 'in consideration of the services rendered by their ancestors to King Charles II in his escape after the Battle of Worcester'; £50 for the daughter of Napoleon's jailer, General Sir Hudson Lowe; £300 to Snow Harris for his diligence in the investigation of electrical phenomena; and £100 to a geographer who had shown much endurance on 'the north coast of America.'

Certainly the children of murdered policemen qualified for the lowest awards of all. Six orphans of a Chief Constable in Ireland received, like the orphans of Deptford, £8 6s 8d a year each.

In some of these awards it is easy to see the cynical hand of Lord Melbourne, who must have chuckled grimly as he signed the papers, though it is only fair to point out that the most hilarious award of all—to the two gentlemen whose distant ancestors had befriended a runaway prince—was one of Peel's; so was that to Mlle d'Este. The young Queen obviously had a personal share in making some of these awards. Although the grants were in the main small the ammunition given to the Radical readers of Black Books was considerable.

A popular butt of Victoria's reign, among the intelligentsia, was the *Court Circular*. This daily chronicle of royalty's movements was instituted in 1803 by George III, who had grown exasperated by the misreporting and misrepresentation of Court affairs in the public prints. At first newspapers headlined the efforts of the Court Newsman according to their individual whims, but from about 1813 the phrase 'Court Circular' became standardised.

Queen Victoria believed that no activities of the royal family were too trivial to interest the public, and she may well have been right. Every day, the nannies of Britain could read how many princes or princesses had been out for an airing, and whether they had been aired in carriages, on pony back or on foot. Even when no princes or princesses were taken out of doors, it was news: 'The foggy and unfavourable state of the weather during the day prevented the Royal Family from taking their usual airings.' Similarly the Queen's failures to catch colds were news: 'Her Majesty has not suffered from the inclemency of the weather during the last week.' Every minor excursion of the Queen and her Consort, whether at Windsor, Balmoral or Osborne, was faithfully recorded. 'The Queen and Prince Albert promenaded in the pleasure grounds adjacent to the Castle this morning. On the return of Her Majesty and her illustrious Consort, his Royal Highness went shooting in the royal preserves, attended by. . .'

The *Court Circular* employed a dreadful language of its own.

The Queen and her Consort never took a walk; they promenaded. They never went riding; they took equestrian exercise. They never took a train to Paddington, but to 'the Paddington terminus of the Great Western Railway.' Guests were not asked to stay for a meal; they were graciously invited to partake of a collation. No one sang to the Queen, but many enjoyed the distinguished honour of singing before Her Majesty. They were not applauded, but their efforts elicited the approbation of the royal circle. The Queen did not have a happy birthday, but an auspicious return of her natal day.

Usually, only the out-of-doors activities of the Queen and her Consort were chronicled. If she and Albert spent an hour in their photographic dark room, dabbling in chemicals, the fact was not recorded. Sometimes, however, the public were honoured with a list of the tunes played by the royal band at dinner.

That such details were insufficient for the public is clear from the reports of royal movements in the newspapers. The Court Newsman was content to report the number of vehicles employed and the number of horses drawing each; but *The Times* gave details of where and when royalty stopped to change horses. On a winter's day in 1845 the Queen and Consort drove from Brighton to Arundel and were met at Worthing by the Duke of Norfolk (a seemlier Duke than 'the Jockey') who rode behind the carriage for the latter part of the journey. 'Her Majesty and Prince Albert conversed with the noble Duke through the open windows for about a mile, when the snow rendered the closing of the windows necessary,' said the newspaper. Was the representative of *The Times*, one wonders, riding muffled on horseback hard behind the royal carriage? Or did he gain his information later from the Court Newsman?

The *Court Circular* invited ridicule and duly received it, notably in the pages of *Punch*. What exactly was meant, it asked, by 'Her Majesty still adheres to mourning attire?' Could it be that the mourning attire adhered to Her Majesty? Thackeray, in his *Book of Snobs*, which first appeared in *Punch*, indulged in parodies like 'The Princess Piminy was taken a drive attended by her ladies of honour and accompanied by her doll.' Finding it hard to believe in the existence of 'that wonderful and mysterious man, the author of the *Court Circular*,'

Thackeray stayed up late in a newspaper office to see him arrive. Unfortunately he does not describe the gentleman in question. Even though the *Court Circular* did not quite descend, like Saint-Simon, to recording when the sovereign took physic, Thackeray had no time for it: 'I promise to subscribe for a year to any daily paper that shall come out without a *Court Circular*—were it the *Morning Herald* itself. When I read that trash I rise in my wrath; I feel myself disloyal, a regicide, a member of the Calf's Head Club.'

28

Not for Tradesmen

THE compilers of the etiquette books which pullulated in mid-nineteenth century usually instructed their readers in behaviour at levees and drawing-rooms. In theory, these functions offered the subject the traditional facility of access to his sovereign. In practice, this facility had long been restricted to the nobility and gentry; and now, under Victoria, it was restricted to such of the nobility and gentry as had not been detected in moral lapses.

In the *Court and Country Companion*, published in the 1830s, are such instructions as: 'If your own carriage and servants should not be in town, you may easily procure a handsome chariot, with a respectable coachman and footman, for the occasion at the principal livery stables.' Although the fuss over feathers and lappets is considerable, it is worth it, since 'a British Court drawing-room is the most fascinating of any in Europe; for, independently of the ladies' tasteful dresses, formed so elegantly neat, with blazes of diamonds, which are the prevailing and distinguishing ornaments of rank and beauty, the *British Ladies* are celebrated throughout the world for the clearness and brilliancy of their complexions, for their graceful forms and for their easy, modest, elegant and enchanting manners.'

The author of *Court Etiquette* (1849), who describes himself as 'A Man of the World', explains apologetically: 'To write a treatise on etiquette is to be condemned everlastingly to the region of tailors, ladies' maids and *parvenus*; though to produce an Act of Parliament on Precedence is a dignified occupation worthy a thousand legislators and a Sovereign.' If, after this, the reader did not feel too small, he could go on to read of the purposes of levees and drawing-rooms. These were designed for the convenience of persons moving in the front ranks of society, who wished to notify any accession of dignity, the contracting of matrimony, the obtaining of any kind of social or professional advancement or merely the fact of arrival in town from abroad. Presentation was not only an authentic announcement of an occurrence but an intimation to a man's acquaintances that he occupied a certain status in society. Only those who had passed before the Queen could, on travelling abroad, obtain a presentation at a foreign court. It was possible to procure a letter from the Lord Chamberlain certifying that one had been presented.

The lists of those attending Victoria's Court contain such reasons as these for seeking presentation: on elevation to the peerage; on marriage and change of name; on change of flag (for an Admiral); on appointment to the Madras Artillery; on appointment as naval *aide-de-camp*; on returning from India (for a colonel); on appointment as librarian to the Foreign Office; on appointment as recorder; on changing name to Simmons (for an ensign called Carlyon); on succeeding to title (for a baronet); on appointment as Queen's Counsel; and on taking the coif (for a barrister). Sometimes an author was privileged to make a presentation of his latest work, but only if he had previously notified the Lord Chamberlain of his intention. Permission, one imagines, was but rarely granted. Uniquely privileged guests at the drawing-room, once a year, were the boys of the mathematical school at Christ's Hospital, whose visits had been a tradition since Stuart times. On these occasions, the *Court Circular* would say: 'The Queen condescended to inspect the charts and drawings of the boys and to express her approbation of their performances.'

The first step for a person wishing to be presented at Court was to find an introducer. For a civil servant, the appropriate nominee was the head of his department; for a young officer, his colonel; for a mayor, the Home Secretary; for persons arriving from the colonies, the Colonial Secretary; for a foreigner, his ambassador; for a newly married woman, her most distinguished relative; for a person entering society, a father, uncle or most distinguished connection.

The rule was that the name of a person wishing to be presented should be submitted two clear days beforehand to the Lord Chamberlain. If not qualified to wear official, professional, military or academic costume, he would present himself in Court attire, consisting of claret-coloured coat, knee breeches, buckled shoes, lace shirt front, ruffles, long white stockings and sword. If he was 'more economical than fastidious,' he might be able to hire such articles.

Persons of high official status entered St James's via the Ambassadors' Court. This *entrée* was much coveted by ladies who abhorred a crush, but that was not a sufficient reason for being granted it. Carriages went straight to the Palace doors, but those in hackney carriages had to dismount at the foot of St James's Street, 'a nuisance which when once known few people incur a second time.'

Presentations were performed, not by the sponsors, but by a lord in waiting. Each gentleman was required to go down on one knee (authorities varied as to which knee) and raise his right arm with the back of the hand uppermost. On this the Queen would lay the palm of her hand. The visitor would 'barely touch' the back of the Queen's hand with his lips, restraining all fervour. 'If he wishes to be particularly absurd and vulgar,' says the author of this guide, 'he will kiss the hand with a loud smack, and if he be very bashful or alarmed he will merely bow down to the hand without the courage to touch it with his lips.' He must not speak, but rise (refraining from hauling on the Sovereign's hand), bow first to the Queen and then to her Consort, then retire backwards, keeping his eyes respectfully on majesty.

At drawing-rooms, ladies were not required to kneel in order to kiss the Queen's hand. As they neared the presence, they dropped their trains, which were spread out for them by officers armed with wands. After presentation, the trains were deftly scooped up again by other officers. Daughters of earls, marquises and dukes did not kiss the hand but were kissed by the Queen on the forehead or cheek.

A book of presentations was kept at St James's, but was not available to the public. By sufferance, the representative of the *Court Circular* stood in the Tapestry Room copying the cards left on the table of the Queen's page. He did so with a mixture of furtiveness and awe, like a junior reporter noting down names on 'floral tributes' in a churchyard.

Under the heading 'Accidental Intercourse With Royalty,' 'Man of the World' offers advice for those uncertain whether to bow, kneel or run. It is merely necessary to stand still, bareheaded, and refrain from conversation. If presented, one should bow twice, the second time in acknowledgement of royalty's bow. The expressions 'Madam' and 'Your Majesty' should be used sparsely, and never as expletives. It is inadvisable to talk to courtiers in the presence of royalty. Attendants on foreign princes and princesses usually keep closely to the person, not presuming to notice anybody or anything which is not at that moment under royal observation. Although Queen Victoria imposes no such restriction on her Court, 'it ought to be the pride of every Englishman not to misuse or overstrain this liberty which Her Majesty allows to every member of her suite by continuously addressing any of them or endeavouring to carry on any lengthened conversation in which the Queen does not choose to participate.'

Finally, 'Man of the World' warns his readers that in society a certain standard of taste, elegance and refinement is set up for the purpose of being immediately pulled down the moment it is recognised as a standard.

On a more exalted level was *Manners and Rules of Good Society*, by 'A Member of the Aristocracy,' which ran through a great many editions in the latter part of the reign. Those readers uncertain of their pretensions to attend Court were in little doubt after they had read this handbook. The honour was open only to the nobility and gentry, and the gentry embraced the officers of the Army and Navy, the clergy, the bar, doctors, professional men and 'the aristocracy of wealth, the aristocracy of art, merchant princes and leading City merchants and bankers.' It was essential that aspirants from the ranks of commerce should be engaged *on a large scale*. 'At trade known as retail trade, however extensive its operations, the line is drawn and very strictly so, as were a person actually engaged in trade to obtain a presentation, his presentation would be cancelled as soon as the Lord Chamberlain was made aware of the nature of his occupation, but the sons of wealthy manufacturers are not precluded from attending levees if their wealth, education and association warrant their so doing.' The same indulgence applied to the wives and daughters of wealthy manufacturers.

In this they had the advantage over wives and daughters of obscure officers in the Royal Navy or in Foot regiments, for such ladies 'would not be justified in attending a drawing-room, although the officer himself might be desirous of attending a levee; and this remark equally applies to the wives and daughters of clergymen, barristers and others.'

It is a sombre thought that there were persons ready to acquaint the Lord Chamberlain that So-and-So had obtained a presentation when he was only a tradesman and that the Lord Chamberlain was willing to act on such information. The best course for a tradesman was to become a Justice of the Peace or a mayor, to join the Volunteer forces, or win a knighthood; it was not then possible to turn him from a levee.

Not the least privilege of ranking with the gentry, according to this pundit, was that one was entitled to address the Queen as 'Ma'am' (never 'Madam') and the Prince as 'Sir.' The lower professional classes, the middle classes and the lower middle classes were expected to say 'Your Majesty' and 'Your Royal Highness.'

'A Member of the Aristocracy' reveals one of the many worries of the Lord Chamberlain in the realm of ladies' dress. 'The regulation respecting low bodices is absolute; though under very exceptional circumstances permission can be obtained from the Lord Chamberlain for a modification of this decree if the application be accompanied by a certificate from the physician as to the inability of the applicant to appear in a low bodice.'

Unmarried ladies are expected to wear white and so are married ladies on first presentation, unless their age renders such a course unsuitable. As a rule married ladies wear lace lappets and unmarried ones tulle veils, but this is a matter of individual taste. Trains are to be not less than three-and-a-half yards in length.

For young and old, married and unmarried, strong-chested or weak-chested, one item of equipment is obligatory: a head-dress of three white plumes. No line from a physician can secure a dispensation from this rule.

Among miscellaneous items of information offered by 'A Member of the Aristocracy' is this: if, at a ball, a Prince of the Blood wishes to dance with a lady he does not know, he sends his Equerry to fetch her. The Equerry presents the lady, saying, 'Mrs A, sir.' The Prince bows to Mrs A and offers his arm. She curtseys and takes it, and does not speak until he does. If a Princess of the Blood wishes to dance with a gentleman, the same procedure is adopted.

Throughout Victoria's reign, great caution was taken against efforts to present ladies of doubtful character. There was an unfortunate episode in 1849 when a colonel of the Life Guards, performing the duties of Silver Stick,* was dismissed from Court for a year for presenting a lady with whom he had lived before marriage, and whom he had wed according to Scots law. Silver Stick, in the Queen's view, ought to have known better.†

The protocol of levees and drawing-rooms was regarded with increasing distaste in the New World. In 1854 William Marcy, Secretary of State, whom no one had ever accused of being a cosmopolite, issued a *Dress Circular* which caused much pained surprise in European capitals. Henceforth, he ruled, American ministers abroad would appear 'in the simple dress of an American citizen,' always provided that non-conformity with usage would not seriously interfere with the conduct of their business. Since John Adams had paid his historic call on George III, the costume of the American envoys had been nothing if not variable. John Quincy Adams, in the Prince Regent's day, had sometimes made himself conspicuous by being the only person at a reception in full Court dress.‡ Other American diplomatic visitors had worn, on occasion, oddly assorted attire. When Secretary Marcy's *Dress Circular* came out, the Ambassador to Britain was James Buchanan, a future President. Though privately amused, he let it be known that he proposed to obey the ruling in the spirit. In the Travellers' Club, London, he happened to meet Sir Edward Cust, the Queen's Master of the Ceremonies, who became greatly agitated when he learned of the Republic's proposed affront to the Court of St James's. Buchanan said that if the Queen expressly requested him to appear in costume he would do so. To this,

---

* In Charles II's day, Guards officers appointed to attend the sovereign were known as Gold Stick and Silver Stick from their symbols of office
† Vera Watson: *A Queen at Home*
‡ Beckles Willson: *American Ambassadors in England*

English Court dress creates a stir at a ball in Moscow

the Master of Ceremonies replied that the Queen would no doubt receive him in whatever costume he chose, but non-conformity with established usage would be disagreeable to her. Surely, Mr Buchanan would not expect to attend a Court ball in plain dress? Would he wish to find himself relegated, along with bishops, to such undress functions as State concerts? The Ambassador retorted that he, personally, did not care whether he appeared at Court or not. He was reminded that a royal invitation was a command.

The Ambassador realised that the problem was more ticklish than he had expected. Writing to Secretary Marcy, he said it was probable that he would be sent to Coventry by London society if he were refused admission to Court. The issue was complicated by the fact that the Sovereign was a lady, who was regarded with 'a mingled feeling of loyalty and gallantry.' Hence the population might regard his refusal to dress as a piece of presumption.

Buchanan learned that a senator visiting St Petersburg had been invited to visit the Czar in costume, but had declined. Asked what dress he put on to call on his President, the senator said that he wore his ordinary dress. Without more ado, the Czar received him. This may have steeled Buchanan to carry out his Secretary's desires. He was determined not to wear diplomatic gold embroidery in any form. Somebody suggested that he should dress in the costume of George Washington, a proposal which the Ambassador appears to have taken seriously; but he decided it would be presumptuous to ape the Father of his Country. While he was still undecided, he received an invitation to attend the opening of Parliament, but as the invitation said that no one would be admitted unless in Court dress, he stayed away, not wishing to be involved in a public scene. His absence did not go unmarked in the press. Happily, the ice was thawed by an invitation to dine in 'frock dress' with the Queen and Consort, an occasion which passed off amiably enough.

Finally, the Ambassador decided that 'the simple dress of an American citizen' could best be interpreted as black coat and pantaloons, white waistcoat and cravat, and a plain sword. He was not happy about the sword, but was persuaded by a Court official that it was 'considered merely as the mark of a gentleman.' Also, as he realised, it was desirable to wear something to distinguish him from an upper Court servant. He had thought of wearing 'United States buttons,' but decided that a neat, black-hilted, black-sheathed sword would be 'more manly and less gaudy.'

In this costume, he attended a levee in February, 1854. The Court officials, having yielded, were now friendliness itself. When he reached the Queen she gave him 'an arch but benevolent smile.' Afterwards he said he had never felt prouder than at that moment, in that glittering throng.* He appears to have basked in the peculiar distinction that a woman in simple well-cut black enjoys at a party where all the other women are loaded with feathers and brilliants. Thereafter he lost nothing in popularity by following Washington's whim. Some of the newspapers were critical, but the Ambassador expressed the belief that he had most of England behind him.

Buchanan's action served as a useful precedent for John Bright, the Radical, who became a minister in Gladstone's government, in 1868. As a working man, he considered it morally wrong to wear gold lace and sword, saying, 'I have never put on livery and I think I never shall.' A compromise was suggested, so he appeared in a Court suit of black velvet, plainly cut but with an old-fashioned elegance. The new minister also had moral objections to kneeling in order to kiss the hand and in this, too, the Queen humoured him. Old courtiers saw in this stiff-backed figure the herald of Revolution.

* G. T. Curtis: *Life of James Buchanan*

29

Smoking up the Chimney

B Y the 1850s, the Baron Stockmar was very gratified with the way the Court was shaping. The Consort continued to improve, morally and politically, and the Queen was honest and above intrigues. In 1854 the Baron summed up his feelings thus:

'How valuable, in and for itself, is the moral purity of the Sovereign, as an example to the public, as moral oil for the driving wheels of the Constitutional machine, as a controlling principle for the highest Government and Court favours. I have had it in my power to observe for 16 years and to compare with what had fallen under my notice under George IV and William IV during the 22 preceding years. Let men like the late Lord Melbourne exclaim as they please, "This damned morality is sure to ruin everything." I, on the other hand, can testify before God that the English machine works smoothly and well only when the Sovereign is upright and truthful, and that when he has been insincere, mendacious and wicked it has creaked and fouled, and jolted to within an ace of coming to a deadlock.'*

The aristocracy still grumbled about 'this damned morality.' They knew that the Consort disliked their raffish habits and that he rejected nominees for Court appointments if he did not care for their way of life. Moreover, they disliked his cold manner and what they assumed to be his foreign arrogance. But to the middle classes, as to Stockmar, the Court commended itself. For 200 years the palaces of England had presented an almost unrelieved pattern of family discord (George III, though he had treated his Queen well, had been at loggerheads with most of his relations); now, Victoria and Albert had established

* Sir Theodore Martin: *Life of the Prince Consort*

a pattern of family decorum. The Court had become what it should always have been: an example instead of a warning.

The public could not, and did not, as yet know that the Prince of Wales, whose sailor suit they had so eagerly copied for their own children, was proving a disappointment to his parents. Like a captive shrinking from an iron maiden, the boy shied from the fearful educational machine prepared for him by the Baron Stockmar. In 1858, when he was 17, three elderly Equerries were attached to him, with most specific orders to make him sit upright, keep his hands out of his pockets, refrain from dandyism, sauntering, slang, banter, mimicry and practical jokes. In the evenings, when not entertaining distinguished elderly gentlemen to dinner, he was expected to look at elevating engravings. The victim of this conspiracy proved oddly intractable.

Then, in 1861, Prince Albert died. He was a much misunderstood man with many sound achievements behind him. His Great Exhibition had done more to thrill and inspire the mass of the nation than a hundred great *bals poudrés* could have done. If, with the Queen's approval, he had meddled in politics, so had every ruler since the Conqueror's day.

The effects of his death on the Queen hardly need telling here. In her name, he had borne the weight of government; now she had to bear it alone. In her wretchedness, she felt incapable of doing this and inspiring a Court as well. So Buckingham Palace became, in effect, Albert's mausoleum. For two years the Queen lived in total seclusion. Then, gradually, the rudimentary Court functions—levees and drawing-rooms—were taken over by the Prince of Wales and family deputies. Not until 1868 did the Queen herself appear at a drawing-room.

The country felt cheated. London grumbled because the sovereign who should have given life to its shuttered palaces pottered about at Balmoral or in the Isle of Wight. Tradesmen deplored a grief which was keeping money out of their pockets. Statesmen deplored a grief which forced them to transact the nation's business from a clammy castle on Deeside. Radicals objected, with some justice, that the only occasion on which the Queen made a public appearance was to rattle the money-box on behalf of her enormous family. She maintained no state; what, then, did she *do* with the money? Men like Sir Charles

Dilke openly agitated for a republic. In fact, the Queen was earning her money in so far as she was attending to the nation's business; she was not earning it in her capacity as figure-head. As an example, visiting monarchs—the Czar, the Shah, the Sultan, the Khedive, to say nothing of the uncouth kings of Pacific Islands—were not being received in the way that a great nation should receive them. The Queen was not at home to visitors, whether house-trained or otherwise. Had she died in, say, 1870, no nimbus would have surrounded her memory. All her glory was yet to come.

Over those gloomy years hovers the enigmatic figure of John Brown, whom the less reverent Press dubbed 'the great Court favourite.' The riddle of this brusque and dominating servant, who never left the Queen's attendance for 18 years, is unlikely to be solved. Brown's papers and diaries were destroyed after his death and the Queen was dissuaded, not without difficulty, from writing a book about her servant. Even if she had been encouraged in this unqueenly enterprise, it does not follow that she would have satisfied the intense curiosity which still surrounds this episode.

The bare facts are well enough known. Brown was a ghillie who had accompanied Victoria and Albert on many outings at Balmoral. He had been attentive, but never obsequious. His naturalness and forthrightness appealed to the Queen, and in her mourning he seemed able to jerk her to life as her own ladies could not. She sent for him from Osborne and thereafter he assumed charge of her person, taking her on airings, straightening her shawl and, when necessary, criticising her for slovenly turn-out. 'Whit are ye daeing with that auld black dress on ye again? It's green-moulded,' was his rebuke on one occasion, in front of guests and servants.* The Queen meekly went away and changed her dress. She did not rebel even when Brown addressed her as 'woman.'

In the upper circle of the Court Brown's presence was furiously resented, save by those who had the wit to see that he was worth more to the Queen than the entire medical staff, from physician in ordinary down to cupper. Disraeli came to terms with Brown, but Gladstone was often snubbed by him; once, when he was lecturing the Queen, Brown is supposed to

* E. E. P. Tisdall: *Queen Victoria's John Brown*

A débutante kisses the Queen's hand: 1893

have tapped him on the shoulder and told him he had said enough. The Prince of Wales loathed Brown, who saw in him the sort of son whose escapades were not such as to add to his mother's peace of mind.

Inevitably, scandalmongers got busy. It was known that John Brown had been moved into an apartment close to the Queen's. He had a special room to himself on the royal train. The irreverent began to call the Queen 'Mrs Brown.' What influence did he really wield? Did the man who stood ready to blot the royal signature read the documents as they were signed? Did the Queen act on his advice as a homespun philosopher?

In the 'sixties scandal sheets thrived on rumours and cartoons about John Brown. One of them was *The Tomahawk*, which showed the Highlander leaning on an empty throne. Even reputable publications began to voice their dismay. *Punch*, still mocking the *Court Circular*, printed this paragraph in 1866:

> *Balmoral, Tuesday*
> Mr John Brown walked on the Slopes.
> He subsequently partook of a haggis.
> In the evening Mr John Brown was pleased to
>   listen to a bagpipe.
> Mr John Brown retired early.

In an earlier day the publisher of such an item would have been set upon on his way home and his nose would have been slit. But no hostile reaction seems to have been aroused from Balmoral.

Brown's unpopularity became so intense that the people of London, though not of Balmoral, were ready to pelt him on sight. His stock went up, however, in 1872 when he boldly grappled with a youth who flourished a pistol at the Queen in her carriage. The Queen was careless of what the public thought. She gave the faithful Brown the rank of Esquire, forgave him his occasional tippling (no small act of forgiveness in Victoria), and, when he died, provided the *Court Circular* with a long obituary notice extolling his virtues and loyalty.

In his biography of Brown, E. E. P. Tisdall mentions the notion, once popular in spiritualistic circles, that Brown was the Queen's medium through whom she consulted the wishes of Prince Albert. This was by no means the oddest theory evoked by the presence of the kilted, bearded figure behind the Throne. In some quarters it was believed that the Queen was mad and that John Brown was her keeper.

In his blunt, possessive way, the Highlander kept the Queen from self-neglect. Then Disraeli, with his old-fashioned courtly approach, helped to rekindle a flame which had burned dangerously low. Whether his tactics were oriental flattery or overblown chivalry does not greatly matter. No one else, in saying thank you for a gift of palace blooms, would have dared to liken the Queen to Titania. Discreetly, he tried to encompass this sad 'Faery' with the old aristocracy who had held aloof. The results of his wooing were slow but gratifying. From the 'seventies onwards the Queen began to resume her public duties. By the year of the Jubilee, 1887, she had become the well-loved matriarch. She had pulled herself together. She might be crusty and old-fashioned, but she was an institution. She stood for honesty, dignity and authority. She was Europe's grandam. In her last years she enjoyed more affection than any sovereign before her.

Her Court remained severe. No changes were made in the palaces unless by stealth. Commands to 'dine and sleep' at Windsor filled the hardiest statesmen with trepidation. At the dinner table, conversation was subdued and nervous. If the Queen noted that animated exchanges were in progress she might demand to know the nature of the topic, and if it was not a seemly one the meal continued in glacial silence. In any event, it did not pay to talk too much, for when the Queen laid down her knife and fork, the plates of all the guests were whipped away, whether they had finished or not. Afterwards, there was the formal parade at which guests were called up one by one to converse with the Queen. In her youth, Greville had mocked the young Queen for the aridities of her small talk. In old age, light conversation came no easier. Guests found it a relief to be dismissed. And if the atmosphere was chilly, so were the rooms. The Queen liked her homes to be as cool as the Prince Regent liked them to be hot.

In all the palaces, smokers had a very difficult time. On the walls of Windsor were framed and glazed notices instructing gentlemen not to smoke. The heir to the Throne might canter across Newmarket Heath with a cigar between his lips, and the

Commander-in-Chief might puff like a chimney all the way to the Horse Guards, but they sucked lozenges before they ventured into the Queen's presence. Of course, there were cases of surreptitious indulgence, as when Count Hatzfeldt was seen lying in his pyjamas on the bedroom floor blowing smoke up the chimney.* Sir Frederick Ponsonby has told how smokers at Windsor had to wait until the Queen retired for the night. Then a vicious procession wound its shamefaced way to the far-distant billiard room. Late-duty pages were on duty to lead the guests back to their bedrooms, for even persons whose brains were unclouded by nicotine were often unable to retrace their steps through the labyrinthine castle.† At least one unescorted guest, hopelessly lost, dossed down for the night in a gallery.

At Osborne, for a long period, the only smoking-room was in the garden, where it enjoyed all the prestige of an outdoor privy. When Prince Christian arrived at Balmoral to seek the hand of one of the Queen's daughters, he was given a small bare smoking-room near the servants' quarters, furnished with a hard chair and table. This was in accordance with the Scots tradition that sensual indulgence must be made as uncomfortable as possible. Later, Prince Henry of Battenberg induced the Queen to provide a retreat less like an opium den which could be reached without going out of doors.

King Albert of Saxony was warned against smoking at Windsor, and held out for two days. Then, having remembered that he was a king, he walked up the grand staircase puffing a long cigar, which shocked the Court ladies deeply.‡ It was a foretaste of the historic scene on the day of the Queen's funeral, when three kings—of Belgium, Portugal and Germany—were seen smoking away before the fireplace in the Grand Corridor.

The older the Queen grew, the more intolerant she became of the stares of her servants. They were liable to dismissal if they looked her straight in the face. When reporting to her, or receiving orders, they were expected to stand with eyes downcast. If she met a servant on her way through the palace she would look through him.

---

* Baron von Eckhardstein: *Ten Years at the Court of St. James*
† *Recollections of Three Reigns*
‡ Baron von Eckhardstein

Nearly all the memoirists of the period testify to the awe which the old Queen spread in her household. It was a crime to be seen by her when she rode through the grounds of Windsor in a pony trap, so Equerries hid behind bushes at her approach. Rebukes were administered in writing, and were delivered in special boxes, marked 'The Queen.' It was a one-way traffic, for an offender was not expected to send his excuse back in the same box.* Like Queen Elizabeth, Victoria did not like to see her courtiers marry. Sir Frederick Ponsonby, an Equerry in the 1890s, waited three years for permission. When, at last, it was grudgingly given, he was told that he must not expect to be offered a house. The Queen's opposition was founded on her conviction that men told their wives every-thing.† At a fairly advanced age, her physician, Sir James Reid, became engaged to one of her maids of honour, without asking permission. The Queen was extremely angry and said that she did not see how a physician in ordinary could devote himself to two ladies. For three days she declined to see him, sending him his commands in writing, then gave him a severe lecture. He apologised, saying he would not do it again, and for once Victoria was amused.‡

---

* Princess Marie Louise: *My Memories of Six Reigns*
† *Recollections of Three Reigns*
‡ Sir Felix Lemon: *Autobiography*

30

The Barriers go Down

IT was 'as if a Viennese hussar had suddenly burst into an English vicarage.' In this agreeable phrase, the Duke of Windsor has described the arrival of Edward VII.*

Edward, in his sixtieth year, had waited a cruelly long time for the Throne. Distrusted by his mother, frozen by the higher aristocracy, he had made up his circle from those elements which were rejected by Victoria's Court, notably the new plutocracy of international bankers, veldt millionaires, Jewish financiers, American magnates and even advertising tradesmen like Sir Thomas Lipton ('my uncle has gone boating with his grocer,' sneered the Kaiser). It did not follow that the womenfolk of this new society were admitted to favour, unless they chanced to be witty and beautiful.

The aristocrats who followed Edward were the sport-loving, hard-living, worldly types his father had despised. Twice, 'Bertie's' name had been involved in resounding scandals. Although, each time, he was personally cleared, moralists judged him by the company he kept. Before he was born, his mother had been hissed at Ascot; in 1870, after his appearance in the divorce court, he had the distinction of being hissed at Epsom. There came a day when a group of coroneted matrons tried to persuade the Archbishop of Canterbury to rebuke, publicly, the Prince and his social set. When he declined, the ladies went out of their way to pray for the Prince.†

As Prince, Edward had held his court at Marlborough House and Sandringham. Now all the palaces were his. For a brief moment he toyed with the idea of reanimating the glories of

* *A King's Story*
† E. F. Benson: *King Edward VII*

Hampton Court, but the cost was unthinkable. So he braced himself to the task of dusting out the 'Sepulchre,' as he described Buckingham Palace, and the junk-filled caverns of Windsor.

His officers went through both palaces systematically, counting, cataloguing, salvaging, condemning. Many a bizarre discovery was made amid the mildew. At Windsor were piles of elephant tusks which had been sent as tribute from far parts of empire. These were sold off and doubtless finished up as billiard balls. One puzzling object was eventually identified as the codpiece from Henry VIII's suit of armour in the Tower. Possibly it had been detached in a moment of prudery by an official who had not dared to destroy so potent a charm. Also unearthed were a large number of statuettes of John Brown which the Queen had been in the habit of presenting to those whom she thought capable of appreciating them. Edward is reported to have demolished these with great energy and satisfaction.

Windsor also had animate oddities in its recesses. In King John's Tower were the old Queen's Indian attendants, living a life of their own withdrawn from the fret of the world, and in a cottage at Frogmore lived a Munshi who had taught the Queen Hindustani. Edward, who spoke French and German fluently, had no further lingual ambitions. The Indian retainers were found new homes.

Buckingham Palace steeled itself to receive motor cars. Soon after his accession the King drove from Sandringham to Newmarket in his new Daimler, the populace cheering as he sped over the dusty roads at rather more than twice the legal speed limit. Anyone who expected the Master of the Horse to be re-titled the Master of the Horseless Carriage was disappointed. Chauffeurs and mechanics came directly under the Crown Equerry, the executive officer of the Master of the Horse. Many were sorry to see the monarch encourage mechanisation. In *The Tatler*, in 1902, a critic of manners wrote: 'Men go to the levee in cabs or on (sic) motor cars and send their ladies to the palace ball in the products of the Coupé Company.' In all London, he complained, there was hardly a carriage with wigged footmen to be seen.

Both Windsor and Buckingham Palace were ludicrously

short of bathrooms. For this reason alone, foreign royalties in Victoria's reign may have been glad to stay in hotels. Edward sent in a wave of plumbers, and followed them up with ventilation, electrical and telephone engineers. Reluctantly, Victoria had allowed two telephones to be installed at Buckingham Palace in order to facilitate the calling of guests' carriages. Now all the departments of the palace were linked to a central switchboard.

The King also remembered the long-neglected Palace of Holyrood, where he had spent some months as a boy, and sent Sir Lionel Cust to report on its furniture and treasures. Unexpectedly, the monarch found himself embroiled in an old-fashioned dispute with a proud noble. The Duke of Hamilton, who had hereditary rights in Holyrood, was unwilling to give the King permission to reorganise the palace. His trustees argued that the bulk of the treasures and furniture were ducal property. Finally a committee was set up to determine the ownership of every item.*

At the instigation of a Parliamentary Select Committee, various economies were made in the Household, both in salaries and appointments. Henry Labouchère was one of those who rose in the Commons to protest that the Committee did not go far enough; there were, he said, still far too many 'ornamental sinecurists.' The temptation to 'do a Burke' was irresistible. A sum of £28,000, Labouchère pointed out, was allocated to cover the expenses of the Lord Steward's department. 'The Treasurer of the Household received £700, the Comptroller £700, the Master £1156, the Paymaster £1130, the Secretary £1000; and at the head of these gentlemen, who certainly could do between them the business of looking after the £28,000, a large portion of which went to themselves, was the Lord Steward, who would not only receive £2000 but had the right of using the carriages of the Court.' Labouchère then waxed irreverent over the establishment of 36 chaplains who received £40 a year each for preaching a single sermon. He understood that they could contract out of their obligation by paying £3, and strongly suspected that most of them did so, thus getting £37 for nothing. If the Church had to be endowed, said Mr Labouchère, this was an unsatisfactory way of doing it.

* Sir Lionel Cust: *King Edward VII and His Court*

In the same debate Keir Hardie rose to speak as a republican, at which Members made the noises which Hansard interprets as 'Oh! Oh!' One foolish king, he said, could wreck the Empire in six months. But Edward, whatever his faults, turned out to be a far from foolish king.*

It had always been a mystery what the Gentlemen Ushers found to do in Victoria's reign. Edward offered them more work for less pay and there was a certain amount of well-bred grumbling. A Gentleman Usher's outfit cost not less than his yearly salary of £100. It was no task for those who shrank from giving orders to, and being shouldered by, ladies of high birth talking in the loud voices for which the English female aristocracy is internationally notorious. Sir Lionel Cust, who allowed himself to be appointed Gentleman Usher as well as Surveyor of the King's Pictures, has expressed himself feelingly on this theme. Usually, he says, 'a few persuasive words, an appealing hand and above all the wave of a cocked hat proved sufficient to guide these ladies into the path of righteousness.' There were, however, blue-blooded dames who were reluctant to yield precedence to ladies of lower birth, even though these might be the wives of cabinet ministers. Sir Lionel had to make speeches like, 'I beg your pardon, Lady ——, but please stand still for a moment and allow Mrs John Burns to pass.'†

The King tried to encourage senior Army and Navy officers to become Gentlemen Ushers, but not every veteran who had ruled a province or commanded a flotilla was eager to end his days clearing dance floors and standing guard over supper tables.

The Equerries, too, had enjoyed a very easy time in the previous reign. It soon became obvious that this appointment was not for the senile. These officers might be called upon to perform such feats as riding on hard roads, in the rain, and wearing top hats, from Windsor to Ascot, a distance of a dozen miles, with a loyal populace doing its best to make the horses shy.‡ The King waged a battle on the subject of Equerries with the War Office, which sought to alter their terms of employment without seeking his permission. He won a complete victory.

---

* May 9, 1901
† Sir Lionel Cust:
‡ B. J. W. Hill: *Windsor and Eton*

The oldest Court institution to be abolished by Edward was that of the Buck Hounds, which had been in existence for some 700 years. Comically enough, the Mastership was a political appointment. 'Sometimes,' says E. F. Benson, 'a Conservative minister chased the stag, sometimes a Liberal.'* It has been suggested that Queen Alexandra, with her humanitarian instincts, was behind this decision; in fact, the recommendation was that of the Select Committee. The Chancellor of the Exchequer, Sir M. Hicks-Beach, told Parliament that the Committee had considered, as an alternative, the establishment of a pack of royal foxhounds, but 'various difficulties' had arisen. It was the view of the Committee that the sovereign alone should decide whether and in what form encouragement should be given to any sport. They thought it undesirable that he should be obliged to subsidise a specific sport by spending Civil List funds on it. The financial saving as a result of disbanding the Buck Hounds would be more than £6000. No objection seems to have been voiced to this economy. It was a historic day in the annals of the Court, for since long before the Conqueror's time it had been expected of a sovereign that he should be a pursuer and slayer of wild beasts. Now, if kings wished to kill stags, they had to stalk them (King Edward shot his first stag in 1858).

The peer who had held the post of Master of the Buck Hounds—Viscount Churchill of Wychwood—did not find himself shorn of all dignity. Since before Victoria's day it had been the Master's additional responsibility, in conjunction with the Jockey Club, to supervise the Royal Heath at Ascot and to sift applications for the Royal Enclosure. At the King's request Viscount Churchill stayed on as Steward of Ascot. The rules governing admission to the Royal Enclosure were in no degree slackened; if anything, they were tightened. No individual could enter the Enclosure as of right. Normally, only those who had been presented at Court were eligible, but at the discretion of the Steward others were occasionally admitted.

As Princess of Wales, Queen Alexandra had inspired a fashionable boycott of the singularly unsporting live pigeon shoots at Hurlingham and elsewhere. If she made any attempt

* *King Edward VII*

Vive le sport: the future Edward VII slays a boar in Germany

to discourage the King's addiction to pheasant *battues* she was unsuccessful, for the royal guns on some of their outings brought down a staggering weight of meat from the skies. The King's hosts felt that they must offer him good sport and their idea of good sport was a sky dark with pheasants at tree-top height. The King had no wish to be called a poulterer and still less had his son, the future George V. Both were chary of being 'bribed' by *nouveaux riches* promising limitless slaughter and champagne. The fact remains that both helped on occasions to pile up some immodest bags. Thackeray would have been happy to join in the criticisms which this kind of sport attracted. He once derided the punctilio which surrounded game shooting at European courts, where no royal shot would accept a gun direct from a loader, but only via his equerry.

In Victoria's reign there had been a good deal of grumbling about the rigours of the royal drawing-rooms. These events were held in the early afternoon, which meant that ladies had to start arraying themselves in jewels and plumes soon after breakfast. Then, in the merciless light of mid-day, they faced stares and jeers and cries of 'Mothballs!' as their carriages were held up in traffic jams. In the palace waiting-rooms they sat in rows on gilt chairs eyeing each other, fierce scrawny duchesses, mountainous marchionesses, terrified or giggling girls. The longer they waited, the more alarming seemed the feat of controlling train, bouquet and veil while curtseying and kissing the royal hand, always with the haunting fear that the three ostrich feathers were behaving treasonably. After backing out of the presence, the guests went straight to their carriages. No refreshment was provided, except for those who succumbed to faintness or fervour. Victoria declined to alter the system. She considered the strain on those who passed before her was trivial compared with the strain on herself.

Edward earned much fashionable gratitude by abolishing the afternoon drawing-rooms and replacing them by evening courts. These were functions of a splendid amplitude, glittering and orchid-scented, with generous refreshments both for ladies and their escorts. George IV could not have contrived them more royally. To be presented was still an ordeal, but it was an enjoyable ordeal. Those ladies not privileged to attend could spend the best part of a morning reading the details in *The*

Queen, which filled up to half a dozen of its huge pages with small-type descriptions of the outstanding gowns.

Of course, there were minor regrets. The writer of the ladies' notes in the *Illustrated London News* was one of those who sighed over the passing of the 'train tea,' a domestic function which used to follow the return from the Palace. 'What a delight it was for the lady who had gone to immense expense and trouble over her Court dress to display it to her friends at home—and what an amusing function it was to the guests! To know three or four people who were going to Court and run round to see them successively "let down their trains" was the best of fun.'*

Many ladies had grumbled, or pretended to grumble, at the cost of embroidering and bejewelling a three-yards train which might be worn only once in a life-time. It was an item of attire for which it was difficult to find any alternative use, though the writer of the notes in the *Illustrated London News* knew of a lady of rank who had converted her superb crimson-and-gold, Viennese-made train into a cover for her grand piano. Few had the temerity to economise on this item of equipment, for ladies at Victoria's Court had been turned back because their trains had been made of mere 'fine supple cloth' instead of the regulation velvet, silk or lace.

Anxious to spare ladies some of this fuss and fret, Queen Alexandra inspired a new regulation which said that trains need be worn only by those who were being presented and by their sponsors. At once a howl went up. The representations of the trade were so urgent that their Majesties 'were moved by them' and the new order was cancelled. This, said the *Illustrated London News*, was a welcome sign of the Court's readiness to change announced decisions. English ladies, it appeared, did not realise how lucky they were, for at the Court of Austria trains might run to nine yards in length, according to the rank of the wearer.

The new-style courts were not popular with fashionable florists. To clutch a bouquet and perhaps also a fan while helping oneself to ingenious delicacies was an exasperation, and the number of bouquets carried at Court began to diminish. On such accidents as these the fate of trades may depend.

* Jan. 11, 1902

Levees in Victoria's day had been held at such a time as to deprive gentlemen of their luncheons. Edward advanced the hour so that they were over by two o'clock. This caused distress only to those young men who had been in the habit of holding 'levee teas.' Now it seemed unlikely that they would wish to remain in levee dress until their lady friends arrived at four or five o'clock. The levee tea, pronounced *The Tatler*, was 'too ladylike, and it is as well that it is ended.' As the reign progressed, it was noticed that a wider range of persons was being presented at levees. Ancient ghosts at St James's were suitably shaken when, in 1904, the Bishop of London presented a distinguished Nonconformist divine.

The dress rules for gentlemen underwent minor relaxation. For a long time the press had been campaigning for the abolition of frills, swords and knee-breeches, which were described by one newspaper as 'a costume of the worst period of English taste.' The rules allowed gentlemen to appear in one of two outfits: black velvet coat and breeches with white waistcoat and sword, or cloth coat of mulberry, claret or green, also with knee-breeches. In a dress guide published in 1903 appeared this useful tip:

'With black stockings it is advisable to wear a *thin* pair of black cotton hose under the black silk. Both pairs should be well pulled up over the knees and should fit closely.'

This guide also warned against wearing wafer-thin pumps. 'It is not easy to cross a sanded road or courtyard with befitting dignity if very thin shoes are worn.'*

Dinner guests at Windsor mostly wore evening dress with knee breeches, though pantaloons were sometimes tolerated (Gladstone used to wear them). Any departure from strict formality was liable to be met with a royal observation like, 'I see you have come in the suite of the American Ambassador.'

Numerous stories have been told of the discomfiture of those who entered Edward's presence improperly dressed. Gentlemen Ushers saved many from ignominy. A famous lawyer, for example, appeared at a levee with his sword on the wrong side. To switch it to the correct side was not so simple, for his household, fearing he might lose it, had contrived to stitch it

* H. Graham Bennet: *Dress Worn by Gentlemen at H. M. Court*

to his underwear. He was hustled away to a bedroom and the necessary adjustments were made. The Queen herself was ordered back when she appeared wearing the Garter star on the wrong side. It had clashed, she explained, with her other jewels; but the King rejected this excuse.

Although, in a few minor ways, etiquette was slackened, the King was capable of acting as his own Master of Ceremonies. Sir Frederick Ponsonby tells how he would walk through the public rooms late in the evening, counting heads, to ensure that no ladies and gentlemen had gone to bed without permission. Once, finding that he was a courtier short, he sent a page to root out the absentee. It turned out to be the venerable General Sir Dighton Probyn, who had retired because he felt ill. The King thought this a great joke, but the General was hurt.

Among functions discontinued by Edward were the twice-yearly State concerts. These were intended for the entertainment of persons too staid to attend State balls. Edward had no wish to encourage persons as staid as that. If they wished to attend concerts, they must make their own arrangements. The King's attitude towards music clearly showed up the clash between the old and the new. On a notorious occasion his mother, hearing her military band playing a new tune, sent a page to ask the bandmaster the name of the piece. He returned slightly red, and reported that it was called 'Come where the booze is cheaper.' Edward's Master of the Musick was Sir Walter Parratt, who had been private organist to Victoria. He was not the man to be caught out like this, and resolutely declined to play frivolous tunes on ceremonial occasions. If the King wanted Sousa, he is credited with saying, he should hire him (in due course, Sousa's band paid a visit to Sandringham). Sir Frederick Ponsonby also objected to frivolous music being played at Courts and investitures. 'What I disliked,' he writes, 'was seeing eminent men being knighted while comic songs were being played by the band outside.' The King got his way by employing military bands when he wanted light music. Even today visitors to investitures are sometimes surprised at the lively nature of the repertoire played by the scarlet bandsmen in the gallery.

The lightness of the King's tastes was reflected in his patronage of the theatre. It was a grievance of the intelligentsia that the King gave no encouragement to serious drama and that the Lord Chamberlain did his best to thwart it. Edward's liking was for musical comedies (he went to theatres notorious for their unvirginal promenades) and stylish comedies of manners. He was the first sovereign to visit the theatre for something like half a century, but he was happier when the theatre visited him. Not, perhaps, since the days of James I had a monarch commanded so many plays to be performed under his roof. The resources of Edwardian sea and land travel were sorely stretched, at times, to bring companies to Windsor and Sandringham on schedule. For the players, it was an exciting experience to ride through palace gates in a royal carriage, to peer through curtains at King and Kaiser, and afterwards, with luck, to penetrate into royal kitchens. For producers, the task of adapting plays to inadequate stages was a considerable worry. It is evident that the cost of bringing the Martin-Harveys, the Dan Lenos and the Albert Chevaliers to the royal footlights must have been a heavy drain on the Privy Purse. Edward was the last Sovereign to indulge freely this old-fashioned form of patronage.

The Lord Chamberlain's right to censor the drama, through his Examiner of Plays, was assailed, in 1908, by an army of more than 70 playwrights and authors, among whom were Shaw, Wells, Hardy and Swinburne. In a letter to the press they said it was monstrous that the labours of a serious drama-tist should be at the mercy of a Court functionary, answerable neither to the law nor to Parliament. The office of Examiner of Plays had been introduced 'for political and not for so-called moral ends to which it is perverted.' Not only was the system contrary to justice and common-sense, it was one which relieved the public of the onus of passing their own moral judgments. Under pressure, the Prime Minister set up a Select Committee to investigate theatre censorship. Its sessions produced much wit, nonsense, insincerity and self-advertisement. The serious dramatists complained that the Examiner was licensing only those plays which measured up to his own limited intelligence; on the other hand he was sanctioning any number of 'naughty' farces, some of which in Shaw's opinion were 'disgusting to the very last degree,' thus showing that he did not have a

mind dirty enough for his job. It was an embarrassing period
for Mr G. A. Retford, the Examiner in question, who had
turned down Shaw's *Mrs Warren's Profession*, Shelley's *The Cenci*,
H. Granville-Barker's *Waste* and Ibsen's *Ghosts*. Theatrical
managers were quite convinced (as they still are) that the
licensing system was a sound one, for once the Lord Chamberlain had passed the script of a play no policeman or busybody
could initiate a prosecution. Having heard all the evidence,
the Committee decided that the anachronism should be perpetuated. Soon afterwards a new Examiner of Plays was
appointed in the person of Charles Brookfield, author of one
of the naughtiest farces of the period, *Dear Old Charlie*.* After
this, no one could complain that the Examiner had too innocent
an outlook.

Edward was far from being an easy king to serve, but those
who did so respected him. Sir Frederick Ponsonby's reminiscences give a good idea of the strain involved in attending a
cosmopolitan, peripatetic monarch. Not the least of the Private
Secretary's worries was fending off the deluge of decorations
which foreign Courts were anxious to bestow on Edward's suite,
and at the same time resisting solicitations for honours, which
Edward gave sparingly. It was a world in which the gift of
a not-quite-good-enough cigarette case could cause a worse
wound than no gift at all. Ponsonby wrangled with his master
on such issues, attended to correspondence and a hundred
and one matters, and changed in and out of uniforms all day.
If he had an easy time under Victoria, he earned every half-
penny under Edward.

In the entourage, there were those whose function was purely
to amuse. Among them was the Marquis de Soveral, the
Portuguese minister, a witty grandee who could chaff women
in all civilised languages. He was an arbiter of feminine elegance, a considerable wit and a polished dancer. His nickname,
inspired by his swarthy complexion, was 'the Blue Monkey.'
Like William IV, the King had a marine painter in the person
of the Chevalier Martino, a former officer in the Italian Navy,
who was happy to be at the receiving end of the royal
witticisms.

The royal friendship with Sir Thomas Lipton surprised many

* A. E. Wilson: *Edwardian Theatre*

besides the Kaiser. As the King drove through the streets, seeing his own name blazoned in lights and flowers, he must have glimpsed hundreds of times the name of his favourite more durably installed on bridges and gable-ends and sides of omnibuses. Lipton owed his favour to many things: he was, like the King, a keen ocean yachtsman and one of the few men able to indulge in that sport; he was a good *raconteur;* and he was no sycophant. As his biographer, Alec Waugh, points out, he was so wealthy that he could hardly be accused of cultivating the King's society in the hope of gain; and furthermore he was a bachelor, free from potentially tiresome relatives.*

That other self-made favourite, Sir Ernest Cassel, also had nothing to gain by following the King, though it is no secret that the King had much to gain by following Sir Ernest. In appearance he closely resembled the King. While hospitable and generous, he was as reserved as Lipton was flamboyant.

If Saint-Simon had been attached to the Court of King Edward he would have found no lack of sillinesses in the society which revolved round it. Various observers have noted how gentlemen imitated the King's stiff, rheumatic handshake and ladies strove to copy the Queen's limp. It has even been argued that the King's operation for appendicitis encouraged the *beau monde* to expose their paunches needlessly to the knife. Sir Richard Holmes, Librarian of Windsor Castle, says that carriage-borne ladies, seeing the Queen riding out with her grandchildren in her lap, tossed the dogs out of their laps and replaced them with children.†

In other ways, imitation of the Court—its hats, its suits, its dresses, its tastes in food and wine—was markedly good for trade and prestige. Like the Prince Regent, Edward made the Court once more an influence in the world of fashion.

It was a short reign and a popular one. The working classes, remembering that, on his accession, Edward had spent £30,000 to give a dinner to half a million London poor, were content to cry 'Good old Teddy!' He was a King who acted according to their conception of a king and did all the things they would have liked to do. It was a pleasure to back his horses; just as,

* *The Lipton Story*
† *Edward VII: His Life and Times*

twenty years on, it would be a pleasure to sample the 'King's No 1 Special Brew' inaugurated by him at Burton-on-Trent. To Labour leaders, like John Burns, he was affable, always provided that they refrained from unduly crude assertions. He had a sharp brush with the Parliamentary Labour Party at a time when three of its members, aware that he proposed to visit the Czar, denounced in strong language the vigour of Czarist counter-revolutionary methods. The names of these three objectors, of whom Keir Hardie was one, were struck from a list of Labour guests the King had invited to a function at Windsor. At once the Party sent a message to the King saying that if these three were not to be invited, all the names must be struck from the list. The names were restored.*

The upper classes, save in the more glacial reaches, were grateful to Edward for reanimating the Court. The Duchess of Devonshire showed what she thought of him by sending 300 torchmen to light him to the fiery gates of Chatsworth, which was picked out in lights and glittering monograms under a rocket-filled sky. A few observers thought this spectacle a trifle overdone, verging on the oriental.

To the middle classes, the Court was rather too rich and hearty and perfumed and fond of its belly. Also, the phenomenon of Mrs Alice Keppel disconcerted them. Hostesses invited her when they invited the King; it was a social procedure which fitted ill into their conception of the orderly life. Eventually the world learned that the Queen had led Mrs Keppel by the hand to the King's death-bed. This, too, the narrow-minded found difficult to understand. To intellectuals, the Court was beneath notice. They saw a King who did not read books and who thought that actors were the be-all and end-all of the theatre.

But even the intellectuals had to admit that the King had broken down the old exclusiveness of the Court and let gusts of daylight into it. If in so doing he had admitted undesirables, these would be extruded by his successors.

* Emrys Hughes: *Keir Hardie*

31

Socialists in Breeches

EDWARD VII had dreamed of reanimating Hampton Court. His son, George V, also had his dream: it was to pull down Buckingham Palace, sell the gardens, and use the proceeds to rebuild Kensington Palace as the town residence of the Sovereign. Viscount Esher says that no one knew better than the King that this idea was a visionary one.*

It was some time before the new King could be broken of his attachment to York Cottage, the one-time bachelors' annexe on the Sandringham estate. The skylarking, skylark-eating society which had revolved round Edward barely concealed its disappointment at a King who hankered to live in a cottage. The worldly days of the Court, they began to suspect, were over, and they were right. It was the turn of the middle classes to hail a monarch who, as they liked to think, was an idealised projection of themselves; though not many perhaps, could picture themselves wearing a crown of diamonds and receiving the tribute of Indian princes in a camp of 40,000 tents.

If the King wished to live modestly, there was still a band of Burkes eager to help him to do so. When the Civil List came up for discussion in the Commons, in July 1910, Mr G. N. Barnes, a future Pensions Minister, described the Household as a nest of parasites battening on the nation under the shadow of the Throne. The Lord Steward's department, he thought, required investigation. One official in it drew £700 for showing people to their places on State occasions, and there were certain lords in waiting, 'some of whom may be in hearing of my own voice,' who were paid £600 or £700 for fancy duties. 'These men are kept men of the Government

* *The Girlhood of Queen Victoria* (introduction)

and they are given fancy names to hide the real nature of the deal.'

The reply of Mr A. J. Balfour* was that the Lord Steward operated under a system which made him both a Court official and a member of the Government. If Mr Barnes thought that Court officials should no longer be members of the Government, that was an arguable proposition; but, given a monarchy, ceremonial duties had to be performed, and they might as well be performed properly. In his view, ceremonial was admirably handled and no one could seriously argue that it was excessive. Mr Balfour little knew how soon the Lord Steward was to be lifted clear of politics.

Palace ceremonial received its rudest shock for generations on a June evening in 1914. Thanks to the suffragettes, who had reached the stage of burning down chapels and trying to blow up the Coronation chair, Buckingham Palace was in a state of siege. The King has been forced to abandon his daily ride in Rotten Row. Police patrolled the Palace approaches, turning away demonstrators, but failed to prevent two of them from chaining themselves to the royal railings. Within the grounds another force of police kept day and night vigil. Apprehensions were not decreased when it was learned that Mrs Pankhurst was occupying a house in Grosvenor Place overlooking the Palace grounds. It was a harassing time for the Lord Chamberlain's officials who had the task of approving applications from women wishing to be presented. Thanks to their vigilance, several of 'the furies,' flourishing forged invitations, were successfully frustrated. On June 4 the King, in the uniform of a Coldstream colonel, and Queen Mary took up their usual positions in the Throne Room to receive feminine homage. The ritual proceeded smoothly until a handsome young woman, instead of rising from her curtsey, spread her arms and in 'a well-modulated voice' cried out, 'Your Majesty, for God's sake stop torturing women!' The words were hardly uttered before the Comptroller of the Household, Brigadier-General Sir Douglas Dawson, and another official stepped forward and half led, half carried the offender from the presence. If these gentlemen were Mr Barnes's 'parasites,' they performed an unpleasant task with notable efficiency. The King,

* Later Lord Balfour

the Queen, three princes and three princesses took no apparent notice and the function went on without a pause; but it was as if a four-letter word had been used at a polite dinner table.

The 'Wild Woman in the Throne Room' (to quote the *Daily Mail* headline) was Miss Mary Blomfield, the 26-year-old daughter of a knight who had performed artistic services at Sandringham. At once her mother issued a statement to the press saying that the family were 'sick and disgusted to a degree' by the girl's performance. It turned out that the offender and her younger sister, who had tried to silence her outburst, had been in the habit of marching with suffragettes. They were described as quiet girls of rather unusual tastes. The Lord Chamberlain's officials at once re-examined the names of those women still to be presented and special messengers were sent to inform three of them that permission to attend Court had been withdrawn. Police precautions were further strengthened; but in spite of all, on June 7, a convivial citizen was able to climb into the grounds and enter the Palace. He was not detected until he opened the door of a bedroom on the top floor, when a page got up and chased him. His story was that he wanted to show up the inadequacy of the police guard.

The King's comment on the Throne Room episode summed up the view of 99 per cent of the nation. He said he did not know what things were coming to.

During the 1914–18 war the Court was quick to impose its own sumptuary laws. As early as April 1915 the King forbade the serving of wine, spirits and beer under his roof, but most of his subjects shied at such early sacrifice. In 1917, when the American Ambassador, Walter Haines Page, stayed a night with the King, he was offered 'only so much bread, one egg apiece and—lemonade.' Frugality at table did not save the Court from radical criticism. On April 21, 1917, Mr H. G. Wells wrote to *The Times* to suggest that the time was now ripe to give some clear expression of the 'great volume ' of republican sentiment in Britain. Such a course, he felt, would be 'a thing agreeable to our friends and allies, the Republican democracies of France, Russia, United States and Portugal.' The spirit of the nation, in his view, was 'warmly and entirely against the dynastic system that has so long divided, embittered and wasted the spirit of mankind.' In a leading article, *The Times* said the letter showed that clever men could sometimes write foolishly, and added: 'If we do its author the disservice of making it public it is in order to show the absurdity of the "republican" manifestations in this country.'

Some of the anti-Court feeling was due to the fact that German titles were borne by many members of the royal family. The King decided to remove this source of irritation once and for all. In June 1917 he 'deemed it desirable' that those members of his family who bore German names should relinquish them and adopt British surnames. As a result Tecks became Cambridges, Battenbergs became Mountbattens, and sundry 'highnesses' and 'serene highnesses' vanished. While approving this decision, the *Daily News* said: 'One cannot help speculating what Queen Victoria would have thought could she have foreseen this final severance of the Court from all German associations.' Perhaps, like her grandson, she would have said 'They are my kinsmen, but I am ashamed of them.' In July of that year the King announced that all descendants of Queen Victoria would henceforth take the name Windsor. The suggestion for this name came from Lord Stamfordham, the King's Private Secretary, who subsequently learned that Edward III had been described as Edward de Windsor.

Through the war years Buckingham Palace modestly entertained a number of persons who in the ordinary way would not have qualified for admission within its walls. Among these were officers of the armed forces, who were regaled with tea and films. Wounded officers enjoyed the privilege of being waited on by royal ladies. After this, could the Court ever go back to its old exclusiveness? If a man was admissible to the Palace in war, why not in peace?

It became clear, after 1918, that Society was being both dilated and diluted. Not all the old Court restrictions could be maintained, and one which went into the discard was that which banned the presentation of actresses, musicians and singers (unless retired and of blameless life). Among the first actresses to be received was Ellen Terry. On the same day that she made her accomplished curtsey, the King received the actress wife of his Librarian at Windsor, John (later Sir John) Fortescue, better known as the historian of the British Army.

M

In 1914, when the couple were married, Winifred Fortescue had tactfully retired to London whenever the Court visited Windsor.*

Unfamiliar faces appeared in the Royal Enclosure at Ascot, where the rule against the admission of innocent parties to a divorce was lifted. This was not necessarily the triumph for common sense that it might appear, for in polite circles husbands were expected to put themselves in the wrong. In further recognition of social changes, the King developed the garden parties which his grandmother had initiated. These were designed to admit thousands when courts could receive only hundreds. An invitation to a garden party did not count as a presentation at Court, but it was a widely sought honour. Few citizens had suspected that Buckingham Palace could boast an attractive rear elevation or such extensive and agreeable gardens. The procedure was for the royal family to circulate without excessive formality among their guests and then retire into a Durbar tent for special presentations. A rained-out garden party provided cruel amusement for the press, for it was impossible to admit thousands of dripping guests into the Palace.

In 1924, traditionalists prepared for the worst when a Socialist Ministry took office. How would Mr Ramsay Mac-Donald fill his Court appointments? Would he put his men into velvet breeches? Or would they carry their cloth caps into the Throne Room?

When the Ministers were due to visit the Palace to receive their seals of office, Sir Maurice Hankey, Secretary to the Cabinet, was anxious that they should parade in frock coats and top hats. His anxiety was shared by Mr MacDonald, who was by no means a hater of ceremonial, but he was doubtful whether he could carry his followers with him. Viscount Snowden says that several of the ministers, whose homes were in the provinces, had only the clothes in which they stood. There was no time to buy new ones and apparently no inclination to hire any. Sir Maurice Hankey was a worried man. The matter was referred to Lord Stamfordham, who agreed that lounge suits would have to be accepted. A few of the ministers were able to unearth old frock coats and silk hats. Hankey

* Winifred Fortescue: *There's Rosemary, There's Rue*

did not let the revolutionaries into the Palace until he had given them two or three rehearsals.*

So much for Lord Snowden's account. Mr Fenner Brockway says that two of the ministers, Mr Fred Jowett and Mr John Wheatley, deliberately declined to wear the panoply of a class to which they did not belong, and went for their seals wearing their ordinary clothes, surmounted by a soft hat and a bowler hat respectively. This action shocked Mr MacDonald far more, in Jowett's view, than it shocked the King. (The legend that the King put on a red tie to make his guests feel at ease may be discounted.) As a result, these two were hailed in the Labour movement as remaining spiritually true to their class.† The controversy over swords and knee breeches was still to come.

The question of Court appointments caused Mr MacDonald much hard thought. Happily, he was not called upon to produce a Socialist Master of the Buck Hounds, but he did not wish to put even his second-best men in decorative appointments. *The Times* helpfully suggested a course of action. The Household offices, it said, had long ceased to be of serious political significance. Doubtless Mr MacDonald would have difficulty in filling the principal vacancies because of Labour's exiguous representation in the Lords. Why not, therefore, leave these posts to the unfettered choice of the King? The time was long past when such appointments were used by 'the King's Friends' to frustrate the ministers of the day. If this course were adopted, future prime ministers would be freed of the temptation to distribute Court posts among place hunters.‡

In due course, Mr MacDonald let it be known that he was willing to allow the King to fill the Court vacancies as he wished. For his part, the King did not want to be accused of surrounding himself with personal friends, answerable to no one but himself. According to Sir Harold Nicolson, the leaders of the other parties were approached for their opinions. Lord Balfour wished to maintain the *status quo*, since it was useful to have sops for those not qualified for ministerial office, but Mr Herbert Asquith§ was in favour of making the Court

* Viscount Snowden: *An Autobiography*
† *Socialism Over Sixty Years: Life of Jowett of Bradford*
‡ Jan. 15 1924
§ Later the Earl of Oxford and Asquith

appointments non-political.* The result was a compromise. Henceforth the Lord Chamberlain, the Lord Steward, the Master of the Horse, the Captain of the Gentlemen at Arms, the Captain of the Yeomen of the Guard and three lords in waiting were to be appointed by the Sovereign, on condition that they took no part in political affairs. The Prime Minister was to have the nomination of the Vice-Chamberlain of the Household, the Treasurer and the Comptroller. In practice, persons appointed to these posts perform only trivial ceremonial duties. Usually they become whips of the party in office.

The Earl of Cromer and the Earl of Shaftesbury were re-appointed as Lord Chamberlain and Lord Steward respectively. To the post of Treasurer of the Household Mr MacDonald appointed Mr Tom Griffiths, Member for Pontypool, who as a half-timer had earned fourpence a day in a tinplate works. The office of Comptroller went to Mr. J. A. Parkinson, representing Wigan, who had entered the pits at the age of ten; and that of Vice-Chamberlain to Mr. J. E. Davison, representing Smethwick, a former foundry worker and sanitary inspector. These appointments were all very romantic, all very dreadful or all very unnecessary, according to individual viewpoint.

The more hard-bitten members of the Labour Party reacted unprintably to the idea of working men becoming courtiers. So did many intellectuals. That Labour ministers should have descended to wearing top hats was bad enough; that they should contemplate wearing knee breeches and swords was the final betrayal. For that matter, the idea of Mr MacDonald wearing a sword was equally distasteful to his enemies. On March 12, 1924, the public opened its newspapers and saw photographs of Labour Ministers making their first appearance at a levee at St James's. The Prime Minister was shown, hatless, in a long cloak, beneath which appeared the tip of a sword. He was wearing trousers with a broad stripe. Two future peers, Mr Sidney Webb and Mr Noel-Buxton, were very obviously wearing breeches (this seemed to dispose of a popular idea that it was Sidney Webb's wife who wore breeches). Mr Tom Griffiths wore the same style of levee dress as the Prime Minister with a plumed hat. Rarely, perhaps, have photographs of

* *King George V*

politicians created such intense feeling at both ends of the political scale.

Two factors induced the Labour ministers to put on Court 'livery.' One was the singular tact and courtesy shown to them by the King; it would have seemed churlish if, in return, they had elected to defy a custom he valued. The other was the desire of their own leader that they should adhere to tradition. Mr MacDonald had the idea that, if his ministers conformed in the matter of dress, it would help to give a sense of continuity. Many of his followers thought that what was needed was a break of continuity, but they did not wish to force a quarrel. 'We drifted into acquiescence,' says Mr J. R. Clynes.*

What irked Mr Clynes, and many of his colleagues, was the need to keep changing uniforms all day—'morning dress for one function, afternoon dress with plumes and sword to consort with some arriving prince and evening dress for a banquet.' He also thought it wrong that civilians should be expected to wear the 'peacock gauds of professional officers,' but felt that Tory gibes on this score could be dismissed as the snarls of those who had hoped to wear the same uniforms. He added that he had seen an ex-docker and an ex-policeman looking more distinguished in their Buckingham Palace uniforms than 'certain immature noblemen sent to Court from very wealthy households.'

From all this controversy (which was rekindled when the second Labour Government came to power) the man to emerge with most dignity was the King. He made it clear from the start that he did not expect any of the ministers to buy expensive full dress. If he showed any prejudice, it was against Mr George Lansbury, who had said some disagreeable things about him, and Mr MacDonald was careful not to include Lansbury in the Cabinet; but later the King came to terms with the old rebel. The two even reached the stage of swopping physical symptoms and discussing the shortcomings of their doctors.†

Across the Atlantic, the subject of knee breeches was always an inflammatory topic. It was usual for the press to ask ambassadors whether they proposed to wear this decadent garb at the British Court. Back in 1913 Walter Haines Page appears to

* *Memoirs*
† Raymond Postgate: *Life of George Lansbury*

have done so at certain functions, for in his correspondence he says that when he goes home he intends to adopt knee breeches for good—'you've no idea how nice and comfortable they are— though it is a devil of a lot of trouble to put them on.'* In 1929, when reporters asked Brigadier-General Charles Dawes whether he proposed to wear 'knickers,' he replied, colourfully, that he did not. If he had read the *New York Times* of June 14, 1929, he would have seen an advertisement by Macy's which began, 'Everywhere these days men are taking to knickers.' The Duke of Windsor tells how perturbation at the General's decision was caused in Court and diplomatic circles. It was felt that the Queen's dignity was at stake, for although dress regulations had been slackened in minor respects it was still regarded as *de rigueur* for diplomats to wear knee breeches if the Queen was present. The Duke, then Prince of Wales, was approached in the hope that he would try to put pressure on General Dawes, with whom he was on terms of friendship. He was reluctant to do so, but suggested to the Ambassador, presumably in jest, that he should wear trousers over his breeches when he set out for the Palace and remove them when he arrived. General Dawes remained intractable and appeared before the Queen in trousers.†

The King's life, whether in palace or shooting box, was one of disciplined and harmonious elegance. In Queen Mary he had a partner who knew the secret of turning palaces into homes. She reclaimed a thousand objects of art from places where they should not have been and installed them where they should have been. The King's intimates were friends of his youth. Lord Stamfordham, his Private Secretary, still wrote the bold script he had adopted to spare the dimming eyes of Queen Victoria. In the 'seventies, as Lieutenant Arthur Bigge, Royal Artillery, he had been a valorous fellow-campaigner of the Prince Imperial against the Zulus. It was this tried and loyal courtier who taught his master the art of being a king, as the pupil very generously attested. Another crony of the 'seventies was Sir Charles Cust, who had been a cadet with the King on board the *Britannia*. His privilege was to be crusty and contradictory, but he would hardly have been retained as

* B. J. Endrick (ed.): *Life and Letters of Walter H. Page*
† *A King's Story*

Equerry for nearly 40 years if he had lacked more estimable qualities. A third veteran was Sir Frederick Ponsonby, now serving his third sovereign.

By the time of his silver jubilee the King was taken aback to find that he was popular, not only with the middle classes, but with the masses. It was the same sort of surprise that Queen Victoria had experienced on her jubilee. One of the tributes paid him on this occasion may be singled out. The thousand holders of the Royal Warrant—the descendants of the pin-makers and spatterdash-makers of an earlier day—clubbed together and presented him with the King's House at Burhill, near Cobham. The roll of royal tradesmen still contained some remarkable entries, among them manufacturers of lamprey pies, rick cloths, Edinburgh rock, Highland ornaments, daylight reflectors, lamb food, wine corks and paper table decorations. There were also jobmasters, *fournisseurs*, purveyors of Japanese goods, purveyors of Norwegian goods, rockworkers, horse milliners, pyrotechnists, and press cuttings agents.

For many, the Court was too old in outlook. But the King and Queen were both eminently honest, courageous and conscientious. In the loose 'twenties they stood for durable values and virtues. Their enthusiasms were not wholly of the upper class. If the King shot pheasants, he also collected stamps. If he presided at Ascot, he also liked soccer cup finals. When, in 1932, he broadcast his first Christmas message—an innovation which did much to alter the whole popular conception of monarchy—he sounded just the bluff, fatherly type his subjects had always imagined him. His Queen never broadcast, never made speeches, never used telephones; but she had the gift of majesty.

When the King died, the Labour leaders who had once thought him a crusted Tory hailed him as a great democrat. Mr Clynes described his reign as 'the finest example in modern times of the supremely difficult art of constitutional kingship. He took the trouble to understand his people and to progress with them through the age in which they lived.'*

Contrary to the hopes of some of his admirers, Edward VIII had no intention of re-shaping the Court to a Hollywood

* *Memoirs*

specification. All he wanted was to reduce the average ages of the courtiers by 20 years or so and to open a few windows.

As a Prince he had been idolised. He had been a good master to his Duchy of Cornwall. As a King his handicap, in the view of his biographer Hector Bolitho, was that he had no solid friends, only a variety of amusing acquaintances. For this, a life spent in travel was partly responsible.* Sir Frederick Ponsonby had cautioned him against making himself too accessible. Royalty, insisted the courtier, should always retain an element of mystery. In other words, royalty should not allow itself to be seen walking out in a raincoat, carrying an umbrella.

The press agreed that it was right and proper for a new king to surround himself with his own friends and acquaintances. Nothing could be more unsatisfactory, said *The Times*, than an attempt to work permanently with a staff selected by others and inevitably disposed to draw comparisons with the methods of a past régime. The old staff, it is clear, *did* draw comparisons, but Edward persevered with his domestic changes. He built a squash court at Buckingham Palace and installed television sets both there and at Fort Belvedere, near Sunningdale. Already he had broken away from the stately Daimler tradition and had been seen in an American station wagon and a long sleek Buick. When he made his Household appointments, he chose the leading amateur huntsman of the day, the Duke of Beaufort, as Master of the Horse. He struck off one or two minor offices and caused mild surprise in some quarters by appointing a manipulative surgeon to his roster of medical men. His happiest innovation by far was to designate his private air pilot Captain of the King's Flight. Wing-Commander Edward (now Air Commodore Sir Edward) Fielden thus secured a place in history as the first flying courtier. During the 1939–45 war the Flight was broken up but was later re-created within the framework of the Royal Air Force.

Writers of Court gossip had the liveliest expectations of this reign. Under Edward's father, they had contented themselves with noting how the wraps of royal guests were always laid carefully on sofas 'and not rolled in a ball as frequently happens at large houses,' or how a footman stood at the foot of the

* *King Edward VIII*

grand staircase offering glasses of lemonade to departing guests. Now, much more piquant details could be expected.

One of the first of the piquant discoveries was that the list of royal guests in the *Court Circular* included the name of Mrs Ernest Simpson, without that of her husband. The rest of the story need not be told here.

32

A New Pattern?

I T was not surprising if George VI, whose elder brother had so callously slipped the Throne under him, looked back at the well-ordered, dignified life of his father and sought to model his own life on it. The country had been disappointed in its unorthodox king; now it wanted an orthodox one again. The call was for a family man with strength of character and a sense of dignity. The third king of 1936 had these qualities. His Queen was all that a consort should be.

When the Civil List came up for debate, in May 1937, the country was still suffering from the hangover of the coronation, which Sir Stafford Cripps had described as 'bunting and bunkum.' A number of Labour peers did not attend it, being unwilling to spend £150 or so on robes. In the Commons, Labour Members found a good deal to criticise in the Court as an institution. It was time, they thought, to re-shape it to the needs of a classless state. Mr Clement Attlee said he did not mind occasional displays of ritual but he was opposed to continual ritual. Mr James Maxton, the firebrand from the Clyde, wanted to see Buckingham Palace, Windsor Castle and Holyrood used as 'social institutions for the benefit of the people of this country.' Colonel J. C. (later Lord) Wedgwood thought the Royal family would prefer to live in simple dignity like the Swedish or Danish royal families, rather than carry on their backs for ever a greedy gang of flunkies. In a burst of revelation, he said:

'My experience when we were in office was that when the Labour Party surrounded the Throne they behaved exactly as any other party. Their knees trembled and they confined their conversation entirely to "Yes, sir," or to "No, sir." ' They were not allowed to start any topic of discussion.

Asked whether his own knees had trembled in his days as a Court flunkey (he was Chancellor of the Duchy of Lancaster in 1924), the Colonel said he did not claim any exemption from the common failings of humanity.

Other members professed to have difficulty in explaining to their constituents why they must work for ten years to make as much as the King was paid in a day. Mr J. J. Jones said he noticed that a Court official still received £300 a year for looking after the swans. Was it not time for the swans to look after themselves? He added: 'There are Ladies of the Bedchamber, too. I have seen some of them. They would not be ladies in my bedchamber.'

Labour demands for a committee to investigate ways of simplifying the Court fell on stony ground. Mr Winston Churchill said there was no evidence of any strong feeling that the Court needed profound simplification. Another member told the sad tale of how Edward VIII in a bowler hat had been greeted by a dressed-up provincial mayor, a spectacle which inspired a small boy to exclaim, 'Isn't the King lovely in his red coat and gold chain?' Was this what Labour wanted?

In the second world war the Court came down to skeleton proportions. It adapted itself to living in a train, in which it covered some 40,000 miles. Because of security restrictions, the King's movements had to go unannounced. Nine times in all Buckingham Palace was bombed and in one week it was hit twice. In the palace baths a line was drawn at the five-inch level. Corn grew in Windsor Great Park.

The King showed himself willing to break precedents. He personally decorated uncommissioned ranks for gallantry; he appointed young officers of outstanding distinction to his personal staff, an innovation which was to have resounding repercussions; and he went to Windsor railway station to meet the American Ambassador, Mr John Winant, thus making a concession which would have appalled the third George. He also paid visits, as a guest, to No. 10 Downing Street.

After the war the Court once more began to adjust itself to a social revolution. In 1946 many of the Household servants formed themselves, for the first time, into a trade union. Among diehards, and not only among diehards, the idea of the Lord

Steward's power passing to the shop steward was peculiarly horrifying. But all was not lost. Slowly, as austerity permitted, the old pattern of the Court was restored. Even the débutantes' parties came back.

It was clear, however, that a new pattern had been evolved for royal progresses. On the strenuous South Africa tour, in 1947, the Court once more adapted itself to dwelling in a train (in telephonic touch with London), and the royal movements were speeded as required by Viking aircraft of the King's Flight.

So, in 1952, the second Elizabeth came to a Court which drew both strength and glitter from its anachronisms. Her great officers held appointments dating from Norman times. Her bodyguard was Tudor, her horsed escort was Stuart. She had almoners and play examiners, a bargemaster and a press secretary, a staff of motor mechanics, a Bedchamber complete with ladies and women, and the premier Duke of England to administer Queen Anne's racecourse. The ritual of this Court went back until it vanished in a haze of mysticism. Its etiquette, though much eased, was still the timeless etiquette of sovereigns. Very noticeably, it was a Court of retired soldiers, who filled the ranks of Gentlemen Ushers, Equerries, Yeomen of the Guard, and Gentlemen at Arms, besides holding a variety of other posts.

From the start it was a newsworthy Court. Not only had it a young and popular Queen, but it had a restless royal duke who hovered above it in a helicopter, fluttering the ghosts at the Board of Green Cloth. For further piquancy, it contained an Equerry who had fallen in love with the Queen's sister.

The press decided that this was the new Elizabethan age. So, on the Court, all the pitiless machinery of modern publicity was turned. Life was lived in an electronic flash. Television cameras tracked down on to tiaras, lingered on corsages, microphones multiplied on the royal board. 'Peeping Tom' lenses were levelled at balconies. What the lenses did not see, the reporters did, or fancied they did. On the Queen's highway press cars tore after royal cars. In the palace, clever young men, and clever middle-aged men, posed the royal family for endless photographs. The birth of the Elizabethan age coincided with conspicuous improvements in colour printing, which in turn coincided, ironically enough, with a slump of interest in popular magazines. In an effort to stave off collapse, the royal family was processed and re-processed in polychrome.

The Court of George VI had possessed strong and sober virtues, but the demand now was for something more sprightly, more socially adventurous. All had their own idea of what the Court ought to be. Some wanted it to encourage art and letters, opera and music, to prise itself from the grip of the variety artists and of Wardour Street. Some wanted the Queen to lay fewer foundation stones and visit more colonies. Some wanted to be able to troop into Buckingham Palace and look at the pictures. Others hoped the Court might become less horsy. Others, again, wished it to discountenance blood sports, or to show more respect for the Sabbath. Still others wanted to see the royal children sent to ordinary schools. A few thought it would be a gracious gesture to receive the Duchess of Windsor.

As a rule, the advocates of such changes adopted the easy convention of criticising the Queen's advisers, but the spokesmen and spokeswomen of the League Against Cruel Sports preferred to attack the Queen in person. 'We know who our chief enemies are,' said one of them, 'and the Queen is our worst enemy.' This may be distasteful, but at least it is honest, for it is not the great officers who decide whether the Queen shall attend a hunt or watch Sunday polo.

Among the first criticisms of the Court was a three-day lambasting administered by the *Daily Mirror*, starting on September 26, 1956. The series was entitled 'The Royal Circle,' and the headlines included 'Are These The New Elizabethans Or Is It The Mixture As Before?' and 'When Will The Duke Send The Old Gang Packing?' The contention was that the Court was still living in an age of golden cobwebs. 'In this day and age the friends of the Royal Family should be democratic, modern, representative of the century we live in, drawn from all walks of life.' Instead, they were aristocratic, insular and 'toffee-nosed.' Out of 50 members of the royal circle, 31 were peers, or the wives, sons and daughters of peers. How these 50 members were selected, since they did not all hold Court appointments, is obscure; the total seems to have included those who merely 'rubbed horses' with the Duke at Cowdray Park.

Lord Altrincham mounted the next set-piece in the *National and English Review* of July 1957. The royal family's choice of friends, he said, was not a legitimate matter for comment, but it was fair to point out that the Queen's personal staff were drawn from a single 'tweedy' social type. They were of the United Kingdom not of the Commonwealth, 'a tight little enclave of British "ladies and gentlemen".' What was needed was a truly classless and Commonwealth Court. Lord Altrincham described presentation parties for débutantes as 'a grotesque survival from the Monarchy's "hierarchical" past.' The Crown's benison should be reserved for those who earned it by public service.

It was for his personal criticisms of the Queen, rather than of the Court, that Lord Altrincham had his face slapped, his house daubed and was disowned by the town of Altrincham. Newspapers which had assumed their readers would be against him on all counts were surprised to find, on taking polls, that some of his criticisms of the Court were widely supported.

The third storm broke, shortly afterwards, with the publication of Malcolm Muggeridge's article 'Does England Really Need a Queen?' in the *Saturday Evening Post* of October 19, 1957. This described the pageant of royalty, as presented by press and television, as a royal soap opera in which interest must never be allowed to flag. Its appeal was to the gallery rather than to the stalls. Monarchy, he said, was a generator of snobbishness and a focus of sycophancy. 'The worthy alderman kneels ecstatically with creaking joints before the Queen to receive the accolade; the aged party hack finds one more canter in him when it is a question of being elevated to the peerage by Her Majesty in person.' The Queen ought to be put across as a unifying element of society. This could not be done until she had new men about her—'men who understand what the twentieth century is about . . . men who can deal with the ink and television side of her existence subtly and sensibly without losing sight of the great symbolic utility of the institution she embodies.'

To what extent, if any, these criticisms influenced Court changes will not be known for a long time, if ever. From about

1954 it became clear that the pattern of Court entertainment was being re-examined. In October of that year it was announced that a new system would be adopted at Ascot. In the new Royal Enclosure then under erection the rules governing divorce would cease to operate; but there would be an enclosure within the enclosure, to be known as the Queen's Lawn, to which access would be by invitation alone, and in which the rules on divorce would continue to apply.

In May 1956 was inaugurated a new type of private luncheon designed to bring to the royal table leaders of all walks of life. The choice of the first six guests was a cautious one, including as it did the Bishop of London, the Editor of *The Times*, a titled banker and a titled civil servant. The second set of guests included the Headmaster of Eton, the Vicar of St Martin's and another titled banker, but was varied by the chairman of the National Coal Board (an ex-miner), the Master of the Queen's Music and the managing director of Wembley Stadium. Since then the choice has varied very widely. It has included wits like Sir Alan Herbert and Osbert Lancaster; Lord Rank and Michael Balcon, from the film world; stage stars like Sir Alec Guinness and Flora Robson; record-breakers like Donald Campbell and the late Mike Hawthorn; and sportsmen like Chris Brasher and Billy Wright. The names of Billy, Mike, Alec and Chris make a change in the *Court Circular*. There is still hope, perhaps, for Lord Altrincham and Malcolm Muggeridge.

In November 1957 came the decision to end débutante presentations at Court. These functions had long been a legitimate subject for attack, not only because they bestowed an unmerited privilege on the daughters of birth and wealth, but because parasites were battening on the system. Those who lacked sponsors could obtain them by paying fees of anything up to £1000 to aristocratic matrons willing to market their qualifications. A further objection was that the whole social pattern of which 'coming out' was a part had vanished. The number of wealthy young idlers waiting to snap up the season's matrimonial prizes was trivial. Of the potential husbands of these girls, few had made much way in the world. The débutantes themselves could no longer be maintained in idleness by their parents, so they went to work in stores, dress shops and espressos. That this system should require a royal benison was patently absurd, yet much ingenuity had been expended in defence of it. The historically bemused still saw it as the ultimate refinement of that ancient privilege whereby the subject had right of access to the sovereign. It was also represented as a female initiation ceremony at which a girl became a woman; but a number of those who passed through the 'gateway of life' gave little sign of having achieved adult status.

Officially the reason given for ending presentation parties was that the number of applications had grown unwieldy. To accommodate all who wished to be presented, it would have been necessary to hold an extra party, and this could not be fitted into the Queen's list of engagements. Instead, the Lord Chamberlain explained that more garden parties would be held, in order that a greater number of persons could be invited to Buckingham Palace. The number of débutantes attending a presentation party was about 250, whereas the Palace lawns could hold as many as 8000 (of whom, however, a number often go home without having glimpsed their sovereign).

Those newspapers which might have been expected to chortle over the end of débutantes' parties came very near to shedding a sentimental tear. *The Times* thought there would be some natural regrets but that they would not be widely felt. It was anxious, however, that this decision should not be taken as an encouragement to those who wished to see a more democratic Court. The new changes 'should not be followed up by any further move made in defence of the illusion that the subjects of the Queen in any part of the Commonwealth wish her life to be conducted as though she were just one of themselves.'

The following month, another royal benison went by the board. It was announced that the Queen's bounty of £3 for triplets and £4 for quadruplets would no longer be granted. Queen Victoria had introduced this award in 1849, having observed the hardships suffered by her more fertile Irish subjects. In days of family allowances, the bounty was clearly superfluous; moreover, in days of devalued currency, the word bounty was scarcely apt. Those parents who felt that the birth of triplets entitled them to some form of royal recognition were still eligible to receive the Queen's congratulations, provided they

The Court: 1958-59

notified the Palace of their desire. Statisticians revealed that in the reign of George VI and of Elizabeth, up to the time of the announcement, payment had been made in respect of 19 sets of quadruplets and 1451 sets of triplets.

On several occasions, the right of the royal family to decent privacy became an issue. Newspapers deeply shocked each other by their speculations as to whether or not Princess Margaret would marry Group-Captain Peter Townsend, the Battle of Britain pilot whom her father appointed as his Air Equerry of Honour and who, on the King's death, became Equerry to the Queen Mother and Princess Margaret. A statement denying the Princess's intention to marry the Group-Captain was made in October 1955. In other ways there was invasion of privacy, as in the publication of books of reminiscences by retired Palace servants, whose jejune memories were stimulated by the waving of cheque-books. None despised this development more than those courtiers and diplomats who are careful to pack their own reminiscences with anecdotes of royal contacts. In 1954, when the Press Council referred to 'a long-standing custom for members of royal households to write books about life therein,' the Queen's Press Secretary, Commander Richard Colville, took the opportunity to clear the air. 'It has long been the custom,' he wrote, 'that those persons who by virtue of their work or other circumstances are brought into contact with the Sovereign or Members of the Royal Family do not make their experiences the subject of books and articles for publication; that a small number have chosen to break the trust reposed in them in this respect does not change the fact that such a trust exists.' The Queen's view was that she was entitled to expect that her family should attain the same privacy in her home that other families enjoyed. The Press Council warmly endorsed these sentiments, but its influence over its members is slight. In 1959 the Palace took action in the courts to restrain a former official at Windsor Castle from writing reminiscences of his royal service for a Sunday newspaper.

The press has professed to see the hand of the Duke of Edinburgh in many of the recent Court changes; not only in the decision to stop the débutantes' parties, but in a greater informality which has crept into royal speeches and in a growing independence of groups and organisations which had fancied they had a secure claim on the Queen's patronage. To his influence, also, has been ascribed the announcement, as these lines are written, of a party at which the Queen is to meet the press. All this is only speculation. But it is obvious that the popularity of the monarchy must depend on the skill with which a compromise is effected between formality and informality.

Meanwhile, the chorus of advice and criticism continues. There are some who will not be satisfied until they see the Queen on continual progress through the Commonwealth. If this day comes, there is a risk that the Master of the Horse will become a movements officer, the Bedchamber will be a cabin on a Comet, and the palaces will end as a collection of art galleries peopled by the ghosts of almoners, swan keepers, masters of the revels and chaplains in ordinary.

Index